Love by the Numbers

Lang Classical Studies

Daniel H. Garrison
General Editor

Vol. 10

PETER LANG
New York • Washington, D.C./Baltimore
Bern • Frankfurt am Main • Berlin • Vienna • Paris

Helena Dettmer

Love by the Numbers

Form and the Meaning in the Poetry of Catullus

PETER LANG
New York • Washington, D.C./Baltimore
Bern • Frankfurt am Main • Berlin • Vienna • Paris

Library of Congress Cataloging-in-Publication Data

Dettmer, Helena.
Love by the numbers: form and meaning in the poetry of Catullus/
Helena Dettmer.
p. cm. — (Lang classical studies; vol. 10)
Includes bibliographical references and index.
1. Catullus, Gaius Valerius—Criticism and interpretation.
2. Love poetry, Latin—History and criticism. 3. Epigrams, Latin—
History and criticism. 4. Cycles (Literature). 5. Rome—In literature.
6. Literary form. I. Title. II. Series.
PA6276.D48 874'.01—dc20 96-41571
ISBN 0-8204-3663-1
ISSN 0891-4087

Die Deutsche Bibliothek-CIP-Einheitsaufnahme

Dettmer, Helena:
Love by the numbers: form and meaning in the poetry of Catullus/
Helena Dettmer. – New York; Washington, D.C./Baltimore; Bern;
Frankfurt am Main; Berlin; Vienna; Paris: Lang.
(Lang classical studies; vol. 10)
ISBN 0-8204-3663-1
NE: GT

Cover design by Nona Reuter.

The paper in this book meets the guidelines for permanence and durability
of the Committee on Production Guidelines for Book Longevity
of the Council of Library Resources.

Printed in the United States of America.

In Memory of

Frank Olin Copley

Teacher
Mentor
Friend

Contents

List of Illustrations

Chapter One

Chapter Two

Chapter 6

Chapter 7

Appendix

PREFACE

The genesis of this book was serendipitous. One day in August of 1978, I was reading through the elegiac epigrams of Catullus in the order in which they appear in the text when I noticed symmetrical patterning in cc. 69–78 of the same sort that I had discovered was operative in later Latin books of the first century B.C. Quite astonished by this discovery, I continued to read through the rest of the epigrams and then the rest of the corpus. The results of that day's investigation are exhibited in Appendix B on pages 267–69. Although I did not know what to make of some of the fragments during this initial inquiry, I nevertheless determined the basic structure of the Catullan corpus. The body of poetry is organized in nine consecutive rings based on thematic reciprocity, and these circular structures coincide closely with the three major metrical groupings in which the poems also are organized. I had a singular advantage in ascertaining order in the poetry of Catullus because of earlier extensive research on arrangement in Latin poetry books. Thus I knew, for example, that Roman poets do not pair poems on a one-to-one basis only, and that they usually do not organize their poems in a pure ring pattern. Variation in structure is as important a feature in book arrangement as variation in theme (this applies especially to works consisting of fifteen poems or more). I was fortunate also in that I knew intimately, in all its structural complexity, the organization of Horace's *Odes I–III,* a collection that is comparable in size to that of the *corpus Catullianum.* As a result, I could often intuit certain features that I thought should be characteristic of Catullus' poetry. For instance, I was confident that the poetry would be textured, that the primary arrangement of the entire work would be complemented by groups of thematically related poems making up secondary schemes. First-rate poets cannot resist ordering a large collection of poems exhibiting a variety of topics in multiple ring patterns. I was fairly certain, too, that mathematical symmetry should accompany and reinforce the organization of the poetry, as it does in later poetry books belonging to the first century B.C.—although I was concerned that the sorry state of the text in places might hinder attempts to ascertain the type of numerical pattern Catullus employed. The eventual discovery of these numerical patterns was a thrilling experience, for they confirmed unequivocally in my own mind that a posthumous editor could *not* be responsible for the arrangement of the poetry.

I began serious work on the arrangement of Catullus' poetry in fall of 1983, on the heels of finishing my book on Horace. Working on this monograph for the past thirteen years has been an incredibly rich and exhilarating experience. Not only have I derived great pleasure from studying Catullus, but my admiration for his technical skill, his genius, and his razor-sharp wit has grown immeasurably over time. Truly he is one of the world's great poets. We are lucky to have his poetry at all, since it survived antiquity by the slimmest of threads; we are equally lucky to have Catullus' own arrangement of his poetry, for, as will become clear in the course of this study, structure and meaning are intimately bound.

There are many to whom I owe thanks. During the past thirteen years the University of Iowa has aided my research by giving me the equivalent of two and a half years of paid leave. It also is assisting financially in the publication of this book. The Classics Department at the University of Texas made me feel welcome during my year's sabbatical there in 1983 and generously gave me library privileges. I have been encouraged by friends and colleagues at the University of Iowa, particularly Professors E.B. Holtsmark and J.F. Finamore of the Classics Department, Professor D.N. McCloskey of Economics and History, and Dr. M. Lindgren, a former student. My editor, Professor D.H. Garrison of Northwestern University, offered many suggestions for improvement of the manuscript. Cindy Smith, now of Loras

College, Paul Kreinheder, and Samuel Huskey all assisted in proofreading at various stages. Dennis McClure transferred the IBM copy of the manuscript to the Macintosh and spent countless hours redrawing the numerous illustrations. Samuel Huskey and my secretary Loretta Milder reformatted the manuscript for publication and also redrew some of the major illustrations. Professor Holtsmark proofread the manuscript before it was reformatted; Dennis McClure and Dr. Marcia Lindgren proofread the book in its final form. Terry Stone, my husband, and daughters, Heather and Anne, gave me moral support. Anne in particular deserves recognition for her understanding of my obsession with Catullus, since my engagement in this book project encompasses almost the entire span of her life. Finally, my dear friend and mentor, Frank Olin Copley, encouraged and supported my research every step of the way. I regret that I was unable to complete this monograph before his death. Out of love, admiration, and gratitude I dedicate this book to his memory.

Helena Dettmer
Iowa City, Iowa
November, 1996

Select Bibliography

J.N. Adams, *The Latin Sexual Vocabulary* (= *LSV*) (London 1982).

E. Adler, *Catullan Self-Revelation* (New York 1981).

B. Arkins, *Sexuality in Catullus* (Hildesheim 1982).

R. Ellis, *A Commentary on Catullus,* 2nd ed. (Oxford 1889).

J. Ferguson, *Catullus* (Lawrence 1985).

C.J. Fordyce, *Catullus: A Commentary* (Oxford 1961).

P.Y. Forsyth, *The Poems of Catullus: A Teaching Text* (Lanham and London 1986).

G.P. Goold, *Catullus* (London 1983).

T.K. Hubbard, "The Catullan Libellus," *Philologus* 127 (1983) 218–37.

H.A. Khan, "Catullus 76: The Summing Up," *Athenaeum* 46 (1968) 54–71.

J.K. King, "Catullus' Callimachean Carmina, cc. 65–116," *CW* 81 (1988) 383–91.

D. Lateiner, "Obscenity in Catullus," *Ramus* 6 (1977) 15–32.

M.H. Lindgren, *Non Bona Dicta: Obscenity in the Poetry of Catullus* (Diss. University of Iowa 1983).

V.P. McCarren, *A Critical Concordance to Catullus* (Leiden 1977).

C.W. Macleod, "Parody and Personalities in Catullus," *CQ* 23 (1973) 294–303.

G.W. Most, "On the Arrangement of Catullus' *Carmina Maiora*," *Philologus* 125 (1981) 109–25.

C.L. Neudling, *A Prosopography to Catullus* (Oxford 1955).

J.K. Newman, *Roman Catullus and the Modification of the Alexandrian Sensibility* (Hildesheim 1990).

K. Quinn, *Catullus: An Interpretation* (London 1973).

_____. *Catullus: The Poems,* 2nd ed. (London 1973).

L. Richardson, Jr., "*Furi et Aureli, Comites Catulli,*" *CP* 58 (1963) 93–106.

A. Richlin, *The Garden of Priapus: Sexuality and Aggression in Roman Humor* (New Haven 1983; rev. New York 1992).

E.A. Schmidt, "Catulls Anordnung seiner Gedichte," *Philologus* 117 (1973) 215–42.

R. Seager, "*Venustus, Lepidus, Bellus, Salsus*: Notes on the Language of Catullus," *Latomus* 33 (1974) 891–94.

C.P. Segal, "The Order of Catullus, Poems 2–11," *Latomus* 27 (1968) 305–21.

M.B. Skinner, *Catullus' Passer: The Arrangement of the Book of Polymetric Poems* (New York 1981).

S.G.P. Small, *Catullus: A Reader's Guide to the Poems* (Lanham and London 1983).

O. Thomsen, *Ritual and Desire: Catullus 61 and 62 and Other Ancient Documents on Wedding and Marriage* (Denmark 1992).

G. Williams, *Tradition and Originality in Roman Poetry* (Oxford 1968).

T.P. Wiseman, *Catullus and his World: A Reappraisal* (Cambridge 1985).

_____. *Catullan Questions* (Leicester 1969).

Chapter One: Introduction

The aim of this study is to address the Catullan Question. I intend to argue that Catullus arranged the poetry in its present order in a sophisticated and purposeful structure; that his claim to originality in c. 1 pertains to the arrangement as well as the composition of the poems; and that since this body of poetry has organizing principles in common with later collections of Latin poems of the first century B.C., Catullus appears to stand at the head of a tradition.

Problems

It is not certain when Catullus was born or when he died. The consensus is that he flourished circa B.C. 84–54. His years as a poet are uncertain, too, since most of the poems cannot be dated. But because the body of poetry is so slender and because the fifteen or so datable poems seem to belong to the period of B.C. 57 to 54, there is general agreement that Catullus' career was brief, terminated by an early death. The view that Catullus died prematurely is one factor that has prompted critics to postulate that the body of poems was compiled, arranged, and prepared for publication by a posthumous editor.

Another factor concerns unusual features of the transmitted text. We know the Catullan corpus only in book form in the modern sense (as against the papyrus roll of Catullus' day) because the poetry survived into the Middle Ages in a single manuscript. Compared to other extant Latin poetry books, the collection seems extraordinary in several respects. First, there is its heterogeneous content. In no other ancient poetry book do poems exhibit such a variety of genres, or are poems of two lines found together with poems of over two hundred lines. Second, in no other body of poetry from that period does meter define the shape. The Catullan collection falls naturally into three distinct parts demarcated solely by meter. Poems 1 through 60 are in a variety of meters; poems 65 through 116 are all in elegiac couplets; and poems 61 through 64 are metrically transitional between the first and the third parts. And there is the size of the collection. Since most books of Latin poetry that we have from the first century B.C. contain between 800 and 1100 verses, the question arises: Was the Catullan corpus (approximately 2300 verses) originally published in three papyrus rolls, which coincide with the three metrical divisions described above? Or was its ancient form accurately reflected in the medieval manuscript, i.e., was it published in a single roll? Ancient references to Catullus' poetry do not refer to separate *libelli*, and thus the citations of poems by "generic affiliations, meters, or available internal headings" offer tantalizingly suggestive but inconclusive evidence.[1] The fragmentary state of parts of the manuscript further complicates the problem, for it raises the issue of whether the extant work contains all that Catullus meant to bequeath to posterity.[2]

The simple division of the poems into three parts based on meter also is considered problematical. A.L. Wheeler saw the segregation of Catullan poems in elegiac couplets from those in various meters as evidence of tampering by a posthumous editor. As an analogue, he pointed to the fate of Meleager's *Garland*, in which poems in elegiac couplets apparently were later separated from those in non-elegiac verses:[3] "[Just as] somebody took the elegiac pieces out of the *Garland* and rearranged them in the *Anthology*...[so] somebody took the elegiac pieces from Catullus' original *libelli* and rearranged them at the end of the collected edition."[4]

Meleager was the first ancient poet to organize and publish a large collection of short poems. Like Wheeler, I am convinced that Catullus drew on the *Garland* (circa B.C. 101–90)[5] as a source of inspiration for his poetry. Catullus, in fact, indicates clearly his indebtedness to Meleager by alluding to the introduction of the *Garland* in the very first verse of his own introductory poem and by alluding to the *Garland* again in cc. 2 and 3; the *passer* poems resemble *A.P.* 7.195

and 196 (=G-P 4058, 4066) and *A.P.* 7.207 (=G-P 4320) of Meleager in theme, form, and language.[6] Emulation, however, does not necessarily indicate imitation. And so my position on the issue of the metrical arrangement is the opposite of Wheeler's. I think Catullus isolated poems on the basis of their meter as a calculated response to Meleager's interspersion of non-elegiac pieces with those in elegiac couplets. His purpose was to experiment with meter as a structural tool to define major sections of a unified corpus.[7]

What students of Latin poetry have overlooked in considering odd features of the transmitted text is that these oddities could in fact enhance the possibility that the poet was their creator. They suggest experimentation, and Catullus was in every way an experimental poet. F.O. Copley described Catullus as "a rebel, a radical,...an innovator, a pioneer." It is a small step to take this characterization beyond the scope of the individual poems and to extend it to the appearance and shape of the corpus as a whole.[8] Catullus may have been the first Latin poet, or one of the first, to integrate a large group of poems of various lengths and of various genres.[9] Further, he deliberately created overlap among the major sections in order to unite these heterogeneous elements. On the basis of meter and length the collection yields 1–60, 61–64, and 65–116; on the basis of meter, length, and theme it yields 1–60, 61–68, and 69–116. Additionally, on the basis of meter alone the collection can be viewed in terms of the polymetrics (1–64) and the elegiacs (65–116). It is important to note that the *carmina maiora* are the poems mainly affected by the slight shift in focus among the three complementary divisions. The structural flexibility of the central poems is intended to reflect their pivotal character as a bridge between the shorter poems on either side.

Indications of Unity

Evidence that each of these three major divisions was consciously contrived can be offered through verbal and thematic cross-references that link first and last poems. The polymetra are framed by poems to faithful and faithless friends. The dedicatory c. 1 thanks the historian Cornelius Nepos for past encouragement of Catullus' literary efforts and praises his *Chronica* as a work characterized by Callimachean qualities; by contrast, c. 60 reproaches a nameless addressee for lack of compassion in Catullus' time of need. At the center of the corpus, real and mythical marriages join cc. 61 and 64. In the one, the god of marriage is invoked to attend a wedding of mortals; in the other, gods attend a wedding of mortal and immortal. These epithalamia exhibit also an opposing relation. In the words of T.P. Wiseman, "the presence of the god at the wedding of Manlius and Vibia...contrasts sharply with the epilogue of poem 64, on the refusal of the gods to appear on earth in modern times when *pietas* is held in contempt."[10] A striking verbal reminiscence, *carmina...Battiadae*, signals the connection between the first and last poems written in elegiac couplets. They, too, display an antithetical relation. In c. 65, instead of an original poem, Catullus sends a friend a translation of Callimachus; in c. 116, instead of translating a poem of Callimachus, Catullus responds to an enemy by sending him an original poem (of invective).[11] If the long poems are conceived as a whole, opening and closing poems are related through the same recipient, Manlius Torquatus, whose happy circumstances in c. 61 turn tragic in cc. 68a/b as a result of the loss of his bride. Cc. 69–116, all elegiac epigrams, are enclosed by invectives against Rufus and Gellius, successful rivals for Lesbia. Finally, if cc. 1–64 are considered a unity (just as 65–116 were above), the Rhamnusian *virgo* at the end of 64 (v. 395), who is associated with death and destruction, corresponds inversely to the *patrona virgo* at the end of c. 1, who is associated with creation and preservation. Poems that begin and end major sections, therefore, are related principally by antithetical themes.

In conjunction with this point, it is worth noting that another pair of opposites, cc. 1 and 116, act as a frame for the entire corpus. Not only are the first and last of Catullus directed to men of opposite character, a good friend and bitter enemy, but c. 116 forms the mirror image of c. 1 by inverting motifs characteristically found in dedicatory poems.[12]

There is other evidence that the poems in their present form show a careful and deliberate structuring. The polymetra and elegiac epigrams are organized similarly so that poems occupying the same key positions exhibit the same themes. Both groups of short poems begin with a series of Lesbia poems. The opening sequence in the polymetra (2–11) tells the story of a love affair gone wrong; the opening sequence in the elegiac epigrams (69–77) tells a story of double betrayal by a lover and by a friend. Both cc. 1–60 and 69–116 center on the theme of an unanticipated violation of *fides* with regard to a love affair. In c. 30 Catullus expects loyalty from Alfenus but does not receive it. In c. 91 he expects the utterly immoral Gellius to be loyal to him, too, but not for the usual reason of friendship; even so Gellius disappoints him.[13] Finally, not only do both sections of short poems close with a series of attacks against political figures (52, 53, 54, 56, 57; 105, 108, 112, 113, 114, 115), but they culminate in an attack against the same political figure, Caesar's henchman Mamurra (57, 114, 115).

Organizing Principle

Critics have long recognized that at various places throughout the collection clusters of poems treat similar themes.[14] Cc. 2–11 are constructed around the progression of Catullus' relationship with Lesbia.[15] The disintegration of the love affair in c. 11 is followed by a mini-sequence on male friendship in cc. 12–14, whose purpose is to set the stage for the coming homosexual love poems in cc. 15–24.[16] Furius' seduction of Catullus' boy friend in c. 24 anticipates the theme of petty theft and grand larceny with which the next group, cc. 25–33, is largely concerned. Eight of the ten poems in cc. 35–44 involve writing in one form or another (35, 36, 37, 38, 40, 42, 44).[17] Cc. 52–60, which conclude the polymetra, consist mostly of short political invectives that appear to belong to the same general period of B.C. 55–54.[18] Cc. 61–68b all deal directly or indirectly with the theme of marriage.[19] As for the elegiac epigrams, T.P. Wiseman suggests that they comprise two groups of equal length that are defined by the distribution of the themes of love and politics. The first half, cc. 69–92, "is devoted to 'Lesbia' and the various men in her life," while the second half, 93–116, attacks Caesar and his partisans, with Mamurra "The Prick" singled out as the principal object of vituperation.[20]

The notion that the collection is organized in sequences of thematically related pieces is strengthened by poems generally recognized as pairs, for they occur in close proximity: the *passer* poems, 2~3;[21] the Lesbia kiss-poems, 5~7; the *scorta* poems, 6~10; the Furius poems, 23~24; the Egnatius poems, 37~39; the Amiana poems, 41~43; the *otium* poems, 50~51; the marriage hymns, 61~62; poems to and for Hortalus, 65~66; poems to and for Manlius, 68a~68b; the stinking Rufus poems, 69~71; Lesbia poems on verbal commitment, 70~72; the "foul mouth" poems, 97~98; the reconciliation poems, 107~109; and the Mentula poems, 114~115. The unity of theme displayed by clusters of poems and the clear correspondences of neighboring poems within these clusters suggest the underlying principle of arrangement. Catullus organized his entire work in ring structures of paired corresponding pieces.

The Dominant Pattern

The diagrams on pages 267–69 of Appendix B exhibit the collection in nine successive rings or cycles of thematically related poems. The arrangement coincides closely with the three major metrical sections. The polymetra are ordered in five rings, 1–14, 15–24, 25–33, 34–44, and 45–60; the longer poems in one, 61–68b; and the elegiac epigrams in three, 69–78, 78b–99, and 100–111. A five-poem tag, 112–116, rounds off the corpus.

Catullus avoided a rigid or static structure in two ways. He varied the types of circular arrangements that unify the poems (cf. the chiastic structure of 1–14 and the interlocking-ring structure of 15–24), and he created imbalance by excluding several poems from the circular schemes (17, 30, and 48 lack symmetrical counterparts). The formal patterning resembles that found in later Latin poetry books of the first century B.C., where ring arrangements based on thematic reciprocity function as the chief unifying principle.[22]

Catullus indicated the structural integrity of six of the nine rings by having the first and last poems feature themes or personages that do not occur elsewhere. The first cycle, 1–14, is enclosed by the motif of a gift of a *libellus,* a motif peculiar to cc. 1 and 14. Cc. 25 and 33 of the third cycle unite petty thievery with passive homosexuality. Cc. 34, 35, and 44 of the fourth cycle exhibit another singular combination, by joining the themes of prayers to deities with "what literature can do to you." Cc. 78b, 79, and 99 of the eighth cycle are joined by the themes of oral sex and kissing, which are not explicitly brought into relation elsewhere. Manlius Torquatus figures in cc. 61 and 68, and in no other place.[23] Likewise, Aufillena makes her only appearances in the poems that enclose the final cycle, cc. 100, 110, and 111. Of the remaining three cycles, two open and close with principals who have a common love interest. Aurelius (c. 15) and Furius (c. 24) of the second cycle are rivals of Catullus for the favors of Juventius; Rufus (c. 69) and Gellius (c. 78) of the seventh cycle are rivals of Catullus for the favors of Lesbia (cf. cc. 77 and 91). Finally, the connection between cc. 45 and 60 also involves love. The ostensibly happy or ideal love of Septimius and Acme in c. 45 is contraposed to the unhappy situation of the lover betrayed in c. 60.

Verbal/Structural Clues

The question that now arises is this: Assuming that the structural units have been identified correctly, how does one determine which poems within each ring Catullus intended as pairs? As an example, both T.K. Hubbard and I see cc. 1–14 as forming a unified block.[24] But our analyses of the structure differ. The schemes shown in figure 1.1 below have three pairs only in common, 1~14, 2~3, and 5~7. I suggest that it is possible to demonstrate that one analysis is preferable to another by carefully examining the clues the poet himself provided.

Catullus usually signals correspondences through verbal cross-references so striking that they must have been intended to be *heard* by an audience accustomed to having their poetry read aloud. To take as a point of departure the three pairs common to Hubbard's and my schemes, the expression *passer, deliciae meae puellae* occurs only in cc. 2~3; the expressions *tantum basiorum, quot basiationes* only in cc. 5~7; and the notion of a *novus libellus* as a gift only in cc. 1~14.[25] Catullus indicated the relation of cc. 6~10 and 12~13 by elaborating on his usage of striking verbal reminiscences. As figures

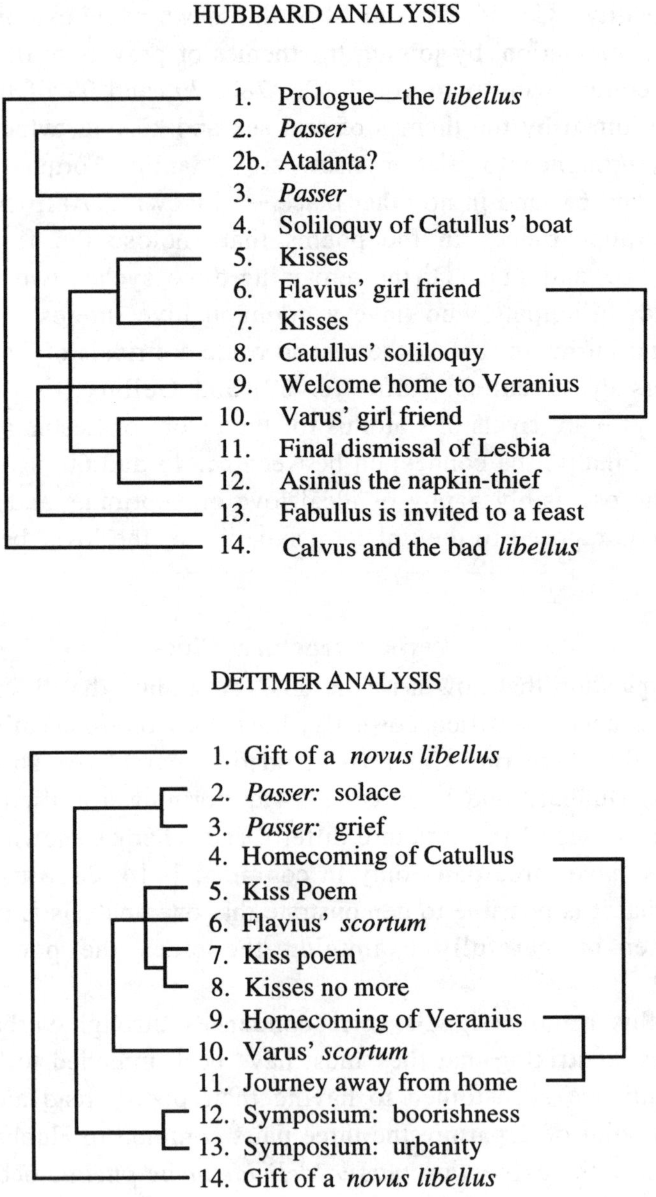

Figure 1.1 Comparison of Structural Schemes for Poems 1–14

1.2 and 1.3 on pages 10–11 illustrate, the *scorta* poems and the symposia poems complement each other structurally as well as thematically. A parallel arrangement of words and ideas, or interlocking-ring pattern (A A^1 B B^1 C C^1, etc.), joins each set of poems and results in their forming, in essence, a single poetic entity.[26] For example, both cc. 12 and 13 begin with an address to the recipients and with an enumeration of the accoutrements of the symposium, and both end with Fabullus. Within this frame there is a similar development of the same or antithetical ideas. The systematic patterning of verbal parallels in cc. 6~10 and 12~13 is too contrived to be anything but intentional. It therefore provides strong, if not definitive, evidence that these poems (and not 6~11, 10~12, and 9~13) were written to function as counterparts. In addition, by having 13.12 repeat the phrase *Veneres Cupidinesque* from 3.1 Catullus perhaps was indicating the symmetrical relation of the erotic 2~3 and the sympotic 12~13, pairs of consecutive poems that hold the second and third places from each end of the cycle.[27]

Poems 4, 8, 9, and 11 remain to be considered. Cc. 4 and 9 are related by the themes of foreign travel and homecoming. And, I think, c. 11 is to be taken with them. This bitter poem, a large portion of which is concerned with the theme of foreign travel, neatly inverts the theme of joyful homecoming found in the earlier two poems. Loss of Lesbia's love prompts thoughts of leaving Rome to join expeditions to dangerous and remote places. The epic adventures to be experienced by Furius and Aurelius, companions of Catullus in c. 11, correlate with the epic adventures of the boat in c. 4. Further, just as the boat retires from the sea, so Catullus contemplates retiring from love as he considers exchanging his posture as a *homo otiosus* for the life of the soldier-adventurer. As for c. 8, Catullus indicated through a striking verbal cross-reference that it belongs with 5 and 7. *Quem basiabis* (8.18) not only "vividly recalls" the countless kisses of 5 and 7,[28] but placed at the end of c. 8, the phrase rounds off the *basia*-cycle.[29] All three poems focus on the intensely physical side of the love affair.

	C. 6	C. 10
SIMILAR PRINCIPALS	Flavi, delicias tuas Catullo (1)	Varus me meus ad suos amores (1)
SCORTA	ni sint illepidae (2)	non sane illepidum (4)
RETICENCE VS. LOQUACITY	tacere (3)	incidere nobis / sermones varii (5 ff.)
BEDS IN A STATE OF COLLAPSE	attritus, tremulique quassa lecti / argutatio inambulatioque (10–11)	fractum qui veteris pedem grabati / in collo sibi collocare (22–23)
SPEECH	quidquid habes... dic nobis (15–16)	istud quod modo dixeram me habere (28)
REVERSAL OF EARLIER QUALITIES	lepido (17)	insulsa male (33)

Figure 1.2 Parallel Structure of Poems 6 and 10

It is important to observe that the connection of c. 8 with 5 and 7 does not preclude a relationship with c. 11.[30] The poem clearly anticipates both verbally and thematically Catullus' "final" repudiation of Lesbia, and for this reason it is instructive to read the two pieces together. (The Lesbia and Juventius poems form one of several subpatterns that complement the primary structure.) There are other instances, too, where Catullus elected not to pair poems with similar themes, as, for instance, cc. 12 and 25, which deal with the theft of his Spanish napkins. This does not mean, however, that an analysis of the interplay of these poems, or of other thematically related poems, is not illuminating. We need to bear in mind that it would have been physically impossible for Catullus to have created relationships among all his poems that show thematic affinities. The intent of this study is to suggest that the ring ordering of the collection is one way to look at the poems; it is not the only way.

The point likewise should be made that not all corresponding poems are closely related. Those that exhibit numerous similarities

	C. 12	C. 13
OPPOSITION OF FABULLUS TO ASINIUS	Marrucine Asini,... non belle (1–2)	bene, mi Fabulle (1)
SYMPOSIUM	in ioco atque vino ...salsum (2, 4)	et vino et sale et omnibus cachinnis (5)
ILL-BRED ASINIUS VS. WELL-BRED FABULLUS	tollis lintea (3) invenusta (5) furta (7)	attuleris...cenam (3–4) venuste (6) attuleris (6)
NOTION OF FULLNESS	est enim leporum / differtus puer ac facetiarum (8–9)	nam tui Catulli / plenus sacculus est aranearum (7–8)
INVECTIVE AGAINST AMATORY POETRY	hendecasyllabos trecentos / exspecta (10–11)	accipies meros amores (9)
PRICELESS GIFTS	nam sudaria... miserunt mihi muneri (14–15)	nam unguentum dabo,...meae puellae / donarunt (11–12)
FABULLUS	ut...Fabullum (17)	ut..., Fabulle (14)

Figure 1.3 Parallel Structure of Poems 12 and 13

probably were written (or rewritten) for the express purpose of functioning as counterparts. Conversely, those that show few similarities probably were not originally conceived as a pair. There are three poems, too, that lack counterparts in the primary pattern of organization (17, 30, and 48). This slight inconcinnity was carefully calculated to effect variation and to avoid a precision characteristic of "a machine rather than a work of art."[31] Non-corresponding poems also are a characteristic feature of ring structures in later collections of Latin poems where they serve a similar purpose.[32] In addition, it seems reasonable to assume that Catullus revised and possibly re-ordered some of the poems before the collection was issued in its final form. Therefore, although it may be interesting to try to determine whether a poem is early or late, the actual chronology is not of paramount importance to this study. Our concern is with the chronology that Catullus created, as it unfolds in c. 1, develops and ends with c. 116.

This monograph has as its main focus the interaction of poems that function as counterparts in the ring arrangement of the corpus (shown on pages 267–69 of Appendix B) and the significance of that interaction for the interpretation of the poetry. Chapters Two, Three, and Five deal with the ordering of the polymetra, the central poems, and the elegiac epigrams. Chapter Two shows how verbal clues and parallel structures (as in cc. 6~10 and 12~13) signal and support corresponding poems. Chapters Three and Five introduce another type of documentation. Like his Augustan successors, Catullus devised numerical schemes to accompany and reinforce the design of his poetry. In addition to their function as a tool of interpretation, these schemes are highly significant because they provide incontrovertible evidence that the transmitted text contains almost all that Catullus intended to preserve. Chapter Four has as its subject the Caelius and Rufus poems. The six poems that belong to this series illustrate dramatically how structure elucidates meaning. Chapter Six considers other evidence—both internal and external—that indicates our modern edition closely resembles the deluxe edition sent by Catullus to Cornelius Nepos. The Epilogue speculates on how and why Catullus organized his poetry in groups of interrelated poems, and it assesses his achievement.

Chapter Two:
The Polymetra

In Chapter One it was proposed that Catullus may have been the first ancient poet to integrate a large collection of poems of various lengths and of various genres.[1] A remarkable feature of cc. 1–14 lends support to this proposal. Parallel structures join a proportionally high number of corresponding poems in this unified sequence, eight of the fourteen.[2] To the best of my knowledge, in no other cycle of Latin poetry or book of comparable size are the correspondences of so many poems reaffirmed by their similar organizations. This point is significant because it appears that Catullus meticulously indicated the ring arrangement of the first fourteen poems in order to intimate the pervasive organizing principle for the entire work.

Poems 1–14

Figure 2.1 below illustrates the chiastic arrangement of cc. 1–14.[3] The theme of a gift of a *novus libellus* encloses the cycle. The programmatic 1 and 14 set Catullus' polished verse against the less-than-polished verse of inferior poets such as Caesius, Aquinus, and Suffenus. The second and third places from each end are held by pairs of consecutive poems that exhibit responsive relationships.[4] In the one pair, the solace that Lesbia derives from her love for the sparrow (c. 2) is answered by the grief she experiences as a result of its death (c. 3); in the other pair, Asinius' boorishness (c. 12) is answered by Fabullus' urbanity (c. 13). Cc. 6 and 10 deal with the subject of urbanity *(venustas),* too, but here the theme is combined with that of the *scortum*. Cc. 4, 9, and 11 hold in common the motif

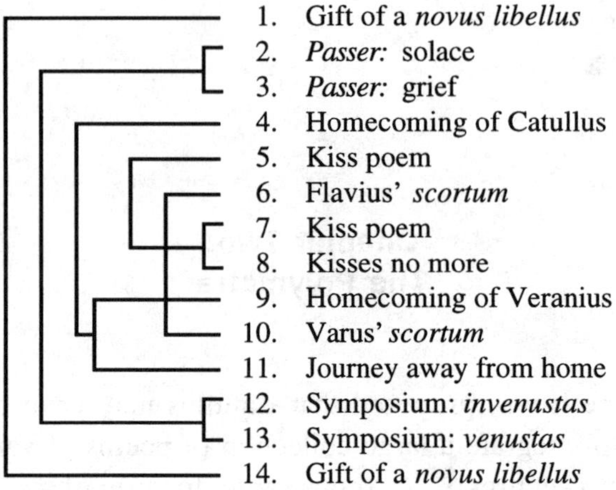

Figure 2.1 Ring Structure of Poems 1–14

of foreign travel. The dangerous journey away from home that Furius and Aurelius are to make in the intensely bitter c. 11 is contraposed to the happy homecomings of Catullus and Veranius in cc. 4 and 9. Lastly, the Lesbia kiss-poems 5 and 7, together with c. 8, form the pivot of the cycle. As C.P. Segal observes on their connection, c. 8 shares with 5 and 7 the *basia* theme as well as enlarging on "the momentary awareness of [Poem] Seven's *vesanus Catullus*."[5]

Poem 1

Cui dono lepidum novum libellum
arido modo pumice expolitum?
Corneli, tibi: namque tu solebas
meas esse aliquid putare nugas
iam tum, cum ausus es unus Italorum
omne aevum tribus explicare cartis
doctis, Iuppiter, et laboriosis.
quare habe tibi quidquid hoc libelli
qualecumque; quod, <o> patrona virgo,
plus uno maneat perenne saeclo.

The amount of secondary literature on c. 1 is enormous.[6] Despite the considerable attention lavished on this poem, only two of several controversial issues seem to be resolved. Most critics now interpret the description of the *libellus* in verses 1–2 as having a double significance, as referring not only to the external appearance of the book but to the contents of the book as well.[7] And a consensus appears to have been reached regarding the intent of verses 5–7. The laudatory character of these verses is nearly incontrovertible once it is recognized that Catullus describes Nepos' achievement and his own in similar terms.[8]

Two other major points of contention, however, continue to be re-examined and re-explored. The first concerns what is to be read at the end of verse 9, *patroni ut ergo* or *<o> patrona virgo*. The second has to do with the prefatory character of c. 1: precisely which poems does it introduce, 2–14, 2–50 or 2–51, 2–60, or 2–116? The correspondence of cc. 1 and 14 will assist in resolving the textual problem. The issue of which poems c. 1 introduces will be taken up again later.[9]

Poems 1~14

Cc. 1 and 14 are the only poems in the corpus to have as their theme a gift of a *novus libellus*.[10] The highly original, exquisitely polished, deluxe edition of c. 1 is a gift from a grateful Catullus to his friend Cornelius Nepos. The book of c. 14 (an anthology of very bad poets) also is a gift in gratitude, presumably from Sulla the *litterator* to his patron Licinius Calvus. The quality of Sulla's gift sets in motion a further development in the theme of book-giving, whereby the anthology of atrocious verse finds its way into Catullus' possession. It appears that Calvus cannot resist passing on this *novum ac repertum / munus* (8–9) as a Saturnalian gag-gift to a friend and fellow neoteric poet. Catullus' reaction to Calvus' practical joke is one of feigned horror, "Great gods, what a horrible and accursed little book" (*di magni, horribilem et sacrum libellum* 14.12). This hyperbolic expression of disdain finds its analogue in c. 1 in Catullus' exclamatory praise of Cornelius' *Chronica* as "a work of great erudition, Jupiter, and of immense effort" (*doctis*, *Iuppiter*, *et laboriosis* 7). Because Cornelius had acted as mentor to the young poet (*namque tu solebas / meas esse aliquid putare nugas* 3–4), he

	C. 1	C. 14
LITTÉRATEURS ADDRESSED	Corneli, tibi: namque (3)	iucundissime Calve,... te...: nam (2–4)
GIFTS OF NEW POETRY	Cui dono lepidum novum libellum / arido modo pumice expolitum? (1–2)	hoc novum ac repertum / munus dat tibi (8–9)
EXCLAMATIONS OF PRAISE AND FEIGNED HORROR	doctis, Iuppiter, et laboriosis (7)	di magni, horribilem et sacrum libellum (12)
GIFTS OF POETRY	habe tibi quidquid hoc libelli (8)	te his suppliciis [= carminibus] remunerabor (20)
NEW ADDRESSEES	<o> patrona virgo (9) maneat (10) saeclo (10)	pessimi poetae (23) abite (21) saecli (23)

Figure 2.2 Parallel Structure of Poems 1 and 14

is now to receive this presentation copy of neoteric poems as an expression of Catullus' gratitude (*quare habe tibi quidquid hoc libelli / qualecumque* 8–9). By contrast, in the corresponding poem Calvus is to receive as a "gift" poetry of quite a different sort. Catullus plans to get even with his witty friend by sending him an anthology of poetry as bad as (or perhaps even worse than) that which he sent to Catullus (*te his suppliciis* [= *carminibus Caesiorum, Aquinorum, Suffeni*] *remunerabor* 18–20).

Figure 2.2 above shows how the sections directed to the littérateurs Nepos and Calvus exhibit a parallel structure. The same figure illustrates that the parallelism continues into the final verses. Here both poems introduce another addressee, the relationship between whom conforms to the pattern of contrast found in the preceding sections. 1.9–10 are directed to the Muse; 14.21–23 to her antithesis, the *pessimi poetae*, described earlier in the poem as violators of "the rites of the Muse" (*impiorum* 7).[11] The connection between the Muse and the awful poets is strengthened by verbal ties. The noun *saeclum* occurs in the final verse of both poems, and *maneat* at 1.10 is echoed by its opposite *abite* at 14.21.

The similar structure of cc. 1 and 14 has important implications for the textual problem at 1.9. In the *textus receptus* the penultimate verse has suffered the loss of a syllable. The simplest way to repair the meter is to adopt the Renaissance supplement of an "o" before *patrona virgo*, as Mynors does in the *OCT:*

> quare habe tibi quidquid hoc libelli 8
> qualecumque; quod, <o> patrona virgo, 9
> plus uno maneat perenne saeclo. 10

Some critics find this emendation unsatisfactory and prefer instead the conjecture of Bergk/Munro/Goold, in which a reference to Cornelius Nepos as patron replaces the patron Muse:[12]

> quare habe tibi quidquid hoc libelli 8
> qualecumque quidem patroni ut ergo 9
> plus uno maneat perenne saeclo. 10

The past few years have witnessed an inundation of secondary literature for and against each of the two readings. In figure 2.3 below arguments against *o patrona virgo* are catalogued with their counterarguments in A–A^1 through G–G^1; major objections adduced for both emendations follow in H–H^1 through J–J^1.[13] The enumeration of arguments and objections is instructive because it makes clear why this textual problem remains unresolved. First, the arguments for and against *o patrona virgo* seem equally weighted, and, second, neither emendation is without difficulties.

The objections to *o patrona virgo* in A through G fall under two categories: (1) the vagueness of the expression and (2) the poem's double addressees. The reason for the second addressee has already been suggested: structurally, c. 1 is meant to mirror c. 14. The description of the Muse as a *patrona* may serve a similar purpose. Catullus may simply be creating another point of convergence between the two poems. Sulla is a client of Calvus, Catullus is a client of the Muse (the legal language *habe tibi* at verse 8 paves the way for the reference to a patron-client relationship at verse 9). Accordingly, although neither reading of 1.9 is without difficulties, the

ARGUMENTS AGAINST READING *<o> patrona virgo*	COUNTERARGUMENTS
A. Change of addressee from *tibi* to *o patrona virgo* is quite "difficult" (Fordyce *ad loc.*; Singleton 195).	A[1] Legal and religious expressions (*habe tibi, quidquid, qualecumque, quod*) pave the way for the appearance of the Muse, who is the natural addressee of a prayer for the immortality of a literary work (Carins 157–58).
B. In other dedicatory/introductory poems, "we find that whether the Muse, the patron, or the book is addressed, the addressee remains the same throughout" (Singleton 195).	B.[1] The addressee in a dedicatory/introductory poem need not remain the same throughout; cf. Horace, *Odes* 2.1 (Cairns 157–58).
C. "The phrase *patrona virgo* is incongruous.... The reader surely expects the poem to end with some explicit reference to Nepos as *patronus*; he does not expect the introduction of a rival patron to steal Nepos' thunder" (Singleton 195).	C[1]. "A sufficient number of such near-contemporary prologues including both Muse and patron have survived to show that Catullus' readers would not have been surprised to come upon the Muse in line 9" (Cairns 156). Also, it is unlikely that Catullus would have used the term "patron" to describe his association with Nepos, because "in classical Latin, *patronus* is not used in speaking of literary relationships" (White 79).
D. "Nowhere is the Muse ever referred to as 'patron'" (Goold 256).	D[1]. Poets are described elsewhere as clients of the Muses (Levine 215, note 27).
E. We always meet Catullus' Muses in the plural (Goold 256).	E[1]. The singular [*virgo*] aptly accords "with the correlative association...between the Muse and Nepos" (Levine 215, note 27).

F. *Virgo, virgineus*, and *virginitas* occur only in the long poems (Goold 256).

F^1. The word *virgo*, applied to the Muses or a Muse-equivalent, connects cc. 1, 61, and 65. Catullus' purpose is to relate the three poems that head a major division of the corpus (Arkins 18–19; Dettmer 74–75).

G. After Catullus depreciates his poetry, it seems odd to find him asking for its immortality. Further, "who is the Muse for a *libellus* of *nugae*?" (Fordyce *ad loc.*; Goold 256; Singleton 196).

G^1. Catullus' modesty is all part of a pose to receive a "dispassionate judgment" of his poems from his Roman audience. The prayer to an indiscriminate Muse is entirely consonant with the self-disparaging language found in the rest of the poem (Copley 205).

ARGUMENTS AGAINST
<o patrona virgo>

H. The stop after the fourth syllable gives an enjambment unparalleled in the hendecasyllabics (Fordyce *ad loc.*; Goold 254).

I. The use of "o" with "an adjective and noun combination" is unparalleled in the poetry of Catullus (Goold 254).

J. *Patrona virgo* "can be construed only as a vocative, which is very strange, because in Catullus…vocatives normally have some formal connection with the sentence" (Goold 255).

ARGUMENTS AGAINST
quidem patroni ut ergo

H^1. Not only is the elision *patroni ut* quite harsh (Ellis *ad loc.*), but elision of -i before u- very rarely occurs (Monbrun 35, note 18).

I^1. *Ergo* either as preposition or conjunction does not appear elsewhere in Catullus. Further, the genitive with *ergo* occurs rarely in Latin poetry (Clausen 38, note 2).

J^1. In all Latin literature except for one instance (Arnobius) "*ergo* follows immediately on the genitive" (Clausen 38, note 2).

Figure 2.3

close relation of cc. 1 and 14 tips the scales in favor of the virgin Muse.

A final point. It has not been noticed that the prayer to the Muse at the end of c. 1 makes good sense from a linear perspective by providing a transition to the very next poem. C. 2 parodies the form and content of a Roman hymn to a god.[14] The juxtaposition of cc. 1 and 2 also is significant regarding the question of whether the end-rhyme couplets in c. 1 are intentional or accidental (libellUM~expolitUM 1–2; solebAS~nugAS 3–4; cartIS~laboriosIS 6–7; virgO~saeclO 9–10).[15] From c. 1 to c. 2 the conscious artistry shifts from the end of the line to the beginning. In c. 2, the initial words or consonants in verses 2–9 display an elaborate structure:[16]

QUICUM LUDERE	2
Cui primUM	3
ET	4
Cum desiderIO	5
Carum nescIO	6
ET	7
Credo, ut tUM	8
TECUM LUDERE	9

Poems 2~3

Catullus' love affair with Lesbia is the unifying theme of this body of poetry. The poet signifies the importance of the woman and the theme by introducing his lady in the very first poems of the collection proper. Although cc. 2 and 3 are ostensibly about his mistress' pet bird, they reveal much about "Lesbia," who is referred to simply as *mea puella* in both poems (2.1; 3.3, 4, 17), and Catullus' relation to her:[17]

Passer, DELICIAE meae puellae,
quicum LUDERE, quem IN SINU TENERE,
cui primum digitum dare APPETENTI
et ACRIS solet INCITARE MORSUS,
cum DESIDERIO meo nitenti
carum nescio quid lubet IOCARI,

et SOLACIOLUM SUI DOLORIS,
credo, ut tum GRAVIS acquiescat ARDOR:
tecum LUDERE sicut ipsa, posse
et TRISTIS animi levare CURAS
tam gratum est mihi quam ferunt puellae
pernici aureolum fuisse malum,
quod zonam solvit diu ligatam.

The amorous language indicated in the passage above suggests that Lesbia is playing erotic games with the sparrow.[18] From this play she apparently derives complete sexual satisfaction. Catullus, however, cannot achieve the same satisfaction from playing with the bird. In order to relieve his *ardor* and *dolor*, nothing short of "full sexual relations with Lesbia" will do.[19]

The second *passer* poem reverses the situation in the first; solace provided by the bird is replaced here by grief caused by the death of the bird:

Lugete, o Veneres Cupidinesque,
et quantum est hominum venustiorum:
passer mortuus est meae puellae,
passer, deliciae meae puellae.
quem plus illa oculis suis amabat.
nam mellitus erat suamque norat
ipsam tam bene quam puella matrem,
nec sese a gremio illius movebat,
sed circumsiliens modo huc modo illuc
ad solam dominam usque pipiabat;
qui nunc it per iter tenebricosum
illud, unde negant redire quemquam.
at vobis male sit, malae tenebrae
Orci, quae omnia bella devoratis:
tam bellum mihi passerem abstulistis.
o factum male, quod, miselle passer,
tua nunc opera meae puellae
flendo turgiduli rubent ocelli.

Catullus calls upon all the Venuses and Cupids and men blessed by love to mourn, for Lesbia's pet sparrow is dead. As a result, she can no longer use the bird to relieve her sexual desires as she used to do. In contrast to c. 2, therefore, she is unhappy and sexually unfulfilled.

The connection between cc. 2 and 3 is signaled by the expression *passer, deliciae meae puellae* (2.1; 3.4), which occurs only here.[20] In addition, *nec sese a gremio illius movebat* in 3.8 echoes *quem in sinu tenere* in 2.2; *tam...quam puella* in 3.6 recalls the similar collocation of *tam...quam...puellae* in 2.11—the correlatives *tam...quam* do not occur often in the poetry;[21] and the impersonal *negant* in 3.12 parallels its positive counterpart *ferunt* in 2.11.

2b

I have indicated in the preceding paragraph, as well as elsewhere, my opinion on the problematical 2b; I think these verses were meant to form the close to c. 2.[22] The symmetry of 2/3 and 12/13 in the ring structure of the cycle strengthens this view. In a collection of poetry, when two pairs of consecutive poems balance each other by their parallel position in a ring pattern, as 2/3 and 12/13 do, no poem ever intrudes between the first and second member of the pair because each set of corresponding poems functions as a unit.[23] This symmetrical relationship thus eliminates the possibility that 2b represents a fragment of a lost poem that once separated the first *passer* poem from the second, a solution that some critics have found very attractive.[24] Consequently, two options remain. Either the fragmentary 2b somehow strayed into this position of the text, or, more likely, the three verses belong to c. 2.

For those strongly opposed to integration, the point is worth making that the mythological tag may well represent a later addition to c. 2, made prior to the publication of the entire work.[25] This proposal is prompted by details suggesting artistic refinement. Not only do references to myths in which apples overcome opposition to love connect the poems that head each half of the corpus (2 and 65),[26] but the theme of virginity (and its loss) serves to link the opening poems of each tripartition.[27] An issue of even greater controversy than the unity of c. 2 will be considered later. This concerns the question of whether cc. 2 and 3 can sustain an obscene interpretation (i.e., does *passer* signify *mentula*?).[28]

C. 2 provides an excellent introduction to the love affair with Lesbia by foreshadowing the painful direction that the relationship is to take. While Lesbia's sexual desires seem easily satisfied, Catullus' are not. It is notable, too, that verse 5 of c. 3 represents the only instance in the corpus where Lesbia is said to love something more than she loves herself (*quem* [= *passerem*] *plus illa oculis suis amabat*).[29] If the "bird" is interpreted literally as Lesbia's pet, the statement seems to suggest a certain emotional shallowness. If the "bird" is interpreted metaphorically (*passer* = *mentula*), then Catullus indicates, albeit humorously, that from the outset Lesbia's interest in him was chiefly physical (i.e., she loved the part of him from which she derived sexual pleasure).[30] The next Lesbia poem takes up this intensely physical side of their relation. Catullus' exuberant exhortation "to live and to love" follows naturally on a pair of poems that illustrate the brevity of both life and pleasure.[31]

Poems 5, 7, and 8

The Lesbia kiss-poems 5 and 7 have long been recognized as companion pieces. In this instance, however, perhaps because the relation is so obvious, critics have focused their attention not on the similarities but on the differences.[32]

To begin, the *basia*-poems are dissimilar in mood and complexity. C. 5 is simple, immediate, and exuberant; c. 7 is elaborate, distant, and quiet, with geography, learned references, and formal language all contributing to create an atmosphere of detachment. C. 5 speaks of Catullus and Lesbia as a pair; c. 7 speaks of them separately. In c. 5 Catullus urges Lesbia to indulge in physical expressions of love, and their passion is conceived of as an answer to life's brevity. By contrast, in c. 7 the lovers merely talk, and Catullus' passion is equated with madness. Both poems employ the language of calculation but to opposite ends. While in c. 5 Catullus uses finite numbers to express the notion of infinity, in c. 7 he uses images of infinity, the sand and the stars, to respond to Lesbia's request for a finite number. Both poems too refer to evil spells in their final verses; but the close of c. 7, with its vividly personified *mala lingua*,[33] appears more ominous than the close of c. 5, with its corresponding but vague *ne quis malus*. Likewise, although both poems appeal to nature by way of illustration, the nature of c. 5, which

	C. 5	C. 7
ADDRESS TO LESBIA	mea Lesbia (1)	Lesbia (2)
COUNTING LANGUAGE	unius aestimemus assis (3)	magnus numerus...harenae (3)
NATURE AND DEATH:		
HEAT	soles	Iovis...aestuosi
DEATH	occidere/occidit	sepulcrum
DAYLIGHT/STARS	lux	sidera
NIGHT	nox (4–6)	nox (5–7)
MULTITUDE OF KISSES	multa [basia] fecerimus (7–10)	te basia multa basiare (9)
COUNTING LANGUAGE	conturbabimus (11)	nec pernumerare (11)
SUPERSTITION	ne quis malus invidere possit (12)	nec...curiosi / possint nec mala fascinare lingua (11–12)

Figure 2.4 Parallel Structure of Poems 5 and 7

so eloquently reinforced the theme of *carpe diem*, takes on sinister overtones in c. 7, where in the still of the night countless stars observe the illicit love affairs of men. The many differences in detail tend to obscure just how similar cc. 5 and 7 really are. As figure 2.4 above illustrates, in structure the one Lesbia kiss-poem is a carbon copy of the other.

Both poems are directed to Lesbia; both deal with calculation; in both there is an appeal to nature, with the same elements enumerated; both are concerned with an infinite number of kisses; and in both Catullus is anxious to confound the curiosity of those who might curse his and Lesbia's love through their knowledge of the exact number. In addition, a close connection is indicated by the one poem's resuming verbally where the other ends (cf. *tantum...esse basiorum* 5.13 and *quot...basiationes...sint* 7.1–2). The spatial and intellectual distancing and the air of detachment are intended to signify that the passion in c. 5 is starting to cool in c. 7. The underlying conflict adumbrated by this remoteness is made explicit in the very next poem, where a rift has taken place and the lovers are estranged. What is more, by indicating an emotional commitment to Lesbia in the final verses of c. 7 (*vesano Catullo* 10), Catullus sets the stage for the pain, the anger, and the ambivalence toward Lesbia that is to follow. In c. 8 mood and tone are skillfully conveyed through language, meter, and total lack of enjambment, which results in an emotionally dramatic pause at the end of every verse.[34]

Poem 8

C. 8 is about Catullus' contradictory feelings toward Lesbia.[35] In form, the poem is a dramatic monologue in which Catullus presents simultaneously two aspects of his personality: the passionate lover, who clearly is reluctant to reject Lesbia, and the rational poet, who asserts that the affair is over.

C. 8 opens with the theme of the infatuated lover (1–2):

> Miser Catulle, desinas ineptire,
> et quod vides perisse perditum ducas.

The emotionally charged *miser Catulle* creates a link between 8.1 and the final verses of c. 7, where Catullus also describes himself as completely dominated by passion (*vesano Catullo*).[36] In verse 2, *ducas* with its overtones of computation calls to mind the language of accounting that occurred in both cc. 5 and 7. The recollection seems bitterly pointed. While in the previous poems the language of calculation was used to exhort Lesbia to indulge in passion,[37] here it is used to an opposite end, to enjoin the impassioned Catullus to accept the fact that he has lost Lesbia.

The verses that follow recall Catullus' past happiness (3–8):

> fulsere quondam candidi tibi soles,
> cum ventitabas quo puella ducebat
> amata nobis quantum amabitur nulla.
> ibi illa multa cum iocosa fiebant,

quae tu volebas nec puella nolebat,
fulsere vere candidi tibi soles.

The *soles* of verses 3 and 8 echo the *soles* of 5.4, where Catullus, appealing to nature, urged Lesbia to "seize the day." The "suns" of c. 8 may parallel those of c. 5 in another respect. In writing on syllabic wordplay in 5.4–6, F. Ahl observes that "by pluralizing 'sun,' Catullus generates *SOLes*, 'you habitually'."[38] In c. 8 there is an even greater temptation to see Catullus playing on this analogue of the plural "suns," for the notion of repeated action suggested by the *soles* of verses 3 and 8 provides a perfect frame for a section replete with verbs in the imperfective tense.

In c. 5 "living" is synonymous with "loving" (*Vivamus, mea Lesbia, atque amemus* 1). In c. 8 the synonymity of the two ideas seems implicit, as is suggested by the bleak and desolate picture that Catullus paints of Lesbia's life without his love (9–19):

nunc iam illa non volt: tu quoque inpote<ns noli>,
nec quae fugit sectare, nec miser vive,
sed obstinata mente perfer, obdura.
vale, puella. iam Catullus obdurat,
nec te requiret nec rogabit invitam.
at tu dolebis, cum rogaberis nulla.
scelesta, vae te, quae tibi manet vita?
quis nunc te adibit? cui videberis bella?
quem nunc amabis? cuius esse diceris?
quem basiabis? cui labella mordebis?
at tu, Catulle, destinatus obdura.

As critics have observed, by describing what is to come in terms of the past, Catullus is really predicting his (and not Lesbia's) future unhappiness.

The language in verses 14–18 again calls to mind cc. 5 and 7. The questions, "whose will you say you are?" and "whom now will you love," posed in verse 17 recall that Lesbia was once Catullus' and that he loved her (cf. *mea Lesbia* and *amemus* at 5.1). "Whom will you kiss?" in verse 18 looks back to the innumerable kisses in cc. 5 and 7 (*basia multa*); at the same time, by virtue of its position at the end of c. 8, the question *quem basiabis* brings the series of kiss-poems to a close.[39] A last common feature is that the poems conclude with oral imagery, *lingua* in 7 and *labella mordebis* in 8.[40]

The struggle between intellect and emotion informs the shape of c. 8:[41]

1–2	Be firm, Catullus
3–8	His and Lesbia's past happiness
9–13	Be firm, Catullus
14–18	His and Lesbia's future unhappiness
19	Be firm, Catullus

The alternation of resolution and reflection of past joy is intended to suggest that Catullus' ambivalence toward Lesbia is not settled at the poem's end. Rather, the ring structure turns c. 8 back on itself, thus causing the struggle between intellect and emotion to begin again.[42] The closing imperative *obdura*, which contains the UR- element meaning "to burn with passion," is emblematic of Catullus' conflict. At the very moment that he is attempting to steel himself, he longs for Lesbia's love. This lack of resolution looks forward to c. 11, where in contrast to c. 8 the farewell to Lesbia appears final.

C. 11 is the only Lesbia poem in this cycle that is not joined to another Lesbia poem. It functions instead as counterpart to cc. 4 and 9. The three poems are related through the theme of foreign travel.[43]

Poems 4, 9, and 11

Cc. 4 and 9 deal with the homecomings of Catullus and Veranius from their travels abroad in Bithynia and Spain.[44] Their presumably real and safe journeys are set in opposition to a dangerous, projected journey to be made by Furius and Aurelius in c. 11, the purpose of which (on the surface, at least) is to suggest the loyalty of Catullus' friends. Cc. 4, 9, and 11 show some interesting parallels. The three poems hold in common temporal as well as spatial movement (the direction of the poems is to or away from Rome). Within cc. 4 and 9 the temporal sequence is mirrored, as tenses shift from present to past to present (c. 4) and from present to future to past to future to present (c. 9). C. 11, on the other hand, inverts a natural chronological order by beginning with the future, slipping by way of an imperative into the present, and ending with the past. All three poems feature a geographical excursus, which is hinted at in 9.6–7 and is developed in 4.6–24 and 11.1–14. The poems also closely associate travel and danger. In c. 9 Catullus expresses relief that his friend Veranius has returned from Spain unharmed (*incolumem*); in cc. 4 and 11 the element of danger is a natural concomitant to the epic adventures experienced by the ship (6–9, 18–24) and to be experienced by Furius and Aurelius (1–14).

Two additional features link cc. 4 and 11. Both make use of intermediaries. In c. 4 the ship speaks indirectly to the visitors through the poet, while in c. 11 the poet speaks indirectly to Lesbia through Furius and Aurelius. And both contain reminiscences of sepulchral epitaphs. In c. 4 the address to the *hospites*, followed by the life-story of the *phaselus* and the boasts of excellence, elicits details found in Latin funereal inscriptions;[45] in c. 11 the renunciatory *cum suis vivat valeatque moechis* echoes and parodies the valediction *vive ac vale,* which sometimes appears on Roman gravestones.[46]

The question that now arises is this: What is the point of the relation of cc. 4, 9, and 11? The answer appears to lie with c. 11 and the combined themes of epic adventure and rejection of Lesbia.

C. 11 is really about two diametrically opposed ways of life. Verses 1–14 are concerned with the soldier-adventurer; verses 15–24 with the lover. Once this polarity is recognized, it becomes clear that loss of Lesbia's love prompts thoughts of joining expeditions to the ends of the world. As D.O. Ross, Jr. observes, "the opposition between the lover and the soldier,...could be used to represent the unhappy end of an affair."[47] His observation is important for the connection of cc. 4 and 11. Catullus appears to be using Lesbia's utter and complete betrayal of his love in the one poem to justify serving on Memmius' praetorial staff in the other, a justification prompted by a violation of his ethico-literary posture as a *homo otiosus*.[48] Regarding the interplay of cc. 9 and 11, Catullus' great affection for Veranius and his obvious joy at his return contrast sharply with his contempt for Lesbia, whom he repudiates through intermediaries. Presumably the purpose of this opposing relation is to point forward to cc. 12 through 14, where Veranius and other male friends will "fill the gap left by Lesbia."[49]

Furius and Aurelius

Much has been written on the question of whether Furius and Aurelius are true or false friends.[50] Their names are suggestive regarding this issue. In other poems concerned with Furius and Aurelius, Catullus seems to be playing on their *nomina* to indicate a Tweeddledum/Tweeddledee relationship. He associates madness with Aurelius (instead of Furius) and lack of money chiefly with Furius (instead of Aurelius, whose *nomen* has pecuniary overtones).[51] In view of this witty, semantic enallage, I think it is possible to construe the names together as "Mad for gold" or "Money-mad." The paronomasia thus illuminates the choice of Furius and Aurelius as *comites Catulli* in c. 11. This twosome are exactly the sort who would willingly go with Catullus on campaign to the far corners of the earth in pursuit of wealth, but who are unlikely to have been numbered among his closest friends.

Poems 6~10

Sandwiched between the travelogues of 9 and 11 and the kiss-poems of 5 and 7 occur a pair of *scorta* poems.[52] Cc. 6 and 10 are joined by two related themes. The poems are concerned specifically with the demimondaines of Flavius and Varus, and generally with the larger issue of whether the girl friends possess that indefinable yet highly desirable quality of *lepor*.[53] In fact, each poem is framed by the notion of charm and its opposite: c. 6 begins with *illepidum* and ends with *lepidum*, while c. 10, inverting the order, begins with *non illepidum* and ends with *insulsum*. The progression from one extreme to the other is accompanied by a parallel ordering of words and ideas (shown in figure 2.5 below, page 32), the purpose of which is to indicate that cc. 6 and 10 function as companion pieces.

Cc. 6 and 10 begin similarly by introducing the same principals—a male friend, his girl friend, and Catullus:

Flavi, | delicias tuas | Catullo (6.1)

Varus | me meus | ad suos amores (10.1)

The transposition of the order of the girl friend and Catullus in the initial verse of c. 10 was deliberately contrived to reflect a change in focus. While the first of the pair is about a friend's mistress, the second is really about Catullus.

The next verses describe the current mistresses of Flavius and Varus:

ni sint illepidae atque inelegantes,
velles dicere nec tacere posses.
verum nescio quid febriculosi
scorti diligis: hoc pudet fateri. (6.2–5)

visum duxerat e foro otiosum,
scortillum, ut mihi tum repente visum est,
non sane illepidum neque invenustum. (10.2–4)

Catullus speaks of both women as *scorta*, and hints that both are unhealthy *scorta* at that. In c. 6, *febriculosi*, in addition to its metaphorical sense of "hot little tart," literally means "sick of a fever"; the view that Flavius' lover is truly ill, very likely the victim of malaria, has been revived by M.G. Morgan.[54] In c. 10, the infirmity of Varus' girl is suggested both by *visere ad*, an expression commonly used of visiting the sick,[55] and by the later reference in verse 26 to Serapis, a god of healing. The language in the passages quoted above further indicates that Catullus is consciously connecting the demimondaines. *Scortum* and its diminutive *scortillum* do not occur elsewhere,[56] and only here is *illepidus* used with reference to people.[57] The contrasting pairs of adjectives in 6.2, *illepidae atque inelegantes*, and 10.4, *non sane illepidum neque invenustum*, are instructive because they account for the divergent attitudes of the male principals. Flavius is disinclined to speak about his lady, Catullus would have us believe, presumably because she is "unrefined," while Varus introduces Catullus to his lady, presumably because in his opinion she is not "unsophisticated."

The theme of speech joins the verses that follow. Although Flavius refuses to be lured into kissing and telling, Catullus asserts that the furnishings of his bedroom (in vain mute) loudly proclaim how he has been spending his evenings. Further, the condition of the bed and of Flavius' thighs attests to the type of woman with whom he has been consorting, all details meant to induce Flavius' discomfiture. In c. 10 Catullus, almost a foil to Flavius, voluntarily speaks of his experience in Bithynia as a member of Memmius' praetorial staff. And Catullus' loquacity (in contrast to the reticence of Flavius) leads to his discomfiture. In order to make himself appear better off than he actually is, Catullus lies—and is later caught in his white lie—about owning a litter with litter-bearers, a local product of Bithynia.

The description of the *lectica* in Catullus' aside in 10.21–23, where he reveals the truth,

> at mi nullus erat NEC HIC NEQUE ILLIC,
> FRACTUM qui VETERIS pedem GRABATI
> in COLLO sibi COLLOcare posset.

is strongly reminiscent of the description of Flavius' bed in 6.9–11:

> pulvinusque peraeque ET HIC ET ILLE
> ATTRITUS, TREMULIque quassa LECTI
> arGUTATIO inamBULATIOque.

The first verses of each passage hold in common the expressions *et hic et ille* and *nec hic neque illic*. Not only does this similar phraseology occupy the same position in the line, but it also does not appear elsewhere in the poetry.[58] The second verses are parallel in thought and structure. Words conveying "disintegration," *attritus* and *fractum*, open the lines (*fractum* also parallels *quassa*); words for "bed" in the genitive close the lines; and adjectives modifying words for "bed," *tremuli* and *veteris*, appear in the same metrical position in the center. The third verses feature Catullan wordplay, *ar-gutati(o) inam-bulatio-que* in c. 6 and *collo sibi collo-care* in c. 10.

The next points of coincidence initiate the process of bringing the verbal echoes full circle. *quidquid habes...dic* (6.15–16) and

	C. 6	C. 10
SIMILAR PRINCIPALS	Flavi, delicias tuas Catullo (1)	Varus me meus ad suos amores (1)
SCORTA	ni sint illepidae (2)	non sane illepidum (4)
RETICENCE VS. LOQUACITY	tacere (3)	incidere nobis / sermones varii (5 ff.)
BEDS IN A STATE OF COLLAPSE	attritus, tremulique quassa lecti / argutatio inambulatioque (10–11)	fractum qui veteris pedem grabati / in collo sibi collocare (22–23)
SPEECH	quidquid habes… dic nobis (15–16)	istud quod modo dixeram me habere (28)
REVERSAL OF EARLIER QUALITIES	lepido (17)	insulsa male (33)

Figure 2.5 Parallel Structure of Poems 6 and 10

istud quod modo dixeram me habere (10.28) recall the motif of speech that occurred at 6.6ff. and 10.5ff. (see figure 2.5 above). As a result of this verbal framing, the notion of beds in a state of collapse becomes the centerpiece of the parallel structuring of cc. 6 and 10. Catullus emphasizes this particular theme to reaffirm the lighthearted and comic intent of the poems.[59]

The chiastic arrangement of each poem is completed by the reversal of the opening theme of *illepidum* or *lepidum*. In c. 10, because Varus' girl embarrasses Catullus by resoundingly outwitting him, he revises his initial impression of her as *non sane illepidum neque invenustum* (4); he now considers her *insulsa male et molesta* (33). In c. 6 Catullus promises to transform the "unrefined" affair of Flavius through his "refined" verses.[60] In other words, what was previously *illepidum* (2), his poetry will render *lepidum* (17). The parallelism of cc. 6 and 10 illuminates the subtlety of Catullus' artistry. Although the poet employed essentially the same elements to shape his poems, he skillfully concealed the close resemblance by highlighting different aspects of their themes. Prominent in the one is the amusing anecdote that Catullus tells at his own expense. Pre-eminent in the other is the playful treatment of a conventional motif derived from Hellenistic poetry: In c. 6 the theme of the lover's sorry appearance that betrays his infatuation is transferred from Flavius to the bedroom furnishings where the love-making took place.[61]

Finally, it is worth observing that cc. 6 and 10 are perfectly placed between cc. 5~7 and 9~11. C. 10 continues the theme of foreign travel from 9 and carries it over into 11. C. 6 casts Catullus in the role of voyeur, the very sort of person who arouses his own fear at the end of both 5 and 7. In addition, the inclusion of the *scorta* poems in this initial sequence of Lesbia poems is meant to anticipate Catullus' painful revelation in the final stanzas of c. 11 that his own Lesbia is no better than a whore.[62]

Poems 12~13

In cc. 12 and 13 Catullus again attempts to define the elusive qualities of *lepor* and *venustas*. As in the earlier cc. 6 and 10, the poet illustrates what he means by sophistication through antithesis.[63] The lack of *urbanitas* of the provincial Asinius Marrucinus in the one piece is contrapuntal to the *urbanitas* of Catullus and his friend Fabullus in the other. Cc. 12 and 13 also resemble cc. 6 and 10 in that although the poems are joined by various elements, such as a symposiac setting and the motif of gift-giving, a parallel structure (shown below, page 37) provides the most compelling evidence of their complementary character.[64]

Both cc. 12 and 13 open by addressing the recipients, whose names seem well suited to the predominant theme of the poems. The *nomen* Asinius (< *asinus*) may connote boorishness,[65] the very subject of c. 12, while the *cognomen* Fabullus has gastronomical associations (< *faba*),[66] which neatly coordinate with the dinner-invitation of c. 13. The backdrop for each poem is a symposium, which is taking place or is to take place at Catullus' house. The point of the common setting is to sharpen the focus on the characters of the two protagonists:

Marrucine Asini, manu sinistra
NON BELLE uteris: IN IOCO ATQUE VINO
TOLLIS lintea neglegentiorum.
hoc SALSUM esse putas? fugit te, inepte:
quamvis sordida res et INVENUSTA est.
non credis mihi? crede Pollioni
fratri, qui tua FURTA vel talento
mutari velit:... (12.1–8)

Cenabis BENE, mi Fabulle, apud me
paucis, si tibi di favent, diebus,
si tecum ATTULERIS bonam atque magnam
cenam, non sine candida puella
et VINO et SALE et OMNIBUS CACHINNIS.
haec si, inquam, ATTULERIS, VENUSTE noster,
cenabis bene;... (13.1–7)

The contrasting language in the opening sections indicates that Fabullus is acting as foil to Asinius. The negative terms describing Asinius' theft in c. 12, *non belle* (< *bonus*) and *invenusta* (2, 5), are echoed by their positive equivalents used in association with Fabullus in c. 13, *bene* (< *bonus*) and *venuste* (1, 6). Likewise, the etymological relationship between *tollis/furta* (< *fero*) and *attuleris* (12.3, 7; 13.3, 6) makes clear that Asinius' act of thievery in c. 12 is being set in opposition to the contributions to be provided by Fabullus in c. 13. Presumably, too, Fabullus possesses the intangible qualities of wit and gaiety that he is to bring, unlike his ill-bred counterpart.

At the center of cc. 12 and 13 the focus shifts from Asinius to his brother Pollio ("the Polished One") and from Fabullus to Catullus. Both the language and the structuring of the language here are very similar:

EST ENIM leporum
DIFFERTUS PUer ac facetiarum. (12.8–9)

NAM tui Catulli
PLENUS saccULUS EST aranearum. (13.7–8)

nam and its postpositive derivative *enim* (*e* + *nam*) are followed by trisyllabic masculine nouns in the genitive, *leporum* and *Catulli*. At the beginning of the next line occur masculine adjectives in the nominative signifying "fullness"; *differtus* and *plenus* are in turn followed by masculine nouns in the nominative, *PUer* and *saccULUS*, which through their stem or suffix convey the idea of "smallness";[67] and the passages are completed by pentasyllabic feminine nouns in the genitive plural, *facetiarum* and *aranearum*. This extremely contrived verbal parallelism closely associates Catullus of c. 13 with Pollio of c. 12, a young man "stuffed full" of witty pranks. The purpose is to indicate that Catullus too possesses a high degree of urbanity in order to justify his criticism of Pollio's older brother. The verbal parallels at 12.8–9 and 13.7–8 also are significant for a reading in the text. The correlation between the adjectives for "full" strongly suggests the superiority of Passertius' emendation of *differtus* at 12.9 over the manuscript's reading of *disertus*.[68]

The next verses are linked by the notion of anticipation:

> quare aut HENDECASYLLABOS TRECENTOS
> EXSPECTA, aut mihi linteum remitte, (12.10–11)
>
> sed contra ACCIPIES MEROS AMORES (13.9)

If Asinius does not return Catullus' napkin, he will receive as punishment a few hundred hendecasyllables; as recompense for Fabullus' bringing nearly everything to the dinner-party, he will receive "the essence of love." The phrase *meros amores* is troublesome: is it to be taken as synonymous with *unguentum* in verse 11, or do *meros amores* and *unguentum* mean two different things?[69] Recently, M. Marcovich and W.H. Bernstein, arguing independently that *meri amores* is distinct from *unguentum*, suggest that the phrase signifies "love poetry."[70] The interplay of 12.10–11 and 13.9 lends support to their proposal, for it seems only logical to link the objects of *accipies* and *exspecta* also. The correlation of *hendecasyllabos exspecta* and *accipies meros amores*, then, represents another incidence of contrast between the poems' principals. As it is fit and proper, *invenustus* Asinius, who displays his uncouth behavior to all, will receive the poetry of invective, while *venus-tus* Fabullus, a person of elegance, wit, and charm, will receive the poetry of love.

At 12.12ff. Asinius disappears, and the focus shifts entirely to the purloined napkin:

> quod me non movet aestimatione,verum est
> mnemosynum mei sodalis.
> NAM SUDARIA Saetaba ex Hiberis
> MISERUNT mihi MUNERI FABULLUS
> ET VERANIUS: haec amem necesse est
> ut Veraniolum meum et Fabullum.

Here we discover that the value of the napkin derives from its being a gift, a keepsake, given to Catullus by his friends, Fabullus and Veranius. The final verses of c. 13 likewise are concerned with a gift of inestimable value (10–14):

> seu quid suavius elegantiusve est:
> NAM UNGUENTUM DABO, QUOD MEAE PUELLAE
> DONARUNT VENERES CUPIDINESQUE,
> quod tu cum olfacies, deos rogabis,
> totum ut te faciant, Fabulle, nasum.

In addition to poetry, Fabullus is to receive scented perfume, which Catullus claims was given to his lady by the Venuses and Cupids. The last sections of the two poems thus neatly invert the roles of giver and receiver. The Spanish napkin is a present to Catullus from Fabullus (and Veranius); the divine perfume is to be a present to Fabullus from Catullus. Fabullus, who appears in the final verse of both poems (12.17; 13.14), completes the parallel structure.

A puzzling feature of c. 13 remains to be considered. Why, after the scathing dismissal of Lesbia in c. 11, does Catullus make mention of his lady at 13.11? The answer to this question is that the reference serves a multiple thematic and structural purpose. First, it creates a contrasting balance between cc. 2 and 13, where Lesbia first and last appears in the cycle.[71] Second, it indicates to a new reader of the poetry that Catullus' bitter renunciation of Lesbia in c. 11 does not

	C. 12	C. 13
OPPOSITION OF FABULLUS TO ASINIUS	Marrucine Asini,... non belle (1–2)	bene, mi Fabulle (1)
SYMPOSIUM	in ioco atque vino ...salsum (2, 4)	et vino et sale et omnibus cachinnis (5)
ILL-BRED ASINIUS VS. WELL-BRED FABULLUS	tollis lintea (3) invenusta (5) furta (7)	attuleris...cenam (3–4) venuste (6) attuleris (6)
NOTION OF FULLNESS	est enim leporum / differtus puer ac facetiarum (8–9)	nam tui Catulli / plenus sacculus est aranearum (7–8)
INVECTIVE SET AGAINST AMATORY POETRY	hendecasyllabos trecentos / exspecta (10–11)	accipies meros amores (9)
PRICELESS GIFTS	nam sudaria... miserunt mihi muneri (14–15)	nam unguentum dabo,...meae puellae / donarunt (11–12)
FABULLUS	ut...Fabullum (17)	ut..., Fabulle (14)

Figure 2.6 Parallel Structure of Poems 12 and 13

truly mark the end of the love affair.[72] The notion that 13.11 hints that Catullus' obsession with Lesbia will continue beyond these initial poems is borne out by the very next poem to refer to Lesbia. C. 36, a poem that speaks of reconciliation, picks up where c. 13 leaves off, both verbally and thematically, by reversing the genealogy of ownership from c. 13:

> nam unguentum dabo, quod MEAE PUELLAE
> donarunt VENERES CUPIDINESQUE,... (13.11–12)

> Annales Volusi, cacata carta,
> votum solvite pro MEA PUELLA.
> nam sanctae VENERI CUPIDINIQUE
> vovit,... (36.1–4)

In c. 13 Catullus will give Fabullus perfume, which the Venuses and Cupids gave to Lesbia and which Lesbia in turn gave to him; in c. 36 Lesbia is on the point of being "the giver of the gift of poetry" to Venus and Cupid—poetry which presumably she received earlier from Catullus. What is more, the transference of ownership of the divine *unguentum*, which once belonged to Catullus' mistress, to an intimate male friend in c. 13 appears to point forward to his coming involvement in a homosexual love affair in cc. 15–24.

Linear Structure of Poems 1–14

The circular structure of cc. 1–14 is complemented by a linear structure that links one poem with the next. C. 1 concludes with a request to the Muse for the immortality of the work. The prayer at the end paves the way for the parody of a hymn in c. 2. From c. 2 to c. 3 the thought shifts from the unhappiness of Catullus, who is unable to satisfy his desire, to the unhappiness of Catullus and Lesbia, both of whom are affected by the sparrow's death. The mock dirge and the journey of the bird to the underworld in c. 3 anticipate the reminiscences of the sepulchral epigram at the beginning of c. 4, as well as the adventures of the ship on the high seas. The fourth poem ends with the theme of old age and with a reference to the Dioscuri, who symbolize light and darkness, life and death. This combination provides an excellent transition to the opening verses of the next poem, where are found an urgent appeal to live and love in verse 1, rather censorious old men in verse 2, and the imagery of light and darkness in verses 3–5. C. 5 focuses on the physical side of love. Catullus' exhortation to Lesbia to yield to passion is thus preparatory to the theme of sexual abandon in c. 6. Here Catullus, relentless inquisitor of the debauched Flavius, plays the part of busybody, the very sort of person who arouses his own fear at the end of both 5 and 7. C. 7 is the pivotal poem of the cycle. Spatial and intellectual distancing suggests a cooling in the relation between Catullus and Lesbia, a cooling made explicit in c. 8. Unfortunately, because by this stage Catullus the lover is emotionally committed, he finds it difficult to come to terms with the dissolution of the love affair. Self-admonitions "to be strong, to endure" give way to memories of past happiness and physical pleasure. C. 8 is in turn joined to c. 9 by references to future kisses (*quem basiabis, [Lesbia]?* 8.18; *iucundum os oculosque [Verani] suaviabor* 9.8–9). The interplay between Lesbia's lack of affection for Catullus and Catullus' genuine affection for Veranius appears to anticipate the role to be played by male friends as surrogates of sorts for Lesbia after Catullus breaks off the attachment.[73] C. 10 picks up the theme of foreign travel from c. 9, an exuberant poem that celebrates Veranius' homecoming, and combines it with that of the *scortum*. This combination of themes, in turn, looks forward to "the not dissimilar combination" in the very next poem.[74] The geography of foreign places in c. 11, however, is exotic, no doubt to provide the proper backdrop for the coming description of Lesbia as a Scylla-like monster.[75] The motif of travel abroad continues into c. 12, with the reference to Spain at verse 14, and it may subtly continue into c. 13 as well. Perhaps the dinner-party that Fabullus is expecting is a *cena adventicia,* traditionally given on the safe return of a friend from abroad.[76] In addition, both cc. 13 and 14, which share with c. 12 the themes of wit (*sale* 13.5; *salse* 14.16), friendship, and gift-giving, provide an answer to the implicit question raised by c. 12, "By Catullus' standards, what constitutes an amusing prank?"[77] Surely it is witty to invite a close friend to a dinner-party that he must cater himself—if he is to dine well. Equally witty is to send a good friend a collection of god-awful poetry as a Saturnalia gift. This triad of lighthearted pieces that explore the issue of urbanity offer contrast and comic relief from the intensely bitter c. 11, a climactic *tour de force*, which draws together the principal themes of cc. 2–10: Lesbia, the *illepidum scortum*, and travel abroad/homecoming.[78]

Cc. 1–14 are the subject of a massive amount of secondary literature. Two reasons in particular account for their continuous popularity. The first has to do with the quality of the poems themselves. As a group they represent some of Catullus' finest pieces. The second reason concerns the endless fascination with the Lesbia poems. This opening cycle quite literally is built around the poems that deal with Lesbia (2, 3, 5, 7, 8, 11, 13). Catullus' purpose in giving prominence to the love affair here is to indicate that love, and especially love for Lesbia, is to be the principal theme of the entire *oeuvre*. In addition, the Lesbia poems together with the other poems of the cycle serve an important general function. As we shall see, cc. 1–14 act as an overture to the rest of the polymetra, which repeat and vary the opening themes.

14b

Si qui forte mearum ineptiarum
lectores eritis manusque vestras
non horrebitis admovere nobis.

Over the years critics have attempted to find a home for the presumably displaced 14b.[79] The fragment has been attached to the beginning of 2b and of c. 16, and to the end of c. 14. None of these transpositions, however, has proved satisfactory. The current view is that 14b represents a remnant of a longer poem that is now lost. Yet, despite its fragmentary character, the content of 14b provides just enough information to make some probable conjectures regarding the part that the complete poem once played in the structure of the corpus.

Because 14b is concerned with the poetry of Catullus, it is reasonable to suppose that the poem in its entirety had poetry as its subject. Indeed, this supposition is supported by verbal parallels that link the fragment with two earlier programmatic pieces, 1 and 14. C. 1 and 14b similarly describe Catullus' poetry in a self-deprecatory fashion as "trifles" (*meas...nugas* 1.4) and "foolishness" (*mearum ineptiarum* 14b.1). C. 14 and 14b associate poetry with the notion of "bristling" (*horribilem...libellum* 14.12; *non horrebitis...nobis [= carminibus]* 14b.3),[80] and they also identify poets closely with their poetry (14.21–23; 14b.3).[81]

Through the verbal interplay of 14b and c. 15, we can guess where the fragment once belonged in the lost poem. If the surviving verses occurred at the end, the phrase *manusque vestras* in the penultimate verse would anticipate *commendo tibi* (*con* + *manus* + *do*), "I put in your hands," at the beginning of c. 15. Actually, I am convinced that *si qui...nobis* served as the conclusion. Since the poems of Catullus often are organized in a ring-composition structure, it seems highly probable that the omission of verses is the result of a scribe's eye straying from an "if clause" occupying the same metrical position at the start of the poem to *si qui forte* at the end.

The language, programmatic character, and content of the fragment permit further speculation about its original purpose. A relationship with cc. 14 and 15 suggests that the once complete poem was meant to act as a transition between the first and second cycles. It is important to emphasize again the experimental nature of the arrangement. Catullus *wants* the reader to see how he organized his poems. If 14b had survived in its entirety, its dual function of rounding off the themes of cc. 1–14 and of anticipating the homosexual themes of the following poems undoubtedly would be clear.[82]

Poems 15–24

The first and second polymetric cycles are closely connected. The dismissal of Lesbia and the emphasis on male friendship in cc. 11 through 14 pave the way both dramatically and psychologically for the series of poems in cc. 15–24 that concern Catullus' love affair with the boy Juventius. The figures of Furius and Aurelius provide a direct link between the two groups of poems. The pair who are associated with the bitter "conclusion" of the affair with Lesbia in cc. 1–14 play the part of rivals for Juventius in cc. 15–24.[83] The purpose of this deliberate connection is to suggest a narrative continuity. The reader is to assume that "emasculated" by his lady and, as a result, utterly disillusioned with womankind, Catullus becomes involved in a homosexual relationship.[84] The series differ, however, in emphasis and intent. The Juventius poems do not have as their primary focus either the beloved or love for the beloved; rather they spotlight rivals for the boy's affections (15, 21, 24, 40, and 81). Their comic intent is indicated from the outset, for in the very first poem Catullus entrusts his boy to a flagrant pederast.

Aurelius and Furius, the principal characters in cc. 15–24, appear in five of the seven poems.[85] They are lampooned separately in two

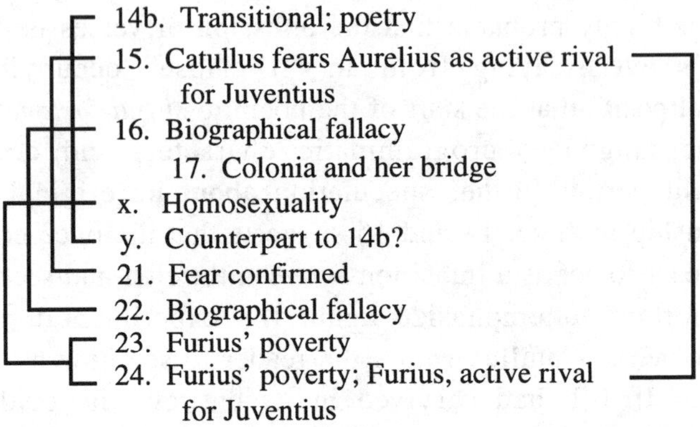

Figure 2.7 Ring Structure of Poems 15–24

poems apiece. Cc. 15 and 21 contain dire threats to Aurelius to stay away from Catullus' lover. Cc. 23 and 24, tame by comparison, ridicule Furius for his poverty. Aurelius and Furius are attacked together in the colorfully programmatic c. 16, which like c. 22 rejects the biographical approach to literature. In the role of rivals for Juventius, they also join beginning and end of the cycle. C. 17 appears to lack a counterpart. This unusual poem to a provincial town with a rickety bridge inverts a common theme of cc. 15, 21, and 24: here the lover (the complaisant husband) is not keeping a wary eye on his beloved.[86]

The second cycle of polymetra is problematical because there appears to be a major gap in the text, quite remarkably, precisely where Muretus inserted into the Catullan manuscript a fragment and two Priapea, which he numbered 18 through 20 in his 1554 edition. (The traditional numbering of the poems is owed to him.) Experience with other circular compositions suggests that cc. 23 and 24 should have a counterpart in the other half of the ring structure.[87] The only place in a collection where a sequence of poems functions as a tag is at the very end. What is more, if 14b belongs to this cycle, its symmetrical complement is missing, too. The loss of two poems is indicated in figure 2.7 above, where I speculatively completed the ring pattern. The problem of a gap in the text will be taken up again later when other evidence can be offered in support of this proposal.[88]

Poems 15~21

In form, c. 15 is a parody of a *commendatio*, a practice by which one person is entrusted to the safekeeping of another. The poem opens innocently. Catullus places his boy friend in the care of Aurelius with the request that he preserve his lover's purity (1–8). Catullus' modest favor, however, turns out to be highly ironic. At verses 9f. it is revealed that Aurelius is an incontinent pederast, the very person from whom Catullus has the most to fear (*verum a te metuo tuoque pene / infesto pueris bonis malisque*). The purpose of the poem is to warn off Aurelius, a potential rival, by making outrageous threats. In Catullus' mind his relationship with the boy is exclusive like a marriage. And so assuming the pose of an injured husband, he promises a painful penalty against the adulterer should Aurelius fail to comply: anal rape with radishes and mullet-fins as penis-substitutes (18–19).

C. 21 is written in response to c. 15. Catullus' fear that Aurelius will seduce his beloved is confirmed in the second member of the pair: Aurelius is openly pursuing Juventius (*pedicare cupis meos amores. / nec clam* 4–5). Again Catullus warns Aurelius to keep "hands off," to desist while his virility is intact. As in c. 15, the consequence of non-compliance is punitive rape (12–13).

Numerous parallels indicate that cc. 15 and 21 were conceived as counterparts.[89] The poems open by addressing Aurelius (15.2; 21.1), they appeal to his modesty (15.2, 5, 13; 21.12), and they describe his treachery as *insidiae* (15.16; 21.7). In each, Catullus' lover (who similarly plays a minor role) is referred to indirectly in precisely the same fashion, first as *meos amores* (15.1; 21.4), then as *puer* (15.5; 21.11).[90] Each poem closes with Catullus threatening Aurelius with sexual assault (15.18–19; 21.12–13). Finally, food imagery combined with buggery links the beginning of c. 21 with the end of c. 15.

C. 21 differs, however, from c. 15 in that it unites the incongruous figures of the rival and parasite. The elaboration of Aurelius' role from the one poem to the other accounts, too, for the shift in sexual retribution from *pedicatio* to *irrumatio*; oral sodomy is intended to complement the earlier references in the poem to hunger and thirst.[91] A further difference concerns the change in Aurelius' role from potential to active rival.[92] In the first poem Aurelius is threatened with a stiff penalty if he should seduce the boy; in the second he is threatened because he is actively engaged in the seduction. Catullus' overzealousness in c. 21 stems from his fear that association with Aurelius will corrupt Juventius' character.

Poems 16~22

In accordance with "ancient poetic literary criticism...the kind of poetry a poet wrote and the kind of life he lived were interchangeable equivalents."[93] Cc. 16 and 22 dismiss the tradition of *qualis vir, talis oratio* by claiming that the character of a poet cannot be judged by the poetry he writes (16.3–6, 12–13; 22.9–16).

In c. 16 Catullus uses himself and his poetry to illustrate the folly of a biographical approach to literature.[94] Furius and Aurelius apparently think that because Catullus' verses are *molles*, so is he (used of verses, *mollis* suggests love poetry; used of a man, *mollis* suggests effeminacy, that Catullus is the passive partner). Catullus asserts that a poet dedicated to the Muses must be "decent"; his verses, on the other hand, need not be so. In fact, *versiculi* have no wit and charm unless they are suggestive and indecent. Such verses provoke sexual excitement. Because Aurelius and Furius have read about the thousands of kisses in c. 5 and nothing more sexually explicit, they assume that Catullus is sexually inadequate.[95] The poet will demonstrate his virility in no uncertain terms by sodomizing anally and orally his very accusers.

In contrast to the outrageous c. 16, c. 22 is a reflective poem that criticizes the poetaster Suffenus for superficial elegance and self-satisfaction. Here a protest against the biographical approach to literature is combined with the aesthetic ideal of *venustas*.

The poem begins with a characterization. Suffenus is charming, witty, and urbane, qualities that Catullus esteems (*venustus et dicax et urbanus* 2). But the fellow is a bad poet, judged by Callimachean standards, because he writes too many verses (*idemque longe plurimos facit versus* 3). Consequently, the moment you read his poetry, the sophisticate is transformed (9–11):

> haec cum legas tu, bellus ille et urbanus
> Suffenus unus caprimulgus aut fossor
> rursus videtur: tantum abhorret ac mutat.

He appears a goat-milker or a ditch-digger; as a writer he is more countrified than the countrified country (*idem infaceto est infacetior rure* 14).

Suffenus has an additional failing of conceit. Thinking his poetry is splendid, he publishes the atrocious verses in deluxe editions. Catullus ends the poem by excusing Suffenus: "We do not see the part of the knapsack that is on our back" (*sed non videmus manticae quod in tergo est* 21). The double knapsack in the closing generalization neatly coordinates with the dual character of Suffenus and his verses. "Suffenus [is] a polished man but an unpolished writer....His books are polished externally and unpolished internally."[96]

In c. 22, therefore, the poet is both associated with and dissociated from his poetry. Like the author, the books are attractive but, unlike the author, the verses lack charm. In c. 16 Catullus dealt with the effect that poetry could have on the reader: it can arouse sexual excitement ([*versiculi*] *quod pruriat incitare possunt* 9). In c. 22 he inverts this idea by considering the effect that poetry has on its writer: as soon as he turns his hand to poetry, the otherwise urbane Suffenus becomes a country bumpkin (*bellus ille et urbanus....idem infaceto est infacetior rure, / simul poemata attigit* 9, 14–15).

Cc. 16 and 22 form perfect complements in that good and bad poet alike illustrate the fallacy of a biographical approach to literary criticism.

Cc. 16 and 22 are similar, too, in that they look back to earlier poems. C. 16 is related to c. 11 by several parallels. Most obviously, these are the only poems that feature Aurelius and Furius as a pair: the twosome appear prominently, and are addressed jointly, in the opening verses (11.1; 16.2); in both poems Aurelius and Furius are associated with Catullus' love affair with Lesbia (11.15–24; 16.12–13), and in both obscenity is a characteristic element (11.17–20; 16.1, 16).[97] C. 16 also is reminiscent of c. 14. The two pieces on poetry use the same language drawn from ritual to express literary doctrine. In 16.5 Catullus asserts that he is *pius*, "a priest of the Muses," while in 14.7 he condemns poets like Caesius, Aquinus, and Suffenus for being *impii*, violators of the rites of the Muses.[98] The passing reference to the poetaster Suffenus at 14.19 prepares for his next and final appearance in the *oeuvre* in c. 22, where his poetry illustrates the antithesis of Callimachean aesthetics. C. 22 is related, too, to c. 1 through the similar description of the physical appearance of Catullus' and Suffenus' works: the book of both poets is new and is smoothed with pumice (*cartae regiae novae bibli, / novi umbilici,...pumice omnia aequata* 22.6–8; *novum libellum...pumice expolitum* 1.1–2).[99] The likeness ends, however, with their outward appearance, for the quality of Suffenus' poetry, unlike that of Catullus', is at variance with the external elegance. C. 22 recalls another programmatic piece, 14b, in that it combines the idea of reading with the verb *(ab)horreo* (*haec cum legas tu,...abhorret* 22.9, 11; *lectores eritis manusque vestras / non horrebitis admovere nobis* 14b.2–3; cf. also *horribilem...libellum* in 14.12). Lastly, although the theme of *venustas* links c. 22 with cc. 1, 6, 10, 12, and 13, its relation to c. 10 is particularly close. Not only are cc. 10 and 22 the only poems to feature Varus, but they similarly illustrate how, in the case of the *scortillum* and of Suffenus, first impressions of *venustas* prove to be false.[100] The charm and wit of both individuals are more apparent than real.[101]

The next pair in the cycle concern another flawed *bellus homo,* but, unlike Suffenus, Furius falls short because of his extreme poverty.

Poems 23~24

C. 23, directed to Furius alone, begins by cataloguing what he does not possess. He has no servant, no money-chest, no bug, spider, or fire (*Furi, cui neque servus est neque arca / nec cimex neque araneus neque ignis* 1–2). Lack of money and property, Catullus continues tongue-in-cheek, can actually be beneficial. Furius and family have nothing to fear of fires, collapsing buildings, impious deeds, deceits of poison, or other risky occurrences (8–11):

> ..., nihil timetis,
> non incendia, non graves ruinas,
> non facta impia, non dolos veneni,
> non casus alios periculorum.

What they do possess, however, is bodies drier than horn from sun, cold, and hunger (*atqui corpora sicciora cornu / ...sole et frigore et esuritione* 12–14). Presumably as a result of this dryness, Furius lacks normal bodily fluids: sweat, saliva, mucus, and runny nose (*at te sudor abest, abest saliva, / mucusque et mala pituita nasi* 16–17). As a member of a family who can eat stones (3–4), the excreta of the juiceless Furius are harder than pebbles or beans (*durius est faba et lapillis* 21). The final verses contain the punchline. Catullus reveals that the occasion of the poem is Furius' repeated requests for a loan (*sesteria quae soles precari / centum* 26–27). Catullus' answer: You have so many blessings; you're rich enough (*haec tu commoda tam beata, Furi, / noli spernere nec putare parvi, / ...nam sat es beatus* 24–25, 27).

The question arises, why does Catullus dwell on Furius' juicelessness (12–23)? The explanation proposed by L. Richardson, Jr. is surely right, that Furius' lack of salt humors is meant to suggest lack of charm and wit: "Many of the terms for indicating wit and its appreciation are words like *sucus* and *saliva*," and in the specialized vocabulary of Catullus, *sal* is a highly desirable quality.[102]

Furius, then, might be perceived as a foil to Catullus. This is an important point because in several of its details c. 23 recalls c. 13.[103] Both are non-food poems, and both are concerned with "poverty." But while Catullus has a wallet full of spiders, Furius doesn't have a spider to his name. Furius' lack of salt humors recalls the salt/wit that Catullus asks his charming friend Fabullus to bring to their future dinner-party. Another point of contrast is that, unlike the poverty-stricken Furius, Catullus claims to have something to offer, Heaven's Scent and *meros amores* (13.9–12). The point of the interplay between cc. 13 and 23 is to set up an implicit contrast between Furius and Catullus in preparation for c. 24, the companion piece of c. 23, where the two appear as rivals.

C. 24 combines Furius' poverty with the theme of love. Although Furius is not named in the poem, his identity as Catullus' rival is indicated through the repetition of the phrase *neque servus est neque arca* (23.1) in verses 5, 8, and 10. The phrase, in fact, acts as a frame for the two poems:

> Furi, cui neque servus est neque arca (23.1)
>
> nec servum tamen ille habet neque arcam. (24.10)

The purpose of this emphatic verbal cross-reference is to suggest a close relation. In c. 23 Catullus gave an ostensible reason for his derision of Furius, the repeated request for a loan. In c. 24, I believe, he gives the real reason: Furius has seduced his boy friend. It is on the pretext of Furius' poverty that the jealous Catullus objects to the liaison. In chiding Juventius, he assumes the pose of a madam lecturing a "tender-minded courtesan": "Yes, the guy's classy, but he has no dough."[104]

C. 24 is the first poem to name Juventius. Catullus appears to have postponed revealing the identity of the *puer* until the close of the cycle for dramatic effect. The final piece resolves the tension raised in cc. 15 and 21 by Catullus' fear that his darling will be seduced by another. In c. 24 Juventius betrays Catullus just as Lesbia had earlier in c. 11.[105]

Interestingly, other parallels connect cc. 11 and 24. Both equate flowers and love. In the one, love for Lesbia is compared to a flower at the edge of a meadow (*velut prati / ultimi flos* 11.21–22), while in the other Juventius is addressed as a small flower (*flosculus... Iuventiorum* 24.1). Both depict the beloved as a prostitute (Lesbia low-class, Juventius high-class). Both associate Furius (and Aurelius) with the theme of betrayal. In c. 11 Furius and Aurelius are to deliver Catullus' vitriolic message to the faithless Lesbia, while in c. 24 Furius steals Juventius from Catullus. A final feature of both poems is the issue of money. In c. 11 the reason that Furius and Aurelius would be willing to go to far and distant places is presumably to acquire wealth; in c. 24 Catullus suggests that the desperately poor Furius can be corrupted by money (*mallem divitias Midae dedisses / isti...quam sic te sineres ab illo amari* 4–6).

The point of the relation between the two poems seems to be to indicate that Juventius, to a certain extent, is a pale imitation of Lesbia.[106] The homosexual poems show important differences from the heterosexual poems in focus, in range of topics, and in degree of intensity. These differences coordinate with purpose. The Juventius poems are intended to provide "light relief" from Catullus' grand passion for Lesbia.[107] After Catullus is betrayed by his male lover in c. 24, the stage is set for a reconciliation with Lesbia (albeit brief) in c. 36. Further evidence of deliberate interplay between the homosexual and heterosexual love poems can be offered by the disposition of the first and last Juventius poems. The first Juventius poem (15) occurs after c. 11; the last Juventius poem (99), in which Catullus is cured of his love for the boy, occurs before the final reconciliation with Lesbia in cc. 107 and 109.

Poem 17

C. 17 is a *jeu d'esprit* about a laggard husband who is indifferent toward his pretty, lascivious wife. Catullus deals with this topos in a highly imaginative fashion by creating a correlation between the ostensible subjects of the poem, Colonia and her dilapidated bridge, and the real subjects of the poem, the *insulsissimus homo* and his *nupta puella*.

Colonia wishes to play on her bridge, but she is afraid that it might collapse on its back and sink into the depths of the swamp below. Catullus suggests a propitiatory sacrifice to restore the bridge magically. A certain *municeps*, complaisant to the sexual needs of his young wife (who, like Colonia, likes to play), should be thrown into the swamp. This treatment, if effective, will restore the vitality of the bridge and husband alike.

C. 17 is one of three non-corresponding poems in the polymetra.[108] The reason for the poem's place here is that it combines two major themes of the cycle, retributive punishment and social ineptness.

Linear Structure of Poems 15–24

14b appears to have been a slight piece whose combined themes of poetry and homosexuality effected a transition from cc. 1–14 to cc. 15–24. C. 15, however, seems to provide the real start of the cycle. The poem begins in a manner reminiscent of c. 1. The opening words, *Commen-do tibi*, recall the earlier *Cui dono* from the dedicatory poem. Further, just as c. 1 introduced major themes of the cycle, gift-giving, the quality of *lepor,* male friendship, the slight, erudite, polished poem, and the notion of reckoning (*puto* in 1.4 seems to anticipate the numerical references in cc. 5, 7, 9, 11, and 12), so c. 15 serves a similar function. The poem introduces a new love, an unidentified *puer*, who is to be the object of male rivalry, and it sets the tone for the general lightheartedness of the Juventius poems. The reference to *raphanidosis* (15.18–19) also may subtly foreshadow the theme of poverty in cc. 21, 23, and 24. According to the scholiast on Aristophanes' *Plutus*, this painful penalty was paid by poor men caught in the act of adultery; rich men paid a fine.[109] The theme of retributive punishment, which concludes c. 15, is resumed in the first verse of c. 16 (*Pedicabo ego vos et irrumabo*). A close relation to c. 15 is further indicated through several verbal reminiscences.[110] A central concern of c. 16 is the issue of sexual adequacy (*male marem*). This theme recurs in the very next poem (*nec se sublevat ex sua parte* 18), in which drastic measures are suggested to restore the potency of the *insulsissimus homo* who is indifferent toward his pretty, young wife. Unlike the Veronese *municeps* in c. 17, Catullus in c. 21 watches his beloved carefully, as he attempts to preserve the boy's integrity. The themes of pederasty and poverty (*pater esuritionum*) in c. 21 form a strong link with cc. 23 and 24. C. 22 also is related to these last pieces through the figure of the flawed *bellus homo.*

Poems 25–33

The next poems form the pivot of the polymetra. As the center, cc. 25–33 share an interesting feature with the coming cc. 61–64.

25. To the thieving *cinaedus,* Thallus
26. Catullus' villa
27. Hard drinking
28. Misuse of gubernatorial power; hunger/lack of money
29. Misuse of gubernatorial power; gluttony/prodigality
30. Betrayal by a friend
31. Catullus' villa
32. Hard loving
33. To the thieving *cinaedi,* Vibennius, Sr. and Vibennius, Jr.

Figure 2.8 Ring Structure of Poems 25–33

Here, as there, the reader is to be provided with a respite from Catullus' major love affairs, for this cycle contains no direct references to either Lesbia or Juventius.

Cc. 25–33 are organized in a ring-composition structure, shown in figure 2.8 above. Eight poems make up four pairs, with a ninth poem lacking a counterpart. Cc. 28~29 deal with misuse of gubernatorial power; cc. 26~31 concern Catullan villas; cc. 25~33 combine thievery with homosexuality; and cc. 27~32 treat separately the complementary motifs of hard drinking and hard loving.

Poem 25

Cinaede Thalle, mollior cuniculi capillo
vel anseris medullula vel imula oricilla
vel pene languido senis situque araneoso,
idemque, Thalle, turbida rapacior procella,
conviva cum ebriosior se tendit oscitanter,
remitte pallium mihi meum, quod involasti,
sudariumque Saetabum catagraphosque Thynos,
inepte, quae palam soles habere tamquam avita.
quae nunc tuis ab unguibus reglutina et remitte,
ne laneum latusculum manusque mollicellas
inusta turpiter tibi flagella conscribillent,
et insolenter aestues, velut minuta magno
deprensa navis in mari, vesaniente vento.

The opening poem resumes virtually where the first cycle of polymetric poems, cc. 1–14, ends. In theme and in many of its details, c. 25 recalls c. 12. The setting of both poems is a banquet, during which Catullus' highly esteemed Spanish napkins are stolen (*sudaria/-um Saetaba/-um* 12.14; 25.7); the thieves Asinius and Thallus take advantage of dinner guests who are inattentive (12.3; 25.5); and the culprits, denounced as *inepte* (12.4; 25.8), are threatened with punishments that involve writing if the stolen items are not returned (*hendecasyllabos trecentos / exspecta, aut mihi linteum remitte* 12.10–11; *remitte, / ne... tibi flagella conscribillent* 25.9, 11).[111] But while c. 12 focuses on the boorishness of Asinius, a topic that leads to the intrinsic value of the item he has taken, c. 25 emphasizes the effeminacy and rapacity of Thallus, whose petty larceny provokes threats of physical punishment.

C. 25 differs also from c. 12 in that as the lead poem it introduces themes that are to occur in the rest of the cycle.[112] The reference to the Spanish napkins and Bithynian embroideries in 25.7, acquired by Catullus, Fabullus, and Veranius during their service abroad on praetorial staffs, looks forward generally to the topic of provincial administration in cc. 28 and 29 and specifically to the association of Catullus' own experiences in the provinces with those of his friends in c. 28.[113] The mention of Bithynia also relates c. 25 to c. 31, an exuberant poem that celebrates Catullus' joyful return home from that very province. Interestingly, Catullus' cloak, one of the pilfered objects (*pallium,... quod involasti* 25.6), makes its only other appearance at 32.11, where it again is subjected to violent assault (*pertundo...palliumque*).[114] A sympotic setting anticipates that in c. 27, in addition to connecting with the themes of gluttony in cc. 29 and 32 and hunger in c. 28. Thallus' breach of trust in taking advantage of the inattentiveness of his friends foreshadows a more serious violation of friendship in c. 30, where Alfenus has deserted Catullus in his time of need.[115] The motif of homosexuality (*Cinaede Thalle*) figures also in cc. 28, 29, and 33. Finally, the last phrase in c. 25, *vesaniente vento* (13), forms a link with the gusts of wind at the beginning of c. 26 (1–3), to which Catullus' villa is not exposed.

Poems 25~33

The themes of effeminacy and thievery join cc. 25 and 33. In the one poem they are united in the single figure of Thallus, the effeminate thief, while in the other they are combined in a pair of individuals, the bath-thief Vibennius, Sr. and his effeminate son.

The poems begin in the same way, with an unflattering address to the recipients:

> Cinaede Thalle, mollior cuniculi capillo
> vel anseris medullula vel imula oricilla
> vel pene languido senis situque araneoso,
> idemque, Thalle, turbida rapacior procella, (25.1–4)
>
> O furum optime balneariorum
> Vibenni pater et cinaede fili
> (nam dextra pater inquinatiore,
> culo filius est voraciore),... (33.1–4)

Verses 1–4 of c. 33 resemble verses 1–4 of c. 25 in their syntactical patterning of an apostrophe followed by comparative adjectives (*cinaede Thalle*, *mollior*... *rapacior* 25.1, 4; *o furum optime balneariorum / Vibenni pater et cinaede fili*... *inquinatiore*, ...*voraciore* 33.1–4). Similar language provides further coincidence. The second of the two comparatives refers to the greed of Thallus and Vibennius, Jr. (*rapacior*; *voracior*), and the femininity of the same individuals is underscored through the collocation of *cinaede* with Latin and Greek words that derive from roots meaning "to suck," *fili* from the Latin *fel*- and *Thalle* from the Greek cognate θηλ-. It is tempting, too, to see a parallel between *culo* in 33.4 and *cuni-culi* in 25.1 (the *cun*- element also suggests *cunnus)* as well as between the juxtaposed *natis pilosas* in 33.7 and *cuni-culi capillo* in 25.1.

C. 33 is structured so as to identify the Vibennii. As D. Lateiner observes, "the first line refers indifferently both to father and son," and the interchange of epithets just one line later creates a similar ambiguity: "Prosaic thought would imagine that *voracior* applies to *dextra* (*manus*) and *inquinatior* applies to *culus*."[116] Catullus' purpose is to tar *père* and *fils* with the same stick. As a result, Vibennius, Jr. and Sr. alike are to be perceived as "thieving queers."

It is true that in theme c. 33 is "a spin-off from the napkin thieves of poems 12 and 25."[117] But as a scathing imprecation c. 33 lacks the charm of c. 12 and the energy and splendid imagery of c. 25, which is a miniature *tour de force.* The difference in tone perhaps has to do with the recipients of the poems. The thievery of Asinius and Thallus, who moved in Catullus' social circle, shows them to be merely deficient in social graces while as professionals the Vibennii are wholly contemptible.

Poems 26~31

The motivation behind c. 26 is Furius' poverty. Presumably, as in c. 23, Furius has asked for a loan. But while in the earlier poem Catullus refused his request on the grounds that Furius was "rich enough," here he offers a humorous variation of that excuse by claiming that he himself is not well off financially:[118]

> Furi, villula nostra non ad Austri
> flatus opposita est neque ad Favoni
> nec saevi Boreae aut Apheliotae,
> verum ad milia quindecim et ducentos.
> o ventum horribilem atque pestilentem!

Although C.J. Fordyce is right that c. 26 largely serves as "a vehicle for a verbal joke on the two meanings of *oppositus*, 'facing' and 'pledged'" (i.e., "mortgaged"), there are other humorous elements.[119] The catalogue of winds culminates in a grandiloquent-sounding "obscure Greek name," *Apheliotae*,[120] and Catullus' excuse for refusing Furius' appeal for money is comically transparent, for a debt of 15,200 sesterces was not considerable.[121] It may seem odd that Catullus did not place *Furi, villula nostra* in the preceding cycle with the other two poems that deal with the theme of Furius' poverty. I suspect the reason he did not is that c. 26 is not a Juventius poem. (C. 23 is connected with the series through its relation to c. 24.)

The villa of c. 26 is probably the house in the Sabine country, which Catullus himself bought and which he addresses in c. 44. The villa of c. 31, located on Sirmio near Verona, was most likely a family estate.

C. 31 is an exuberant poem that celebrates Catullus' homecoming after an unpleasant year spent in Bithynia on Memmius' praetorial staff. In form, the poem is a personal *epibaterion*, a "disembarkation poem," in which Catullus joyfully greets Sirmio on arriving home from abroad.[122] For our purposes it is important to note that c. 31 does more than merely personify Catullus' native land. The poem so closely associates Sirmio the peninsula and the *domus* located on it that the two entities become almost one. Their dual character is suggested by the language of the poem, which abounds in doublets.[123] Sirmio is the jewel of islands and peninsulas alike; she (for Sirmio is personified as Catullus' mistress[124]) is viewed both happily and gladly, as Catullus comes to see and gaze on her in safety, having left behind Thynia and the Bithynians; and Sirmio and the Lydian waters are to rejoice at the return of their master.

In addition to the theme of Catullan villas, c. 31 shares with c. 26 a humorous intent, as is suggested, for example, by "the word-plays and jingles" (*paene insularum,...insularumque* 1; *uterque Neptunus* 3; *Thuniam atque Bithunos* 5; *gaude / gaudente* 12–13) and, of course, by the personification itself.[125]

Furi, villula was placed here, presumably, to be near the earlier poems concerned with Furius' poverty, cc. 23 and 24. In addition, by identifying his own lack of money with that of Furius, Catullus foreshadows his financial setback as a member of Memmius' praetorial staff in c. 28. C. 31 also relates to c. 28 by recalling the theme of provincial service in Bithynia. At the same time, the close association between Catullus' *domus* and the personified Sirmio as *amica* points forward to the close association between the *meretrix* Ipsithilla and her *domus* in c. 32.[126]

Poems 27~32

The complementary themes of love and the symposium join cc. 27 and 32. The occasion of c. 27 is a drinking party. The poem opens with Catullus requesting cups of stronger wine in accordance with the dictates of the toastmistress Postumia. The presence of an aristocratic woman at a drinking party is remarkable (only *hetairae* attend *convivia*), but even more remarkable is her function as symposiarch. "According to traditional Roman usage women were not allowed to drink wine,"[127] and the role of the *arbiter bibendi* is to maintain order, a role Postumia disdains by virtue of her generous decree and by her own condition of inebriation. In the second part of the poem, Catullus banishes water. The *lymphae* are to go into exile to the *severi*, to those individuals who do not know how to enjoy life. Here is undiluted Bacchus. C. 32 also features a woman, but one whose identity is veiled under a pseudonym coined by Catullus. As in c. 27, the time is postprandial, and the poem involves a request. Catullus asks Ipsithilla to stay at home (don't bar the door) and prepare for him nine continual fucks. Not only does the sexual gluttony of c. 32 complement the gluttonous winebibery of c. 27, but the reference to the theme of the *exclusus amator* at 32.5 suggests a closer connection.[128] The elements of drunkenness and the shut door, which often are combined in the *paraclausithyron*, have been severed here and set forth in separate poems.[129]

Cc. 27 and 32 share the following features. Both are requests, the one to a slave boy to pour cups of stronger wine, the other to a young woman to provide sexual relief, for Catullus' need is urgent. In both poems, the women command, while Catullus' role is subordinate or passive. Postumia is *magistra bibendi*; Ipsithilla herself will decide whether or not to invite Catullus to her house for a midday siesta. The time of the poems is similarly postprandial. Lastly, as figure 2.9 below illustrates, the poems exhibit a parallel structure.

The relation of the central three pairs in figure 2.9 is self-evident. The notion of women commanding joins 27.3 (*lex Postumiae iubet*) and 32.3–4 (*iube…iusseris*); and antithetical imperatives link 27.5–7 and 32.6–7 (*vos…hinc abite~neu…foras abire* and *ad severos migrate~domi maneas*). The relation of the first and last pairs, however, requires explanation. The correspondence of *calices amariores* at 27.2 and *dulcis Ipsithilla* at 32.1 involves more than the pairing of the opposites of bitter and sweet, for Ipsithilla (if this is the correct form of the name[130]) also can be taken with *calices*, since the

	C. 27	C. 32
BITTER VS. SWEET WINE	calices amariores (2)	dulcis i-PSITH-illa (1)
COMMANDING	lex Postumiae iubet (3)	iube...iusseris (3–4)
DOUBLE ANTITHETICAL IMPERATIVES	vos quo lubet hinc abite (5)	neu tibi lubeat foras abire (6)
	ad severos / migrate (6–7)	domi maneas (7)
VIOLENCE SUGGESTED	THYON-ianus (7)	pertundo (11)

Figure 2.9 Parallel Structure of Poems 27 and 32

Greek adjective for a kind of grape or "the wine made from it" (ψίθιος) is contained within her name.[131] The correlation between the epithet of Bacchus at 27.7 and *pertundo* at 32.11 is equally subtle and learned. *Thyonianus*, which calls to mind the Greek verb θύειν ("to rage"), accords with the image of assault that concludes c. 32.[132]

Critics suggest that c. 27 attacks a real person named Postumia, possibly the wife of Servius Sulpicius Rufus, who at one time was a mistress of Julius Caesar.[133] Whether this identification is correct or not, the correspondence of c. 27 to c. 32 makes quite clear that the point of the poem is to insult Postumia. Through the parallels that link her with Ipsithilla, Catullus intimates that she has the morals of a high-class working girl.

From a structural perspective, the identification of Postumia as a mistress of Caesar is attractive because it provides a transition to cc. 28 and 29, where Catullus censures Piso, Caesar's father-in-law; Mamurra, Caesar's henchman; Pompey, Caesar's son-in-law; and Caesar himself.

Poems 28~29

Cc. 28 and 29 are attacks on the Roman system of patronage. In the one, Piso and Memmius fail to reward members of their praetorial staff, while in the other Mamurra is over-rewarded for his services as a result of the perverse generosity (*sinistra liberalitas*) of Caesar and Pompey.[134]

C. 28 focuses on the disappointment of Catullus and of Fabullus and Veranius at their failure to make money from their service abroad. The poem opens with his friends returning to Rome empty-handed,[135] having endured cold and hunger, and without any financial reward to show for their time on the staff of Piso in Macedonia:

> Pisonis comites, cohors inanis,
> aptis sarcinulis et expeditis,
> Verani optime tuque mi Fabulle,
> quid rerum geritis? satisne cum isto
> vappa frigoraque et famem tulistis? (1–5)

Catullus can sympathize with their situation, for his own experience in Bithynia under Memmius was financially disastrous, too:

> ecquidnam in tabulis patet lucelli
> expensum, ut mihi, qui meum secutus
> praetorem refero datum lucello? (6–8)

The poem takes an unexpected turn at the center; thoughts of lack of profit lead to the topic of sexual violation:

> o Memmi, bene me ac diu supinum
> tota ista trabe lentus irrumasti. (9–10)

"Memmius, with that whole shaft of yours you raped me long and well as I lay on my back, and you took your time about it." Catullus then suggests that Fabullus and Veranius have suffered a similar fate:

> sed, quantum video, pari fuistis
> casu: nam nihilo minore verpa
> farti estis. pete nobiles amicos! (11–13)

"With no less a prick have you been stuffed." *Farti estis* in verse 13 responds to the earlier imagery of emptiness and hunger in verses 1 and 5 (*inanis*; *famem*). The final section shifts from Catullus' friends to a curse against Piso and Memmius, the perpetrators of their financial failure:

> at vobis mala multa di deaeque
> dent, opprobria Romuli Remique. (14–15)

The lack of financial compensation and the disappointment of Catullus and his friends in c. 28 is answered by the success and enrichment of Mamurra in c. 29. This poem, like its counterpart, combines the themes of sex, money, and food. But whereas Catullus and friends, hungry and penniless, are "screwed" by niggardly political governors, Mamurra, depicted as a sexual and material glutton, "screws" his patrons Pompey and Caesar, and all Rome as well, through his squandering of wealth, which was acquired on campaigns in Gaul, Britain, Spain, and Pontus. The responsive relation of the two poems is further suggested by a parallel structure.

Cc. 28 and 29 both begin with a series of questions. 28.1–8 address Veranius and Fabullus, who have just arrived home from abroad; 29.1–10 address Pompey, whom Catullus attacks for his indulgent passivity with regard to Mamurra's profligacy.[136] The first five verses contrast the hunger/poverty of Veranius and Fabullus with the gluttony/enrichment of Mamurra. A form of *fero* closes the opening sections (*tulistis, feres*):

> Pisonis comites, cohors inanis,
> aptis sarcinulis et expeditis,
> Verani optime tuque mi Fabulle,
> quid rerum geritis? satisne cum isto
> vappa frigoraque et famem tulistis? (28.1–5)

> Quis hoc potest videre, quis potest pati,
> nisi impudicus et vorax et aleo,
> Mamurram habere quod Comata Gallia
> habebat uncti et ultima Britannia?
> cinaede Romule, haec videbis et feres? (29.1–5)

The next three verses oppose Catullus' debit to the newly acquired wealth of Mamurra. While Mamurra overflows with wealth (*superbus et superfluens*),[137] Catullus counts as profit the money he expended in following Memmius:

> ecquidnam in tabulis patet lucelli
> expensum, ut mihi, qui meum secutus
> praetorem refero datum lucello? (28.6–8)

> et ille nunc superbus et superfluens
> perambulabit omnium cubilia,
> ut albulus columbus aut Adoneus? (29.6–8)

The excess suggested by the repeated *super-* in *superbus* and *superfluens* at 29.6 coordinates with the opposite idea in the repeated diminutive *lucelli/ -o* at 28.6, 8. (Also, the bookkeeping language in 28.6–8 is recalled by *eo nomine* in 29.11 and 23.)

At this point both poems change addressees. C. 28 shifts from Fabullus and Veranius to Memmius; c. 29 shifts from Pompey to Caesar.[138] Additionally, the change of addressee in each instance is followed by references to oral acts:

> o Memmi, bene me ac diu supinum
> tota ista trabe lentus irrumasti. (28.9–10)

> eone nomine, imperator unice,
> fuisti in ultima occidentis insula,
> ut ista vestra diffututa mentula
> ducenties comesset aut trecenties? (29.11–14)

In c. 28 Memmius shafted Catullus with that entire beam of his (i.e., screwed him out of money), while in c. 29 Mamurra, that lecherous prick of Caesar (and Pompey, *vestra*), has devoured 20 or 30 million sesterces.

Continuing the theme of oral sodomy, the next verses of c. 28 also relate to 29.13–14:

> sed, quantum video, pari fuistis
> casu: nam nihilo minore verpa
> farti estis.... (28.11–13)

The noun *verpa*, which may indicate "a *mentula* with foreskin drawn back as a result of...excessive sexual activity,"[139] parallels the phrase *diffututa mentula* in meaning and in its holding the final position in the verse. In both passages, too, references to exhausted penises are combined with metaphors of eating (*farti*; *comesset*).

The final verses of the two poems show similar language and technique:

> at vobis mala multa di deaeque
> dent, opprobria Romuli Remique. (28.14–15)
>
> quid hunc malum fovetis? aut quid hic potest
> nisi uncta devorare patrimonia?
> eone nomine urbis o piissimi
> socer generque, perdidistis omnia? (29.21–24)

Both close with a conjoint address: 28.14–15 are directed to Memmius and Piso (the real subject of 28.1–8) and 29.21–24 to Pompey and Caesar; the description of Mamurra as *hunc malum* at 29.21 echoes the *mala multa* of the curse at 28.14; a set of "twins," Romulus and Remus and father-in-law/son-in-law, occurs in the last verse of both poems; and, lastly, the sarcastic apostrophe *urbis o piissimi*, "o most honorable men of Rome," corresponds to the equally unflattering apostrophe *opprobria Romuli Remique*, "you who disgrace Romulus and Remus."

The parallel structure of cc. 28 and 29 (shown in figure 2.10 on page 62) is significant for the interpretation and text of c. 29 in the following respects. There has been much discussion regarding whether 29.1–10 address Caesar or Pompey. Since both poems appear to be organized so that the recipients of the poems are addressed successively and, at the end, conjointly, this parallelism lends support to the view that verses 1–10 of c. 29 are directed to Pompey and verses 11–20 to Caesar.[140] Another point of dispute concerns *quid hunc malum* in 29.21. Should *malum* be construed as a neuter interjection ("Why the devil...") or as a masculine accusative ("Why do you pamper this evil person")? The connection between 28.14 and 29.11 is suggestive. It is tempting to see *hunc malum*

C. 28	C. 29
Poverty/Hunger of Fabullus and Veranius (1–5)	Gluttony/Enrichment of Mamurra (1–5)
Catullus' debit (6–8)	Mamurra's newly acquired wealth (6–8)
Addressee shifts to Memmius (9)	Addressee shifts to Caesar (11)
References to oral acts (9–10)	References to oral acts (13–14)
Exhausted penis combined with metaphors of eating (13–14)	Exhausted penis combined with metaphors of eating (13–14)
Conjoint address to Piso and Memmius (14–15)	Conjoint address to Pompey and Caesar (21–24)
Twins: Romulus and Remus (15)	"Twins": father- and son-in-law (24)
Disparaging apostrophe (15)	Ironical apostrophe (23)

Figure 2.10 Parallel Structure of Poems 28 and 29

(= *Mamurram*) in c. 29 as answering Catullus' prayer in c. 28 that the gods may give many evils to military commanders like Piso and Memmius and Caesar and Pompey.[141] A third difficulty involves the text at 29.23. The *communis opinio* is that the manuscript reading of *opulentissime* is corrupt.[142] The superlative adjective is problematical for two reasons. First, the third syllable violates the pure iambic trimeter in which the poem appears to be written;[143] second, the vocative *urbis opulentissime,* which must refer to Crassus, introduces another person at the very end of the poem. Such an intrusion disturbs the obvious symmetry in which the recipients of verses 1–10 (Pompey) and 11–20 (Caesar) are addressed jointly in the final verses.[144] Most attempts to repair the line involve reading an interjection "*o*" and a masculine plural superlative adjective to agree with *socer generque* in verse 24.[145] The close relation of cc. 28 and 29 suggests that this approach is exactly right. A sarcastic or disparaging apostrophe to Caesar and Pompey, allied by marriage at 29.23–24, would complement the disparaging apostrophe to Caesar's father-in-law Piso at 28.15. Of the several emendations that have been proposed, Haupt's *o piissimi* is attractive from a structural perspective because the entire apostrophe *urbis o piissimi* is similar in language and meaning to *opprobria Romuli Remique. Romuli,* the founder of Rome, parallels *urbis* = *Romae*, while *opprobria*, "disgrace" parallels *piissimi*, which here is used ironically to signify "dishonorable." The emendation accords well also with the sacerdotal language of 28.14–15 (*at vobis mala multa di deae / dent*), thus providing another link between the two passages. And a small, additional point in favor of the reading is that *o piissimi* in an ironical sense forms a verbal pivot to the phrase *facta impia* in the opening verses of the very next poem.[146]

Poem 30

C. 30 is about broken faith. The poem is directed to a certain Alfenus who has abandoned Catullus in his time of need. The "ruined friendship with Alfenus" is described in terms of a love affair.[147] Numerous verbal echoes relate Catullus' lament in c. 30 to Ariadne's lament in c. 64 (vv. 132–201), the point of which is to suggest a similarity in their situations.[148] Like Ariadne, Catullus feels seduced and deserted by his friend. Catullus is not specific about the exact nature of Alfenus' offense because such information would detract from the principal theme of betrayal, which, as D.W.T.C. Vessey observes, occurs in virtually every verse of the poem.[149]

As the centerpiece of the polymetra, c. 30 stands out by virtue of its status as a non-corresponding poem, by virtue of its meter—the greater asclepiadean occurs nowhere else in the corpus—and by virtue of its combination of themes. Catullus' *pietas*, betrayal by a friend or lover, and the threat of divine retribution for promises unkept are not joined in a single poem elsewhere in the polymetra. This also is the first instance in which Catullus speaks of an *amicitia* in terms of a *foedus*.

The language of political or aristocratic obligation (*impia*, *fides*) links c. 30 with its neighbors, all of which directly or indirectly can be viewed as political poems. The point of c. 27 is to attack Postumia, who, in all likelihood, was a mistress of, if not Caesar, then some other prominent political figure; cc. 28 and 29 attack gubernatorial abuses, "the first from an immediate personal perspective, the second for ostensibly disinterested patriotic motives";[150] and c. 31, picking up the theme of Bithynia from c. 28, turns the bitterness of the earlier poem into joy, as Catullus celebrates his return from abroad to his family estate.

Catullus' passive or insubordinate role is another element that relates c. 30 to other poems of the cycle. In c. 28 he is shafted by Memmius; in c. 29 he, along with the rest of Rome, is shafted by Mamurra; in cc. 27 and 32 women are in charge of the drinking and the sex; in c. 25 he is the victim of Thallus' thievery; and in c. 30, whenever "Catullus refers to himself, it is always as the object or recipient of Alfenus' actions."[151]

Much space has already been devoted to c. 28. But before we complete discussion of this cycle by turning to the linear structure, it is worth considering why c. 28 is the only poem in the corpus that unites Catullus' experiences in the provinces with those of his friends. The reason is shown in figure 2.11 on the next page. The poem functions as the centerpiece of the Veranius/Fabullus and Bithynia poems, which are combined and organized in a ring-composition pattern.[152]

Cc. 4 and 46 have as their subject Catullus' return to Italy. The one describes the geographical excursion from Bithynia to Italy, while the other, which is set just prior to the departure from Bithynia, depicts Catullus' eagerness to return home. Since the dramatic time of c. 46 precedes that of c. 4, the order of the poems is slightly curious. C. 31 also concerns Catullus' return to Italy, but this poem is linked with c. 9. They share the combined themes of homecoming and reunion with a close friend (Catullus and Veranius in c. 9, and Sirmio = *amica* and Catullus in c. 31). Similar language and a similar mood of unbounded joy underscore the poems' relationship.[153] The Veranius and Fabullus poems 12, 13, and 47 are joined by the theme of a dinner party. The theme is admittedly misleading, for in none of these poems do Catullus' friends enjoy a sumptuous repast, even vicariously. In c. 47 they are scrounging for an invitation to dinner at

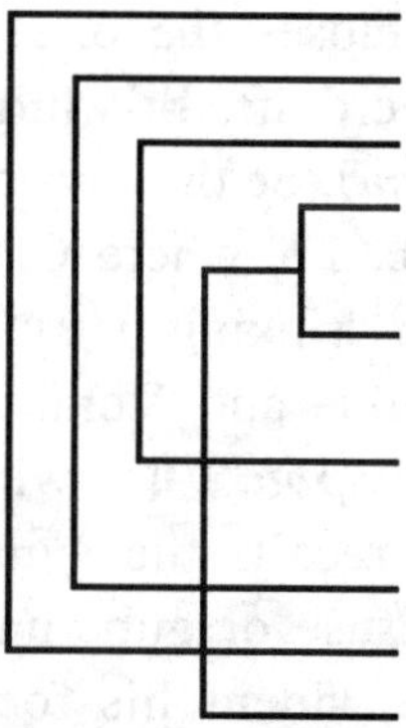

4. Catullus' return from Bithynia
9. Reunion: Veranius and Catullus
10. Memmius *irrumator*; no profit
12. Fabullus and Veranius: theft of Spanish napkins dissociates them from food
13. Fabullus expects a dinner party; no food; poverty of poet
28. Catullus and friends "irrumated" by provincial governors; no profit; hunger
31. Reunion: Catullus and Sirmio
46. Imminent return from Bithynia
47. Fabullus and Veranius scrounge for dinner invitations

Figure 2.11 Ring Arrangement of the Provincial Poems

crossroads; in c. 13 Fabullus, who presumably has just returned from the provinces, will have to cater his own *cena adventicia* if he wishes to dine at all (to say nothing of "well") because Catullus professes poverty, and in c. 12 Fabullus and Veranius are dissociated from food as a result of the theft of the napkins they sent to Catullus. Finally, the remaining cc. 10 and 28 form obvious counterparts. They are the only poems to mention Memmius, the governor of Bithynia (who is similarly described as an *irrumator)*, and they are the only ones to indicate that Catullus' year spent abroad was disappointing financially. In addition to joining the unhappy experiences of Catullus and his friends, c. 28 unites themes found in the other eight poems. These include: oral rape (10), hunger (12, 13, 47), poverty or lack of profit (10 and 13), and homecoming (4, 9, 13 [implied], 31, and 46).

Nearly one-sixth of the polymetra is devoted to the theme of Bithynia, Spain, and Macedonia. This figure, taken with the position of prominence that these poems occupy at the beginning, middle, and end, suggests that the time spent abroad by Catullus and his friends is to be construed as representing a major event in their lives.

Linear Structure of Poems 25–33

As for the linear sequencing, cc. 25 and 26 are linked by the motif of winds (*vento*, 25.13; *Austri, Favoni, Boreae, Apheliotae, ventum* 26.1, 2, 3, 5). The raging gale that closes the one poem (*vesaniente vento)* humorously shifts to an overdraft, bristling and pestilent (*ventum horribilem atque pestilentem)*, at the end of the other. The theme of destructiveness recurs in c. 27, where Catullus banishes ruinous water, *vini pernicies*, from the drinking party. The exiled water contrasts with the returning Fabullus and Veranius of c. 28, who have just come home from abroad (*vappa,* "flat wine"—Catullus' abusive term for Piso in 28.5—also recalls the sympotic theme of c. 27). While Catullus deals with misuse of gubernatorial power from a personal perspective in c. 28, he widens his focus in c. 29, as he implies that all Romans are getting shafted by the likes of Mamurra. In c. 30, the use of language of political alliance with reference to Alfenus suggests that, in Catullus' eyes, his friend's behavior is as dishonorable as that of Rome's unscrupulous politicians. The unhappiness and misery caused by the disloyal friend is contrapuntal to the joy of homecoming in c. 31 (cf. also *quasi tuta omnia mi forent* at 30.8 with *in tuto*, referring to Catullus, at 31.6). The close connection between *venusta* Sirmio and Catullus' *domus* anticipates the same close connection between Ipsithilla and her *domus* in c. 32. Lastly, the sexual gluttony of Catullus (*paresque nobis / novem continuas fututiones* 32.7–8) anticipates the voracious sexual appetite of Vibennius, Jr. in c. 33 (*culo...voraciore*). What is more, the proximity of *pallium,* the final word of c. 32, to *O Furum*, the first words of c. 33, appears deliberately designed to call to mind that at the start of the cycle Catullus' cloak was one of the pilfered items (25.6).

Poems 34–44

The next sequence begins with a poem that is conspicuous because of both its meter and theme: c. 34 is the only polymetric to be written in stanzas of three lines of glyconics and a fourth of pherecratean, and it is the only genuine hymn in the first part of the corpus. The poem has two counterparts. The one, c. 44, is a parody of a hymn/prayer that invokes Catullus' villa as though it were a god. The other, c. 35, concerns Cybele, whose associations as giver of fertility and mistress of wild nature parallel those of Diana in c. 34.

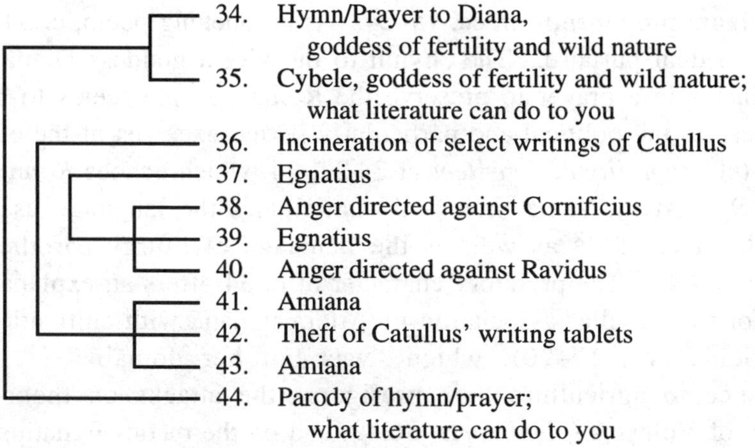

Figure 2.12 Ring Structure of Poems 34–44

C. 35 in turn is related to c. 44 through the theme of literary criticism. Together cc. 34, 35, and 44 act as a frame for four pairs that are largely denunciatory. Cc. 37~39 and cc. 41~43 abuse the provincials Egnatius and Amiana, both of whom are given to self-delusion. Cc. 38~40 are directed against individuals who have angered Catullus regarding matters of the heart (*meos amores*). And cc. 36 and 42 are *jeux d'esprit* that concern the fate of Catullus' poems, which in both instances are in the possession of a woman.[154]

Poems 34~35~44

The very formal hymn to Diana, in which "a chaste goddess," is invoked "by a chorus of chaste boys and girls,"[155] seems an odd piece to be included in the polymetra in general. Even more remarkable, however, is its presence among a series of obscene and scatological pieces (32, 33, 36, 37). P.Y. Forsyth describes the poem as "somewhat un-Catullan";[156] other critics attempt to explain its *raison d'être* by suggesting that Catullus wrote the poem for performance.[157] Although it *is* possible that c. 34 was composed for an actual occasion, its appearance here can be explained without resorting to elaborate hypotheses. We have already seen how c. 15, the real start of the second cycle, both recalls the dismissal of Lesbia just four poems earlier and introduces the theme of pederasty, which is to figure prominently in cc. 15–24. As an opening poem, c. 34 also serves a dual purpose. The hymn to the virgin goddess Diana that culminates in a prayer to preserve the Roman people seems to be in response to the political and particularly sexual excesses of the earlier c. 29 (cf. *Romulique,...gentem* at 34.22, 24, which echoes *Romule* at 29.5, 9). At the same time c. 34 anticipates the language used of Cybele in c. 35[158] as well as the language of liturgy parodied in cc. 36 and 44. The prefatory character of c. 34 offers an explanation, too, for the peculiar association of Artemis/Diana with cultivation of the fields (vv. 17–20), which "was not her domain."[159] The reference to agriculture here prefigures the attacks on the rustic poetry of Volusius (*pleni ruris* 36.19) and on the rustics Egnatius and Amiana (37, 39, 41, 42?, 43). Further, the phrase *rustica...tecta* at 34.19–20 creates a specific link with the villa of c. 44. In the words of C.J. Fordyce, the Sabine pedigree of the Catullan country estate suggests "farming and simple, even primitive, ways of life."[160]

C. 34 has other features in common with c. 44. Both poems open with an emotional vocative, followed by a reference to the addressee's origins (34.5–8; 44.1–5), and both close with a prayer (34.21–24; 44.18–21). In addition, c. 44 resumes where c. 34 ends by parodying the religious "escape-clause" formula that protects the worshipper in case he did not use the right name:[161]

sis quocumque tibi placet
sancta nomine, Romulique,... (34.21–22)

O Funde noster seu Sabine seu Tiburs
(nam te esse Tiburtem autumant, quibus non est
cordi Catullum laedere; at quibus cordi est,
quovis Sabinum pignore esse contendunt),
sed seu Sabine sive verius Tiburs,... (44.1–5)

This is the point of the concern in c. 44 over whether the farm is Sabine or Tiburtine. Further, the solemn vocative *O Funde*, the repeated *seu...seu*, and the explanatory clause beginning with *nam*, all of which belong to the language of ritual, indicate that Catullus is addressing his villa as though it were a god.

Archaic and religious language sustains the parody in the following verses, where Catullus discloses the circumstances of the invocation, expresses thanks to the villa for his recovery, and utters a curse against Sestius (*grates* 16; *non es ulta* 17; *peccatum* 17; *deprecor* 18; *recepso* 19):

fui libenter in tua suburbana
villa, malamque pectore expuli tussim,
non inmerenti quam mihi meus venter,
dum sumptuosas appeto, dedit, cenas.
nam, Sestianus dum volo esse conviva,
orationem in Antium petitorem
plenam veneni et pestilentiae legi.
hic me gravedo frigida et frequens tussis
quassavit usque, dum in tuum sinum fugi,
et me recuravi otioque et urtica.
quare refectus maximas tibi grates
ago, meum quod non es ulta peccatum.
nec deprecor iam, si nefaria scripta
Sesti recepso, quin gravedinem et tussim
non mi, sed ipsi Sestio ferat frigus,
qui tunc vocat me, cum malum librum legi.

The parody of a hymn to Catullus' villa provides a point of departure and humorous backdrop for literary criticism, the real subject of c. 44. As a precondition of attending one of Sestius' lavish dinners, Catullus was expected to read the latest speech written by his host. The oration against Antius, however, was so "frigid" (a technical term of literary criticism for bad taste) that Catullus caught a terrible cold.[162] As a result, he was forced to retreat to his villa, thereby missing the sumptuous dinner-party for which he "prostitut[ed] his critical and aesthetic faculties."[163]

E.S. DeAngeli advances the notion that certain features of c. 44 suggest the poem is a pastiche that parodies the style of Sestius.[164] DeAngeli's proposal merits consideration, not so much because we know from Cicero that Sestius was a bad stylist (e.g., *Att.* 7.17.2), but because such deliciously malicious wit seems so characteristic of Catullus. The idea that literature can physically affect its reader links c. 44 with its other counterpart, c. 35.[165]

Poem 35

Poetae tenero, meo sodali,
velim Caecilio, papyre, dicas
Veronam veniat, Novi relinquens
Comi moenia Lariumque litus.
nam quasdam volo cogitationes
amici accipiat sui meique.
quare, si sapiet, viam vorabit,
quamvis candida milies puella
euntem revocet, manusque collo
ambas iniciens roget morari.
quae nunc, si mihi vera nuntiantur,
illum deperit impotente amore.
nam quo tempore legit incohatam
Dindymi dominam, ex eo misellae
ignes interiorem edunt medullam.
ignosco tibi, Sapphica puella
musa doctior; est enim venuste
Magna Caecilio incohata Mater.

The subject of c. 35 also is literary criticism.[166] Caecilius, a young poet, has written a poem on the goddess Cybele and sent a copy to Catullus. Catullus reads Caecilius' *Magna Mater* and finds it promising but "unfinished," in the sense that it requires revision. In order that his friend might hear his thoughts on this piece, he invites him to Verona for a visit. There is a sense of urgency about the invitation that suggests Caecilius is on the point of publishing the work (*si sapiet*, *viam vorabit* 7). In writing to his friend, Catullus anticipates that Caecilius will be reluctant to come because of involvement in a love affair. To persuade his friend and his friend's girl of the importance of the trip, Catullus adopts a two-fold strategy. First, he subtly suggests that it is in the best interests of Caecilius' love affair that he hear what he has to say by creating a cause and effect relation between the themes of poetry and love: only after Caecilius' lady read his poetry (according to Catullus) did she fall hopelessly in love with him. Second, in order to assuage Caecilius' *candida puella*, whom he envisions as physically detaining her lover, Catullus resorts to flattery. She is more learned than Sappho's Muse. Presumably, therefore, because of her literary acumen, she will understand that the invitation is not a pretext to lure away her lover. Catullus is genuinely concerned about Caecilius' reputation as a poet. The *Magna Mater*, though charmingly begun, is "just begun."

Cc. 35 and 44 share several common features. Both address Catullus' comments on literary efforts to inanimate objects, a papyrus in the one and a villa in the other. Both combine the themes of invitation and critique of literature. In c. 35 Caecilius is requested to come to Verona in order to hear Catullus' thoughts on his poem. In c. 44 Catullus is invited to a dinner, at which Sestius' speech is certain to be one of the subjects of conversation. Both show a cause and effect relation between the reader and the book, the point of which is comic. After reading the *Magna Mater*, Caecilius' girl friend fell passionately in love with him (*quo tempore legit incohatam / Dindymi dominam, ex eo misellae / ignes interiorem edunt medullam* 13–15). After reading Sestius' pestilent speech, Catullus fell quite ill, racked with cold and cough (*orationem...legi. / hic me gravedo frigida et frequens tussis / quassavit usque* 11–14). The last parallel also offers a neat antithesis, with fire consuming the love-sick girl and cold gripping the sick Catullus. Finally, both poems are concerned with the quality of literature. In c. 35 subtle criticism of Caecilius' poem is tempered with praise. The *Magna Mater*, though charmingly begun, is not finished (*est enim venuste / Magna Caecilio incohata Mater* 17–18). In c. 44, however, no words are minced in the overt condemnation of Sestius' frigid diatribe against Antius: his is a nasty book (*malum librum* 21).[167]

Poems 36~42

The first of the next pair recalls in some of its details the situation of c. 35, where a "Sapphic" girl, who is *docta*, is "inflamed" by her lover's poetry. In c. 36 the girl is Lesbia, the poetry, that of Catullus, and the passion, a combination of anger and love:[168]

Annales Volusi, cacata carta,
votum solvite pro mea puella.
nam sanctae Veneri Cupidinique
vovit, si sibi restitutus essem
desissemque truces vibrare iambos,

electissima pessimi poetae
scripta tardipedi deo daturam
infelicibus ustulanda lignis.
et hoc pessima se puella vidit
iocose lepide vovere divis.
nunc o caeruleo creata ponto,
quae sanctum Idalium Uriosque apertos
quaeque Ancona Cnidumque harundinosam
colis quaeque Amathunta quaeque Golgos
quaeque Durrachium Hadriae tabernam,
acceptum face redditumque votum,
si non illepidum neque invenustum est.
at vos interea venite in ignem,
pleni ruris et inficetiarum
annales Volusi, cacata carta.

C. 36 opens with Catullus invoking Volusius' *Annals* to discharge a vow made by his girl.[169] An explanation follows. Lesbia has pledged to the Gods of Love to burn the choicest writings of the worst poet, if Catullus were restored to her and if he ceased to write attacks against her. The *pessimus poeta* Lesbia had in mind was, of course, Catullus; Catullus wittily misconstrues her words to refer to Volusius. The solemn, ritual language in the first part of the poem (*votum solvite*, *sanctae*, *electissim*a, *tardipedo deo*, *infelicibu*s) coordinates with the parody of the prayer-style in the second part (the introductory *o*, the birth-legend, and the enumeration of cult-centers introduced by anaphora of *quae*).[170] After an extravagant-sounding recital of places of worship—there are numerous elisions in verses 12–17—comes the prayer to Venus. Using language drawn from commerce, Catullus requests that the goddess enter the vow of his lady, as he has reinterpreted it, as received and duly paid.

In c. 36 Catullus thus appears to have outwitted the woman who threatens his writings. In the corresponding poem, however, he loses the battle with the fairer sex.[171]

In c. 42 Catullan *scripta* are again in the possession of a woman and are again in jeopardy. In this instance the *puella* refuses to return writing tablets on which presumably a poem of solicitation is inscribed. In order to get back his *pugillaria,* Catullus resorts to a form of extralegal redress whereby a victim of injustice calls together his friends who seek out the transgressor and assault him verbally in a public place. In the *flagitatio* of c. 42 Catullus' poetry is summoned (instead of his friends) to assist him in retrieving their common property. After identifying the thieving culprit, he urges his verses to surround and dun the woman by chanting the refrain, *moecha putida, redde codicillos, / redde, putida moecha, codicillos.* The loud, insulting language, however, proves totally ineffectual in bringing about the return of the *pugillaria.* As a result, a drastic change in strategy is adopted at the poem's end, from abuse to praise. Instead of calling the woman "a filthy slut," the hendecasyllables should call her "chaste and pure."

Cc. 36 and 42 stand out as the only pair in the collection to have poetry as their recipient. Moreover, the personified addressees play a similar part. Both are invoked to assist Catullus in difficult situations that involve a woman, the fate of his poems, and the notion of restoration. In the one poem, Lesbia has vowed to the Gods of Love to burn the worst writing of the worst poet, if Catullus were restored to her (*restitutus essem* 36.4). In the other, the hendecasyllables are summoned to help Catullus dun an unnamed *puella*, who refuses to give back his writing tablets (*reddituram* 42.4). But while Catullus views Lesbia's vow as witty, he clearly views the theft of his *pugillaria* as lacking wit, as the abusive language directed against the *puella* indicates. This observation is important because the qualities of sophistication and lack of sophistication are inverted between the first and the second poems. As the diagram below illustrates, c. 36 features "unsophisticated poetry" and a sophisticated girl, while c. 42 features "sophisticated poetry" (presumably, since it is Catullus') and an unsophisticated girl; Catullus' role as victim remains the same in the two poems:

C. 36	C. 42
unsophisticated poetry (*Annales Volusi*)	sophisticated poetry (that of Catullus)
sophisticated girl (Lesbia)	unsophisticated girl (identity unknown)
Catullus, the victim	Catullus, the victim

It is significant that the characters of the *puellae* are contrasting. Catullus may despise Lesbia for her inability to make a commitment and he may loathe her for her sexual promiscuity, but he never castigates her for lack of urbanity. For this reason the view that Lesbia is the anonymous woman of c. 42 seems improbable.[172] Who is she, then? Critics are perhaps right in identifying her as Amiana, who (to her great disadvantage) is explicitly compared to Lesbia in the very next poem, c. 43.

G. Williams has called attention to the complexity of c. 36, which combines the themes of literary criticism, parody of religious language, personification of an inanimate object, and Catullus' relationship with Lesbia.[173] Curiously, however, a particularly fascinating aspect of this poem, concerning the liaison, has failed to attract comment. C. 36 is the first poem to refer to Lesbia since c. 13, and it is the first to refer to the love affair since c. 11. The subject of reconciliation, therefore, is significant for the issue of a narrative continuity. It suggests that Catullus is linking the Lesbia poems that occur later in the polymetra with those that occur in the opening sequence (for the arrangement of the love poems, see Chapter Six).

Although the witty *Annales Volusi* may have been successful in effecting a reconciliation with Lesbia,[174] the renewed relation is short-lived. Just one poem later, the lovers are estranged again. What is more, although Catullus outwits his girl in c. 36, he appears to have won the battle but lost the war. In c. 37 we find Lesbia playing with a different kind of fire, Egnatius (< *ignis*) the Spaniard.[175]

Poems 37~39

The first half of c. 37 is devoted to attacking the habitués of a certain drinking-house:

> Salax taberna vosque contubernales,
> a pilleatis nona fratribus pila,
> solis putatis esse mentulas vobis,
> solis licere, quidquid est puellarum,
> confutuere et putare ceteros hircos?
> an, continenter quod sedetis insulsi
> centum an ducenti, non putatis ausurum

me una ducentos irrumare sessores?
atqui putate: namque totius vobis
frontem tabernae sopionibus scribam.

Catullus threatens the clientele with oral rape and the tavern itself with figurative rape, the scribbling of obscenities on its front wall.[176] At verses 11–16 we discover why the tavern and its salacious customers are the victims of such vicious verbal assault:

puella nam mi, quae meo sinu fugit,
amata tantum quantum amabitur nulla,
pro qua mihi sunt magna bella pugnata,
consedit istic. hanc boni beatique
omnes amatis, et quidem, quod indignum est,
omnes pusilli et semitarii moechi;

In a word, the reason is "Lesbia." Catullus' lady has taken up residence in the tavern and is consorting with its customers. What really hurts is that her lovers include not only Rome's privileged class (*boni beatique*), but back-street lechers as well and particularly the provincial parvenu Egnatius. The poem builds to one of the most memorably obscene punch lines in all of Latin literature (17–20):

tu praeter omnes une de capillatis,
cuniculosae Celtiberiae fili,
Egnati, opaca quem bonum facit barba
et dens Hibera defricatus urina.

Egnatius of *cun-i-cul-osa Celtiberia* brushes his teeth with Spanish piss. (Catullus is probably punning here on both *cun(n)us* and *culus.*)

C. 39 continues the attack on Egnatius by enlarging on the theme of his lack of elegance and sophistication. The opening section of the poem is concerned with Egnatius' quite annoying habit of smiling constantly whether the occasion is appropriate or not (1–8). The next verses maliciously account for his being *inurbanus* (9–16). The point of the catalogue of Italian nationalities, with whom Egnatius the Spaniard is contrasted, is to suggest that one really should not expect urbanity from an individual who obviously is *so* provincial. As in c. 37, thoughts of Egnatius' homeland lead naturally, in Catullus' mind, to thoughts of the oral hygiene practiced by the Celtiberians. In fact, the repetition of the same language from 37.18–20 at 39.17–19 (*Celtiber*[*–ia*], *dens*, *defricare*) seems to be preparing the reader for a similar scatological joke at the end.[177] The blow delivered in the final verses is devastating. The more dazzling Egnatius' smile, the more piss it can be assumed he ingested (*ut, quo iste vester expolitior dens est, / hoc te amplius bibisse praedicet loti* 20–21).

The disposition of the two Egnatius poems merits attention, because Catullus could have created a responsive relation by inverting their order. *Salax taberna,* which reveals Egnatius is Lesbia's lover, then would have accounted for the vicious assault on him in *Egnatius, quod candidos.* The reason that the second Egnatius poem does not precede the first is this: C. 37 is intended to answer c. 36; by signifying that the reconciliation of Catullus and his lady lasts but a brief time, c. 37 sets the tone for the coming poems of disillusion and rejection that characterize the second group of Lesbia polymetra.

Poems 41~43

Cc. 41 and 43 form a double attack on Amiana (or Ameana), who is named in the one poem and alluded to in the other:[178]

C. 41

Amiana puella defututa
tota milia me decem poposcit,
ista turpiculo puella naso,
decoctoris amica Formiani.
propinqui, quibus est puella curae,
amicos medicosque convocate:
non est sana puella, nec rogare
qualis sit solet aes imaginosum.

C. 43

Salve, nec minimo puella naso
nec bello pede nec nigris ocellis
nec longis digitis nec ore sicco
nec sane nimis elegante lingua,
decoctoris amica Formiani.
ten provincia narrat esse bellam?

tecum Lesbia nostra comparatur?
o saeclum insapiens et infacetum!

Part of the reason that Amiana is the victim of Catullus' abuse lies in the repeated phrase *decoctoris amica Formiani* (41.4; 43.5), placed prominently at the center of each poem.[179] She is the girl friend of the bankrupt Formian Mamurra, whom Catullus appears to be attacking indirectly by assailing his lady.[180] The other part of the reason has to do with Amiana and her own self-delusion. In c. 41 the woman, who fancies herself to be quite beautiful, apparently is demanding an outrageously high price for her favors. Catullus responds to the exorbitant fee of 10,000 sesterces by impugning her attractiveness and suggesting she's lost her mind.

C. 43 in turn begins by recalling the theme of mental illness. The opening salutation *salve* wittily echoes the opposite idea of *non ...sana* from the close of c. 41. The second of the pair, however, does not expand on this theme; rather, it develops the subject of Amiana's physical shortcomings, taking as its point of departure her prominent nose, mentioned at 41.3 (*turpiculo puella naso*). Verses 1–4 of c. 43 list her imperfections: her nose is not very small, her feet are not pretty, her pupils are not black, her fingers are not long, her mouth is not dry, and her tongue is none too refined. The litotic enumeration of physical flaws simultaneously suggests qualities of ideal feminine pulchritude, thereby foreshadowing the reference to Lesbia at 43.7, who in Catullus' eyes epitomizes true beauty.

Cc. 41 and 43 thus deal with a figure familiar from comedy and satire, the repulsive prostitute who is sexually unworthy.[181] Although the two poems of eight lines each hold in common Catullus' rejection of Amiana, they differ in their emphasis and complexity. While c. 41 deftly combines the themes of greed, unattractiveness, and mental health, c. 43 focuses on the single subject of Amiana as a paragon of feminine imperfection.[182]

M.B. Skinner observes how the description of Amiana as a *puella defutata* at 41.1 recalls and complements the earlier description of Mamurra as a *diffututa mentula* at 29.13.[183] M.H. Lindgren sees a verbal parallel within the poem that links the lovers. The participle *de-fututa*, "wasted or consumed" (by frequent sex) in verse 1, is similar in meaning to the substantive *de-coctor*, "he who has wasted or consumed" (his property or money) in verse 5: "Equal in their appetites for money and sex, Ameana (*puella defututa*) and Mamurra (*diffututa mentula, decoctor*) make a perfect pair. By constantly indulging in sexual relations, he consumes fortunes, she amasses them."[184]

The similar language in verses 1 and 5 suggests a further resemblance:

Am-iana	puella	de-fututa	(v. 1)
Form-iani	amica	de-coctoris	(v. 5)

It appears that in order to complement *Formiani,* Catullus coined the name *Amiana* from AM–, the root for "love," and the suffix *–iana,* an adjectival suffix (cf. also *Vatinianus* in 14.3 and *Sestianus* in 44.10). The interpretation of *Amiana* as a neologism is attractive because it eliminates the prosopographical difficulty of the name's being unattested in antiquity.[185]

Several parallels relate the attacks on Egnatius and Amiana. Both individuals are ridiculed because of their provincial background, their lack of sophistication, their sexual profligacy, and their self-delusion. The motivation behind the attacks is similar, too, their association with Lesbia.[186]

The final pair to be considered, cc. 38~40, are short variations on the earlier themes of cc. 35 and 36. All four poems involve lovers, passion, and poetry, but cc. 38~40 differ from the earlier pieces in that the passion (of anger) is displayed by the lover (instead of the beloved).

Poems 38~40

C. 38 is a versified letter addressed to the neoteric poet Q. Cornificius:

> Malest, Cornifici, tuo Catullo,
> malest, me hercule, et laboriose,
> et magis magis in dies et horas.
> quem tu, quod minimum facillimumque est,
> qua solatus es allocutione?
> irascor tibi. sic meos amores?
> paulum quid lubet allocutionis,
> maestius lacrimis Simonideis.

The poem begins with Catullus stating that he is deeply distressed. His pain is compounded by bitter disappointment because Cornificius has failed to console him in his hour of need. Catullus closes by asking his friend to write a little something for him, something "sadder than the tears of Simonides." The source of Catullus' pain is problematical, since the poem only hints at what it might be. Critics, however, have narrowed the possibilities to three: a physical illness, the death of Catullus' brother or a close friend, or infidelities of a lover.

The once favored interpretation of c. 38 as a deathbed poem was dismissed as improbable years ago by F.O. Copley, who has written the only in-depth study of the poem.[187] Copley argues that the occasion is the loss of someone dear to Catullus and that the key to the occasion lies in the reference to Simonides in the final verse, whose "songs were for the *survivors* of the dead, to console them for their loss."[188]

There are two difficulties with this view. First, the punning allusion to "the labors of Hercules" at verse 2 (*hercule, et laboriose)* seems discordant in a poem in which Catullus apparently is devastated by the death of a close friend or relative. Second, *magis magis in dies et horas* at verse 3 appears to indicate that "Catullus' unhappiness arises from a situation in which he is still embroiled."[189]

The hyperbole in the opening verses better suits the occasion of a failing love affair, the third possibility enumerated above. Accordingly

1 Malest, CORNIFICI, tuo Catullo,
2 malest, me hercule, et laboriose,
3 et MAGIS MAGIS in dies et horas.
4 quem tu, quod MINIMUM facillimumque est,
5 qua solatus es ALLOCUTIONE?
6 irascor tibi. sic meos amores?
7 PAULUM
7 quid lubet ALLOCUTIONIS,
8 MAESTIUS lacrimis
8 SIMONIDEIS.

Figure 2.13 Ring Structure of Poem 38

I propose that the key to the source of Catullus' distress lies not with *lacrimis Simonideis* in the final verse, but with *meos amores*, which occupies the structural center of the poem. As figure 2.13 above illustrates, c. 38 is organized in a ring-composition pattern. In this scheme writers of dirge, Cornificius in verse 1 and Simonides in verse 8, form the outermost pair. The next pair consists of the comparative adjective *maestius* in verse 8 and the comparative adverb *magis* in verse 3. The circular structure is completed by two obvious pairs, *minimum* and *paulum* in verses 4 and 7 and the repeated *allocutione* and *allocutionis* in verses 5 and 7.

The interpretation that c. 38 is about a disintegrating love affair, rather than about the death of someone dear, has additional merit in that it makes Cornificius appear less insensitive for not complying with Catullus' request for a *consolatio*. The question that now arises is this: to which relationship does *meos amores* refer, that with Lesbia or that with Juventius? The interplay of c. 38 and its counterpart, c. 40, points to a solution.

C. 40

Quaenam te mala mens, miselle Ravide,
agit praecipitem in meos iambos?
quis deus tibi non bene advocatus
vecordem parat excitare rixam?
an ut pervenias in ora vulgi?
quid vis? qualubet esse notus optas?

eris, quandoquidem meos amores
cum longa voluisti amare poena.

Cc. 38 and 40 are linked by the elements of poetry, anger, and the beloved. But while in c. 38 Catullus wanted sympathy for a failing love affair, and was angry when his friend failed to provide it, here he wants revenge. Catullus threatens to pillory a rival with invective verse because he is in love with his *meos amores.* The close resemblance of c. 40 to c. 15 in theme, tone, and especially language[190] indicates that it belongs to the series of Juventius poems. And if *meos amores* at 40.7 refers to Juventius, it seems logical that *meos amores* at 38.6 refers to a love affair with the same individual.[191] If this conclusion is correct, cc. 38 and 40 exhibit a responsive relation, in which the second poem elucidates the source of depression in the first: it appears that Ravidus has supplanted Catullus in Juventius' affections.[192]

In this cycle, therefore, both Catullus' homosexual and heterosexual love affairs are going badly. The poet connects the two amatory series here through the proximity of one failed relation to the other (cc. 37, 38, 40). The point of the failures is to anticipate Catullus' rejection of love in the next and last polymetric cycle.

Linear Structure of Poems 34–44

In addition to introducing the language of ritual and the topic of rusticity that are to figure prominently in this sequence, the hymn to Diana looks forward to c. 35, to the reference to Cybele, another nature-goddess, who is the subject of an "unfinished" work by Caecilius. C. 35 in turn is related to c. 36 by several common features. Both are addressed to papyrus (*papyre* 35.2; *Annales Volusi* 36.1, 20); both are concerned with literary criticism; and in both, poetry arouses the passion of a "Sapphic" girl. The juxtaposed cc. 35 and 36 show a nice touch of Catullan humor, for in the one the girl is inflamed (with passion) by her lover's poetry, while in the other the girl wants to set aflame her lover's poetry. The reconciliation that Catullus appears to be successful in effecting in c. 36, however, is short-lived, as the depiction of Lesbia as a "barroom floozy" in the very next poem indicates.[193] Angered by her promiscuity, Catullus threatens Lesbia's countless lovers with *irrumatio*, and he threatens the *taberna* where they congregate with a correspondingly aggressive punishment, figurative rape, the "scrawling [of] obscenities" on "the front of the tavern."[194] The theme of writing (*scribam* 37.10) in connection with an *affaire de coeur* relates c. 37 to its neighbors, cc. 35, 36, and 38. Furthermore, through the homosexual theme of *irrumatio* (6–8), this same poem subtly prepares for the allusion to Catullus' liaison with Juventius in c. 38 (*meos amores* 6). The impetus behind c. 38 is a friend's omission to provide a poem in consolation for a failing love affair. The tears at the end of this poem (*lacrimis Simonideis* 8) form a link with the weeping and grieving at the beginning of the next (*fletum, lugetur, flet* 39.3, 5), in which Catullus assaults the perpetually grinning Egnatius. C. 38 also allusively introduces the theme of unsound health (*male,...malest* 1–2), which figures in all but one of the five subsequent poems of the cycle, c. 42.[195] The next pieces, cc. 39 and 40, attack rivals, Egnatius and Ravidus, the first of whom suffers from a "social disorder" (*morbum, / neque elegantem*), the second from a mental disorder (*mala mens*). Additionally, just as Egnatius was threatened in c. 37 with *irrumatio* for involvement with Lesbia, so Ravidus is threatened with a "stiff penalty" for seducing Juventius (*poena* at 40.8 is a pun on *pene,* "penis").[196] The juxtaposed *amare p(o)ena*, the closing words of c. 40, in turn provide a neat verbal transition to the opening of c. 41, *AM-iana...DEFUTUTA*. C. 41 and its companion piece, c. 43, attack Amiana, Mamurra's sweetheart. Possibly the same lady may be the victim of Catullus' invective in the intervening poem, c. 42. Finally, the opposition of the urbane Lesbia and the rustic Amiana in the closing verses of c. 43 coordinates with the humorous quibble over the primitive or fashionable pedigree of Catullus' farm in the opening verses of c. 44. The observation is worth making that *O Funde noster* forms the perfect conclusion to this cycle that combines the motifs of illness and vituperation. Somehow it seems not inappropriate that Catullus is laid up after reading someone else's invective.

One question remains. Why is there such a preponderance of poems in this section of the corpus that address inanimate objects?

Part of the answer, of course is that "apostrophe to things" is a predominant theme of the cycle. The other part of the answer is shown in figure 2.14 on page 84. Poems 35 through 44 form the center of a subpattern about, or directed to, personified inanimate objects.[197] Interestingly, each of the ten poems that participates in the scheme concerns a different object—a yacht, a small town, a peninsula and family villa, a sheet of papyrus, an epic of tedious length, a randy drinking-house, Catullan verses, a Sabine villa, a virtuous lock of hair, and a garrulous door. These seemingly diverse pieces are artfully arranged in a chiastic structure.

Cc. 4 and 66 are dedicatory poems. In the one, after a safe return from Bithynia, the *phaselus* offers itself to the Dioscuri, who often are identified with the constellation Gemini. In the other, on the safe return of her husband from Syria, Queen Berenice offers to all the gods a lock of her hair, which is transformed into a constellation. In addition, both objects possess the ability to speak. In c. 4 the yacht speaks through Catullus; in c. 66 the lock speaks for itself. A former long-haired wood (*comata silva*) with talking hair (*loquente coma*), the yacht of c. 4 seems a natural counterpart to the personified subject of c. 66. The next pair appear to share a common setting as well as a common theme. Set in or near Verona, cc. 17 and 67 concern impotent husbands and lascivious wives.[198] These scandalous pieces form perfect thematic complements, with the first poem emphasizing the lethargic husband and the second the neglected wife. The central panel is enclosed by two poems in choliambs that address Catullan villas. Catullus personifies the lovely Sirmio of c. 31 as his mistress, while he elevates the humble Sabine/Tiburtine villa of c. 44 to divine status.[199] The remaining four poems at the center exhibit a close interrelationship. All have in common a poet, a *puella*, and writing in one form or another. Cc. 35 and 42 are clever pieces that invert similar elements. In the one, writing material with hendecasyllabic contents (the papyrus) may assist in the improvement of a poem (Caecilius' *Magna Mater*) that advanced a love affair with a sophisticated *puella*. In the other, hendecasyllabic verses are summoned to assist in retrieving writing material that was

4. *Phaselus* dedicated to a constellation
17. Impotence (lethargic husband)
31. Family villa
35. Papyrus
36. *Annales Volusi*, poetry of an enemy (Lesbia)
37. *Salax Taberna*, hangout of enemies (Lesbia)
42. Hendecasyllables
44. Sabine villa
66. The dedicated hair becomes a constellation
67. Impotence (lascivious wife)

Figure 2.14 Ring Arrangement of Personified Inanimate Objects

not successful in advancing a love affair with a *puella* whom Catullus now views as less than sophisticated. The poems to the *Annals* of Volusius and the whorehouse tavern are joined by the figure of Lesbia and by the condemnation of enemies of Catullus. As the center of the ring, cc. 36 and 37 unite the principal themes found in the other poems. These include dedicatory vows, promiscuity, the quality of literature, the efficacy of poetry in love affairs, and return from Bithynia (36.12–14 appear to suggest the route home).

The linear arrangement of this group of poems is equally contrived. The personified wooden yacht of c. 4, which possibly is a lover-ship, looks forward to the wooden bridge of c. 17, which is identified with the lethargic husband. The association of the *puella* and Colonia in this same poem, in turn, paves the way for the identification of Sirmio as Catullus' *amica* in c. 31. The combination of poet and *puella* will figure in the next four poems, with a sheet or sheets of paper additionally connecting cc. 35 and 36, and with a *puella* sitting in front of a whorehouse and a *puella* being abusively referred to as a whorehouse (*lupanar* 13) additionally connecting cc. 37 and 42. Catullus as victim in c. 42 looks forward to his similar posture in c. 44, where the poet laughs at himself for pimping his critical sensibilities in order to receive an invitation to a sumptuous dinner. The deification of the villa here is transitional to the deification of the severed lock in c. 66. Finally, cc. 66 and 67, which contrapose the virtuous mistress to the promiscuous mistress, are the only poems in which the personified principals speak without intermediaries.

Poems 45–60

The last cycle of polymetra is problematical, for many see the inclusion and arrangement of the last nine or ten poems as the work of an editor who was intent on preserving every scrap of Catullan verse.[200] Because of the prevalence of this view, it seems crucial to initiate discussion of this cycle by showing how cc. 52–60 exhibit an organization that is cohesive and consistent with that found in the preceding poems.

To begin, cc. 52–60 coalesce through several common features. Most of the poems (1) are comparatively short,[201] (2) belong to the same general period of B.C. 55–54,[202] and (3) are politically motivated.[203] Many, too, have their settings "in the streets and squares of Rome."[204] Further, here, as elsewhere in the polymetra, the theme of one poem prepares for that of the very next, and repetition of language strengthens the relationships among consecutive poems. In the exposition to follow, c. 49 will serve as a point of departure for discussing the linear structure of cc. 52–60, for the poem to Cicero appears to initiate this series of political poems.

Poem 49

Disertissime Romuli nepotum,
quot sunt quotque fuere, Marce Tulli,
quotque post aliis erunt in annis,
gratias tibi maximas Catullus
agit pessimus omnium poeta,
tanto pessimus omnium poeta,
quanto tu optimus omnium patronus.

In c. 49 Catullus effusively thanks Cicero. Although the occasion of the poem is the subject of much speculation,[205] several stylistic features make it difficult not to construe the expression of gratitude as ironical.[206] These include the quasi-heroic *Romuli nepotum* (1), the extravagant build-up of *quot sunt, quotque fuere,...quotque post aliis erunt in annis* (2–3), Catullus' formal address to Cicero by both his *praenomen* and *nomen* (2), and the pretentious-sounding superlatives (*disertissime, maximas, pessimus,* and *optimus*) that occur in almost every line and that call to mind Cicero's penchant for using adjectives in the highest degree. The sting of the poem in fact occurs in the final superlative expression, *optimus omnium patronus*, which can possess a secondary nuance of "best advocate of all and sundry." Those who construe the closing verse to imply that Cicero is a lawyer without scruples often ascribe the occasion of the poem to his shift in position from attacking Vatinius in B.C. 56 to later defending him in B.C. 54. The interaction of c. 49 with a Sestius and a Calvus poem, 44 and 53, lends support to this view.

Poems 44 and 49

Verbal expressions that do not occur elsewhere subtly link c. 49 with c. 44, *maximas tibi grates / ago* (44.16-17) and *gratias tibi maximas Catullus / agit* (49.4-5).[207] Owing to the emphasis placed on Cicero's role as *patronus,* the point of the cross-reference appears to be to bring to mind his involvement with Sestius in a well-known trial that took place in B.C. 56. In the *Pro Sestio* "Cicero capped his successful defense of Sestius with a biting invective against Vatinius, a witness for the prosecution."[208] The allusion to Cicero's attack on Vatinius, suggested by the relation of c. 49 to c. 44, is complemented by another allusion to his later defense of the same individual, suggested by the relation of c. 49 to c. 53. The last poem has as its subject Calvus' prosecution of Vatinius in B.C. 54, on which occasion Cicero acted as counsel for the defense.

Poems 49~53

The connection of 49 and 53 is signaled through a striking verbal echo. The adjective *disertus*, which occurs only at 49.1 and 53.5 in the poetry, frames the two poems:[209]

DISERTISSIME Romuli nepotum, 49.1

'di magni, salaputium DISERTUM!' 53.5

The use of the superlative degree of the adjective in c. 49 seems wittily pointed. Apparently Catullus is humorously suggesting to his friend Calvus how it happened that he lost the case: while he was merely *disertus*, Cicero was *disertISSIMUS*.

Similarly, the juxtaposition of poems to Cicero and to Licinius Calvus (49 and 50) appears not without purpose. Although c. 50 is not political, Catullus may be hinting at the occasion of c. 49 by directing successive poems to the chief defender and prosecutor at Vatinius' trial of B.C. 54.

It is worth noting that the "villainous Vatinius" is mentioned in another poem in close proximity; in c. 52 he is vilified along with Nonius. Cc. 49, 50, 52, and 53, therefore, appear to possess an underlying unity, with "their involvement of Vatinius" serving as a common link:[210]

C. 49	Cicero, Defense Counsel for Vatinius in B.C. 54
C. 50	Calvus, Prosecutor of Vatinius in B.C. 54
C. 52	Invective against Vatinius
C. 53	Calvus, Prosecutor of Vatinius in B.C. 54

The question that now arises is this: Does c. 51, a rendition of Sappho's φαίνεταί μοι, fit into this group? K.M.W. Shipton addresses this question in a provocative study in which he proposes that the unidentified *ille* of 51.1–2 is Clodius, who was political mentor to Vatinius.[211] He suggests that the phrase *superare divos* may have a general meaning of "to defeat/overcome the gods," and thus may signify *nefas*. If so, Catullus would be subtly indicating the identity of his rival by alluding to Clodius' sacrilegious invasion of the Bona Dea festival in B.C. 62 and to the rumored reports of incest with his sister "Lesbia." Shipton's highly conjectural proposal is attractive from the perspective of a thematic continuum, for cc. 49 through 53 *en bloc* would be related through a connection with Vatinius. But whether we accept or reject his theory, c. 51 clearly is not out of place in this sequence. By recalling the theme of *otium* from 50.1 only to reject it, 51.13–16 prepare for the antithetical theme of *negotium* in the subsequent poems.[212]

Poems 51, 52

C. 52, a four-line squib, assails Nonius and Vatinius. Several parallels relate this slight poem to c. 51. *Catulle* in 52.1, 4 echoes the Catullan self-address in 51.13,[213] and *moraris emori* in 52.1, 4 picks up the theme of death and destruction from the final two stanzas of c. 51. In addition, Nonius' sitting on the curule chair in 52.2 recalls the posture of Lesbia and the unidentified man who sit opposite each other in 51.3 (*qui sedens adversus...te*). This last reminiscence is important because of a secondary significance of *sella in...sedet.* The phrase may refer to "a common method of soliciting," whereby prostitutes sat in chairs in front of brothels.[214] Not only is the reference to prostituting oneself for political advancement insulting to Nonius,[215] but the verbal cross-reference between 51.3 and 52.2 is unflattering to Lesbia as well. It calls to mind that on the last occasion that we saw Catullus' lady (37.11–16), she was portrayed as a low-class prostitute who was sitting, in the sense of soliciting (*consedit*), in a tavern/brothel nine doors down from the temple of Castor and Pollux.[216] The interplay of cc. 37, 51, and 52 thus suggests that a note of bitterness underlies Catullus' infatuation in c. 51.

Poems 52, 53, 54

C. 53 follows naturally on c. 52, with its mention of Vatinius (52.3; 53.2) and with its setting in the Forum. The poem relates an amusing incident that took place during Vatinius' trial. Apparently one in a crowd of bystanders was so moved by the rhetorical powers of the prosecuting Licinius Calvus that he exclaimed in admiration: "Great Gods, what an eloquent Prick!" (*Di magni, salaputium disertum*). A risqué interpretation of *salaputium* as *mentula salax* gives the poem point.[217] A phallic meaning for *salaputium* also is suggested by the witty juxtaposition of the noun and its modifier—*disertum* according to Varronian etymology derives from the Latin for "sowing seeds" (*L.L.* VI.64). The interplay between the end of c. 53 and the beginning of c. 54, too, would result in an amusing contrast. The small phallus of Otho at 54.1 (*caput* [= *caput mentulae*]*...pusillum*) would be set in opposition to Calvus as a large phallus at 53.5.

Poems 54, 55, 56

The quite corrupt c. 54 continues Catullus' attack on political figures. The references to Hirrus, a kinsman of Pompey,[218] to Caesar, father-in-law of Pompey, and to Libo, father-in-law of Sextus Pompey, all provide a transition to c. 55, in which the Portico of Pompey the Great is the culmination of a list of places in the center of Rome where Catullus has conducted an unsuccessful search for his friend Camerius. Camerius' disappearance and apparent refusal to come out of hiding cause Catullus to suspect him of having a secret love affair. The subtle sexual joke at the end of c. 55—"It's O.K. to remain silent provided that I may share in your love"—looks forward to a similar, albeit more outrageous, comic denouement in the final verses of the next poem. Here Catullus quite literally shares in the erotic activity:[219]

O rem ridiculam, Cato, et iocosam,
dignamque auribus et tuo cachinno!
ride quidquid amas, Cato, Catullum:
res est ridicula et nimis iocosa.
deprendi modo pupulum puellae
trusantem; hunc ego, si placet Dionae,
protelo rigida mea cecidi.

C. 56 probably is directed to Marcus Porcius Cato. The identification is suggested both by the political character of this sequence of poems and by the humorless personality of this particular individual. No doubt the puritanical Cato would have to be told more than once that a certain off-color incident was extremely funny. The punch line in verses 6–7 contains an allusion to *Iliad* 5.375ff., where Diomedes wounds Venus, who in tears hurries off to be consoled by her mother Dione.[220] Catullus' comical identification with the epic hero Diomedes relates back to his quest for Camerius in 55.15ff. (= the displaced 58b), which is described in language that parodies epic.[221] His substitution here of Dione for "gods" in the colloquial expression *si placet dis* also points forward to the appearance of Caesar in 57.2, who claimed Venus, daughter of Dione, as his divine *progenitrix*.[222] In addition, *caedo*, "to penetrate anally," in 56.7 forms a link with the obscene sense of *cinaedis* in 57.1, as well as relating etymologically to *Caesari*, "he who has been cut," in 57.2. The occurrence of all three words at the same point of the verse seems to reinforce a connection:

...hunc ego, si placet Dionae,
protelo rigida mea CECIDI. (56.6–7)

Pulcre convenit improbis CINAEDIS,
Mamurrae pathicoque CAESARIQUE. (57.1–2)

Poems 57, 58, 59, 60

C. 57 lampoons Caesar and his henchman Mamurra. Catullus asserts that they are homosexual lovers, who assume indiscriminately the active and passive roles. Their sexual proclivities include women also. Attempting to satisfy their insatiable appetite for sex, this dastardly duo pursue other men's wives, and compete as friendly rivals for pubescent girls (*vorax adulter / rivales socii puellularum*).[223] The point of c. 57, of course, is to insult Caesar by equating him with a social inferior,[224] by intimating that he sometimes assumes the woman's part, and by depicting him as a rapist of nymphets.

The notion of duality or twinning, which dominates c. 57 (discussed below on page 105), is shared by neighboring poems. Cc. 56 through 60 en bloc exhibit this motif. C. 56 has two sets of "twins," CATo/CATullus[225] and the *pupulus* and *puella* (< PU-); in c. 57 twin first and last lines frame the *gemelli* Caesar and Mamurra; in 58.1–2 occurs the striking gemination of *Lesbia illa, / illa Lesbia*; in 59.1 Rufa services her "twin" Rufulus; and in c. 60 the notion of duality is suggested by the biform Scylla. The related themes of promiscuity and voracious sexual appetite also connect c. 57 with the final three polymetra.

C. 58 initiates a triad of pieces that consist of a single sentence of five lines each and that are concerned with prostitutes.[226] C. 58 depicts Lesbia as a common whore who lends a helping hand to anyone anywhere. Lesbia's debasement is surpassed in the following poem by that of Rufa the *fellatrix*, who frequents cemeteries like

C. 58

Caeli, Lesbia nostra, Lesbia illa,
illa Lesbia, quam Catullus unam
plus quam se atque suos amavit omnes,
nunc in quadriviis et angiportis
glubit magnanimos Remi nepotes.

C. 59

Bononiensis Rufa Rufulum fellat,
uxor Meneni, saepe quam in sepulcretis
vidistis ipso rapere de rogo cenam,
cum devolutum ex igne prosequens panem
ab semiraso tunderetur ustore.

C. 60

Num te leaena montibus Libystinis
aut Scylla latrans infima inguinum parte
tam mente dura procreavit ac taetra,
ut supplicis vocem in novissimo casu
contemptam haberes, a nimis fero corde?

the lowest of prostitutes and who desecrates the dead by stealing food from the burning pyre. The association of food and oral sex in c. 59 splendidly prepares for the mythological reference to Scylla of 60.2, a man-eater *par excellence*. Although the recipient of the last polymetric is anonymous, similar passages in classical literature indicate that Catullus' heartless mistress Lesbia is being alluded to as the offspring of the Scylla,[227] a name "that in [Greek] Middle Comedy and Hellenistic epigram...comes into use as a symbol for greedy prostitutes."[228]

To some, the final poems provide an unsatisfactory close to the polymetra.[229] Yet, it can be demonstrated that the collocation of themes is Catullan by comparing cc. 57–60 to c. 11. The closing sequence sets forth separately themes combined in the earlier poem.

Poems 11 and 57–60

Julius Caesar first appears in the poetry in c. 11, where he is unflatteringly associated with Lesbia. Verbal repetition (*ultimus* 11–12, 23) relates his military conquests to her sexual conquests.[230] Caesar and Lesbia are associated again through the theme of sexual profligacy in the juxtaposed cc. 57 and 58. C. 58 in particular is strongly reminiscent of c. 11.[231] Both are appeals to Catullus' "friends";[232] both deal with Lesbia's utter moral degradation; and both describe her activities in vividly coarse terms (*glubit* at 58.5 and *omnium/ilia rumpens* at 11.19–20). C. 11 is in turn connected with c. 59 through the theme of death. The final image of the flower grazed by the plow and left to die (11.22–24) and the expression *vivat valeatque*, found on grave inscriptions (11.17),[233] accord with the sepulchral setting and the corpses of c. 59. Lastly, cc. 11 and 60 are the only Catullan poems to portray Lesbia as an epic monster. The hyperbolic description of Lesbia holding three hundred lovers "in one Gargantuan embrace" at 11.17–20 evokes the Scylla, with whom she is explicitly identified at 60.2–3.[234]

The parallels shown in the table below thus illustrate that the Lesbia poems in each half of the polymetra build to a similar climax. In both instances Catullus dismisses his lady as a sexually wanton whore, incapable of commitment and unworthy of his love:[235]

C. 11	Caesar-Lesbia are linked by the theme of conquest	Cc. 57/58	Sexual profligacy of Caesar and Lesbia
C. 11	Lesbia, common whore; *omnia / illa rumpens*	C. 58	Lesbia, common whore; *glubit*
C. 11	Theme of death evoked	C. 59	Sepulchral setting
C. 11	Lesbia depicted as a Scylla-like monster	C. 60	Lesbia, offspring of the Scylla

A final piece of evidence indicates that the arrangement of the final polymetra is Catullan. Cc. 55–60 provide closure by reversing the order of themes found in cc. 1–6, as figure 2.15 below illustrates.[236] Cc. 6 and 55 are closely related; only here does

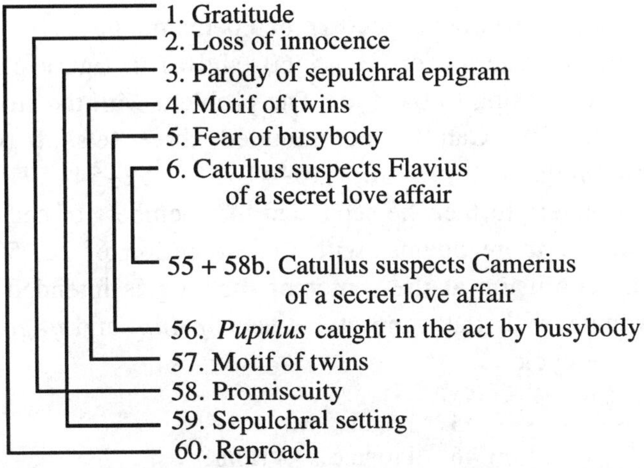

Figure 2.15 Chiastic Ordering of Poems 1–6 and 55–60

Catullus suspect friends of being involved in a secret affair. The fifth poems from each end appear to invert Catullus' role of potential victim and "busybody." In c. 5 Catullus fears that his and Lesbia's love may be threatened by a malevolent meddler; in c. 56 Catullus as meddler catches a *pupulus* in the act of making love. A relation between the next poems is suggested by the diminutive *gemellus*, which occurs only at 4.27 and 57.6 in the poetry.[237] The connection between cc. 4 and 57 is reminiscent of that between cc. 28 and 29, where the theme of return from the provinces is joined to that of the sexual excesses of Mamurra. A sepulchral setting links c. 59 with c. 3, a parody of a sepulchral epigram. These poems only associate eating and death (3.13–14; 59.3–4). Lesbia poems 2 and 58 form a pair through the opposing themes of loss of innocence and promiscuity. Finally, cc. 1 and 60 set gratitude for a past *beneficium* against reproach for neglect of a present appeal for help.

In summary, the linear ordering of cc. 52–60 shows the same meticulous attention to detail among successive poems as that found in cc. 1–51. In light of the exhaustive evidence presented in the previous pages that the arrangement of these poems is Catullan, attention can now be turned to the ring structure of the cycle.

Circular Structure of Poems 45–60

The circular ordering of cc. 45–60 (shown in figure 2.16) is not symmetrically pleasing to the eye. The problem with the structure lies at the center. Here Catullus commingled three sets of two-to-one correspondences (49~53~56; 50~51~55; 52~54~57) and, to complicate matters further, he separated the members of each thematic triad by one or more poems, with the exception of cc. 50 and 51. Perhaps the confusion at the center of the ring is intended to reflect and coordinate with the conflict between *otium* and *negotium* that dominates the cycle.

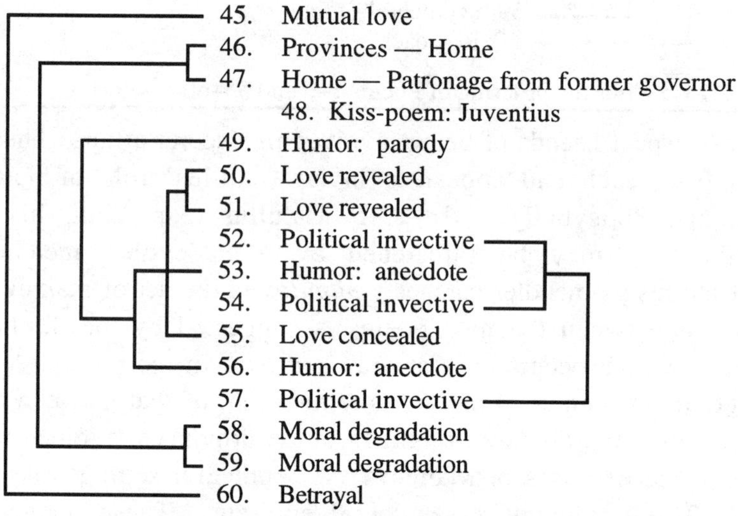

Figure 2.16 Ring Structure of Poems 45–60

Poem 45

The final cycle of polymetra begins with c. 45. In form, the poem is a dialogue between two lovers, in which the girl caps the boy's statement of devotion by asserting that her love is deeper and more passionate. Ostensibly this dramatic vignette appears to be little more than a charming exercise on mutual love; in reality, however, the poem is concerned with a larger issue. Its purpose is to contrast *otium* and *negotium*, to set the life of the lover against that of the soldier.[238] The conflict between making love and war is suggested in the opening speech of Septimius, where his vow of undying devotion to Acme is contraposed to the notion of empire:

Acmen Septimius suos amores
tenens in gremio 'mea' inquit 'Acme,
ni te perdite amo atque amare porro
omnes sum assidue paratus annos,
quantum qui pote plurimum perire,
solus in Libya Indiaque tosta
caesio veniam obvius leoni.'

The tension between these two extremes recurs later at verses 21–22:

unam Septimius misellus Acmen
mavult quam Syrias Britanniasque.

Compelled by the desire to possess just Acme, Septimius rejects the attraction of going on campaign against Syria and Britain.

Thoughts of faraway places, however, do not intrude in Acme's profession of love. The passion she feels for her lover is internalized:

at Acme leviter caput reflectens
et dulcis pueri ebrios ocellos
illo purpureo ore suaviata,
'sic', inquit 'mea vita Septimille,
huic uni domino usque serviamus,
ut multo mihi maior acriorque
ignis mollibus ardet in medullis.'
. . . .
uno in Septimio fidelis Acme
facit delicias libidinesque.

The internalized love of Acme and the externalized love of Septimius also call attention to the implicit opposition between *otium* and *negotium* that operates within the poem: while Acme desires "emotional commitment," Septimius dreams of "exotic adventure."[239]

H.A. Khan is the first to see inherent irony in c. 45 in terms of these two incompatible ways of life.[240] Prior to his study, an ironical reading of the Septimius and Acme idyll depended on interpreting the poem in light of Catullus' own unhappy love affair.[241] Although a biographical approach admittedly is fraught with peril, in this particular instance verbal cross-references to Lesbia poems make it difficult *not* to read c. 45 against the backdrop of Catullus' love poetry. The geographical references to Libya, India, Syria, and Britain in 45.6, 22 are the same as those in the renunciatory c. 11,[242] and the phrase *ut ante* at 45.8, 17 significantly echoes the only other occurrence of the phrase at 11.21.[243] C. 45 also has parallels in common with two Lesbia poems on disillusioned love that occur in this cycle, 51 and 58. Cc. 45 and 58 are the only polymetric poems that describe the sensation of love in terms of a one and only theme (*unam Septimius misellus Acmen.... uno in Septimio fidelis Acme* 45.21, 23; *Lesbia, quam Catullus unam / plus quam...amavit* 58.2–3). And the intensity of Catullus' passion in 51.9–10 (*tenuis sub artus / flamma demanat*) echoes "the description of Acme's emotions" in 45.16 (*ignis mollibus ardet in medullis*).[244]

Poems 45~60

The correspondence of c. 60 to c. 45 provides another indication of implicit cynicism:

> Num te leaena montibus Libystinis
> aut Scylla latrans infima inguinum parte
> tam mente dura procreavit ac taetra,
> ut supplicis vocem in novissimo casu
> contemptam haberes, a nimis fero corde?

The poems are bound by the opposite themes of mutual love and betrayal. The relation, which ostensibly is slight, is signaled by a verbal clue. Mention of Libyan lions (60.1) occurs only here in the poetry.[245] Although c. 60 names neither addressee nor suppliant, it seems certain that Lesbia is being addressed by a disillusioned Catullus. O. Weinreich has convincingly demonstrated the erotic character of c. 60 by comparing the language and imagery in verses 1–3 to similar passages in Greek and Latin literature where the one abandoned abuses his or her callous lover.[246]

Actually it is almost unnecessary to go outside the Catullan corpus to find the key to the interpretation of c. 60. C. 64, just three poems later, indicates the context in light of which c. 60 is to be read (154–57):

> quaenam te genuit sola sub rupe leaena,
> quod mare conceptum spumantibus exspuit undis,
> quae Syrtis, quae Scylla rapax, quae vasta Carybdis,
> talia qui reddis pro dulci praemia vita?

The words of the abandoned Ariadne to her cruel lover, Theseus, echo Catullus' *cri de coeur* to his cruel lover, Lesbia. The function of the Ariadne-Theseus episode in c. 64, which is to undermine a picture of idyllic love (that of Peleus and Thetis), indicates a similar function for c. 60. Accordingly, the disillusion yet to come for Septimius and Acme is intimated by Catullus' setting their bliss against his own unhappy love affair.

Recognizing that c. 45 is concerned with the mutually exclusive activities of political service and pursuit of ideal love is important in order to understand Catullus' motivation, as he wants us to understand it, for going to Bithynia as a member of Memmius' praetorial staff, the subject of the very next poem. A verbal cross-reference between cc. 45 and 46 suggests that the dissolution of a love affair that Catullus had hoped would be as romantic as that of Septimius and Acme prompted him to exchange Service in Love's Camp for Foreign Service: Acme's and Septimius' setting out from a good omen on "the journey of Love" at 45.19 (*ab auspicio bono profecti)* is echoed at 46.10 by Catullus' reference to his setting out from home with male companions for his tour of military duty (*a domo profectos*).[247]

Poems 46~47, Poems 47~59

Cc. 46 and 47 continue the theme of *negotium* introduced in c. 45. C. 46 is concerned with the end of Catullus' term of foreign service in Bithynia. Like Septimius in the previous poem, Catullus dreams of "new experiences far from home,"[248] as he eagerly anticipates visiting the cities of Asia Minor (6–8). C. 47, the counterpart to c. 46, also deals with the subject of political service, but here the focus is on advancement. The poem opposes the success of the thieving and greedy Porcius and Socration in winning Piso's favor to the failure of Fabullus and Veranius in doing so. As in the earlier c. 28, lack of success is expressed through the metaphor of hunger. While Porcius and Socration feast sumptuously at Piso's table, Catullus' friends are reduced to begging for their dinner at the crossroads, "the place of the outcast."[249]

The disappointment and disgraceful posture of Fabullus and Veranius in the one poem is intensified by the opposing picture of Catullus' exuberant happiness in the other. M.B. Skinner is surely right in suggesting that in c. 47 "Catullus ironically censures his friends for snatching crumbs of recognition from the tables of the great."[250]

C. 47 thus appears to be as much an attack on the demeaning behavior of Fabullus and Veranius as it is an attack on the system that encourages such behavior. The relation of c. 47 to c. 59, which also act as counterparts, supports this interpretation.

C. 59 pillories Rufa the *fellatrix*, who, like Veranius and Fabullus, is portrayed as scrounging for dinner. Rufa's situation, however, is more desperate. She is reduced to frequenting graveyards of the poor, where she steals food from the burning pyre. As punishment for her shameless act of desecration, she is raped by a half-shaven corpse-burner.

Hunger, therefore, is the common theme of cc. 47 and 59. A verbal parallel further points up a connection. The language in 47.6–7, *mei solades / quareunt in trivio vocationes,* is echoed by that in 59.2–3, *in sepulcretis...rapere...cenam.* The point of this unflattering association of Fabullus and Veranius with Rufa is to equate quest of patronage with the act of prostitution. And so in their final appearance in the collection even Catullus' closest friends find themselves the victims of implicit attack. Why? I think the answer lies with the setting of c. 47, which, following K. Quinn, I take to be Rome.[251] Presumably Catullus is critical of Fabullus and Veranius for having failed to learn from their unhappy experience in

Macedonia, since now that they are back in Rome they continue to seek patronage from the same villainous scoundrel.[252]

Poems 46~58, Poems 58~59

Catullus, however, does not include himself in his indictment of his friends' pursuit of patronage. In fact, he goes to great lengths to justify his violation of his "ethico-literary"[253] adherence to *otium* by intimating that his tour of duty in the East was the result of his failed love affair with Lesbia. This is the point of c. 46's connection with c. 58, the subject of which is Lesbia's promiscuity (in the polymetra Catullus frequently uses Lesbia's "whoring" as a metaphor for the failed love affair). Catullus does not take great pains to indicate a relation between cc. 46 and 58 because the reader has already seen the themes of return from Bithynia and Lesbia's utter moral degradation joined in an earlier pair, cc. 4 and 11.

It has not passed unnoticed that cc. 58 and 59 concern similar subjects.[254] The five-line poems, each consisting of a single sentence, deal with the habitat and moral shamelessness of Lesbia and Rufa, Roman matrons. As figure 2.17 below illustrates, the poems exhibit a parallel structure (which is discussed in detail on pages 156–58).

	C. 58	C. 59
CAELIUS RUFUS	Caeli (1)	Rufulum (1)
THREE-FOLD IDENTIFICATION OF LESBIA/RUFA	Lesbia nostra (1) Lesbia illa (1) illa Lesbia (2)	Bononiensis (1) Rufa (1) uxor Meneni (= Metelli) (2)
FEM. ACCUS. RELATIVE	quam (2)	quam (2)
TEMPORAL ADVERB	nunc (4)	saepe (2)
UNSAVORY SETTINGS	in quadriviis et angiportis (4)	in sepulcretis (2)
SEX	glubit (5)	tunderetur (5)

Figure 2.17 Parallel Structure of Poems 58 and 59

For the present discussion the significance of the poems' similar strategy is that it lifts the veil of anonymity from Rufa: she is Lesbia, now Rufus' woman. Each of the final three polymetra thus presents a slightly different picture of Lesbia as a common prostitute.

Interestingly, the themes of cc. 46, 47, 58, and 59 recall those of the earlier corresponding cc. 4, 9, and 11:

4/46	9/47	11/58~59
return from Bithynia	Veranius, home from military duty	Lesbia, lowlife whore

Cc. 4 and 46 treat Catullus' journey from Bithynia; in 9 and 47 Veranius has returned to Rome after stints of military duty; and 11, 58, and 59 portray Lesbia as the lowest of prostitutes. A major difference between the two groups, however, concerns Catullus' attitude toward Veranius. By linking Veranius' (and Fabullus') appetite for political advancement in c. 47 with Lesbia/Rufa's insatiable appetite for sex in c. 59, Catullus insinuates that he is as bitterly disappointed in the posture adopted by his friends as he is in the promiscuity of his lady.[255] I suspect that this bitter disappointment is the reason that Veranius and Fabullus make no further appearances in the poetry after c. 47.

Poem 48

In the ring patterning of cc. 45–60, c. 48 lacks a counterpart. The disposition of c. 48, however, is not without purpose. It occupies this particular place for several reasons. A first reason is *variatio*. The Juventius kiss-poem provides a brief respite from the political subjects found in the preceding and following poems. A second reason is transition. Through its food imagery (*mellitos* 1, *numquam…satur* 4, *aridis aristis* 5), c. 48 picks up the theme of feasting from c. 47 and carries over the related notion of planting into the opening verse of c. 49. According to Varronian etymology, *seges* (48.6) and *disertissime* (49.1) both derive from the Latin *sero, serere, sevi, satus* (*L.L.* V.37, VI.64). A third reason concerns the ordering of the love poems. In the circular scheme that integrates these poems, c. 48 functions as counterpart to the Lesbia kiss-poems 5 and 7 (see below, page 232). A fourth and final reason that c. 48 occurs in this place, apparently, is to separate the attack on Piso in c. 47 from the expression of gratitude to Cicero in c. 49, lest any significance be attached to the juxtaposition of these bitter political enemies.

Poem 49

This last observation is important because Catullus has not made clear the occasion of c. 49. And, I would argue, he has done this deliberately in order that the poem might admit multiple interpretations.[256] By relating c. 49 to other polymetra, Catullus indicates three principal reasons why he composed the poem to Cicero.

The interplay of c. 49 with cc. 44 and 53 points to a political motive. The association of Sestius, Cicero, and Licinius Calvus, principal figures in Cicero's two court cases involving Vatinius, suggests that the poem refers to Cicero's volte-face on Vatinius in B.C. 54.[257] At the same time the interaction of cc. 49 and 58 indicates a personal motive. Since the two poems relate Cicero, Lesbia, and Caelius Rufus, the leading characters in the *Pro Caelio*, it seems likely that Catullus is responding also to Cicero's vicious assault on Clodia in the defense of his former protégé (this possibility is explored in Chapter Four). Finally, there appears to be a literary motive.[258] This is suggested not only through the juxtaposition of cc. 49, 50, and 51, which are connected by "poets" and "the making of poems," but through verbal cross-references to earlier poems that deal with literary aesthetics (cf. *pessimus poeta* at 14.23, 36.6; and *maximas tibi grates / ago* at 44.16–17). The subtle recollection of c. 14 through the phrase *pessimus poeta* is especially interesting because Catullus shows in the person of Licinius Calvus that the roles of *patronus* and *poeta*, which are sharply contrasted in c. 49, need not be incongruous. What is the point of Catullus' creating multiple interpretations for this particular poem? I think his purpose is to demonstrate to Cicero, who apparently did not have a high regard for the "New Poets,"[259] that he is anything but a *pessimus poeta*.

49.1	disertissime	53.5	disertum
49.1	Romuli nepotum	58.5	Remi nepotes
49.2–3	quot sunt quotque fuere,... / quotque... aliis erunt in annis	21.2–3	quot aut fuerunt / aut sunt aut aliis erunt in annis
49.4–5	gratias tibi maximas Catullus / agit	44.16–17	maximas tibi grates / ago
49.5–6	pessimus...poeta	14.23; 36.6	pessimi poetae

Figure 2.18 Poem 49 as a Literary Collage

C. 49 is a *tour de force* in another respect. As figure 2.18 above illustrates, Catullus constructed the poem to Cicero out of bits and pieces of other polymetra. Virtually every word and phrase in the first six verses occurs once elsewhere.[260] This literary collage is a showpiece of Catullan ingenuity, for the verbal parallels were carefully chosen, as well as arranged, with an eye to parodying Cicero's own rhetorical style.[261] What is more, by drawing the reminiscences from other poems that are humorous (with the exception of c. 58), Catullus perhaps intended to provide another indication that his expression of thanks to Cicero is insincere. It is the element of wit that links c. 49 with its two counterparts, cc. 53 and 56, as we shall see.

Poems 53~56

Cc. 53 and 56 are anecdotes. The first relates an amusing incident that took place during Calvus' prosecution of Vatinius. The second narrates a risqué tale that apparently is being told for the pure pleasure of provoking the stoic Cato the Younger, a person easily offended by off-color humor.[262] The relation of these two humorous pieces is closer than it might first appear, for cc. 53 and 56 are joined by a parallel structure, shown in figure 2.19 below.

The poems open with the theme of laughter (*risi* 53.1; *ridiculam, ride* 56.1, 3) and close with the image of an erect phallus (*salaputium* [= *mentula salax*] 53.5; *rigida* [*mentula*] 53.7). Both hold in

	C. 53	C. 56
LAUGHTER	risi (1)	ridiculam (1), ride (3)
TEMPORAL ADVERB	modo (1)	modo (5)
ASSOCIATION OF THE POET WITH CALVUS AND CATO	meus...Calvos (3)	Cato, Catullum (3)
THE GODS	di magni (5)	Dionae (6)
ERECT MALE MEMBER	salaputium (5)	rigida mea (7)

Figure 2.19 Parallel Structure of Poems 53 and 56

common the temporal adverb *modo* (53.1; 56.5); in both Catullus associates himself with the chief characters, in the one by using the possessive adjective *meus* to modify Calvus (53.3), and in the other by creating a jingling juxtaposition between Cato's name and his own (56.3). Lastly, both poems make reference to the gods, with the exclamatory phrase *di magni* at 53.5 corresponding etymologically as well as thematically to the goddess Dione at 56.6.[263]

In c. 56 Catullus describes how he caught an unidentified *pupulus* in the act of making love,[264] and "gave him an appropriate form of the punishment decreed for those caught *in flagrante delicto*."[265] W.C. Scott has proposed that *pupulus* of this poem alludes to Clodius Pulcher, who apparently had a nickname of "Little Boy" (*Pusio*).[266] Although the identity of the *pupulus* is not critical to appreciating the joke, Scott's proposal is attractive because the poem gains further point. Presumably even the dour Cato would not fail to derive some pleasure from hearing about Catullus' act of retribution, since his enemy Clodius would be the butt of the joke. In addition, this identification creates another parallel between the corresponding poems. If Clodius is the *pupulus*, both he and his protégé Vatinius of c. 53 would be victims of vicious verbal or physical assault by two friends (Calvus and Catullus) who take on a Priapic pose. The incidents differ, of course, in that the first appears to be based on something that really happened,[267] while the second is sheer fantasy.[268]

Poems 49~53~56

The relation of cc. 49 and 53 was discussed above (pages 86–87). Through their correspondence Catullus wittily suggests why Calvus was unsuccessful in his prosecution of Vatinius. He was only *disertus*, while his opponent Cicero was *disertissimus* (49.1).

Cc. 49 and 56 show a slight connection. Both poems are humorous; both are addressed to orators; and both devote their first three or four verses to a single purpose—the one to addressing Cicero (49.1–3) and the other to preparing Cato for the hilarity of the joke to come (56.1–4). In addition, if the *pupulus* of 56.5 alludes to Clodius Pulcher, presumably Cicero, as well as Cato, would have taken pleasure in the description of the action Catullus took against their common enemy (even if the obscene event is rooted in fantasy).

The next group of corresponding poems, cc. 52, 54, and 56, all are attacks on political figures. Cc. 52 and 54 are directed against henchmen of Caesar and Pompey, while c. 57 includes Caesar as well as Mamurra in its indictment.

Poems 52, 54, and 57

C. 52 is a tiny masterpiece. As figure 2.20 below illustrates, the poem is composed of four perfectly balanced pairs:[269]

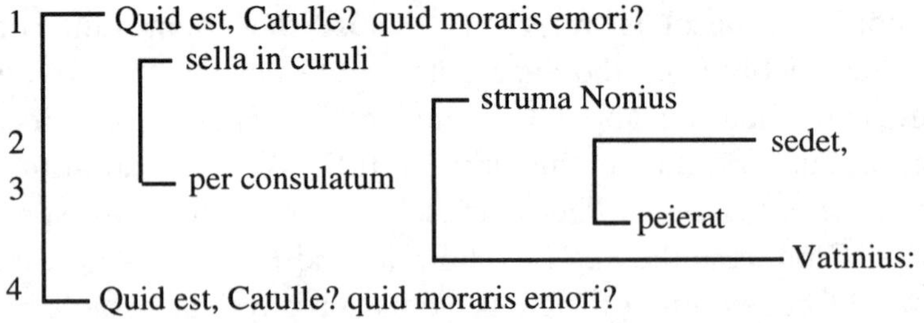

Figure 2.20 Ring Structure of Poem 52

Identifical first and last lines ring a pair of prepositional phrases, a pair of verbs, and a pair of victims of Catullan attack. The obvious purpose of this meticulous symmetry is to create a close relation between Nonius and Vatinius in verses 2 and 3. To the poet's mind, they are twins, twin boils on the body politic.[270]

C. 57 concerns another pair of personages whom Catullus perceives as indistinguishable: Caesar and his chief engineer Mamurra. The two "share the same cultural pretensions, the same lewd dissipations, the same warped tastes. In their homosexual union, each makes love to his own reflection."[271] Catullus emphasizes the oneness of Caesar and his social and military inferior, Mamurra, by devoting two-thirds of the poem to the theme:

> Pulchre CONVENIT improbis cinaedis,
> MAMURRAE PATHICOQUE CAESARIQUE.
> nec mirum: maculae PARES UTRISQUE,
> urbana altera et illa Formiana,
> impressae resident nec eluentur
> morbosi PARITER, GEMELLI UTRIQUE,
> UNO in lecticulo erudituli AMBO,
> NON HIC QUAM ILLE magis vorax adulter,
> rivales socii puellularum.
> pulcre CONVENIT improbis cinaedis.

Like the pair Vatinius and Nonius, Caesar and Mamurra are afflicted with disease (*morbosi pariter*), and, as in the earlier c. 52, identical first and last lines complement the theme of duality.

Although the text of c. 54 is quite corrupt, its function in this triad as a pivot between cc. 52 and 57 seems clear enough:

> Othonis caput oppido est pusillum,
> Hirri rustica et semilauta crura,
> subtile et leve peditum Libonis,
> si non omnia, displicere vellem
> tibi et Sufficio seni recocto...
> irascere iterum meis iambis
> immerentibus, unice imperator.

C. 54, like 52, attacks partisans of Caesar and Pompey. By emphasizing their physical defects, Catullus suggests that these men, just as the scrofulous Nonius and Vatinius, are blemishes on the political organization of the state. At verses 4ff. the poem shifts its focus to Caesar. The closing address to one peerless leader obviously looks forward to the assault of Caesar himself in c. 57. Possibly, too, Catullus may be hinting at a joint attack on both Caesar and Mamurra here through the reminiscence of *unice imperator* from c. 29, where he attacks both individuals.

Poems 50~51~55

The last poems to be considered in the ring structure of the cycle deal with love from three different perspectives. Cc. 51 and 55 have as their subjects "love revealed" and "love concealed," while c. 50 uses the language of love as a metaphor to describe intellectual stimulation. In this last poem, after an exhilarating afternoon spent with Licinius Calvus composing extemporaneously on amatory topics, Catullus cannot sleep; he finds himself experiencing the symptoms of passion for his friend and fellow poet of which they wrote earlier in the day. The theme of c. 50, "what composing literature can do to you," should seem familiar, for it is a variation on "what reading literature can do to you" found in cc. 35 and 44 of the previous cycle. Here, as there, Catullus manipulates the topic for humorous effect.

C. 50 is a *jeu d'esprit* of appreciation to Calvus for a stimulating day spent together composing verses. The humor of the poem lies in Catullus' employing the language of the *sermo amatorius*, which was used in the poetic improvisations of the previous afternoon, to describe his attachment for Calvus.[272] On his return home, inflamed by his friend's wit and cleverness (*tuo lepore / incensus,...facetiisque*), Catullus experiences symptoms of love: he can't eat, he can't sleep; he is reduced to a state of utter exhaustion as he longs for Calvus' conversation and company. The result of this longing is the creation of a poem, which will enable Calvus to see clearly the intensity of Catullus' pain (vv. 16–17):

> hoc, iucunde, tibi poema feci,
> ex quo perspiceres meum dolorem.

We saw in c. 14 that both Calvus and Catullus are pranksters. C. 50, too, I believe involves a joke, which in this obvious burlesque of love poetry[273] lies in the ambiguous language of verses 16–17 (quoted above). The expression *hoc poema* can refer to c. 50 itself ("this poem") or to c. 51 ("the following poem"). Proponents of taking c. 50 as a covering letter to c. 51 point to two features that the poem shares with c. 65, another covering letter. The first feature is similar language: *hoc..., tibi poema feci* at 50.16 parallels [*mitto*] *haec...tibi carmina* at 65.16. The second is a similar position: each occurs immediately before a "translation" from the Greek.[274] Accordingly, if c. 50 can indeed be construed as written to accompany c. 51, verses 7–15 build toward a surprise climax: "I composed this poem for you, my genial friend, so that you might see clearly the agony of my infatuation—for Lesbia."[275]

That cc. 50 and 51 function as companion pieces is further indicated by a ring-composition structure that combines 50 and 51 into what is in essence a single, magnificent poem (see figure 2.20 on the next page). Three striking parallels join the opening of 51 and the close of 50. From the previous poem c. 51 picks up the notion of gods (*est dea, esse deo*) and divine justice (*Nemesis, fas*), while it replaces the idea of seeing the pain caused by infatuation for the beloved (*ex quo perspiceres meum dolorem*) with the actual seeing of the beloved (*qui te / spectat*). The next sections (50.7–17; 51.5–12) deal with the love-symptoms of Catullus. The correspondences here are obvious and self-explanatory (*semimortua~torpet; membra~artus*; *nec somnus tegeret quiete ocellos~gemina teguntur lumina nocte; me miserum~misero mihi*) with one exception, that at 50.12 and 51.6–7. Catullus' longing to see the light of day (*videre lucem*) and his looking at Lesbia (*Lesbia, aspexi*) are related by the notion of brightness as well as seeing. The description of Lesbia, which is suggestive of an epiphany of a god to a mortal, correlates with the light or brightness of the dawn (on the correlation, cf. 68b, where Lesbia, described as a *candida diva* at verse 70, is later addressed as *mea lux* at verse 160). Finally, the beginning of c. 50 and the end of c. 51 are linked by antithesis. The ideas of pleasure and agreeability, implied by *convenerat esse delicatos* at 50.3, are negated by those of

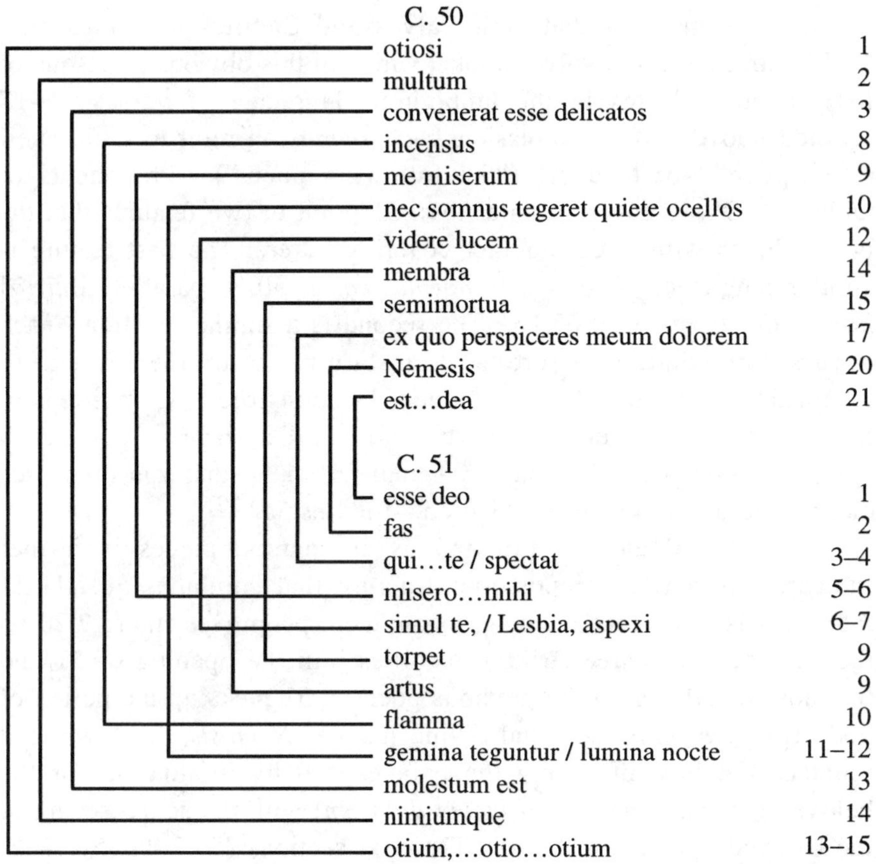

Figure 2.21 Chiastic Structure of Poems 50 and 51

pain and irritation, implied by *molestum est* at 51.13; the neutral *multum* at 50.2 is echoed by the notion of excessiveness, *nimiumque*, at 51.14; and *otiosi*, "being at leisure," at 50.1, a state essential to the writing of poetry, is answered forcefully by a triple *otium* at 51.13–15: the absence of *negotium* results in pain, danger, and destruction. The three pairs of opposing ideas that join 51.13–15 and 50.1–3 are of the highest significance regarding the problematical *otium*-strophe, for they indicate clearly and unequivocally that the final verses form an integral part of c. 51.[276]

Why does Catullus send this adaptation of Sappho's φαίνεταί μοι to Calvus instead of to Lesbia? The answer appears to lie with a unifying principle. After c. 8, Catullus never again directly addresses his lady in the polymetra. What is more, once the *otium*-strophe is recognized as belonging to c. 51, it is difficult to construe the poem, as we now have it, as the first one Catullus wrote to Lesbia.[277] Rather, it seems to be a poem of disillusion. Catullus is still in love with Lesbia; yet he knows that his infatuation is injurious and dangerous. This is what he confesses to Calvus.

Also suggestive regarding the intent of c. 51 is its thematic relation to the preceding and following Lesbia poems, 37 and 58. The description of Lesbia as sitting opposite someone at 51.3 (*sedens adversus...te*) recalls her posture as a prostitute of a brothel at 37.14 (*consedit*). Likewise, the anaphoric *ille...ille...qui* in 51.1–3 is echoed by *illa / illa...quam* in verses 1–2 of 58, a bitter poem which portrays Lesbia as a back-street whore, and which is justly famous for the coarseness of its final verse (*glubit...Remi nepotes*).[278]

The linking of cc. 51 and 58 through anaphora of *ille/illa* may be consequential, too, in providing a clue to the identity of the unnamed rival in c. 51. As we have seen, the notion of "twinning" is a recurrent motif in the final sequence of polymetra (page 90). If the parallelism of *ille...ille...qui* (= rival) and *illa / illa...quam* (= Lesbia) has this significance, it may well be that Shipton's proposal is correct, that the man sitting opposite Lesbia in c. 51 is Clodius, the brother of Clodia/Lesbia (cf. *Lesbius est pulcer* 79.1).[279] The chiastic ordering of cc. 50 and 51, which pairs Lesbia's lover, *ille mi par esse deo* in 51.1, with Nemesis, *est vehems dea* in 50.21, is tantalizingly suggestive in support of this view, for Clodius was well-known for his unrelenting pursuit of vengeance against Cicero, who made the mistake of voluntarily testifying against him in the trial concerning the Bona Dea scandal.

Poem 55 + 58b

Oramus, si forte non molestum est,
demonstres ubi sint tuae tenebrae.
te in Campo quaesivimus minore,
te in Circo, te in omnibus sacellis,
te in templo summi Iovis sacrato.

in Magni simul ambulatione
femellas omnes, amice, prendi,
quas vultu vidi tamen serenas.
'avelli sinite' ipse flagitabam
'Camerium mihi, pessimae puellae.'
quaedam inquit, nudum sinum reducens,
'en hic in roseis latet papillis.'
sed te iam ferre Herculi labos est:
tanto te in fastu negas, amice.
58b non custos si fingar ille Cretum,
non si Pegaseo ferar volatu,
non Ladas ego pinnipesve Perseus,
non Rhesi niveae citaeque bigae:
58b.5 adde huc plumipedes volatilesque,
ventorumque simul require cursum,
quos vinctos, Cameri, mihi dicares:
defessus tamen omnibus medullis
et multis languoribus peresus
58b.10 essem te mihi, amice, quaeritando.
dic nobis ubi sis futurus, ede
audacter, committe, crede luci.
nunc te lacteolae tenent puellae?
si linguam clauso tenes in ore,
fructus proicies amoris omnes.
verbosa gaudet Venus loquella.
vel si vis, licet obseres palatum,
dum vestri sim ego particeps amoris.

C. 55 looks like the sort of metrical experiment that Catullus and Calvus might have tried during their session of writing verses.[280] The normal pattern of the hendecasyllable is varied here. Nearly half of the lines are decasyllables, with a spondee in the second foot replacing a dactyl. The poem reproduced above incorporates fragment 58b, which belongs to it. The text is taken from F. Peachy's excellent study.[281] His arguments for reuniting 58b with its "mother" are worth quoting in full: "The evidence that cries aloud [that 58b has been separated] lies in Camerius' name [which does not occur elsewhere], the repetition of *amice*, the echoes to be heard in *quaeritando*, and the mixture of decasyllabic and hendecasyllabic lines, unique—at least in the *littérature latine qui nous est connue*—to this poem and this fragment."[282] Once the fragment is restored to its rightful place after verse 14, it seems clear that the fourfold anaphora of *te in* at 55.3–5 corresponds to the fourfold anaphora of *non* at 58b.1–4. Catullus' purpose in joining Roman topography to Greek mythology is to enhance the humor by linking the familiar to the world of fantasy.

Another interesting consequence of the restoration is that a direct reference to Hercules at 55.13 is answered by an indirect reference to Hercules' step-father at 55.22–24 (formerly 58.8–10). *Sum defessus quaeritando* are the exact words that Plautus' Amphitruo uses to describe his weariness at the end of a similar "wild-goose chase" (*Amph.* 1014).[283] *Herculi labos* at 55.13 and *defessus ...quaeritando* at 55.24 thus appear to act as points of departure and closure for the mythological excursus.

The symmetry of cc. 46~47 and 58~59 also indicates that 58b has been displaced. Experience with other circular structures indicates that when two pairs of poems balance each other by their parallel position in a ring pattern, as cc. 46~47 and 58~59 do, no poem ever intervenes between the successive corresponding poems because they function as a unit. What is more, cc. 58, 59, and 60 are so closely related thematically and structurally that it seems inconceivable that another poem intruded in this group.

C. 55 has the following features in common with cc. 50 and 51. The opening word *oramus* echoes *oramus* from the end of c. 50 (19), and *non molestum est*, two words later, echoes *molestum est* from the final stanza of c. 51 (13). *Tuae tenebrae* at 55.2 suggests the *vita umbratilis,* "the soft life...of the war-shunning lover/elegist,"[284] and thus coordinates with the *otium* of cc. 50 and 51, and the leisure that allows men to pursue poetry and love. Anaphora of *te in* and of *non* (3–5, 58b.1–4), which together enclose the central section of c. 55, is reminiscent of c. 51, where anaphora of *ille* and of *otium* joins the beginning and end of the poem.[285] In c. 55, as in c. 50, Catullus yearns for an absent friend, and the language used to express this yearning in the two poems is closely parallel:[286]

> at defessa labore membra postquam
> semimortua lectulo iacebant,... (50.14–15)

defessus tamen omnibus medullis
et multis languoribus peresus
essem te mihi, amice, quaeritando. (58b.8–10)

C. 55 also resembles c. 50 in its humorous intent. Catullus' fruitless chase through the streets of Rome in search of Camerius, his interviewing of prostitutes who "look satisfied,"[287] the pun by a *quaedam femella* on Camerius' name (*kamarion* appears to have been a vulgar Greek term for "brassiere"),[288] the high-flown language characteristic of the mythological excursus,[289] and the splendid double entendre on *si linguam clauso tenes in ore, / fructus proicies amoris omnes,*[290] all contribute to the comic effect. C. 55 differs from cc. 50 and 51, however, in that, unlike Catullus, Camerius apparently is unwilling to reveal the object of his love.

In summary, cc. 50, 51, and 55 are connected by the related themes of love, friendship, poetry, and *otium*. The rejection of *otium-amor* at the end of c. 51 serves a two-fold purpose. It prepares for the shift in topic to the serious world of politics in the poems that follow as well as preparing for the ultimate rejection of Lesbia in cc. 58 and 59. In light of this observation, the question must be raised: How does c. 55, which deals with the themes of *otium* and love, coordinate with this change of focus? It appears to coordinate through Catullus' picture of himself as a frustrated lover, who fails to find the object of his longing and ultimately gives up the search for his friend (58b.8–10):[291]

defessus tamen omnibus medullis
et multis languoribus peresus
essem te mihi, amice, quaeritando.

It is important to note that despite the shift to *negotium* in cc. 52ff. and despite the utter condemnation of Lesbia in cc. 58 and 59, there is a suggestion in the pathetic voice of Catullus the suppliant in c. 60 that the infatuation lingers. The picture the poet paints of himself as a man obsessed, unable to let go, is intended to pave the way for c. 68b, the next Lesbia poem, as we shall see.

Earlier it was shown how cc. 1–6 and 55–60 display a chiastic arrangement and how the combination of themes in c. 11 is recalled through the linear ordering of cc. 57 through 60 (page 92). Other parallels in theme join the first and last cycles of polymetric poems. C. 46, like c. 4, has as its subject Catullus' return trip from Bithynia. His experience in the provinces in turn calls to mind that of Veranius and Fabullus, who appear in the very next poem (c. 47) and whose lack of success in accruing wealth Catullus linked earlier with his own (c. 28). The disposition of the Veranius and Fabullus poems is noteworthy because, with the exception of c. 28, they are confined to the first and last polymetric cycles (9, 12, 13, 47). Licinius Calvus, another close friend of Catullus, makes his three appearances in the polymetra in cc. 14, 50, and 53. Although the numerous verbal and thematic parallels common to the programmatic 14 and 50 have been noted,[292] to the best of my knowledge no one has observed that cc. 50 and 53 sever and set forth separately the combined roles that Calvus plays in c. 14 as advocate and poet. A connection between cc. 14 and 53 is further suggested by a verbal reminiscence: the exclamatory *Di magni* (14.12 and 53.5) does not occur elsewhere.[293] Mention of the villainous Vatinius, enemy of Licinius Calvus, also is restricted to the first and last polymetric cycles (14.3, 52.3, and 53.2). The relation of cc. 11 and 51, the only poems in the Sapphic meter, has long been noticed,[294] although critics have just begun to recognize that c. 51, too, is about disillusioned love. In addition, c. 11 has in common with c. 45 the antithetical combination of love and foreign adventure. Kiss-poems (5, 7, 48) are found in the first and last polymetric cycles only, and cc. 1 and 49 express sincere or ironical thanks to littérateurs.

A final point. It is striking that the PU- element occurs in every poem in cc. 53 through 57 (*salaPUtium* 53.5; *PUsillum* 54.1; *PUellae* 55.10, 17; *PUpulum, PUellae* 56.5; *PUellularum* 57.9). I would like to propose tentatively that the purpose of the repetition, which creates an almost stammering effect, is to anticipate cc. 58 and 59, where Catullus makes clear the identity of Lesbia as a member of the PUlcher family through her involvement with Caelius Rufus.[295] If this proposal is correct, the question is worth raising as to whether cc. 58, 59, and 60 together do not function as a sphragis of sorts. Since Catullus uses language that often conflates love and the writing of poems, it seems possible that he intended the allusion to the identity of his beloved, often the source of his inspiration, to seal the end of the polymetra.

Chapter Three: The Central Poems

Cc. 61–68b belong together.[1] Length and similarity of subject combine to make these poems the most well-defined group in the entire corpus: all are comparatively long, and all directly or indirectly concern marriage. What is more, c. 61 clearly marks the beginning of a new movement. So striking is the contrast between this solemn and magnificent piece of 235 verses, purportedly written for the occasion of the wedding of the aristocratic Manlius Torquatus, and the previous three poems of five verses each that scurrilously attack unsavory women (58–60). Because of the prominence to be given to the theme of marriage, Catullus may have intended the elaborate invocation and encomium of the Greek god of weddings in verses 1–75 of c. 61 to serve as a general introduction to the series. This proposal, if correct, may account for the fact that "no other extant epithalamium" begins with a hymn to Hymenaeus.[2] The introductory character of c. 61 may be indicated, too, by the nod to Callimachus in verses 1–2 (cf. vv. 1–2 of c. 1): the references to Helicon and Urania allude to the *Aitia* 1 fr.2a 42–43 (Pfeiffer).[3] The *carmina maiora* divide along metrical lines into cc. 61–64 and 65–68b. The bipartition reflects the function of the central poems as a pivot between the shorter pieces on either side. Like cc. 1–60, 61–64 are written in different meters;[4] like cc. 69–116, 65–68b are all in elegiac couplets.

The thematic arrangement coincides with the metrical, as figure 3.1 below illustrates. In the first half of the *carmina maiora*, the first two poems and the last function as counterparts. Exhibiting traditional features of wedding compositions, cc. 61, 62, and 64 treat marriage from three different perspectives. The wedding celebrated

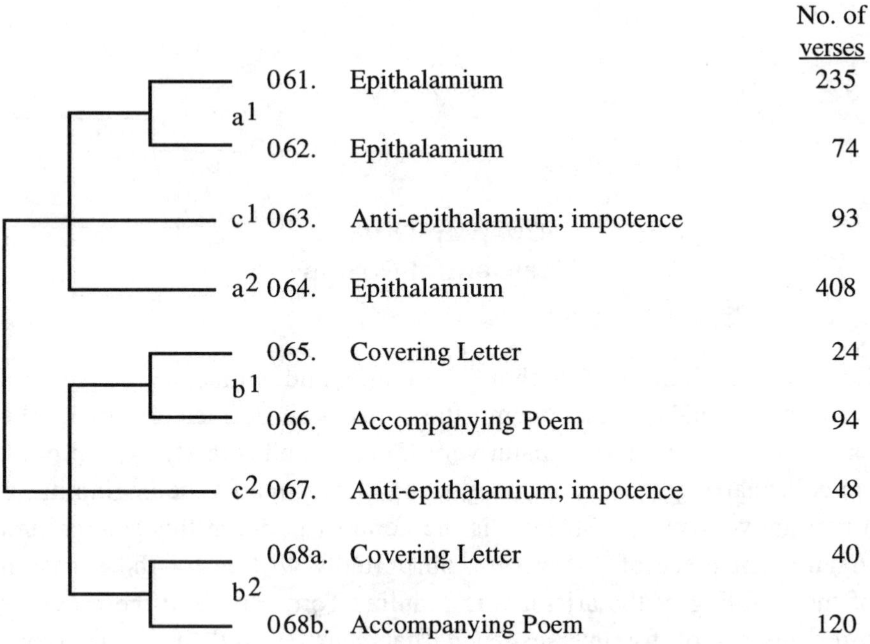

$$[a^2 - a^1] + [b^2 - b^1] = [c^1 + c^2]$$
$$[408 - 309] + [160 - 118] = [93 + 48]$$

Figure 3.1 Ring Arrangement of Poems 61–68b with Numerical Scheme

in c. 61 is real, that in c. 62 is fictitious, while the one in c. 64 is mythical. In the second half of the *carmina maiora,* first and last poems also function as counterparts. The relation of c. 65 to c. 66 and of c. 68a to c. 68b is exactly parallel. Cc. 65 and 68a serve as covering letters to cc. 66 and 68b; their purpose is to explain why Catullus is not sending the sort of poem requested by the recipients. Cc. 63 and 67, which join the two parts, hold in common the theme of impotence or sexual dysfunction. These central poems invert the epithalamic theme. In c. 63 Attis, whose complete devotion to Cybele results in self-mutilation, enters into a perverted form of marriage with the goddess. In c. 67 the wife of Balbus, Jr. undermines the ideals of marriage through her incestuous and promiscuous sexual activity.

A complex numerical scheme, combining addition and subtraction, accompanies and reaffirms the formal arrangement (shown in figure 3.1). It works as follows. If the difference between the number of verses in cc. 61~62 and 64 (a^1 and a^2) is added to the difference between the number of verses in cc. 65~66 and 68a~68b (b^1 and b^2), the total equals the sum of the verses in the central two poems (c^1 and c^2). Thus, [408 – 309] + [160 – 118] = [93 + 48]: 99 + 42 = 141.[5] Simpler numerical patterns, involving either addition or subtraction, occur in later books of poetry, such as Virgil's *Eclogues*, Tibullus, Books I and II, etc., where they perform a similar function of indicating that correspondences have been identified correctly.[6] Mathematical symmetry appears to have been a characteristic feature of the structure of the entire Catullan collection, as we shall see.[7] Both the extensive nature of the numerical schemes and their complexity have important implications regarding the issue of Catullan editorship.

The relation among the poems that define the first half of the *carmina maiora* has not passed unnoticed.[8] The difference among the three epithalamia is largely one of emphasis. As V. Tufte observes, c. 61 focuses on the "benefits [of marriage] to the couple, the family, and the state," whereas c. 62 stresses "the advantage to the maiden and her family"; and c. 64, in turn, rather ambitiously relates "marriage...to the cosmos" by weaving "the two contrasting unions of human beings...into a context involving the gods and the future of mankind."[9]

Poems 61 and 62

C. 61 celebrates the occasion of a real marriage, that of Manlius Torquatus and Vibia Aurunculeia.[10] In form, the poem is a dramatic monologue in which the poet in the role of choragus gives directions and comments on the events as they unfold before him. C. 61 begins with an invocation of Hymenaeus (vv. 1–45), followed by an encomium of the god (vv. 46–75). Although both sections contain traditional formulae of the hymn style, Catullus' conception of the god is slightly unusual. Hymenaeus is summoned to attend the wedding dressed like a Roman bride, wearing an orange-yellow veil and a wreath of fragrant marjoram with yellow slippers on his snow-white feet. Moreover, "his function is not merely that of the spirit of the wedding but that of the presiding genius of married life."[11]

Verses 76–120, in which the guests await the appearance of the bride in front of her home, are transitional to the *deductio*, the next major part of the poem. In verses 121–90 the poet describes the procession of the bride to the house of her husband through a series of addresses to persons participating in the ceremony. Verses 121–55 of this section are arguably the most Roman part of the poem, with the description of the scattering of nuts while Fescennine verses are sung. At verse 166 the bride arrives at her new home where she is immediately escorted to the marriage-chamber. C. 61 closes with an epithalamium in the true sense and with felicitations to the bridal pair (211–35). Marriage in this poem is depicted largely in positive terms.

By contrast, c. 62 is not written for a specific occasion.[12] The scene of the poem is an evening banquet held at the home of the bride's father. The organization of the marriage feast follows Greek custom of separate seating of men and women. The division of the sexes anticipates the amoebean competition to follow, in which choruses of young men and women set forth opposing views on marriage. While the young women reject marriage regarding it as surrender, loss, and violation of their virginity, the young men defend marriage as fulfillment of a woman's fruitfulness. The attitude of the men prevails, who argue that marriage benefits family and society alike. Marriage in this poem is thus depicted in both negative and positive terms.

It is true that cc. 61 and 62 "differ widely in scope and treatment," as R. Ellis observed long ago.[13] Nevertheless, numerous parallels indicate that they were conceived as companion pieces.[14] The poems combine Greek and Roman elements in a complementary manner. In c. 61, the form and technique are Greek, but the ritual is predominantly Roman; in c. 62, the ritual and theme are predominantly Greek, but there are allusions to Roman ideas and marriage customs (e.g., abduction of a reluctant maiden [21–23], the bride's absence from the wedding banquet, the marrying of vines to the tree [54], and "the insistence on law and rights—the bride's duty and the parents' authority [60–65], the 'equal' marriage [57])."[15] The poems complement each other in their dramatic time, too. C. 61

begins at the point at which c. 62 ends, with the procession to the house of the bridegroom about to commence.

The epithalamia share other features. Both refer to the Roman custom of *raptio* in language that is closely parallel:

> qui rapis teneram ad virum
> virginem, o Hymenaee Hymen,... (61.3–4)
>
> tu fero iuveni in manus
> floridam ipse puellulam
> dedis a gremio suae
> matris, o Hymenaee Hymen,... (61.56–59)
>
> [Hespere,] qui natam possis complexu avellere matris,
> complexu matris retinentem avellere natam,
> et iuveni ardenti castam donare puellam.
> (62.21–23)

In the passages cited above Hymenaeus and Hesperus perform similar roles of taking a resistant daughter from the embrace of her mother and handing her over to an ardent youth.[16] The language used in c. 62 to describe the separation of a girl from her mother (*avellere, retinentem*) is stronger, however, with repetition heightening feelings of pathos (*natam...complexu avellere matris, / complexu matris... avellere natam*), a reflection of the general opposition of the female chorus to the idea of marriage. Both poems "survey two generations" in a complementary fashion by looking forward and back.[17] In c. 61 the family relations involve the bridal pair and prospective child (211–30); in c. 62 they involve the bridal pair and parents of the bride (28–29, 59–65). Both poems liken a maiden to a flower in a garden:

> talis in vario solet
> divitis domini hortulo
> stare flos hyacinthinus. (61.91–93)
>
> Vt flos in saeptis secretus nascitur hortis,
> ignotus pecori, nullo convolsus aratro,
> quem mulcent aurae, firmat sol, educat imber; (62.39–41)

In c. 61 the simile is used to reassure the bride of her outstanding beauty,[18] while in c. 62 it serves as a metaphor for virginity. Another nature comparison shared by the two poems concerns viticulture. References to vine and tree occur twice in c. 61, and in each instance the tree does not support the vine but is entwined and embraced by it:

ac domum dominam voca
coniugis cupidam novi,
mentem amore revinciens,
ut tenax hedera huc et huc
  arborem implicat errans.

lenta sed velut adsitas
vitis implicat arbores,
implicabitur in tuum
complexum.... (31–35, 106–09)

The husband or love for the husband is compared to a tree while the bride represents the vine. The symbolism is repeated in c. 62, where "the image appears in its more usual sense of the tree supporting the vine":[19]

at si forte eadem [vitis] est ulmo coniuncta marito,
multi illam agricolae, multi coluere iuvenci. (54–55)

As S. Commager observes, "the conjoined vine and elm (*coniuncta* 54) reaffirm the boys' hopeful image of the joined (*iunxere* 29) bridal pair."[20] Both poems refer to contractual or legal aspects of marriage. While c. 61 "alludes to" *conventio in manus* (vv. 56–58), an ancient custom "obsolete in Catullus' time, when the wife did not normally pass into the legal *manus* of her husband,"[21] c. 62 describes marriage as a contractual agreement entered into by husbands-to-be and parents of brides (27–29).[22] Both poems have in common the motif of the Evening Star; its appearance is alluded to in verses 77–78 of c. 61 and expressly stated in verses 1–2, 7, and 20–37 of c. 62. Both poems identify a god with a member of the bridal pair. In c. 61 Hymenaeus is associated with the bride through costume; in c. 62 Hesperus is associated with the bridegroom through motifs of rising and of heat (*consurgite/tollit* 1–2; *ignis/ardenti* 20, 23).[23] Both use arithmetic in the closing verses—in c. 61 to exaggerate the pleasures of connubial love, in c. 62 to demonstrate that parents have a share in their daughter's virginity:[24]

ille pulveris Africi
siderumque micantium
subducat numerum prius,
qui vestri numerare volt
multa milia ludi. (61.206–10)

virginitas non tota tua est, ex parte parentum est,
tertia pars patrist, pars est data tertia matri,
tertia sola tua est:... (62.62–64)

Both include songs sung by choruses of *virgines* and *pueri/iuvenes*,[25] as well as featuring the traditional refrain of *Hymen o Hymenaee, o Hymen Hymenaee*.[26] Finally, both present "a view of the wedding as a concern almost exclusively of the bride, hardly at all of the bridegroom; it is only the bride who is discussed, and it is only she who is apostrophized."[27]

Poem 64

Poem 64 celebrates the marriage of the mortal Peleus with the goddess Thetis. Because of the watery habitat of the bride, a Nereid, "the wedding..., atypically, takes place in the bridegroom's house: Peleus' palace (64.31ff.), where the wedding banquet, atypically, is held."[28] C. 64 combines the specificity of the occasion of c. 61 with the imaginary character of c. 62, since its story belongs to the world of myth. As was the case with c. 62, too, the setting of the poem is Greek, but there are allusions to Roman features, such as *conventio in manus* in verses 29–30 and the description of the palace in verses 43–49.[29] The marriage song in c. 64, which occupies a proportionally small part of the poem (59 verses), exhibits many of the same topics found in cc. 61 and 62; the song differs from those in the earlier two poems, however, in that it is sung by aged Fates who unite felicitations to the bridal pair with prophecy.

The Fates begin with praise of the husband, a traditional feature of wedding compositions. As in c. 61 (212–15), the groom is complimented on his ancient (and noble) lineage: *o decus eximium magnis virtutibus augens, / Emathiae tutamen, Opis carissime nato* (64.323–24). Peleus, who traces his family back to Jupiter, will enhance "the inherited distinction of [his]...race."[30] In the next verses mention is made of Hesperus, a conventional figure in epithalamia (*adveniet tibi iam portans optata maritis / Hesperus, adveniet fausto cum sidere coniunx* 64.328–29). His arrival foreshadows the imminent appearance of the bride, just as it did earlier in the opening verses of c. 62 (*Vesper adest,...iam veniet virgo* 1, 4). Regarding this last detail c. 64 differs from c. 62 in that Thetis will be escorted directly to the bridal chamber, since the wedding takes place in Peleus' palace. The Fates next turn to the pleasures of love-making and the harmonious love between husband and wife (64.330–36). These topics recall similar ones in c. 61 (31–35, 104–05, 146–53, 206–10). Also, here as there, the motif of connubial love is closely linked with that of procreation. C. 64, however, subverts the innocent and joyful picture of the baby sitting on his mother's lap (61.216–20). The prophetic description of the heroic deeds of the grown son of Peleus and Thetis emphasizes the slaughter and death attendant on Achilles' accomplishments and the sorrow he will bring to the mothers whose sons are to be his victims. The prophecy of the glory of Achilles concludes with "an allusion to another 'wedding,' for Polyxena was sacrificed in order to provide a 'bride' for the dead Achilles....The reference to Polyxena's virginity is also a standard element in the description of brides."[31] The grotesque mock wedding of Achilles and Polyxena forms a transition to the final part of the song of the Fates, where they resume their prediction of the *concordia* of the newly-wed Peleus and Thetis. In this section consummation of the marriage and the groom eager for his bride (*cupido marito* 374) recall the same motifs in c. 61 (*quod cupis cupis* 204). Likewise, the reference to estrangement in verses 379–80 of c. 64 brings to mind the advice to Vibia in c. 61.101–05 and 151–55 that she should satisfy the needs of her husband lest he seek satisfaction elsewhere (the verb *secubare* in 61.105 and the noun from which it derives, *secubitus* in 64.380, occur nowhere else).[32] Cc. 61 and 64 are similar, too, in that they "show us a bridegroom...awaiting his bride" in the atrium of the house or in the bedchamber (61.171–73; 64.328–32, 372–74).[33] Finally, a refrain (here, *currite ducentes subtegmina, currite, fusi*) is common to all three wedding songs.

C. 64 is composed of an epithalamium, the marriage of Peleus and Thetis, and an anti-epithalamium as well, the desertion of Ariadne by her lover Theseus. In the antinuptial part of the poem, hymeneal motifs also occur. Verses 86–90 describe the youth and innocence of Ariadne in terms reminiscent of several passages in cc. 61 and 62:

> ...virgo
> regia, quam suavis exspirans castus odores
> lectulus in molli complexu matris alebat,
> quales Eurotae praecingunt flumina myrtus
> aurave distinctos educit verna colores,

Ariadne is a virgin, still nurtured in the soft embrace of her mother (cf. 61.56–59; 62.21–23); her maidenhood resembles fragrant myrtle and blossoming spring flowers (cf. 61.21–25; 62.39–41).[34] Several verses later (117–20) the description of Ariadne's leave-taking is reminiscent of passages that describe "the bride's departure from her own family":[35]

> commemorem, ut linquens genitoris filia vultum,
> ut consanguineae complexum, ut denique matris,
> quae misera in gnata deperdita laeta<batur>,
> omnibus his Thesei dulcem praeoptarit amorem.

The language in Ariadne's complaint makes clear, too, that she perceived of her relationship to Theseus as marriage. She twice refers to him proleptically as husband (*coniunx* 123, 182), and in verses 140–41 she speaks of his promise of marriage, which she herself longed for (*non haec miserae sperare iubebas, / sed conubia laeta, sed optatos hymenaeos*). A final nuptial reference occurs in verses 158–63:

> si tibi non cordi fuerant conubia nostra,
> saeva quod horrebas prisci praecepta parentis,
> attamen in vestras potuisti ducere sedes,
> quae tibi iucundo famularer serva labore,

candida permulcens liquidis vestigia lymphis,
purpureave tuum consternens veste cubile.

In fantasizing about what might have been, Ariadne imagines herself in the role of slave/concubine, washing Theseus' feet and tending his bed. The description of the *cubile* in verse 163 recalls that of the marriage bed of Peleus and Thetis in verses 47–49.[36]

Many critics have commented on the similar fate of Catullus' Ariadne and Attis of the previous poem.[37] Both circumstances and language create a strong connection between the two figures. M.C.J. Putnam summarizes their parallel situations as follows: "Each wakes from sleep to bitter truth. Each betakes himself to the shore, which becomes not a symbol for arrival (in the opening lines of 63 the shore is not even mentioned), but of separation from true love. Attis laments the loss of home and family through the excessive *furor* of devotion; Ariadne, while manifestly blaming Theseus, bewails almost exactly the same fate, since she herself has been the victim of mad passion to the detriment of all that remains true and steadfast."[38] Part of the point of the close relation between the situations of Ariadne, "a would-be bride,"[39] and Attis is to suggest the antinuptial character of c. 63. Cc. 61–63 are meant to build toward and culminate in c. 64, which combines an essentially happy and idealized picture of marriage, on the surface at least, with an ill-fated relationship.[40]

C. 63 provides an excellent transition between cc. 62 and 64. The rejection of sexuality by the female chorus in c. 62 is taken to the ultimate limits by the self-emasculation of Attis in c. 63. At the same time, because the act of castration, irrevocable and irreversible, dramatically represents Attis' complete devotion to the goddess Cybele, this "religious commitment" is equivalent to a "conjugal pledge" and thus anticipates the union of god and mortal in c. 64.[41]

Poem 63

In interpreting the Attis poem, students of Catullus must skirt Scylla and Charybdis. On the one hand it is wrong to approach the poem exclusively against a background of biography and to insist that Catullus is to be identified as Attis and Lesbia as Cybele; on the other hand it seems equally wrong to divorce Catullus from a poem in which the emotions, mental state, and relation of the protagonist to a woman strongly suggest his own experience with Lesbia. Several points are important to bear in mind in considering the issue of a quasi-autobiographical interpretation.[42]

First, Catullus recast the traditional story of Attis and Cybele. His Attis is not a Phrygian shepherd but a beautiful Greek youth who sails to the Trojan Ida with a group of companions. There, in a moment of religious frenzy, he demonstrates his total commitment to Cybele through self-mutilation. This irrevocable act motivated by *furor* results in Attis' becoming the goddess' slave. The combination of the predominant motifs of madness and servitude is significant because, as T.P. Wiseman observes, they represent "two of the metaphors Catullus used for his own love."[43] The adjective *vesanus* refers to Catullus in love in c. 7 and to his hopeless love affair in c. 100; in 68b his lady resembles Cybele in being a *domina* and "goddess manifest."[44] Another suggestive link involves the *domus*, its loss and restoration through transference. In c. 63 the woods of Ida and the goddess serve as substitute for the home and family Attis left behind (20). In c. 68b through a series of complex images Lesbia is ascribed a similar role as substitute; she becomes Catullus' *domus*, by implicitly replacing the one he lost forever when his brother died.[45]

Second, historical and political events connect Clodia with Cybele. A distant ancestress of Clodia's, Quinta Claudia "was found worthy to pull the goddess ashore [when she arrived] at Ostia and to convey the goddess, in the form of a black stone, to Rome. The arrival of the Magna Mater was commemorated annually by the *ludi Megalenses*, and Claudia's role in it, according to Ovid, was ritually reenacted on stage as part of the festivities."[46] The fame of Quinta Claudia was later matched by the notoriety of her progeny, Clodia Metelli, who in her own lifetime was indirectly associated with the festivities in honor of Cybele. On the opening day of the *ludi Megalenses* in B.C. 56, the irrepressible Marcus Tullius Cicero publicly pilloried Clodia Metelli as a sexually insatiable, and morally bankrupt noble woman in his defense of his friend and protégé Caelius Rufus. (Cicero in fact expressly relates Clodia to her famous ancestress at *Pro Caelio* 34.)

It is also worth observing in this connection that geographical proximity links Clodia with Cybele. Apparently Clodia's house was located near Cybele's temple on the Palatine. For G. Highet this proximity offers a partial explanation for Catullus' portraying his relation to Clodia/Lesbia in mythical terms: "Often in that house, during his ecstasies and agonies, Catullus must have heard the clash of cymbals, the wild cries and the weird rhythms of the drums echoing from the temple, and must have compared the destiny of those fanatics, devotees of a powerful goddess at once lovable and hateful, to his own life as the slave of a cruel but irresistible mistress."[47]

Third, that c. 63 indirectly refers to Catullus' unhappy love affair is suggested by his intrusion at the end of the poem. In verses 91–93 Catullus prays to the goddess to keep her madness far from his house:

> dea, magna dea, Cybebe, dea domina Dindymi,
> procul a mea tuos sit furor omnis, era, domo:
> alios age incitatos, alios age rabidos.

The word order of verse 92, however, appears to belie the meaning, for the framing of *tuos sit furor omnis, era* with *mea...domo* suggests that the madness is already within. What is more, the noun *era*, which Catullus uses to address Cybele here, he uses later in 68b.135–36 to refer to his divine beloved in a passage that is remarkable—indeed unparalleled—because there and only there Catullus expresses his willingness to accept a relationship on Lesbia's terms (as humiliating as that must have been):

> quae tamen etsi uno non est contenta Catullo,
> rara verecundae furta feremus erae,...

The moods of fanatical devotion and despairing disillusion that dominate the Attis poem characterize Catullus' experience with Lesbia.[48]

Finally, the place of prominence that c. 63 holds in the structure of the corpus should be taken into account. As was indicated in Chapter One, the collection was deliberately designed to admit fluidity among its major parts. If the poems are defined by meter and length into 1–60, 61–64, and 65–116, c. 63 forms the centerpiece of the entire work, framed by the epithalamia 61, 62, and 64. Clearly this poem is intended to stand out, for it is a *tour de force* written in an extremely difficult meter that treats the myth of Attis and Cybele in a highly original way. It seems inconceivable that this most personal poet would place at the center of his *oeuvre* a poem that has no relevance to the single theme that gives coherence to the whole, his love affair with Lesbia.[49]

Poems 63~67

If the collection is defined by length and theme into 1–60, 61–68b, and 69–116, cc. 63 and 67 function as counterparts.[50] These central pieces, which hold in common the theme of impotence or sexual dysfunction, invert the epithalamic theme characteristic of the other poems. In c. 63 language, metaphor, and imagery suggest that Attis has entered into a perverse kind of marriage with Cybele. In c. 67 the ideals of marriage are corrupted through the incestuous and promiscuous conduct of the wife of Balbus, Jr.

The relation of these antinuptial poems is closer than it might first appear. In a sense c. 67 supplements c. 63 by dealing with the subject of sexual treachery, the very subject that Catullus elected to omit from his own account of Attis. In the version of the story that provides the impetus for c. 63, Cybele drives her consort to madness and to self-emasculation because he was untrue to her. C. 67 neatly reverses the causal correlation found in the myth: here the wife is untrue to her husband presumably because he is impotent. Similar language used to describe the castrated Attis and the sexually dysfunctional Balbus, Jr. also suggests a connection between the poems. *Sterilis*, which modifies *vir* in 63.69 and *semen* in 67.26, occurs only here in the corpus.[51]

Cc. 63 and 67 share other features. The *domus* is an important motif in both. In c. 63 the *domus* is emblematic of Attis' former life, of what he sacrificed in order to devote himself to Cybele: now his home is the woods of Ida, where he, a slave of Cybele, will serve the goddess for the rest of his life. In c. 67, the personified *ianua*, metonymy for the *domus* itself, functions as the central figure.

Moreover, the house door, like Attis, is portrayed as female and its role is servile (1–6). Cc. 63 and 67 are connected, too, through the theme of the *exclusus amator*. In c. 63 an allusion occurs in verses 65–67:

> mihi ianuae frequentes, mihi limina tepida,
> mihi floridis corollis redimita domus erat,
> linquendum ubi esset orto mihi Sole cubiculum.

This is the only instance in the Roman paraclausithyron to make reference to a boy as the object of suitors' affections.[52] The paraclausithyron in c. 67 is notable as well but for a different reason: it displays none of the traditional elements associated with the literary genre. As P. Murgatroyd observes, the poem is a variation on and adaptation of the "locked-out lover's serenade" in which Catullus inverts "the standard form."[53] The poems coincide also in setting the past against the present. C. 63 contrasts Attis' former sanity and discipline with his present madness and frenzy; c. 67 contrasts the former loyalty of the door with its present disloyalty.

The poems differ, however, in the treatment of the central character, who is personified in the one poem and depersonified in the other. Attis of c. 63 is dehumanized in word as well as deed, with animal imagery repeatedly applied to him and his companions;[54] by contrast, the house door of c. 67 is humanized to such an extent that it is described as possessing the human attributes of ears and tongue. The poems diverge, too, in their attitude toward impotence. In c. 63 Attis' self-castration is viewed in tragic terms as loss of identity, whereas in c. 67 the description of the inability of Balbus, Jr. to rise to the occasion makes light of the subject (20–23). This opposition of mood is a characteristic feature of the central poems, in which Catullus consistently joins comic or happy themes with sad or tragic ones.

By way of an introduction to the remaining poems in the second half of the cycle, the observation is worth making that cc. 65–68b repeat the sequence of themes in cc. 61–64. The parallel ordering indicates a close relation between the two parts and thereby reaffirms the structural integrity of these nine central pieces. Cc. 61 and 65~66 were all written for specific individuals—c. 61 for Manlius Torquatus and cc. 65 and 66 for Q. Hortensius Hortalus. Cc. 61 and 66 further converge in that they treat marriages of actual persons, the Roman Manlius and Vibia and the Alexandrian Ptolemy III and Berenice. Cc. 62 and 67, both dialogic in form, take place within a *domus* and outside of one; the hair-raising stories of adultery in c. 67 correspond inversely to the emphasis placed on virginity in c. 62. Cc. 63 and 68a combine sexual or intellectual impotence with aversion to Venus or disinterest in love affairs. Finally, cc. 64 and 68b exhibit a similarly complex structure of enclosing a tale within a tale as they treat the topics of loss through death and through infidelity.

Poems 65~68a

C. 65 returns to the personal themes of 1–60. In fact, the first poem in elegiac couplets picks up precisely where the final polymetric ends, with the subject of personal misfortune. But while c. 60 was vague about the nature of the *novissimus casus*, c. 65 is specific: Catullus has lost his brother to an untimely death.[55] The poet reveals his deep sorrow to Q. Hortensius Hortalus in a verse epistle in which he apologizes for not composing an original composition for him as he had promised to do earlier. Stricken with grief, he finds himself incapable of complying with his friend's request (1–8). Nevertheless, so as not to disappoint Hortalus entirely, Catullus sends him a translation of Callimachus' *Coma Berenices*, c. 66, so that he would know that the poet had not forgotten his promise (15–18). For Catullus forgetfulness was a serious offense, equivalent to betrayal, to violation of a *fides*.[56]

C. 68a also is a verse epistle written in response to a request for poetry. Manlius in Rome (presumably Manlius Torquatus, the bridegroom of c. 61), greatly distressed because he has been abandoned by his beloved, writes to Catullus in Verona seeking help (1–4). In his letter he claims to be unable to fall asleep in an empty bed or to derive pleasure from reading classical Greek poets (5–8). Accordingly, he asks two favors of Catullus: that he compose a Latin poem for him, apparently a translation or rendition of a Hellenistic poem,[57] and that he provide assistance with his loveless condition (9–10). Catullus' response indicates that his own situation closely parallels that of Manlius (11–24). He, too, is deeply distressed and apparently sleeping alone, since he asserts that he no longer has any interest in love (or in writing love poetry) as a result of intense grief over the death of his brother.[58] Catullus tells his friend that he should not seek happy gifts from one who is miserable (14) and later concludes his response by protesting that he is unable to fulfill either of Manlius' requests (31–40). Yet because of the duty imposed by friendship (cf. cc. 30 and 38), Catullus felt obliged to send Manlius something—that something presumably is c. 68b.[59] Since c. 68a does not announce c. 68b, as c. 65 announced c. 66, and since cc. 68a and 68b concern different friends (Manlius in the one and Allius in the other), Catullus indicated a responsive relation between the consecutive poems in a striking and rather ingenious fashion: He placed virtually identical passages that lament the loss of his brother in identical places of prominence, the structural center of each poem (22–24, 92–96).[60]

In cc. 65 and 68a Catullus excuses himself from fulfilling a prior or present request for poetry because of preoccupation with his brother's death. Strong moral obligations nevertheless compel Catullus to send Hortalus and Manlius some poetic composition. Interestingly, both individuals receive exactly what the other desired (Catullus is playing with the theme of the *recusatio*, which he adapted here to his personal situation).[61] Hortalus apparently wanted an original poem; he instead receives a translation from the Greek. Manlius apparently wanted a translation or adaptation of a Hellenistic poem of the sort sent to Hortalus; he instead receives a highly original poem. Perhaps because so much attention has been paid to the connection between cc. 65 and 66 and that between cc. 68a and 68b, the close relation of the verse epistles has passed unnoticed. As figure 3.2 below illustrates, cc. 65 and 68a display a parallel structure.

Cc. 65 and 68a begin similarly by describing individuals overwhelmed by calamitous circumstances. In c. 65 Catullus is worn out from constant grief; in c. 68a Manlius is crushed by misfortune and bitter chance:

> Etsi me assiduo confectum cura dolore (65.1)
>
> Quod mihi fortuna casuque oppressus acerbo (68a.1)

	C. 65	C. 68a
GRIEVING CATULLUS AND MANLIUS	assiduo confectum ...dolore (1)	fortuna casuque oppressus acerbo (1)
WITHDRAWAL VS. RESTORATION	sevocat (2)	restituam (4)
INABILITY TO CREATE OR ENJOY POETRY	nec potis est dulcis Musarum expromere fetus (3)	nec veterum dulci scriptorum carmine Musae / oblectant (7–8)
NAUTICAL METAPHORS	tantis fluctuat ipsa [mens] malis (4)	naufragum ut eiectum spumantibus...undis (3)
WATER IMAGERY	Lethaeo gurgite fratris...alluit unda pedem (5–6)	quis merser... fluctibus ipse (13)
DEATH OF THE BROTHER	namque mei...fratris fata gemens Ityli (5–14)	sed totum hoc studium ...omnes delicias animi (19–26)
GRIEF–STRICKEN CATULLUS FULFILLS OR DENIES REQUESTS FOR POEMS	in tantis maeroribus, ...mitto / haec... tibi carmina (15–16)	quae mihi luctus ademit, / haec tibi non tribuo munera (31–32)
COMBINATION OF GIFTS, POETRY, AND LOVE	missum sponsi furtivo munere malum [= carmen] (19)	munera [et Musarum et Veneris] (32)

Figure 3.2 Parallel Structure of Poems 65 and 68a

As the reader will learn or surmise, Catullus' sorrow stems from the loss of his brother to death; Manlius' sorrow results from a temporary *discidium* from his wife. The first verses of cc. 65 and 68a have in common, too, that Catullus places himself prominently near the beginning of the verse. His purpose, apparently, is to indicate that he is the principal figure in both poems.

The next parallel involves withdrawal and its opposite, restoration. In c. 65 sorrow calls Catullus away from the learned Muses; in c. 68a Manlius asks to be restored from death's threshold:

> [cura] sevocat a doctis, Ortale, virginibus, (65.2)
>
> [te]...a mortis limine restituam, (68a.4)

The inhibitive effect of emotional stress, similarly described in terms of nautical imagery, on the creation and enjoyment of poetry creates another link between Catullus and Manlius. In c. 65 Catullus' inability to bring forth the sweet offspring of the Muses—his mind is tossed on so great a sea of troubles—is paralleled in c. 68a by the inability of the Muses to delight the "shipwrecked" Manlius with the sweet song of the ancient poets when his troubled mind keeps him awake:

> nec potis est dulcis Musarum expromere fetus
> mens animi, tantis fluctuat ipsa malis (65.3–4)
>
> naufragum ut eiectum spumantibus aequoris undis
> . . . .
> nec veterum dulci scriptorum carmine Musae
> oblectant, cum mens anxia pervigilat: (68a.3, 7–8)

What is the point of Catullus' identifying himself with Manlius through their similar circumstances? I think it is to anticipate the fact that despite what he says in 68b about his inability to fulfill Manlius' request for *munera Musarum et Veneris*, Catullus is going to relent and not disappoint a friend in his time of need. (Catullus, of course, can relate to Manlius' situation since c. 38 shows him in a similar predicament.)

Parallels in the next verses shift to Catullus and his brother. Here water imagery joins the siblings in a sort of cause and effect relation. Because in c. 65 the slowly rising wave of Lethe's stream recently has lapped the pale dear foot of his brother, in c. 68a Catullus is engulfed by waves of misfortune:[62]

namque mei nuper Lethaeo gurgite fratris
  pallidulum manans alluit unda pedem, (65.5–6)

accipe, quis merser fortunae fluctibus ipse, (68a.13)

The passages on the death of the brother offer the most striking parallel common to cc. 65 and 68a. Nearly equal in length, they form the structural center of the two pieces:

namque mei nuper Lethaeo gurgite fratris
  pallidulum manans alluit unda pedem,
Troia Rhoeteo quem subter litore tellus
  ereptum nostris obterit ex oculis.
. . . .
  numquam ego te, vita frater amabilior,
aspiciam posthac? at certe semper amabo,
  semper maesta tua carmina morte canam,
qualia sub densis ramorum concinit umbris
  Daulias, absumpti fata gemens Ityli. (65.5–14)

sed totum hoc studium luctu fraterna mihi mors
  abstulit. o misero frater adempte mihi,
tu mea tu moriens fregisti commoda, frater,
  tecum una tota est nostra sepulta domus,
omnia tecum una perierunt gaudia nostra,
  quae tuus in vita dulcis alebat amor.
cuius ego interitu tota de mente fugavi
  haec studia atque omnes delicias animi. (68a.19–26)

Both pivotal sections contain an apostrophe to the dead brother, both describe him as "snatched away" (65.8; 68a.20), and both connect him with the ideas of love and life. Additionally, cc. 65 and 68a present complementary views of fraternal love. While 65.11–12 describe Catullus loving his brother *(te, vita frater amabilior,... amabo)*, 68a.24 describes a brother's love nurturing Catullus (*tuus in vita dulcis alebat amor*). Although these central verses are in many ways similar, they show an important difference regarding poetic activity. While in c. 65 Catullus states that he will always sing songs saddened by his brother's death, in 68a his brother's death has rendered him intellectually impotent. The inconsistency can perhaps be attributed to the function of c. 65 as an introduction to all the poems in the elegiac meter. As J.K. King observes, the phrase *maesta carmina* brings to mind "the association...of elegy with sadness."[63]

The next sections employ similar language to express antithetical ideas:

sed tamen in tantis MAERORIBUS, Ortale, mitto
  HAEC expressa TIBI CARMINA Battiadae, (65.15–16)

ignosces igitur si, quae mihi LUCTUS ademit,
  HAEC TIBI non tribuo MUNERA, cum nequeo. (68a.31–32)

In c. 65 a grief-stricken Catullus fulfills Hortalus' request for a poem (even though it is not the original composition that he desired), while in c. 68a a grief-stricken Catullus asserts he is incapable of fulfilling Manlius' request either for a poem or for help with his loveless predicament. Finally, the apple, a lover's gift in 65.19–24, to which Catullus compares Hortalus' request for a poem, forms a link with the gifts of love and poetry that Catullus cannot give in 68a.32 and also with the horticultural metaphor in *carpitur* in 68a.35.

In cc. 65 and 68b, therefore, "Catullus explores the relation between his brother's death, his own poetic productivity, and the office of a friend."[64] The close connection between the epistles may contribute to a definitive resolution regarding the autonomy of c. 68a. Since similar theme, function, and structure suggest that cc. 65 and 68a were conceived as companion pieces, clearly verses 1–40 of c. 68 should be regarded as a distinct entity from verses 41–160.[65]

Cc. 65 and 68a also, of course, are closely related to the poems that immediately follow them, cc. 66 and 68b.

Poems 68a~68b

C. 68b is a poem written for Manlius, but which celebrates the benefaction of Allius. The resemblance of the two gentile names not surprisingly has caused much confusion. Its purpose was not to indicate that Manlius of c. 68a (whose name appears in the manuscripts as *Mali*) and Allius of c. 68b refer to the same individual, but rather, as P. Levine observes, "to suggest, somewhat whimsically, a poetic relationship between them."[66] For this reason, too, both men are described as bound to Catullus by ties of friendship involving *hospitium*, although their roles are inverted. While Allius gave help to Catullus stormed-tossed on the seas of love, Manlius in a similar erotic predicament seeks help from Catullus.

Cc. 68a and 68b are linked by other parallels. The Muses, addressed at the beginning of 68b (vv. 41–46), recall the Muses who appear near the beginning of 68a (7–10). Although in both instances the goddesses are connected with Catullus' friends, they serve in different capacities and with opposite effect. In 68a they have the power to provide diversion (which, however, they are unsuccessful in doing):

> nec veterum dulci scriptorum carmine Musae
> oblectant, cum mens anxia pervigilat. (7–8)

In 68b they have the power to immortalize (which they will succeed in doing):

> sed dicam vobis, vos porro dicite multis
> milibus et facite haec carta loquatur anus.
> . . . .
> notescatque magis mortuus atque magis, (45–48)

Both poems join references to past or fleeting time with the notion of *studium*. In 68a Catullus admits that as a young man he often wrote love poetry, an activity he no longer pursues because of his brother's death:

> tempore quo primum vestis mihi tradita pura est,
> iucundum cum aetas florida ver ageret,
> multa satis lusi:...
> . . . .
> sed totum hoc studium luctu fraterna mihi mors
> abstulit.... (15–17, 19–20)

By contrast, in 68b Catullus will immortalize in song the task Allius performed (which advanced his love affair) lest the passage of time shroud his kind act in black night:

> ne fugiens saeclis obliviscentibus aetas
> illius hoc caeca nocte tegat studium. (43–44)

Both poems describe the bittersweet character of Catullus' love in similar terms:

...non est dea nescia nostri,
quae dulcem curis miscet amaritiem. (68a.17–18)

...mihi quam dederit duplex Amathusia curam,
scitis,... (68b.51–52)

In the passages quoted above, *nostri* is echoed by *mihi, curis* by *cura, non...nescia* by *scitis*, and *dea [= Venus]...quae dulcem miscet amaritiem* by *duplex Amathusia [= Venus].* Both poems employ shipwreck metaphors in reference to amatory predicaments (68a.3–4; 68b.63–65), and both make mention of the tears of love's victims—Manlius weeps because of his abandonment, Catullus because of unrequited love (68a.2; 68b.55–56). Both poems have the *domus* as a principal theme (22, 34, 68, 74, 94, 144). In 68a the *domus* is presented as a negative force, thwarting poetic activity. Because his spiritual home was buried with his brother, Catullus now has no interest in the pleasures of love or in composing love poetry; what is more, because his physical home in Rome contains his library of books, Catullus claims not to have a large collection of writings at hand in Verona (that he might translate or use as models). By contrast, in 68b the *domus* is presented in both negative and positive terms. The borrowed *domus* of Allius inspires poetry, as Catullus commemorates the service his friend performed for him by providing a place where he could meet and make love to Lesbia. But Catullus' own home, which is linked with that of the mythological figures Protesilaus and Laodamia, is *inceptam frustra* because his brother died at Troy and because his love affair with Lesbia is adulterous.[67] The *domus*, which thwarts or inspires poetry, relates closely to the motif of the *munus* granted or withheld. The gift of love, which Lesbia gave Catullus in the borrowed house (*furtiva...munuscula* 145), and the gift of poetry, with which Allius is repaid for lending the house (*hoc...confectum carmine munus* 68b.149), recall the gifts of love and poetry that Catullus denies Manlius (68a.31–32, 37–40) because his house figuratively has been destroyed.[68]

The laments for the dead brother form the most striking feature common to cc. 68a and 68b. The two passages of nearly equal length (68a.19–26; 68b.91–100) not only serve the same function as the central panel of their poems, but verses 94–96 of 68b repeat verbatim verses 22–24 of 68a. The point of the extensive repetition, otherwise unparalleled in Latin poetry, is to signal a responsive relation between 68b and 68a. This elaborate verbal signaling was a brilliant maneuver, which probably would have achieved its intended result of clarity instead of confusion, if it had not been for the resemblance between the names of Manlius and Allius. Although the brother passages are virtually identical in language and sentiment, they serve different purposes. The lament in 68a provides an excuse for Catullus' refusal to satisfy Manlius' requests; the lament in 68b is preparatory to establishing an equivalence between Lesbia and the brother. She is to become Catullus' spiritual *domus*, the light of his life, his reason for living.[69] In the course of the poem Catullus "subconsciously" transfers "his love for his dead brother to a 'rehabilitated' Lesbia."[70] At verses 135–48 he resolves to accept the few indiscretions of his lady, admitting that his relation with her is adulterous: he is not her husband. In other words, Catullus accepts a relationship "on her terms."[71] Why? For one reason, I think he desperately needs Lesbia's love as a result of the loss of his brother. For another, I think this new-found tolerance is intended to foreshadow a change in attitude toward Lesbia that will characterize the love poems in the elegiac epigrams.[72] In this part of the corpus, unlike the polymetra, we do not find violent outpourings of rage. The poetry is less abusive; it is "cooler and more analytical."[73]

Before we can conclude discussion of 68b, it is important to recognize that verses 149–54 (and not 149–60) round off the ring-composition structure begun by verses 41–50. Closure is indicated by verbal echoes (*possum/potui, officiis, nomine/nomen, deae/divi, nocte/dies, magis/plurima,* and *anus/antiquis* printed in capital letters below) and by the repeated theme of immortalizing Allius' name:[74]

> Non POSSUM reticere, DEAE, qua me ALLIUS in re
>   iuverit aut quantis iuverit OFFICIIS,
> ne fugiens saeclis obliviscentibus aetas

illius hoc caeca NOCTE tegat studium:
sed dicam vobis, vos porro dicite multis
milibus et facite haec carta loquatur ANUS.
. . . .
notescatque MAGIS mortuus atque MAGIS,
nec tenuem texens sublimis aranea telam
in deserto ALLI NOMINE opus faciat. (41–50)

hoc tibi, quod POTUI, confectum carmine munus
pro multis, ALLI, redditur OFFICIIS,
ne vestrum scabra tangat rubigine NOMEN
haec atque illa DIES atque alia atque alia.
huc addent DIVI quam PLURIMA, quae Themis olim
ANTIQUIS solita est munera ferre piis. (149–54)

The final six verses, then, appear to function as a coda that unites the chief principals of cc. 68a and 68b. The closing benediction represents one of the most remarkable features of this remarkable composition:[75]

sitis felices et tu simul et tua vita,
et domus <ipsa> in qua lusimus et domina,
et qui principio nobis terram dedit auctor,
a quo sunt primo omnia nata bona,
et longe ante omnes mihi quae me carior ipso est,
lux mea, qua viva vivere dulce mihi est. (155–60)

May all of you be happy: you [Manlius] and your wife, together,
and the house itself, in which we made love, and its mistress,
and [Allius] the one who first supported us (buffeted on the seas of passion) by giving us land,
from whom all our blessings originate,
and, by far beyond all, the one dearer to me than my very self,
my light, whose life makes living sweet for me.

We saw how in 68a Catullus repeatedly equated Manlius' situation with his own. This apparently holds true, too, for the final verses, where in essence Lesbia is Catullus' *vita* just as Manlius' lady is his *vita*. (Verse 155, of course, looks forward to their reconciliation.) The center of the six-line coda is held by Allius, who helped Catullus and who indirectly now helps Manlius. The poem in Allius' honor, which presumably was sent to Manlius, is indeed *munera et Musarum et Veneris*. It is a gift of the Muses, and of Venus also, in that its subject is love. Catullus' on-again off-again relation with Lesbia made him an expert of sorts on lovers' quarrels. Thus perhaps through 68b the poet is subtly suggesting that Manlius adopt an attitude of tolerance similar to his own in order to patch things up. The course of love never runs smoothly in the poetry of Catullus, either in his own case or in that of others. Thus it is not surprising that the happy picture of Manlius and his bride in c. 61 is subverted in 68a through their *discidium*, which Catullus optimistically indicates at the end of 68b will be only temporary.

Poems 65~66

Cc. 65 and 66 form an obvious pair. In c. 65 Catullus indicates that he is sending Hortalus a translation of a Callimachean poem, which immediately follows as c. 66. In addition, epistle and accompanying poem are joined by "the themes of love, separation, and the keeping of promises,"[76] through which themes Catullus identifies Berenice's circumstances with his own. Both Catullus and Berenice love a "brother" from whom they are separated by distance (Troy/Syria) and, in the case of Catullus, by death; as a result of this separation, both experience feelings of anguish and sorrow. Both Catullus and Berenice fulfill promises that they made earlier. Catullus sends Hortalus a translation of a poem from Callimachus in order to comply with his friend's request for poetry. Berenice dedicates a lock of her hair to the gods in order to pay a vow for her husband's safe return. The poem and the offering of the lock similarly are viewed as a *munus* (65.19; 66.38). Finally, the closing simile of c. 65, with its allusion to the love story of Acontius and Cydippe told in Book 3 of Callimachus' *Aitia*, foreshadows the story of Berenice's love for Ptolemy in c. 66, taken from Book 4 of the same Callimachean poem.

C. 65 also coordinates with c. 66 stylistically. There is the "abnormal" repetition of words that are not nouns,[77] "the use of uncommon geographical and mythological names (*Rhoeteo* 7,

Daulias, Ityli 14), mannered separation of nouns and adjectives throughout,...[and] use of a fifth-foot spondee (23)."[78]

Poems 66~68b

Cc. 66 and 68b, the poems that accompany cc. 65 and 68a, share common features, too. Both have as a principal theme "the anguish of separation from a loved one."[79] In c. 66 "it is repeatedly stressed in the case of Berenice when the king goes off to Syria, and again in the feelings of the Hair when severed from the royal head."[80] In c. 68b it occurs in the description of Laodamia's longing for her absent spouse (79–86), and again in Catullus' apostrophe to the dead brother, which is placed prominently at the poem's center (91–100). Both poems describe the passionate devotion of Berenice and Laodamia to their husbands (66.19–38; 68b.105–30), and in both poems Ptolemy and Protesilaus depart for war in Asia directly after marriage. Laodamia lost Protesilaus to death at Troy through a ritual error of failing to placate the gods with blood sacrifice (68b.75–86). By contrast, Berenice secured the safe return of her husband from war by vowing a lock of hair and blood sacrifice to the gods (66.33–38). Both poems combine the theme of love in marriage with that of adulterous love. In c. 66 the hair desires a libation from faithful brides, but not from those given to adultery (79–88). In c. 68b Catullus describes Lesbia's coming to him as though she were a bride but later concedes that his relation with her is adulterous (131–46). In both poems Catullus and Berenice experience separation from a "brother" and grief as a result (66.21–22; 68b.91–100). For Catullus the separation is permanent; for Berenice it is only temporary. Also in both, love causes sorrow (*cura* 66.23; 68b.51) and the crying of copious tears (66.29–30; 68b.55–56). Berenice is unhappy because of *discidium* from her beloved, Catullus because of unrequited passion for Lesbia. Both refer to excavation in the proximity of mountains. C. 66 alludes to Xerxes' cutting a canal through the isthmus behind Mt. Athos in his second invasion of Greece (43–46); c. 68b alludes to Hercules' building underground channels at Pheneus to drain off flood water from a low-lying plain by Mt. Cyllene (109–12). Both contain parenthetical asides to the goddess Nemesis; in these asides she is similarly addressed as the Rhamnusian virgin (66.71–74; 68b.77–78). Both link catasterism and deification. In c. 66 the humanized lock achieves immortality by becoming a constellation; in c. 68b Lesbia, a *candida diva*, is described affectionately as Catullus' "star," for the noun *lux* (vv. 132, 160) often signifies "the light of the sun and other heavenly bodies."[81] Finally, the poems employ "the same structural pattern to convey benediction in 68b.155–60 and cursing in 66.48–50":[82]

Iuppiter, ut Chalybon omne genus pereat, (66.48)

sitis felices et tu simul et tua vita,
  et domus <ipsa> in qua lusimus et domina, (68b.155–56)

et qui principio sub terra quaerere venas
  institit... (66.49–50)

et qui principio nobis terram dedit auctor, (68b.157)

The lock's distress at being severed from the head of her mistress in c. 66 (48–50) finds its antithesis in Catullus' happiness and gratitude to Allius for his help in advancing his love affair with Lesbia in c. 68b (157–58).

Cc. 66 and 68b are thus parallel in function and in theme. Written in response to requests for poems, both integrate the themes of love, marriage, separation, death, and immortality. As C.W. Macleod observes, the significance of their relation is that "the tragic element in 68 is pointed up by the contrast to the mock pathos and the courtly compliments of 66."[83]

The preceding discussion thus illustrates that the connection among poems 65, 66, 68a, and 68b is closer and more involved than has been recognized. In addition to the responsive relation between the consecutive poems, it seems clear that cc. 65 and 68a were intended to function as companion pieces, as their parallel structure indicates, and that Catullus wrote or selected cc. 66 and 68b as their concomitant poems because of the many similarities that they too hold in common. This elaborate interrelationship gives additional texture, depth, and significance to these complex pieces.

C. 67, the pivot of the ring structure, is linked thematically with the other long poems in elegiac couplets.

Poem 67

C. 67 has closest affinities with c. 66.[84] The poems are similar in form (both are *aitia* set in the context of marital relations), and they are similar in subject. Both feature inanimate objects "directly engaged in speaking."[85] There is further coincidence in that the artifacts relate tales about women, who, however, happen to be of opposite character. The one is a paragon of marital love and devotion while the other violates the sanctity of marriage through her indiscriminate sexual activities. Both severed tress and door are depicted as "the guardians of true marriage" (66.79–88; 67.1)[86] and, to a certain extent, they are made to reflect the qualities of their mistresses. Like Berenice, the lock is loyal and, faced with separation from someone she loves, experiences great distress; like the wife of Balbus, Jr., the house door is disloyal, for in defending itself from charges of negligence, the *ianua* betrays its mistress by engaging in slanderous gossip. Cc. 66 and 67 are thus studies in contrast that contrapose a wife noble and faithful to one common and promiscuous. As P. Levine observes, in c. 67 Catullus adopted form, theme, and mechanism of talking artifact from Callimachus' *Lock of Berenice*, but he thoroughly "invert[ed] in his portrayal of the dark side of love and marriage almost every aspect of these subjects as treated in c. 66."[87]

One of the most shocking revelations made by the house door in c. 67 is that the father, substituting for his impotent son, slept with his future daughter-in-law. The combined themes of impotence and substitution occur also in c. 65. There intellectual dysfunction, the consequence of the death of the brother, is described in terms of inability to procreate (*nec potis est dulcis Musarum expromere fetus / mens animi* 65.3–4); this inability results in Catullus' substituting a translation from the Greek for an original poem. Intellectual impotence, again the consequence of the loss of the brother, recurs in c. 68a, where it is joined to the notion of total disinterest in love, a variation, it appears, on the subject of sexual dysfunction found in

c. 67. C. 68a also departs slightly from the previous poems in that the theme of substitution is implied, rather than expressly stated, through its relation with c. 68b. Catullus sends an original poem in place of the translation(s) that Manlius requested. It is worth observing that c. 68a shares two additional features with c. 67. Each is set in Northern Italy, in or near Verona, and each concerns a *domus* ruined by either infidelity or death.

Cc. 67 and 68b give prominence to inanimate objects that are virtually synonymous,[88] for the Roman house door was a "metonymic representative of the entire *domus*."[89] Traditionally, the *ianua* functioned as guardian of the house and of its moral integrity. In light of this role, it is ironic that both poems associate the *ianua* and *domus* with adulterous "brides." The *domina* of c. 67 was no virgin when she married nor was Lesbia when she (like a bride) came to Catullus. Set against a backdrop of the paraclausithyron, c. 67 as a whole inverts a standard situation of this genre as does c. 68b in part (vv. 51–72). In both instances lovers succeed, instead of fail, to gain admittance to the house.[90] Finally, both cc. 67 and 68b are Roman variations of the Greek *aition*, with the comic circumstances of c. 67 set in contrast to the tragic circumstances of c. 68b.[91]

C. 67 forms a perfect centerpiece for the second half of the *carmina maiora*. Not only does it incorporate many of the themes of its neighboring poems, but it provides comic relief from the sad and serious topics of loss and separation found in 65, 66, 68a, and 68b.

Relation of Poem 61 to Poems 62–68b

At the beginning of this chapter it was suggested that c. 61 acts as a general introduction to the long poems. By way of a conclusion, the following discussion will elaborate on this idea by showing how c. 61 functions more specifically as an overture by interweaving various themes that are to occur in cc. 62–68b.

Poems 61 and 62

C. 61 has a particularly close connection with c. 62, which functions as its thematic complement. In form, c. 61 is a dramatic monologue in which the poet acts as a master of ceremonies who participates in and comments on the festivities. By contrast, c. 62 is a dialogue, a singing contest between a chorus of young men and one of young women, who hold antithetical views on the subject of marriage. The wedding celebrated in c. 61 is real and historical; that in c. 62 is literary and fictitious. In c. 61 the description of the wedding ceremony is predominantly Roman, while in c. 62 it is predominantly Greek. In c. 61 the bride is the central figure, with the hemichoruses of young men and women playing a smaller role; in c. 62 the hemichoruses are the central figures, while the bride plays a relatively minor role, mostly that of off-stage character (she enters near the end of the poem, shortly before verse 59). Finally, the poems correspond inversely in the attitudes they present toward marriage. In c. 61 marriage is viewed largely in positive terms as benefiting the couple, the families, and the state,[92] whereas in c. 62 the female chorus see marriage in negative terms of loss, surrender, and violation. Although the male chorus win the singing competition, the arguments that are remembered are those of the women,[93] who reject marriage with such vigor that they in essence reject their own sexuality.

Poems 61 and 63

Like cc. 61 and 62, c. 63 is concerned with the subject of rite of passage. But, unlike the bride of c. 62, who overcomes her resistance to marriage, Attis apparently found himself incapable of making a similar transition. In verses 64–67 of a poignant soliloquy of regret, Attis gives a glimpse of his earlier life in Greece where he was a well-known *eromenos*:

> ego gymnasi fui flos, ego eram decus olei:
> mihi ianuae frequentes, mihi limina tepida,
> mihi floridis corollis redimita domus erat,
> linquendum ubi esset orto mihi Sole cubiculum.

It is reasonable to infer that an inability to make the change "society demanded from the role of *puer delicatus* to that of husband"[94] motivated Attis' flight to Phrygia and his self-emasculation. The transition from premarital homosexual love to marital heterosexual love was treated earlier in the *fescennina iocatio* of c. 61.[95] There (vv. 126–50) the male chorus teased Manlius that as a married man he must relinquish love for his male concubine, who, in any event, is now too mature to play the part of *puer delicatus*.

Cc. 61 and 63 are connected additionally through similar descriptions and attributes of Hymenaeus and Attis. Both figures are depicted as sexually ambiguous. In the case of Hymenaeus, this ambiguity is suggested by his identification with both bridegroom and bride. The god is described as a ravisher of brides (3–4, 56–59), and he is also invoked to come to the ceremony dressed as a bride (6–10). In the case of Attis, the ambiguity is suggested morphologically in the poem by the shift between masculine and feminine genders.[96] Both Attis and Hymenaeus have their home in Greece but make their way elsewhere. Hymenaeus is to come to Rome (61.26–35); Attis goes to Phrygia (63.1–2). Both have skin described as *niveus*. Hymenaeus has snow white feet, Attis snow white hands (*niveo pede* 61.9–10; *niveis manibus* 63.8). Both celebrate rites of passage similarly. Hymenaeus is invited to participate in the marriage hymn by singing and shaking a pine torch (61.11–15); Attis celebrates his initiation by singing to his companions and shaking the tambourine (63.10–11). Both are connected with flowers, symbols of virginity, and both are identified with brides. Hymenaeus is to wreathe his temples with flowers (61.6–7), as he comes to the wedding of Manlius and Vibia dressed as a bride. Attis describes his former self as a flower and his home in Greece as wreathed with garlands of flowers (63.64, 66)—Attis, who, like a bride, left a father's *domus* for the *domus* of a "beloved." G.N. Sandy, in fact, observes a parallelism between the expression *ad domum Cybebes* (20) and "the epithalamial formula *deductio in domum*," and adds that "the irony of the situation is that Attis is not the *maritus*, who anxiously awaits his bride, but the *sponsa*, complete with the physical features of the Roman brides pictured in the epithalamia, who is led to the *erus*."[97] Actually, Attis' situation holds even greater irony in that, as pseudo-betrothed of Cybele, he has entered into the very type of relationship that he left Greece to avoid. The parallels linking Hymenaeus and Attis are significant because they reaffirm the interpretation of c. 63 as anti-epithalamic.

Poems 61 and 67

The section dealing with the *fescennina iocatio* appears to relate c. 61 also to c. 67. In the view of several critics,[98] the poem to the house door owes its dramatic occasion to this traditional part of the Roman marriage ceremony, whose purpose, like that of c. 67, is to ridicule and lampoon. The key to the setting of the poem is indicated in the very first couplet:

> O dulci iucunda viro, iucunda parenti,
> salve, teque bona Iuppiter auctet ope,
> ianua,...

Picking up on the language which identifies the door with a new bride,[99] the reader is to presume that, like c. 61, c. 67 is set on the day of a wedding and that the dramatic time, here as there, is the *deductio* or procession to the husband's house. The coarse tale of promiscuity told by the door functions, in the words of L. Richardson, Jr. as "a Fescennine playlet," in which the wedding party en route to the new home of the bride indirectly attack "the bridegroom, Caecilius,...for bringing his bride to a house with a murky past."[100]

Poems 61 and 66, Poems 61 and 64

C. 61 depicts marriage in ideal terms. The marriage of Manlius and his bride is to be characterized by fidelity and *concordia*. This perfect Roman marriage is complemented by both the Callimachean tale of Berenice's lock and the epic Greek tale of Peleus and Thetis.

In c. 66 Berenice is portrayed as a new bride who is in love with and deeply devoted to her husband. Her devotion is such that when Ptolemy III is compelled to go off to war, she vows a lock of her hair to the gods for his safe return. Although it has not generally been recognized, the dedication of the lock coordinates with rites of marriage. It was common practice for brides to sacrifice a portion of their hair shortly before their weddings.[101] Accordingly, Berenice's offering of the lock, which was made in fulfillment of a vow shortly after her marriage, constitutes a deliberate literary modification of this hair-cutting ritual.[102]

C. 66 coordinates with c. 61 in two other respects. First, verses 15–17 (*estne novis nuptis odio Venus? anne parentum / frustrantur falsis gaudia lacrimulis, / ubertim thalami quas intra limina fundunt?*) attempt to correct the impression left by c. 61 (and c. 62) that all brides are nervous and reluctant.[103] Second, the combined themes of disappearance and resurrection in the poem may be anticipated by myths associated with the divine principals in c. 61 (and c. 62). Hymenaeus, Hesperus, and the lock are all translated to heaven through the agency of Venus; the fates of Hesperus and the lock further coincide in that both undergo catasterism.[104]

Ostensibly, the occasion of the marriage of Peleus and Thetis is a happy one. M.C.J. Putnam goes so far to describe the event "as [the] epic counterpart [to the]...Roman portrayal [of a perfect marriage] in 61."[105] The wedding celebration in c. 64, however, is undermined by the episode of Ariadne's abandonment by her lover Theseus, by Ariadne's curse, which results in the death of Theseus' father, and by the song of the aged Parcae that seemingly praises the accomplishments of Achilles, but in reality emphasizes his brutality and bloodthirsty nature. These ominous elements, which detract from the joyful union of Peleus and Thetis, may subtly detract also from the blissful picture of an ideal marriage on a strictly human plane in c. 61 (which c. 64 complements thematically) in anticipation of the coming estrangement of Manlius and his bride in 68a.[106]

Catullus' account of the marriage of Peleus and Thetis omits the intrusion of the uninvited Eris, Goddess of Strife, who threw into the assembled company a golden apple inscribed "for the Fairest," and it omits as well the consequences of her intrusion: the judgment of Paris, which led "inexorably" to the Trojan War.[107] Interestingly, what is omitted in c. 64 is alluded to in c. 61. Catullus indirectly refers to the "unstated climax" of the wedding feast by way of a simile that compares the beauty of Vibia to that of Venus, when she appeared before her Phrygian judge (16–19). Perhaps the purpose of this allusion in c. 61 is to foreshadow the marriage of Peleus and Thetis in c. 64 and the prophetic song sung by the Fates there about the prowess of Achilles at Troy.

Poems 61 and 65

In c. 65 the reference to Troy near the beginning of the poem and the apple simile at the end create a suggestive link with the same reference to the judgment of Paris in c. 61. As in c. 61, too, c. 65 presents a tableau of a mother and her nubile daughter. In this instance the daughter is not being torn from her mother's bosom on her wedding day (*a gremio suae matris* 61.58–59); instead, the girl, surprised by the arrival of her mother, leaps up and accidentally lets slip from her bosom (*casto virginis e gremio* 65.20) an apple, a secret gift from her lover. It is common practice in wedding compositions to make mention of the virginity of the bride and to refer to the couple's begetting of children. These topoi, which occurred in cc. 61 and 64, occur also in c. 65, but in slightly different form. In verses 1–4 Catullus describes his Muses as *virgines* and his poems as progeny. Another feature of ancient wedding compositions is the frequent use of similes,[108] which in c. 65 constitute a third of the poem. The first comparison refers to the tale of Procne, Philomela, and Itys (13–14), while the second is meant to recall the myth of Acontius and Cydippe (19–24).

Poems 61 and 68a/68b

Cc. 68a and 68b, poems to and for Manlius, look back to c. 61, which is written for Manlius and sometimes is directed to him.[109] These final pieces invert the blissful circumstances of c. 61 and the ideals of marriage expressed there. While c. 68a strongly hints that Manlius and his bride are now estranged, c. 68b undermines the notion of a perfect marriage characterized by fidelity by commemorating the adulterous, ill-fated pseudo-marriage of Catullus and Lesbia.

Specific details link the descriptions of the marriages in cc. 61 and 68b, the point of which is to compare and contrast Lesbia and Vibia. Both "brides" are associated with divinities. C. 61 likens the beauty of Vibia to that of Venus (16–19); c. 68b likens the arrival of Lesbia to an epiphany of Venus (132–34). What is more, Cupid, Lesbia's divine escort, wears a saffron tunic (68b.134), which recalls the garb worn by the god Hymenaeus in c. 61 (8, 10), who is closely identified with Vibia. A common detail of the usual marriage ceremony is referred to in 61.166–68, where the choragus advises Vibia to avoid ill omen by lifting her feet over the threshold. His admonition is called to mind in 68b.71–72 by Lesbia's unlucky act of stepping on the threshold. Finally, while Vibia is escorted by friends and family to her husband's house, Lesbia comes without escort to Catullus (except for attendance by Cupid). The reason is that Catullus' lady is a bride in his fertile imagination only, for in 68b.145–46 the poet reveals for the first time that Lesbia has a husband.[110]

A final connection between cc. 61 and 68b concerns the number of similes found in the two poems. Seven similes in c. 61 are matched by seven similes in c. 68b.[111] "Analogy-construction," writes D.C. Feeney, "…[is] intimately linked with the wedding song."[112] The comparisons from nature and myth, which pervade and "overtake" c. 68b, therefore, consciously reflect a characteristic feature of wedding compositions.[113]

Marriage is the particular concern of women. Perhaps because all the *carmina maiora* treat the theme of marriage, the female voice dominates throughout this series of poems. In c. 61 Hymenaeus is invited to come to the wedding of Vibia and Manlius dressed as a bride; in c. 62 "it is the girls' case against marriage that stays in the reader's mind";[114] in cc. 63 and 64 Attis and Ariadne are pseudo-brides; in c. 65 Catullus is like Procne, who grieves the loss of her son, Itys (13–14), and he is like the nubile maiden who forgets about her concealed gift (19–24); in cc. 66 and 67 the talking lock and door are depicted as women; and, finally, in 68b Catullus identifies himself in love and loss with the mythical heroine Laodamia.

The function of the *carmina maiora* is to act as a transition between the polymetra and the elegiac epigrams. While cc. 61 through 64 provide a respite from the personal poetry of cc. 1–60 and particularly the unhappy love affair, cc. 65–68b prepare for, and culminate in, the reconciliation of the lovers in 68b. The death of his brother (c. 65) is the catalyst that motivates Catullus to accept a relationship on Lesbia's terms. What is more, his perception of his love for her in a context of marriage, to his mind, legitimizes the affair and his exclusive claim on her. Since married men must put aside homosexual activities of youth (61.126–50), Catullus' new role as "understanding husband" in c. 68b (135–36, 147–48) foreshadows also the few references to, as well as the end of, his liaison with Juventius in the elegiac epigrams.

The concerns of the *carmina maiora* are universal and timeless. They explore proper and improper relationships between children and parents, and parents and children, between husbands and wives, between men and women, between brother and brother, and between mankind and gods. Individually the poems are exceptional; together they constitute a *tour de force*. In the words of J.K. Newman, "the audacity of these central poems, the quality of imagination and intellectual strength displayed in them, their technical brilliance and variety, raise their author to major rank in Latin literature."[115] Clearly cc. 61–68b are Catullus' greatest achievement and his most important contribution to Latin literature.

Chapter Four: Caelius Rufus

The opening sequence of elegiac epigrams is almost entirely concerned with Lesbia and Rufus. Therefore, before we turn to the last major division of the corpus, it seems appropriate to consider (1) whether Caelius and Rufus in the poems of Catullus refer to the same individual and (2) whether that individual is the celebrated man about Rome M. Caelius Rufus, opponent of Calpurnius Bestia, lover of the notorious Clodia Metelli, defendant of Cicero's *Pro Caelio*.

The question of the identity of Caelius/Rufus is tantalizing because his identity and that of Catullus' Lesbia are intimately bound. We know from Cicero's *Pro Caelio* that M. Caelius Rufus was romantically involved with the widow of Metellus, and we know from c. 77 that Catullus was supplanted in the affections of Lesbia by a certain Rufus. Thus, if it can be proven that Caelius of cc. 58 and 100 and Rufus of cc. 59, 69, 71, and 77 refer to the same person,[1] the traditional identification of Lesbia as Clodia Metelli could be established.[2] The single most important difficulty in identifying Caelius and Rufus as M. Caelius Rufus concerns his place of birth. While Caelius of c. 100 seems to be Veronese (*Caelius Aufillenum et Quintius Aufillenam / flos Veronensum depereunt iuvenum*), the defendant of the *Pro Caelio* is now generally believed to have come from Interamnia in Picenum. This obstacle, however, is not insurmountable; the view that Caelius was a native of Interamnia is conjectural, based on an emendation of a textually corrupt passage in *Pro Caelio* 5.[3] A second difficulty of lesser import has to do with a distinct difference in tone that sets the Caelius poems apart from the Rufus poems. While Caelius of 58 and 100 is addressed as a friend,

Rufus of 59, 69, 71, and 77 is the target of derision and invective. Since critics vary in the significance (if any) that they attach to these discrepancies, a spectrum of views on the prosopography of Caelius/Rufus has arisen that encompasses virtually every possibility.[4] For example, T.P. Wiseman believes that none of the Caelius and Rufus poems relates to M. Caelius Rufus.[5] E.T. Merrill, on the other hand, sees all references to Caelius and to Rufus as pertaining to M. Caelius Rufus.[6] The position of later unitarians is more tentative. While acknowledging the difficulty of 100.1–2, K. Quinn and P.Y. Forsyth would nevertheless like to believe that the Caelius and the Rufus poems refer to the same individual.[7] Still other views fall somewhere in between the two extremes. For instance, J. Briscoe believes that "certainly the Caelius of poems 58 and 100 is not Caelius Rufus, but the Rufus of poems 69 and 77 is a different matter," whereas R.G. Austin sees only c. 77 as possibly referring to M. Caelius Rufus.[8]

The discussion to follow will offer a new approach to this complex prosopographical issue. An examination of the poems in the order in which they appear in the transmitted text will show that the Caelius and Rufus poems together form a single movement and that they are related one to another by a linear structure. The viewing of the poems as a structural entity will make clear how choice of *nomen* in cc. 58 and 100 and of *cognomen* in cc. 59, 69, 71, and 77 was determined by the poems' position and theme.[9]

Poem 58

The first poem of the series opens with a grief-stricken Catullus calling upon a certain Caelius. With this Caelius Catullus shares the depths of the sorrow to which he has been plunged by the utter depravity of Lesbia, the great love of his life:[10]

Caeli, Lesbia nostra, Lesbia illa,
illa Lesbia, quam Catullus unam
plus quam se atque suos amavit omnes,
nunc in quadriviis et angiportis
glubit magnanimos Remi nepotes.

Caelius, our Lesbia, that Lesbia,
that Lesbia whom alone Catullus
loved more than himself, more than his entire family,
now on street corners and in back alleys
lends a helping hand to the great-hearted sons of Rome.

The recipient of Catullus' anguished outpourings is the subject of much controversy. Is the confidant merely some friend, who happens to have the same *nomen* as Catullus' chief rival and successor, or is he in fact M. Caelius Rufus, a confrere, who like Catullus has experienced the agony and the ecstasy of a tempestuous love affair with Lesbia? The connection between c. 58 and c. 49, the only poem in the collection addressed to Marcus Tullius Cicero, is suggestive.

Poems 49 and 58

C. 58 is related to c. 49 by a striking verbal echo. The expressions *Romuli nepotum* and *Remi nepotes*, which hold the same place in their verse, occur only at 49.1 and 58.5 of the poetry.[11] The point of this verbal play appears to be to join two individuals of long-standing relation. Cicero served as teacher, patron, and guardian to Caelius Rufus in his early years, and in his later years he was his

C. 49 Disertissime ROMULI NEPOTUM,
quot sunt quotque fuere, Marce Tulli,
quotque post aliis erunt in annis,
gratias tibi maximas Catullus
agit pessimus omnium poeta,
tanto pessimus omnium poeta,
quanto tu optimus omnium patronus.

C. 58 Caeli, Lesbia nostra, Lesbia illa,
illa Lesbia, quam Catullus unam
plus quam se atque suos amavit omnes,
nunc in quadriviis et angiportis
glubit magnanimos REMI NEPOTES.

Figure 4.1 Interaction of Poems 49 and 58

friend and legal counselor.[12] Both because of this long-standing association and because c. 58 evokes Cicero's own memorably vivid portrait of Clodia as a *meretrix* in his speech on Caelius' defense, it seems almost certain that Catullus is linking Cicero with none other than his protégé Caelius Rufus. Indeed, the interaction of cc. 49 and 58 seems designed to recall the occasion of Caelius' trial.[13] The framing of the two poems with the phrases *Romuli nepotum* and *Remi nepotes* (see figure 4.1 above) effects a logical connection between the end of c. 49 and the beginning of c. 58, and thus between Cicero the lawyer (*tu optimus omnium patronus*) and Caelius his client, the victim, according to Cicero, of Clodia/Lesbia scorned. Another reason, as we shall see, is that Catullus used the interplay of cc. 49 and 58 as a point of departure to foreshadow veiled references to Caelius' trial in two later Rufus poems, 69 and 77.

Poems 58~59

Catullus also intimates the identity of Caelius through the relation of c. 58 and its companion piece, c. 59. In the penultimate polymetric a Rufus and his Rufa are victims of scurrilous attack:

> Bononiensis Rufa Rufulum fellat,
> uxor Meneni, saepe quam in sepulcretis
> vidistis ipso rapere de rogo cenam,
> cum devolutum ex igne prosequens panem
> ab semiraso tunderetur ustore.

> Rufa of Bononia obligingly fellates Rufus,
> noble wife of Menenius, whom often among the tombs
> you've seen stealing food from the burning pyre.
> When she pursues bread that rolls down from the flames,
> she is pounded by a half-shaven corpse-burner.

Catullus brilliantly exploits several senses of the proper nouns in the graffito-like first line. Rufa and Rufus are personal names and they also are epithets of reproach.[14] Similarly, on one level *BONoniensis* means simply "from Bononia"; on a second level it suggests "sexually obliging," the meaning of *bonus* at 89.1 and 110.1.[15] And on yet a third level *BONoniensis* may signify "she who belongs to the *boni*," the upper class of Rome.[16] That the BON- element possesses socio-political overtones is hinted at through the close relation of 58.5 and 59.1. C. 59 not only begins with the striking sexual imagery that closes c. 58, but the first and final verses appear to be ordered chiastically:

glubit (a)	Remi nepotes (b)	58.5
BONoniensis (b^1)	fellat (a^1)	59.1

The primary obscenities *glubit* and *fellat* enclose *BONoniensis* and *Remi nepotes*, the last also an expression with political implications.[17]

Other verbal and structural features join the close of c. 58 to the beginning of c. 59. The adverb *nunc* in 58.4 parallels *saepe* in 59.2, and the phrase *in quadriviis et angiportis* in 58.4 parallels *in sepulchretis* in 59.2. What is more, the poems proceed in a like chronological fashion from past to present and from present to past, with the same number of verses written in each tense:

C. 58 Caeli, Lesbia nostra, Lesbia illa,
illa Lesbia, quam Catullus unam
plus quam se atque suos amavit omnes, (Past)

NUNC IN QUADRIVIIS et ANGIPORTIS (Present)
GLUBIT magnanimos REMI NEPOTES.

C. 59 BONONIENSIS Rufa Rufulum FELLAT,
uxor Meneni, SAEPE quam IN SEPULCRETIS (Present)

vidistis ipso rapere de rogo cenam, (Past)
cum devolutum ex igne prosequens panem
ab semiraso tunderetur ustore.

The resemblance between cc. 58 and 59 goes beyond the first and final verses. Indeed, if it were not for the unfortunate intrusion of 58b in the transmitted text, the poems might long have been recognized as companion pieces. Single sentences of five lines each, cc. 58 and 59 are similar in subject and in structure, as figure 4.2 below illustrates.[18]

	C. 58	C. 59
CAELIUS RUFUS	Caeli (1)	Rufulum (1)
THREE-FOLD IDENTIFICATION OF LESBIA/RUFA	Lesbia nostra (1) Lesbia illa (1) illa Lesbia (2)	Bononiensis (1) Rufa (1) uxor Meneni (= Metelli) (2)
FEM. ACCUSATIVE RELATIVE	quam (2)	quam (2)
TEMPORAL ADVERB	nunc (4)	saepe (2)
UNSAVORY SETTINGS	in quadriviis et angiportis (4)	in sepulcretis (2)
SEX	glubit magnanimos …nepotes (5)	ab…tunderetur ustore (5)

Figure 4.2 Parallel Structure of Poems 58 and 59

Discussion of the parallel organization will start from the end of the figure. *Glubit*, "skin, strip the bark from," used metaphorically in 58.5, corresponds to *tunderetur*, "hammer, beat repeatedly," used metaphorically in 59.5.[19] The same pairing sets the politically noble of Rome (*magnanimos Remi nepotes*) against one of the city's most abject denizens, a squalid undertaker's slave (*ab semiraso ustore*).[20] The antithesis of the great-hearted sons of Rome to the half-shaven corpse-burner to a certain extent reflects a change of milieu. Between the first and the second poem, there is a logical progression in descending order from Rome's busy street corners (*in quadriviis*), where people go to socialize, to see and be seen, to her back alleys (*in angiportis*), the trysting places of lovers of the lower class, to her public graveyards (*in sepulchretis*), the burial places of the poor. The adverbs *nunc* and *saepe* in 58.4 and 59.2 are obvious counterparts, as are the feminine, accusative, singular relatives *quam*, which hold the same position in verse 2. The most important correspondences in the parallel structuring, however, occur at the beginning of the two poems.

As a pair cc. 58 and 59 are unique in the collection because of the preponderance of personal and geographical names that fill the opening verses. C. 58.1–2 in particular have attracted the notice of critics for two reasons. First, c. 58 is the only invective in the polymetra to mention Lesbia by name. Second, it is the only poem in which the name Lesbia occurs three times.[21] Both of these unusual features appear to have been motivated largely by structural considerations. As figure 4.2 above illustrates, the anaphora of Lesbia in c. 58 (*nostra Lesbia* | *Lesbia illa* | *illa Lesbia*) corresponds to the three-fold identification of Rufa in c. 59 (*Bononiensis* | *Rufa* | *uxor Meneni*). The point of this parallelism, I believe, is to indicate that Rufa, Rufus' woman, is a veiled allusion to Lesbia.[22] Another detail in c. 59 enhances the identification. The verb *fello* occurs only once in the poetry of Catullus, at 59.1.[23] In light of the interplay between cc. 58 and 59, it seems highly probable that Catullus is glossing Rufa with *fello*, the Latin for the Greek λεσβιάζω. He is thus suggesting the identity of Rufa by playing on the obscene connotation of the name Lesbia, "she who practices fellatio."[24] *Uxor Meneni*, then, would be a veiled allusion to the metrically equivalent *uxor Metelli*.[25] Caelius and Rufulus coalesce to form the last of the pairs under discussion. Their correspondence was inspired, for it enabled Catullus to signify the identity of Caelius in 58.1 and Rufus in 59.1 simultaneously: they are one and the same person.[26]

The parallel structure of cc. 58 and 59 thus indicates that the latter poem is operating on two levels. On one level c. 59 is about an unidentifiable Rufa who is married to an unidentifiable Menenius and who hails from Bononia. On another level c. 59 is about Lesbia. As was suggested earlier, the reason that Catullus associates Rufa-Lesbia with Bononia, a city of his homeland, is to play on the BON- element of *BONoniensis*, and as much on the socio-political implications that the element elicits as on the sexual. As T.P. Wiseman observes, Clodia "was not merely a member of an ornamental social élite, but at the heart of the ruling class of the Roman Republic."[27] *Bononiensis Rufa* thus appears to be a contemptuous jibe at Clodia the *mulier nobilissima*, whose demeanor contrasts sharply with her aristocratic station. In addition, the geographical adjective is proleptic. The

BON- of *Bononiensis* looks forward to the circumlocution by which Catullus will refer to Lesbia in 68b.158 as *omnia...bona* as well as in 77.4 (*omnia nostra bona*), where he accuses Rufus of stealing Lesbia from him.

In summary, c. 59 paints a less than flattering picture of both Rufulus and Rufa. To describe the parvenu Caelius Rufus, reputedly something of a lady's man,[28] as being fellated by a woman who is associated with the lowest type of whore (a *bustuaria moecha*) undoubtedly was intended to be insulting. The principal target of the *diffamatio*, however, is Rufa-Lesbia. In the penultimate polymetric Catullus depicts Lesbia's moral degradation as having sunk to its lowest depth.[29] A Roman matron of noble lineage performs oral sex in public cemeteries, steals her supper from the dead on a regular basis, and is raped as punishment for her theft by the unsavory likes of a former runaway slave. This poem surely represents Catullus' most damning portrait of the great love of his life.[30]

Poem 69

The next poem of the series focuses its attack on Rufus. Like c. 59, the *diffamatio* involves his sex life. In c. 69 Rufus is depicted as entirely unsuccessful in his pursuit of women. That there is a worsening in Rufus' affairs of the heart between cc. 59 and 69 is suggested by a verbal reminiscence. The thought in 59.1, *Rufa Rufulum fellat*, is maliciously echoed by its opposite, *femina* (<*fello*) *nulla*, / *Rufe* in 69.1–2, which etymologically suggests *Rufus non fellatur*.[31]

Noli admirari, quare tibi femina nulla,
  Rufe, velit tenerum supposuisse femur,
non si illam rarae labefactes munere vestis
  aut perluciduli deliciis lapidis.
laedit te quaedam mala fabula, qua tibi fertur
  valle sub alarum trux habitare caper.
hunc metuunt omnes, neque mirum: nam mala valde est
  bestia, nec quicum bella puella cubet.
quare aut crudelem nasorum interfice pestem,
  aut admirari desine cur fugiunt.

Do not wonder why no lady is willing,
  Rufus, to be laid by placing her tender leg under yours,
not even if you were to bribe her with gifts of finest silk
  or shimmering jewels delicately wrought.
A certain ugly rumor is doing you harm, according to which
  a fierce goat is said to dwell in your armpits.
This everyone fears. And no wonder, for it is quite a nasty
  Beast, nor one with whom a Beauty would wish to sleep.
Therefore, either kill the cruel pest of our noses,
  or cease to wonder why the ladies run away.

C. 69 opens with Rufus apparently puzzled as to why he cannot even bribe a woman, any woman, to sleep with him (1–4). Verses 5–8 supply the reason. Lack of romantic success stems from deficient personal hygiene. In the words of Catullus, "a fierce goat is said to dwell in his armpits." The image of the goat in verse 6 deftly captures the notion of both rankness and randiness: goats were proverbial in antiquity for their lustfulness. In addition, the combined themes of lust and malodor look both forward and backward. They recall the burning corpses and the concomitant stench in c. 59, which serve as the backdrop for Rufa's voracious sexual appetite, reflected by her insatiable appetite for food.[32] And they anticipate the theme of the profligacy of the still foul-smelling Rufus in c. 71.

Poem 71

C. 71 does not name Rufus.[33] That it belongs to the sequence of Caelius Rufus poems, however, is suggested by its picking up from c. 69 and developing further the theme of the ill-smelling lover. A verbal tie further indicates that cc. 69 and 71 are companion pieces. The expressions *alarum trux caper* and *sacer alarum hircus* do not occur elsewhere.[34]

Si cui iure bono sacer alarum obstitit hircus,
  aut si quem merito tarda podagra secat,
aemulus iste tuus, qui vestrum exercet amorem,
  mirifice est apte nactus utrumque malum.
nam quotiens futuit, totiens ulciscitur ambos:
  illam affligit odore, ipse perit podagra.

If ever awful B.O. hurt a "man of social standing"
and if ever crippling gout deservedly afflicted anyone,
that rival of yours who makes time with your love,
has happened on both misfortunes amazingly aptly.
For how often he screws, so often he punishes them both:
she swoons from the stench, he explodes from the gout.

C. 71 continues the saga of Rufus' love life. In this poem we discover that Rufus (somehow) has managed to procure a mistress, but his romantic efforts are hampered by yet another malady. In addition to his disagreeable odor, he is afflicted with gout. Consequently on each occasion that he engages in sexual intercourse, both he and his partner pay the penalty: while Rufus afflicts the lady with his foul odor, he himself perishes from the pain.[35]

Who is the unidentified victim of Rufus' passion? The language in verse 3 (*vestrum exercet amorem*), which recalls *communes exercemus amores* at 68b.69, suggests that we are to think of Lesbia.[36] Like c. 59, c. 71 is pure invective, a malicious fantasy of a man who would like to see his friend and his former lover pay for hurting him.

It is worth observing that Catullus appears to allude to his lady in all four Rufus poems, and in each of the other three instances he associates her with the Latin root BON-. In c. 59 she is *Bononiensis Rufa*; in c. 77 she is *omnia nostra bona*; and in c. 69 she is a *bella* (< *bona*) *puella,*[37] as we shall see. Interestingly, the epithet shifts in c. 71 to Catullus' rival, who is sarcastically described as *bono* in verse 1. It is worth noting, too, that while Catullus connects Lesbia with the root BON-, he connects Rufus chiefly with MAL-, the Latin root for "bad" or "evil." He is a *mala bestia* at 69.6 and earlier at 69.5 a *quaedam mala fabula* is doing him harm; his double malady is referred to as a *utrumque malum* at 71.4; and the pain resulting from Catullus' misguided trust in Rufus is described as *magno cum...malo* at 77.2. Through the linguistic play on BON- and MAL-, Catullus seems to be subtly indicating that he holds Rufus and Rufus alone responsible for the dissolution of his love affair. Rufus' accountability, which is implied through the repetition of MAL-, is made explicit in c. 77.

Poem 77

Rufe mihi frustra ac nequiquam credite amice
(frustra? immo magno cum pretio atque malo),
sicine subrepsti mi, atque intestina perurens
ei misero eripuisti omnia nostra bona?
eripuisti, heu heu nostrae crudele venenum
vitae, heu heu nostrae pestis amicitiae.

Rufus, I believed you a friend in vain and for nothing
(for nothing? On the contrary, the price was great,
the pain severe).
So this is how you sneaked up on me and burned my viscera
through and through
and robbed me in my misery of all that was dear?
You robbed me, alas alas cruel poison of our life,
alas alas deadly bane of our friendship.

C. 77 is concerned with betrayal of friendship, as is indicated by the framing expressions *nequiquam credite amice* and *pestis amicitiae* in verses 1 and 6. The poem read in relation to its predecessor, c. 71, can be described as a reaction to a devastatingly hurtful situation. Rufus' seduction of Lesbia in c. 71 (*aemulus iste tuus, qui vestrum exercet amorem* 3) is answered by indignation and disbelief in c. 77. Rufus was a trusted friend, who repaid Catullus' trust by stealing his most precious possession (*ei misero eripuisti omnia nostra bona* 77.4). The bitter invective directed against Rufus and his lady in c. 71 thus appears to give way here to anger and disillusion.[38] Although it has not been generally recognized, c. 77 also is maliciously witty. The element of humor is revealed through interplay with c. 69, in which veiled references to the prosecution of Caelius Rufus link the two poems.

Poems 69 and 77

In a brilliant study of c. 69, J.D. Noonan argues persuasively that the phrase *mala bestia* in verses 7–8 is a punning allusion to Lucius Calpurnius Bestia.[39] The double-entendre depends on knowledge of parallel predicaments faced by Bestia and Rufus in the early months of B.C. 56 (which are schematized in figure 4.3 below). In February

Trial of L. Calpurnius Bestia (February B.C. 56)

PROSECUTOR:	M. Caelius Rufus
ACCUSED:	L. Calpurnius Bestia
DEFENSE:	M. Tullius Cicero
CHARGE:	*de ambitu* (poisoning of wives alleged during the trial)

Trial of M. Caelius Rufus (April B.C. 56)

PROSECUTOR:	L. Sempronius Atratinus (*filius Bestiae*) and L. Herennius Balbus
ACCUSED:	M. Caelius Rufus
DEFENSE:	M. Tullius Cicero
CHARGE:	*de vi* (attempted poisoning of Clodia)

Figure 4.3

of this year, Caelius Rufus brought Bestia to trial on charges of electoral bribery. In attacking his moral character, Caelius alleged that Bestia had killed his wives with the poison aconite, which he administered vaginally while they slept.[40] Bestia won acquittal of *de ambitu*—not surprisingly, for he had a superb lawyer, Marcus Tullius Cicero.

Within two months the roles of the players in this courtroom drama were exchanged. Caelius now found himself in the defendant's seat (with Cicero a legal counselor); his accuser, Bestia's son Sempronius Atratinus; one of the allegations connected with the charge of *de vi*, attempted poisoning of Clodia. *Quaedam mala fabula* at 69.5 of Catullus' poem, "a certain ugly rumor," may in fact echo *obscaenissima fabula* (*Pro Cael.* 69), the very expression Cicero used to describe the story being circulated prior to the trial about this "attempted poisoning."[41] It is no wonder, then, why no pretty girl wants to endanger her life by sleeping with Rufus, whose armpit harbors a "venomous beast" (= the uxoricide Bestia).

Noonan detects another double-entendre in verse 9. After demonstrating that *pestis* can signify “poison,” he proposes that *interfice pestem* “may be a humorous translation of one of the colloquialisms for aconite. The poison, known most widely as *thelyphonon* or ‘lady-killer,’ was also called, among other names, *therophonon* or ‘beast-bane’.”[42] Catullus is thus wittily suggesting that Caelius get rid of the *mala bestia* by using the very substance that Bestia allegedly used to murder his wives. Contributing to the humor, too, is that aconite is a foul-smelling poison, which accords neatly with the theme of malodor in verses 6–10.[43]

A final point. Noonan’s prosopographical interpretation of Bestia makes it tempting to see another punning reference in the same verse. The joke would be enhanced if in addition to its general sense the *bella puella* (who does not wish to sleep with a *mala bestia*) is intended to suggest the victim of Rufus’ attempted poisoning, Clodia *Pulchra*.

The theme of poisoning recurs in c. 77. That this motif in particular joins the two Rufus poems is indicated by a verbal reminiscence. The adjective *crudelis* occurs in the shorter poems only at 69.9 and 77.5,[44] where in both instances it modifies words for “poison” (*crudelem pestem; crudele venenum*). A connection between *pestis* of c. 69 and *venenum* of c. 77 is further indicated by Catullus’ placing the nouns in the same metrical position; both occupy the final place in the penultimate line of the two poems. What is more, *venenum* is called into prominence in c. 77 by a striking usage: the word is not used in reference to a person elsewhere in Latin literature.[45] As a result of this manipulation of language, it is now impossible to overlook in c. 77 a sardonic allusion to (Caelius) Rufus’ attempted poisoning of Catullus’ Lesbia (Clodia),[46] whom the poet here as elsewhere equates with his life (*nostrae vitae*).[47] And if *nostrae vitae* in verses 5–6 can refer to Lesbia as well as to Catullus, then it follows that the phrase *nostrae amicitiae* can refer to Catullus’ love affair with Lesbia as well as to his friendship with Rufus.[48] This two-fold interpretation of verses 5–6, if correct, enhances the mordant humor of c. 77 by charging Rufus with two counts of poisoning.

Rufus is guilty of attempting to poison Lesbia in addition to poisoning Catullus' love affair with her.

The exploiting of the double sense of *amicitia* as love for Lesbia and friendship with Rufus was a brilliant stroke. By so doing Catullus combined the principal themes of poem 77 in the very last word: Rufus betrayed his friendship with Catullus by destroying Catullus' idealized friendship with Lesbia.

Poems 76 and 77

The connection of c. 77 with c. 76 also suggests that the poem admits a secondary, sardonic level of meaning. Commenting on the similar language of cc. 76 and 77, H.A. Khan offers the interesting proposal that the second poem is meant to respond to the first.[49] In c. 76 Catullus prays to the gods to release him from his unrequited love for Lesbia (*eripite hanc pestem* 20). In c. 77 the lover's prayer is answered, although perhaps not exactly in the way he had anticipated: Rufus has stolen Lesbia from him (*eripuisti omnia nostra bona, / eripuisti* 4–5). Khan further proposes that if his analysis of the relation between cc. 76 and 77 is correct, Catullus may be combining the notion of jealousy and cautery in *intestina perurens* of 77.3, for the entrails were "the seat of passion healthy and unhealthy." In ancient times "cautery was used as a cure for illness, and love was considered a malady admitting this remedy."[50] Accordingly, Rufus "cures" Catullus of his love sickness by depriving him of Lesbia—but not, of course, without some bitterness on the part of the patient.

Poem 100

Khan sees Catullus alluding to the act of cautery, too, in the last poem of the series, where the metaphor of fire in 100.6–7 echoes that in 77.3.[51] There is another verbal reminiscence, however, that points up the principal theme joining cc. 77 and 100. The noun *amicitia* occupies the same position in verse 6 of each poem.

> Caelius Aufillenum et Quintius Aufillenam
> 　flos Veronensum depereunt iuvenum,
> hic fratrem, ille sororem. hoc est, quod dicitur, illud
> 　fraternum vere dulce sodalicium.

cui faveam potius? Caeli, tibi: nam tua nobis
perspecta est igni tum unica amicitia,
cum vesana meas torreret flamma medullas.
sis felix, Caeli, sis in amore potens.

Caelius and Quintius, the flower of Veronese youth,
are madly in love with Aufillenus and Aufillena,
the one with the brother, the other with the sister. This is
truly a sweet instance of proverbial brotherly love.
Whom do I support more? Why, you, Caelius: for your
singular devotion was demonstrated to me through the test of
fire at that time
when fiery passion burned the core of my being.
All success and potency, Caelius, in your love affair.

C. 100 pairs Caelius and a certain Quintius. The pairing is interesting chiefly because earlier in the elegiac epigrams Catullus had connected Quintius with Rufus through a verbal cross-reference. Quintius' attempted seduction of Lesbia in c. 82 (*eripere ei noli, multo quod carius illi / est oculis* 3-4) is described in language reminiscent of Rufus' seduction of Lesbia in c. 77 (*ei misero eripuisti omnia nostra bona* 4).[52] The point of Catullus' earlier association of Quintius and Rufus by theme and language seems clear. He meant to foreshadow the combined appearances of the same individuals in c. 100, where Rufus is addressed by his *nomen* Caelius.[53]

In c. 100 Catullus depicts both Quintius and Caelius as desperately in love, Quintius with Aufillena and Caelius with Aufillenus, her brother. But, out of gratitude for an unspecified service rendered, the poet states his support for the romantic success of Caelius, for he proved to be a *true-blue friend* when Catullus himself was in the throes of passion. The issue that this poem raises is one of sincerity: Does Catullus really mean what he says or is he being ironic? The linear structure of the Caelius Rufus poems offers a definitive answer. Since Caelius must refer to Caelius Rufus and since "the act of friendship" very likely looks back to the "service" he performed for Catullus in c. 77,[54] the intent of c. 100 is surely ironical.[55] In accordance with this view, verse 8 is a skillfully executed parting shot. The last verse reverberates with sarcasm as Catullus wishes Caelius success in his suit of a young man: "May you be suc(k)-cessful—taking *felix* in its etymological sense—and potent in your homosexual love affair."[56]

C. 100 forms a perfect conclusion to the Caelius Rufus poems. The theme of friendship relates the final poem not only to the penultimate poem (77) but to the first (58) as well, thereby bringing the series full circle. In both cc. 58 and 100 Catullus depicts Caelius ironically as an intimate friend. The pair of Caelius poems in turn act as a frame for the four invectives against Rufus. Catullus' choice of *nomen* and *cognomen* for the six poems of this cycle was thus determined by theme and position, as figure 4.4 on page 167 illustrates.

The lines on the right show the linear arrangement of the Caelius Rufus poems. The lines on the left show how the disposition of the themes lends itself to a circular arrangement.[57] C. 58 corresponds to c. 100, 59 to 77, and 69 to 71. The connection between the members of the first and third pairs has been discussed above and thus requires no further amplification. Cc. 59 and 77 of the second pair have in common the same principals, Lesbia and Rufus, and the same theme, that of thievery. In the one, *Bon*oniensis Rufa (= Lesbia) is the thief who steals her dinner from the pyre (*rapere...cenam*). In the other, Rufus is the thief and Lesbia the stolen goods (*eripuisti omnia nostra bona*). The poems also share the motif of the burning of human flesh—real in c. 59 (*ipso...de rogo...ex igne* 3-4) and metaphorical in c. 77 (*intestina perurens* 3). The Caelius Rufus poems are thus interconnected by a complex system of thematic cross-references. Cc. 59, 69, and 71 are related by the motif of malodor (implicit and explicit); 58, 77, and 100 by the theme of friendship; 59, 77, and 100 by the imagery of fire; and 58, 59, and 71 by descriptions of Lesbia's sexual activities. Cc. 58, 69, and 77 allude to the trial of Caelius Rufus. Cc. 59, 69, and 100 are connected by derivatives of the FE- root (*fellat*, *femina*, and *felix*), all of which occur prominently in the first or last verse. Cc. 58, 71, and 77 similarly use the plural possessive *noster* or *vester* to modify "Lesbia."[58] Finally, three of the six poems associate Lesbia with the Latin root BON- (59, 69, and 77), and three associate Rufus with the Latin root MAL- (69, 71, 77), its opposite in meaning.[59]

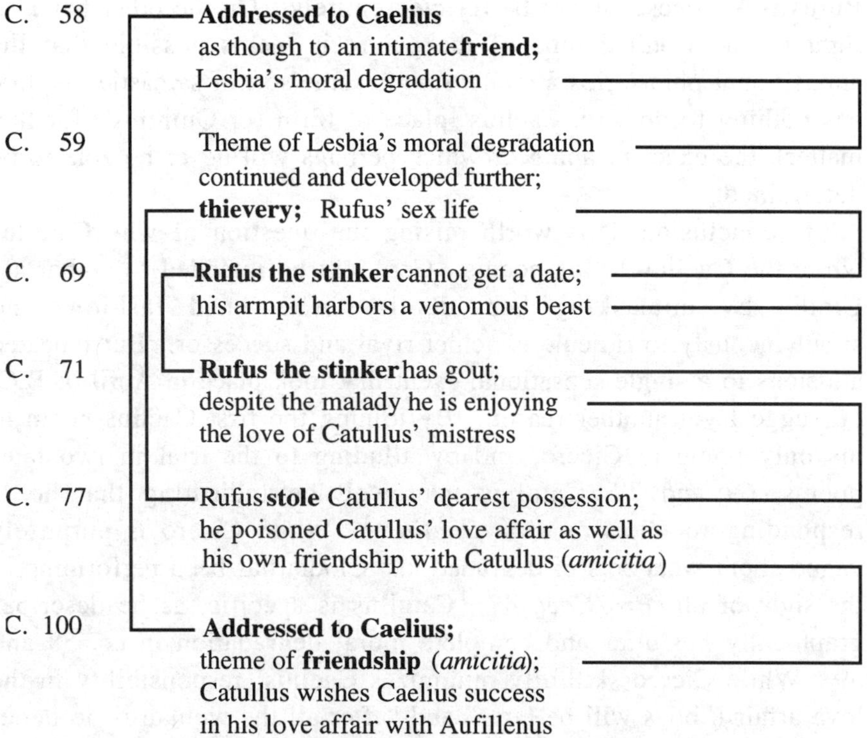

Figure 4.4 Linear and Circular Arrangement of Caelius Rufus Poems

One question remains to be addressed: In light of the knowledge that Caelius and Rufus refer to the same individual, how are we to construe the phrase *flos Veronensum* in 100.2? Does it in fact mean that Caelius (and Quintius) are Veronese? C.L. Neudling interprets the appositional phrase in precisely this manner: "The birthplace of M. Caelius Rufus is uncertain and depends upon reconstruction of the corrupt passage in *Cael.* 5; it could have been Verona as easily as any of the other suggestions."[60] G.P. Goold, on the other hand, in order to identify Caelius as Caelius Rufus and yet not contradict the prevailing opinion that Caelius' homeland is Interamnia in Picenum, proposes that "in the context of this poem he is considered as a resident."[61]

Since inscriptions indicate that there were Caelii in Verona[62] and since the text of *Pro Caelio* 5 is corrupt, the possibility that Caelius

Rufus is Veronese cannot be rejected entirely. On the other hand, in light of the ironical tone of the poem, it seems possible that the appositional phrase *flos Veronensum* is some sort of sarcastic jibe that has nothing to do with Caelius' place of birth (or Quintius', for that matter), the exact meaning of which perhaps will never be able to be determined.

In conclusion, it is worth raising the question of why Catullus wrote the Caelius Rufus poems. Certainly he intended to embarrass Clodia by unmasking her identity in a lurid fashion, and simultaneously to ridicule his chief rival and successor. But repeated allusions to a single sensational event that took place in April of B.C. 56 suggest yet another reason. By joining the first Caelius poem to his only poem to Cicero, and by alluding to the trial in two later poems, 69 and 77, Catullus may well be indicating that he is responding to Cicero's *Pro Caelio*.[63] While Cicero is purposely vague about what acts of degraded lust Clodia has been performing in the sight of all (*Pro Cael.* 47), Catullus is specific, as he describes graphically her utter and complete moral degradation in cc. 58 and 59. While Cicero skillfully minimizes Caelius' responsibility in the love affair ("boys will be boys" and "after all the woman is no better than a whore," *Pro Cael.* 48–50), Catullus makes Caelius fully accountable. He poisoned Catullus' love affair; he stole Lesbia from him. An issue that apparently was raised in the course of the trial was the question of Caelius' loyalty. Lucius Herennius Balbus in fact joined the prosecution because he felt so strongly that Caelius had betrayed an *amicitia* of long standing by prosecuting Calpurnius Bestia (*Pro Cael.* 25–26): just the summer before, the summer of B.C. 57, Caelius, a personal friend of Bestia and fellow member of the Luperci, had supported his candidacy for praetorship. Catullus saves the issue of disloyalty for last and finds Caelius guilty as charged.

This group of six poems demonstrates in a striking fashion how structure elucidates meaning. Generally speaking, the individual Caelius/Rufus poems do not appear terribly interesting or significant or profound.[64] But interpreting the poems as a thematic and structural unity is another matter. The *carmina* acquire dimension and texture; together they well illustrate the poet's wit, ingenuity, and finely developed sense of irony. In short, they provide an excellent example of Catullus' delightfully wicked playfulness.

Chapter Five:
The Elegiac Epigrams

Catullus consciously arranged his collection so that cc. 65–68b belong to cc. 69–116 as well as to cc. 61–64. Catullus indicated the structural unity of cc. 65–116 in several ways. First and most obviously, he composed all the poems in elegiac couplets. Second, he created a thematic and verbal link between the opening and closing elegiac pieces. The only poems in the collection concerned with translations from Callimachus, cc. 65 and 116 exhibit a striking verbal reminiscence. The expression *mitto/mittere tibi carmina Battiadae* occurs only in 65.15–16 and 116.1–2.[1] Third, Catullus involved all the poems in the elegiac meter in two numerical patterns, as we shall see. Fourth, he introduced important themes in cc. 65–68b that are to recur in the subsequent poems. These include: poetry; disloyalty of friends and lovers with the concomitant feelings of betrayal; "gross unfaithfulness in general, applied by extension to politicians"; violation of marriage and family relationships; and love for Lesbia, with an adjustment in perception and attitude on Catullus' part.[2] By depicting his relation with his lady as marriage in c. 68b, Catullus legitimizes the love affair in his own mind. His resolution to play the part of understanding husband here by turning a blind eye to her infrequent lapses from fidelity (*rara furta*) foreshadows the absence of rage and obscenity to be directed against Lesbia in the elegiac epigrams. This marks an important difference between the Lesbia poems in the first and third part of the corpus.

The elegiac epigrams form three complete cycles, cc. 69–78, 78b–99, and 100–111; cc. 112–116, a tag of five poems, rounds off the whole (see figure 5.1 on pages 172–73). The structure of cc. 78b–99

69. Rufus the stinker
70. Lesbia's preference for Catullus
71. Rufus the stinker
72. Lesbia's former preference for Catullus
73. Disillusionment
74. Gellius and Uncle
75. Betrayal by Lesbia
76. Disillusionment
77. Rufus' affair with Lesbia
78. Uncle and Gellius

RIVALS

78b. Oral sex; kissing
79. Oral sex; kissing
80. Paleness; oral sex
81. Paleness; oral sex
82. Seduction of Lesbia
83. Lesbia abuses Catullus
84. Hyperaspiration and rusticity
85. Intensity of Catullus' love
86. Discriminating taste
87. Catullus' love and fidelity toward Lesbia
88. Gellius: *scelus;* oral sex
89. Gellius: *nefas*
90. Gellius: *nefas*
91. Gellius: *scelus:* seduction of Lesbia
92. Lesbia abuses Catullus and Catullus Lesbia
93. Indifference toward Caesar
94. Undiscriminating taste
95 + 95b. Prolixity and rusticity
96. Calvus' love and devotion to Quintilia
97. Stinking Aemilius; oral sex
98. Stinking Victius; oral sex
99. Oral sex; kissing

---

and 100–111 is ring composition while that of cc. 69–78 is interlocking ring. Cc. 69–78 differ further in their ordering from 78b–99 and 100–111 in that, like the long poems, they display a binary structure (69–72/73–78). Catullus deliberately organized 69–78 to resemble 61–68b in order to suggest a close connection between the consecutive cycles. Continuity is the reason, too, that cc. 70 and

100. Aufillena
101. Brother's death
102. Pledge of silence
103. Prostitution
104. Catullus has never written obscenities against Lesbia
105. Mentula, symbolic of obscene verse
106. Prostitution
107. Reconciliation with Lesbia
108. Cominius' tongue to go first
109. Reconciliation with Lesbia
110. Aufillena
111. Aufillena

112–116 form a five-poem tag.

Figure 5.1 Ring Structure of Poems 69–116

72 take up the language of marriage from c. 68b to describe Catullus' relation with Lesbia and that this pair recall the Jupiter-Juno comparison from verses 138–40 of the same poem.

The elegiac epigrams also resemble the central poems in that they feature mathematical symmetry. Here the distribution of cc. 69–111 into three complete cycles is confirmed by a numerical pattern exhibiting exact equality. The difference between the total of verses in the first and second cycles (A and B) equals the total of verses in the third (C): B (148) – A (82) = C (66).[3]

Two other numerical patterns involve all the poems in the elegiac meter. The one illustrates that Catullus ordered this entire section symmetrically. If cc. 65–116 are divided into two equal groups of twenty-seven poems on the basis of their distribution into thematic units, a pattern of 5 – 10 – 12 – 10 – 12 – 5 emerges:[4]

65–68b	(69–78)	(78b–89 //	90–99)	(100–111)	112–116
5 poems	10 poems	12 poems	10 poems	12 poems	5 poems

This scheme makes clear for the first time why four Gellius poems occur successively. Cc. 88–91 function as the centerpiece of this third major section of poems. Another numerical pattern reaffirms the structural integrity of cc. 65–116. The difference between the total of verses in 65–68b, the long poems in elegiac couplets, and that in 69–111, is nearly equal to the total of verses in the five-poem tag: thus, 326 (65–68b) - 296 (69–111) nearly equals 28 (112–116).[5]

This numerical scheme and the perfect proportion among the parts of cc. 65–116 have important structural implications. First, they provide particularly compelling evidence that cc. 65–68b do double duty and should be taken closely also with cc. 69–116. Second, they illustrate that despite the fact that cc. 112–116 do not participate in the ring ordering of cc. 69–116, the poems form an integral part of the design. They function as a five-poem conclusion that complements the five-poem introduction of cc. 65–68b.

Poems 69–78

The first complete cycle of elegiac epigrams consists of five pairs arranged in an interlocking ring (shown in figure 5.2 below). Two poems on Rufus the stinker, 69 and 71, interlace with two Lesbia poems on verbal commitment, 70 and 72, to begin the final major section of the corpus. A poem expressing Catullus' disenchantment with his fellowman follows on c. 72. The enigmatic c. 73 depends on its counterpart, c. 76, to reveal that the unstated reason for Catullus' unhappiness is disillusionment with Lesbia. A poem introducing Gellius and one of his uncles intrudes between Lesbia poems 73 and

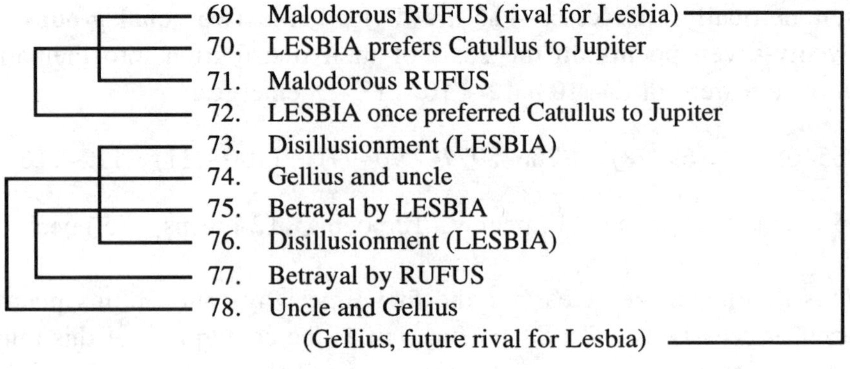

Figure 5.2 Ring Structure of Poems 69–78

and 75. The subject of c. 74, Gellius' incestuous involvement with his aunt, is picked up and elaborated on four poems later in c. 78. Cc. 75 and 77 pair the disloyal Lesbia with the disloyal Rufus. In the one Lesbia betrays Catullus through her infidelity; in the other Rufus betrays Catullus by stealing Lesbia. Cc. 69–78 are thus unified by the same principals, Catullus, Lesbia, and Rufus, who constitute the chief players in a tale of love and betrayal. Gellius and his outrageous escapades offer comic relief from the emotional intensity of the other poems. In addition, Catullus indicates Gellius' coming role as rival by linking him with Rufus through the expression *bella puella cubet* (69.8; 78.4). The verbal reminiscence occurs only in cc. 69 and 78.[6]

Poems 69~71

The first pair under consideration unite the topics of foul odor and sex. Cc. 69 and 71 attack the malodorous Rufus as they deal with his less than satisfactory love life.

Rufus' amatory situation in c. 69 seems to have worsened since his last appearance in c. 59. There he was described as being fellated by a Roman matron whose graveyard activities associated her with the lowest sort of whore. Here Rufus experiences sexual deprivation because he cannot even bribe a woman, any woman, to sleep with him (vv. 1–4). Why is Rufus unable to get a date? According to Catullus, Rufus has an extremely bad case of B.O. The apparent reason for his lack of romantic success, therefore, is deficient personal hygiene.[7]

C. 71 neither names nor addresses Rufus. A relation with c. 69 is indicated by its elaborating on the theme of the foul-smelling lover. In this poem stinking Rufus (somehow) has managed to procure a mistress, but he is hampered in his success as a lover by yet another malady. In addition to his disagreeable odor, he is afflicted with gout. Consequently, when he makes love, both he and his lady suffer. He causes her to swoon from the stench, while he himself perishes from the pain.

Who is the unidentified victim of Rufus' passion? As was proposed in the previous chapter, the language in verse 3 (*qui vestrum exercet amorem*), which echoes *communes exerceremus amores* in verse 69 of c. 68b, suggests that she is Lesbia. Clearly c. 71 is a malicious fantasy of a jealous lover (Catullus) who would like to see both his rival and mistress pay for hurting him.

The point is worth making that Catullus does not allude to Callimachus in c. 69, as he does in other poems that head a major division of the corpus. Instead, he waits until c. 70, which is modeled on Callimachus *A.P.* 5.6 = G-P 1095 ("Ὤμοσε Καλλίγνωτος...).[8] The reason for the slight postponement, I suspect, involves structural considerations, for c. 69 has multiple thematic cross-references.

C. 69 in essence begins where the polymetra end by resuming with the theme of Rufus' sex life (c. 59). At the same time Catullus appears to be creating a parallel between the pieces that begin each group of short poems. The animal imagery in c. 69 (Rufus is compared to a goat) recalls that in c. 2: like sparrows, goats are proverbial for their lasciviousness. Within the elegiac epigrams, in addition to its correspondence to c. 71, c. 69 is related to two Gellius poems. Cc. 69 and 78, the first and last poems of this cycle, are joined by a strong verbal reminiscence (*bella puella cubet*), and c. 116, the last poem of this section, complements c. 69 in attacking a rival for Lesbia.

Poems 70~72

Cc. 70 and 72 are about commitment. The poems have long been recognized as companion pieces because of the striking similarities in language and thought expressed in their opening verses. Both begin with the claim that Catullus' lady prefers him to Jupiter himself:

> Nulli se dicit mulier mea nubere malle
> quam mihi, non si se Iuppiter ipse petat. (70.1–2)

> Dicebas quondam solum te nosse Catullum,
> Lesbia, nec prae me velle tenere Iovem. (72.1–2)

The identity of the *mulier mea* of the first poem is revealed in the second. She, of course, is Lesbia. Catullus employed a similar technique in cc. 69~71, where one of the pair names Rufus while the other merely alludes to him. Besides the obvious verbal parallels in verses 1–2 cited above, another verbal link occurs through the use of the language of marriage to describe Catullus' relation with Lesbia. In 70.1 the infinitive *nubere* means "to marry," as well as, in a comical sense, "to go to bed with," and in 72.1 the phrase *solum te nosse Catullum* suggests the ideal situation for a Roman matrona of being *univira*.[9]

The relation of cc. 70 and 72 is responsive. Catullus' doubt regarding Lesbia's sincerity, expressed at the end of 70 (*sed mulier cupido quod dicit amanti, / in vento et rapida scribere oportet aqua*), is confirmed by the very first words of 72: *dicebas quondam*. What is more, by having *dicebas* in c. 72 echo the three-fold repetition of *dicit* in c. 70 (1, 3), Catullus makes quite clear that "Lesbia's commitment" to him was "essentially *verbal*."[10] Lesbia said what she thought her lover wanted to hear.

The poems differ, however, in their point of emphasis. Whereas c. 70 expresses skepticism about Lesbia's assertion of devotion to Catullus, c. 72 attempts to articulate how Catullus' love for Lesbia once transcended the sexual: "I loved you then not just as common men love their mistresses, but as a father loves his sons and sons-in-law" (3–4). Lesbia's faithlessness, her *iniuria*, however, destroyed the romantic character of Catullus' love. As V. Pedrick remarks on 72.5–8, "his higher feelings are utterly gone, and his 'love' is now at the level of hers."[11] The last four verses describe a paradoxical situation:

> nunc te cognovi: quare etsi impensius uror,
> multo mi tamen es vilior et levior.
> qui potis est, inquis? quod amantem iniuria talis
> cogit amare magis, sed bene velle minus.

Although Catullus respects Lesbia less because of her infidelity, he desires her more. This emphasis on the physical aspect of Catullus' love in the final couplet of c. 70 recalls a similar emphasis in the final couplet of c. 70 (cf. *cupido amanti* with *amantem cogit amare magis*).

C. 72 also indicates that Catullus' resolution in 68b.136 to accept Lesbia's infidelities (*rara verecundae furta feremus erae*) was easier made than kept. Verses 5–8 indicate that he is clearly unhappy in the role of understanding husband. In reality, he cannot accept a relationship on her terms. This inability results in an ambivalence of feelings that pervades the elegiac epigrams. Catullus is physically attracted to Lesbia but simultaneously repulsed by her utter depravity.

Poems 73 and 72

C. 73, a bitter attack on a friend who betrayed Catullus, is a difficult poem. The occasion is unknown, as is the identity of the friend. Further, the language is awkward and the expression of thought so abrupt that the piece almost appears fragmentary. Although Catullus is short on details within the poem, he provides sufficient clues to enable the reader to fill in some of the gaps through c. 73's relation to cc. 72 and 76.

C. 73 concerns ingratitude and disloyalty:

Desine de quoquam quicquam bene velle mereri
   aut aliquem fieri posse putare pium.
omnia sunt ingrata, nihil fecisse benigne
   <prodest,> immo etiam taedet obestque magis;
ut mihi, quem nemo gravius nec acerbius urget,
   quam modo quae me unum atque unicum amicum habuit.

The collocation of *bene velle* in verse 1 recalls the same collocation of words from the final verse of c. 72 (*bene* in 73.1, however, really belongs with *mereri*). The verbal reminiscence creates a strong link between the consecutive poems. In addition, *gravius* at 73.5 echoes *impensius* at 72.5, and "the one and only theme" connects the end of c. 73 (*me unum atque unicum amicum habuit*) with the beginning of c. 72 (*quondam solum te nosse Catullum*). The point of the verbal and thematic interplay of cc. 72 and 73, I think, is to indicate that *Desine de quoquam* also is about disillusionment with Lesbia (and for this reason I read *quae* instead of *qui* at 73.6[12]). Since Catullus conceived of his relation with Lesbia in terms of *amicitia*, it seems appropriate that he describe himself as her *amicus*—an extremely important word here, for it is the only noun in the entire piece.[13] The interpretation of c. 73 as a Lesbia poem receives support from c. 76, its counterpart.[14]

Poems 73~76

C. 76 is a poem of renunciation. In this piece on unrequited love, Catullus describes betrayal by his lover, dwells on his own faithfulness, and in an impassioned appeal to the gods prays for deliverance from a painful love affair. In language and emotion c. 76 closely resembles c. 73.

The poems begin similarly. Verses 1–4 are generalizations about *pietas, benefacta,* and *ingrata* that shift to the particular in verses 5–6:

Desine de quoquam quicquam bene velle mereri
  aut aliquem fieri posse putare pium.
omnia sunt ingrata, nihil fecisse benigne
  <prodest,> immo etiam taedet obestque magis;
ut mihi,... (73.1–5)

Siqua recordanti benefacta priora voluptas
  est homini, cum se cogitat esse pium,
nec sanctam violasse fidem, nec foedere nullo
  divum ad fallendos numine abusum homines,
multa parata manent in longa aetate, Catulle,
  ex hoc ingrato gaudia amore tibi.
nam quaecumque homines bene cuiquam aut dicere possunt
  aut facere, haec a te dictaque factaque sunt.
omnia quae ingratae perierunt credita menti. (76.1–9)

In both poems Catullus is the one who is disillusioned, the one who is suffering because of someone's lack of sensitivity. In c. 73 he states that "nothing gets any return" (*omnia sunt ingrata* 3), and in c. 76 he repeats the notion of ingratitude twice (*ex hoc ingrato amore* 6; *omnia...ingratae...menti* 9). The phrase *ingrato amore* at 76.6 makes clear that Catullus has Lesbia in mind at 73.3. In both poems, benevolence, again with regard to Lesbia, suffers a fate similar to gratitude: all Catullus' efforts have gone unrewarded. Both poems, too, make mention of *pietas* in the same metrical position of the same verses using language that is closely parallel:

[Desine] aut aliquem fieri posse putare pium (73.2)

[voluptas] est homini, cum se cogitat esse pium (76.2)

cogitat esse pium echoes *posse putare pium*, and *homini* echoes *aliquem*. The point is to contrast Lesbia, who is incapable of *pietas*, with Catullus, who is virtually *pietas* personified. Finally, cc. 73 and 76 converge stylistically. Both contain a verse with a double indefinite pronoun (*de quoquam quicquam* 73.1; *quaecumque...cuiquam* 76.7), and both contain an unusually high proportion of elisions (7 in the six verses of c. 73, and 30 in the twenty-six verses of c. 76).

Poems 76 and 77

Verbal echoes link c. 76 also with 77, an angry and bitter poem in which Catullus accuses Rufus of stealing Lesbia from him.[15] C. 76 describes infatuation with Lesbia as a *pestis* (20) that is destroying Catullus. C. 77 describes Rufus as a *pestis* (6) that has destroyed Catullus' love affair. Similarly, in c. 76 the disease of love has insinuated itself into the depths of his being (*mihi subrepens* 21), paralyzing Catullus and removing all his happiness. In c. 77 Rufus is the snake who has crept into Catullus' bosom (*subrepsti mi* 3) and has stolen his dearest possession. The similar language and imagery suggest that Rufus and Lesbia (by implication) are guilty of the same transgression. Through their romantic involvement they betrayed Catullus and thereby violated an *amicitia*. There is a bitterly humorous point, too, to *misero eripuisti omnia nostra bona* in 77.4 echoing *miserum...eripite hanc pestem perniciemque* in 76.19–20. The gods appear to have provided an immediate answer to Catullus' prayer in c. 76 to free him from his love affair by having Rufus (in c. 77) appropriate Lesbia.[16]

Poems 75~77

In c. 77 Catullus blames Rufus for the dissolution of the love affair. Rufus is a thief who stole Lesbia and poisoned and blighted their love.[17] In c. 75 he blames Lesbia—and himself. Lesbia's utter lack of fidelity and Catullus' extreme devotion result in conflicting feelings, which the poet articulated earlier in c. 72: although Catullus cannot respect Lesbia, he still desires her physically.

Cc. 75 and 77 have in common the language of *amicitia* (*officium*, 75.2; *amice, amicitiae* 77.1, 6). Catullus' great sense of duty to

Lesbia in the first poem is set in contrast to Rufus' breach of faith to Catullus in the second. The interaction of the two poems is mutually illuminating. Lesbia's *culpa* of c. 75 must surely be her relation with Rufus of c. 77; likewise, the expressions *omnia nostra bona* and *nostrae vitae* in c. 77 undoubtedly refer to Lesbia, the object of Catullus' love in c. 75.

The point is worth making that verbal cross-references to c. 68b further illuminate Catullus' intense hostility toward Rufus in c. 77. The antepenultimate verses of cc. 68b and 77 are the only instances in the poetry where Catullus calls Lesbia "his dearest possession." Also, the closing verse of 68b is the first occasion prior to 77.6 where Catullus, in essence, equates his lady with his life (*mea lux, qua viva vivere dulce mihi est*). The purpose of the verbal cross-references is to indicate the enormity of Rufus' act of betrayal. By stealing Lesbia, Rufus destroyed Catullus' very reason for living.

Poems 74~78

The final pair have nothing to do with Catullus, Lesbia, or Rufus. Cc. 74 and 78 are about two uncles of opposite character, the one a strict moralist of the sort familiar from comedy, the other a mischievous pervert. Although cc. 74 and 78 are meant to provide comic relief from the emotional intensity of the other poems, thematically they coincide with the rest of the cycle in that they too treat the subject of a love triangle. In both poems, Gellius is sleeping with his uncle's wife.

C. 74 begins by characterizing Gellius' uncle as a stern moralizer: "Gellius had heard that his father's brother was accustomed to reprimand anyone who either had sex or talked about it." So that this would not happen to him, Gellius decided to seduce the wife of his uncle, who consequently would be too ashamed to speak:

> Gellius audierat patruum obiurgare solere,
>   si quis delicias diceret aut faceret.
> hoc ne ipsi accideret, patrui perdepsuit ipsam
>   uxorem et patruum reddidit Arpocratem.
> quod voluit fecit: nam, quamvis irrumet ipsum
>   nunc patruum, verbum non faciet patruus.

The plan was a success; the uncle was transformed into a god of silence. The reference to Harpocrates (v. 4), who usually is represented as a boy with his forefinger near his lips, paves the way for the fellatio joke at the end. "Now, however often Gellius stuffs the uncle himself, the uncle won't say a word" (not only because of his own humiliation, but obviously because he can't).[18]

The plot against the uncle soon thickens. While in c. 74 we are led to believe that Gellius conceived of the idea of seducing his aunt on his own, c. 78 sets the record straight. Gellius has another paternal uncle by the name of Gallus, who is the antithesis of his censorious counterpart in c. 74. Perhaps because Gallus became weary of his brother's endless moralizing, he decided to put an end to it by joining in love his very charming sister-in-law and his charming nephew (*lepidissima coniunx* and *lepidus filius* in vv. 1–2 and *puero bello bella puella* in verse 4 clearly allude to Gellius and his aunt):

> Gallus habet fratres, quorum est lepidissima coniunx
> alterius, lepidus filius alterius.
> Gallus homo est bellus: nam dulces iungit amores,
> cum puero ut bello bella puella cubet.
> Gallus homo est stultus, nec se videt esse maritum,
> qui patruus patrui monstret adulterium.

Gallus thus appears to be the instigator of the incestuous cuckoldry, with Gellius a willing accomplice. Through verbal resonance Gallus is both associated with, and disassociated from, his nephew and sister-in-law. The repeated *bellus* in verses 3–4 suggests that like his relatives Gallus is good-looking, but unfortunately unlike them he is not smart (*lepidus*), since as an uncle he teaches adultery of an uncle.[19]

Cc. 74 and 78, then, are about two brothers of opposite character, the one a moralist, the other a corruptor of morals. Catullus signaled the correspondence by having the poems, of six verses each, similarly center on the cuckoldry of the uncle (vv. 3–4). In addition, the repeated *patruus patrui* in 78.6 recall *patruum,...patruus* in 74.6.

To sum up. Cc. 69–78 display a carefully contrived unity. An interlocking sequence of Lesbia and Rufus poems in 69 through 72 hints at an involvement between the two principals, what the poet describes as Lesbia's *iniuria* in c. 72 and her *culpa* later in c. 75. Cc. 72, 73, 75, and 76, all of which concern Catullus' disintegrating love affair, take the reader through a range of emotions from ambivalence, bitterness, anger, self-pity, disillusion, and self-blame to a desire to be freed from the infatuation. The cycle builds up to and culminates in c. 77. This poem not only reveals the identity of the rival who supplanted Catullus in Lesbia's affections, but charges him with two counts of betrayal: Rufus destroyed his *amicitia* with Catullus by destroying Catullus' *amicitia* with Lesbia. Punctuating the sequence and providing comic relief are the uncle poems, 74 and 78, which, too, are concerned with betrayal—betrayal by a brother, by a wife, and by a nephew.

The opening elegiac epigrams form a closely-knit group. The poems cohere through repetition of theme, language, and imagery,[20] through the recurrence of the same principals, and through the sustaining of a general tone of disillusionment and bitterness. Another unifying feature is characteristic of this cycle only: One poem in each pair consistently illuminates the identity of a person or persons alluded to in the other. The vague *mulier mea* of 70.1 is shown to be Lesbia in 72.1–2. The echo of *alarum caper* (69.6) by *alarum hircus* in 71.1 indicates that Rufus is the subject of c. 71 also. That c. 73 concerns betrayal by Lesbia is indicated through similarity of language and sentiment to c. 76. The relation of Lesbia poem 75 and Rufus poem 77 is mutually illuminating. Lesbia's *culpa* in c. 75 undoubtedly involves Rufus, while the phrases *omnia nostra bona* and *nostrae vitae* in 77.4–6 suggest Lesbia. Lastly, the relation of the uncle poems points to Gellius and his aunt as the referents of the phrases *puero bello* and *puella bella* in 78.4. Cc. 69–78 thus provide a striking instance of how structure illuminates and enriches the meaning of individual poems.

Poems 78b–99

The next cycle (shown in figure 5.3 on the next page) consists of twenty-two poems ordered in a ring-composition pattern. The rather ambitious structuring of cc. 78b–99 may be attributed to mathematical symmetry. Not only does the total of verses contained

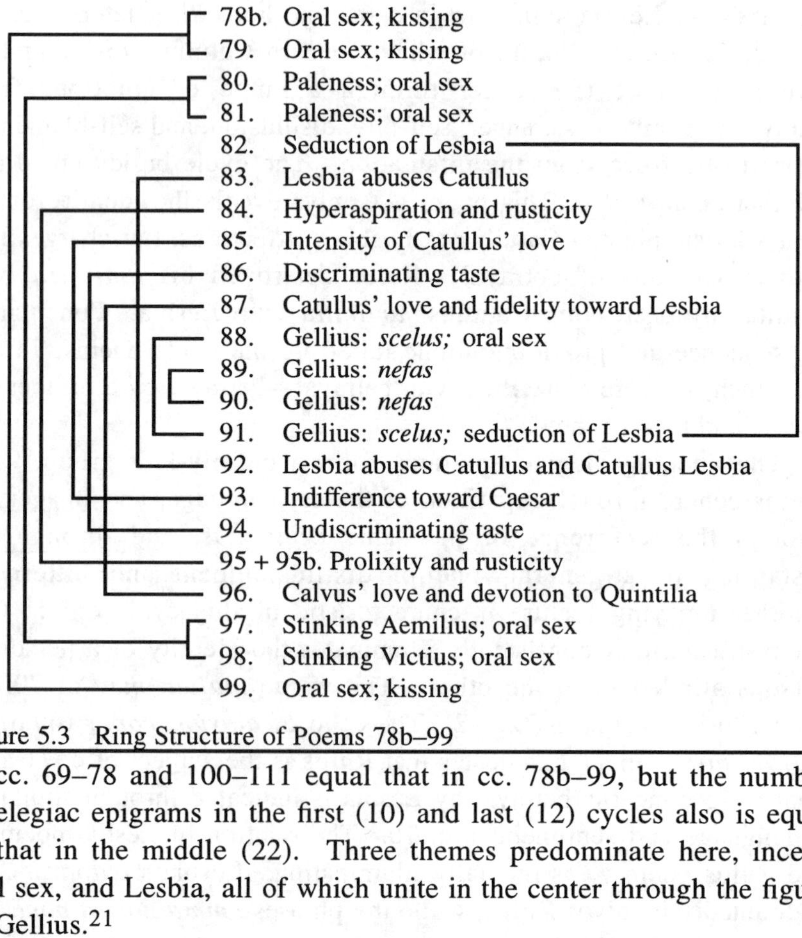

Figure 5.3 Ring Structure of Poems 78b–99

in cc. 69–78 and 100–111 equal that in cc. 78b–99, but the number of elegiac epigrams in the first (10) and last (12) cycles also is equal to that in the middle (22). Three themes predominate here, incest, oral sex, and Lesbia, all of which unite in the center through the figure of Gellius.[21]

Poems 78b, 79, and 99

Cc. 78b, 79, and 99 enclose the second cycle of elegiac epigrams. All three poems combine references to oral sex with the theme of kisses. That this combination of themes does not occur elsewhere is consequential for 78b. A strong connection with cc. 79 and 99 suggests that the incomplete 78b is a remnant of a slightly longer poem that belongs in the position it now occupies; it is *not* a displaced fragment that should be attached to or near the end of poem 77 or poem 78 or poem 80 or poem 88 or poem 91:[22]

sed nunc id doleo, quod purae pura puellae
  suavia comminxit spurca saliva tua.
verum id non impune feres: nam te omnia saecla
  noscent et, qui sis, fama loquetur anus.

Verbal parallels relate 78b to cc. 79 and 99. The noun *suavium/suaviolum* occurs only in 78b, 79, and 99 of the poetry.[23] What is more, verses 2–3 repeat almost verbatim the language in verses 3 and 10 of c. 99 (*verum id non impune tuli: namque....commictae spurca saliva*).[24] Although the repetition has often been noted, to the best of my knowledge no one has recognized the significance. The striking verbal reminiscences are intended to signal interplay between the opening and closing pieces that define this lengthy cycle, the longest in the collection.

78b appears to be a Lesbia poem (*purae pura puellae [= Lesbiae] /suavia*). The lampoon is directed against a rival whom Catullus threatens with eternal infamy. But the question is, which rival? Rufus seems an unlikely candidate because the poem does not fit thematically into the carefully contrived linear structure that joins the Caelius/Rufus poems. Gellius also seems unlikely as the referent because if 78b were addressed to him, his association with Lesbia here would spoil the element of surprise in the climactic c. 91. Quintius (c. 82) and Lesbia's *vir* (c. 83) do not appear threatening enough to merit the abuse of 78b. The only remaining rival is Lesbius of c. 79. That the remnant is directed to him is argued by P.Y. Forsyth, who suggests that 78b functions as poetic prelude to c. 79:[25]

Lesbius est pulcer. quid ni? quem Lesbia malit
  quam te cum tota gente, Catulle, tua.
sed tamen hic pulcer vendat cum gente Catullum,
  si tria notorum suavia reppererit.

C. 79 is a witty attack on Publius Clodius Pulcher. Catullus reveals the identity of his rival by a punning allusion on his *cognomen*: *Lesbius est pulcer*. Lesbia prefers Lesbius to Catullus and his family because he is handsome and because he is her brother. The poem lampoons Publius Clodius for his incestuous relationship with his sister and for indulging in oral sex with her. The final verse indicates that Clodius' sexual practices apparently were well known around Rome, since, according to Catullus, none of his acquaintances is willing to greet him with a kiss of friendship.

Cc. 78b and 79, then, have the following elements in common: Both refer to Lesbia and possibly Lesbius; both concern oral sex[26] and the consequent *os impurum*;[27] and, finally, both conclude with the theme of notoriety, current and future.

In the counterpart to these poems, the poet turns the tables on himself. C. 99 associates oral sex and the theme of the *os impurum* with Catullus. The poem also shares with 78b the theme of retribution (Catullus pays the penalty) and concluding verses couched in the future tense.[28]

C. 99, the last of the Juventius poems, begins with a reminiscence describing the pleasure of a stolen kiss: "I stole from you, while you were teasing me, honeyed Juventius, a tiny kiss, sweeter than sweet ambrosia." The pleasure was clearly short-lived, however, for Catullus was made to pay for his indiscretion. Juventius rejected the kiss by immediately washing off his mouth as though it had been contaminated by the foul spit of a filthy whore (10). Verses 11–14 then describe how Juventius' rebuff continued to torture Catullus to the point that the stolen kiss, initially ambrosial, became more bitter than bitter hellebore. Hellebore was a powerful purgative used by the ancients to treat insanity. Since love was equated with madness, the point of the medicinal reference appears to be to indicate that Catullus is cured of his passion for Juventius. A stolen kiss at the beginning of the poem thus results in the kiss-off of Juventius at the end (*numquam iam posthac basia surripiam* 16).

Critics often comment on the medical flavor of the language which occurs throughout c. 99[29] and which culminates in the reference to hellebore. What has not attracted attention, however, are the numerous echoes of Lesbia poems. As was observed earlier, the expressions *verum id non impune tuli namque* and *commictae spurca saliva lupae* create a close link with c. 78b, the head of the cycle. The verb *excrucior* (99.12) occurs twice elsewhere, in both instances to describe the psychological torture associated with Catullus' love for his lady (76.10; 85.2); the phrase *misero amori* in 99.15 echoes *misero amore* in 91.2, which alludes to the love affair with Lesbia; *surripio*, the opening and closing word of the poem, appears once elsewhere, in 86.6, where *pulcerrima* Lesbia has stolen all sexual appeal for herself; and, finally, *basium*, which is found elsewhere only in the polymetra, is highly charged with erotic associations of Lesbia. *Basium* and the coined *basiatio* occur five times in all, four in the Lesbia kiss-poems 5 and 7 and once in reference to these poems in c. 16. The point of Catullus' combining dismissal of Juventius with reminiscences of Lesbia is to foreshadow his rapturous reconciliation with his lady in c. 107.[30]

There is one other Juventius poem in the cycle. C. 81 concerns the boy's involvement with a rival whom Catullus considers unworthy. The ostensible objection to the unidentified rival is his lack of sophistication. Catullus, however, has another ground for complaint, which the correspondence of c. 81 to c. 80 will make clear.

Poems 80~81

C. 80 is the first in a series of invectives against Gellius. The theme of a lover's pallor, which joins the poem to c. 81, serves as the point of both departure and closure (vv. 1–2, 8):[31]

> Quid dicam, Gelli, quare rosea ista labella
> hiberna fiant candidiora nive,
> mane domo cum exis et cum te octava quiete
> e molli longo suscitat hora die?
> nescio quid certe est: an vere fama susurrat
> grandia te medii tenta vorare viri?
> sic certe est: clamant Victoris rupta miselli
> ilia, et emulso labra notata sero.

Gellius' rosy lips, which are whiter than snow in verses 1–2 (*rosea ista labella / hiberna fiant candidiora nive*), are stained by a milky colored substance in verse 8 (*emulso labra notata sero*). Within this structure Catullus carefully lays the groundwork for the revelation in verse 7 that Gellius is a homosexual who practices fellatio. The poet arouses suspicions of homosexual activity in verses 1–4 by using language that suggests "softness and delicacy" (*rosea ista labella, nive, quiete,* and *molli*).[32] He then heightens our suspicions regarding the indoor activities of the languishing Gellius by the suggestion of rumors in verses 5–6, which turn out to be true (7).[33] The poem also achieves its effect by the careful ordering of *quiete, fama, susurrat,* and *clamant.* Yet Catullus surprises us, for it is not love-sick Victor but his loins that cry out in ecstasy. The closing verse of c. 80, to paraphrase L.C. Curran, explodes "the conventional erotic cliché" of a lover's paleness by disclosing "a shockingly literal reason for the whiteness of Gellius' lips."[34] The vividly obscene language to which the poem builds is drawn from agriculture: "Gellius' lips are stained with whey which he milked from Victor" (*emulso labra notata sero*). The rusticity in the final verse does double duty by paving the way for the jibe in the very next poem that Catullus' beloved is involved with some country hick.

C. 81 is a jealousy poem. The theme of pallor, which enclosed c. 80, occupies the center here. Juventius has fallen in love with a visitor from Pisaurum who is paler than a gilded statue (3–4):

> Nemone in tanto potuit populo esse, Iuventi,
> bellus homo, quem tu diligere inciperes,
> praeterquam iste tuus moribunda ab sede Pisauri
> hospes inaurata pallidior statua,
> qui tibi nunc cordi est, quem tu praeponere nobis
> audes, et nescis quod facinus facias?

The remaining verses are concerned with Catullus' reaction of dismay at being slighted by his lover and replaced by someone who he feels is clearly unworthy. Who is the rival? Echoes of c. 24 suggest that he is Furius (cf. *te sineres...amari* in 24.6 with *tu diligere inciperes* in 81.2, and *non est homo bellus* in 24.7 with *nemone...potuit...esse...bellus homo* in 81.1–2). But whereas there it was conceded that Furius was a *bellus homo*, here a connection with Pisaurum suggests that he is *rusticus*, the antithesis of *bellus*.[35] Why has Catullus' opinion of Furius changed? The correspondence of c. 81 to c. 80 provides an answer. Furius' paleness suggests that he (like Gellius) often engages in oral sex, and this is why Catullus inquires of his lover: *nescis quod facinus facias?*

Despite the similar language and common theme of cc. 24 and 81, few critics regard Furius as the rival attacked in both poems.[36] The reason is prosopographical. We know of nothing that connects Furius Bibaculus with Pisaurum. I would like to propose, however, that the geographical reference conceals some private joke. Not only does the description of Furius as *inaurata pallidior statua* form a link with the earlier allusion to Midas and his golden touch in 24.4, but PisAURi contains the word for gold.[37]

Cc. 80 and 81 are balanced by their position in the ring pattern by another pair of consecutive poems, cc. 97 and 98. The chief principals in this pair also appear to engage in oral sex, as is suggested by the references to foul breath.[38]

Poems 97~98

C. 97 is a coarse attack on a certain Aemilius.[39] Catullus begins the poem on an ambivalent note by stating there is no difference in odor between Aemilius' mouth or his ass (vv. 1–3):

> Non (ita me di ament) quicquam referre putavi,
> utrumne os an culum olfacerem Aemilio.
> nilo mundius hoc, nihiloque immundius illud,...

He then decides that there is in fact a slight difference. The ass is cleaner and better because it lacks teeth (*verum etiam culus mundior et melior* 4). Employing language taken from the barnyard, Catullus then likens Aemilius' gums to a dilapidated cart used for carrying dung and his open mouth to the cunt of a she-mule pissing in the summer's heat (vv. 6–8):

> gingivas vero ploxeni habet veteris,
> praeterea rictum qualem diffissus in aestu
> meientis mulae cunnus habere solet.

Finally, at verses 9–10 the reason for the viciousness of Catullus' assault is revealed. Aemilius is a victim of self-delusion. He *thinks* he is *venustus* (*et se facit esse venustum*); yet the truth is, like Mentula of c. 94, he is undiscriminating (*hic futuit multas*). Consequently, the quality of *venustas* cannot possibly apply to him. The point of the usage of rustic and obscene language, therefore, is to suggest the crude and unsavory character of Aemilius.[40] The poem concludes with Catullus assailing any woman who would sleep with him. Her mouth is equally foul:

quem siqua attingit, non illam posse putemus
  aegroti culum lingere carnificis?

C. 98 abuses another foul-mouthed individual, stinking Victius. A verbal echo, conspicuous because of its obscene nature, signals a connection with the preceding poem. The phrase *culum lingere* occurs only in 97.12 and 98.4 of the poetry:[41]

In te, si in quemquam, dici pote, putide Victi,
  id quod verbosis dicitur et fatuis.
ista cum lingua, si usus veniat tibi, possis
  culos et crepidas lingere carpatinas.
si nos omnino vis omnes perdere, Victi,
  hiscas: omnino quod cupis efficies.

Victius is commonly identified with the notorious perjurer L. Vettius.[42] The identification is attractive because the poem gains point. As M.H. Lindgren observes, "Victius' tongue is doubly harmful, for he is capable of destroying everyone simply by opening his mouth, either by informing against them or by subjecting them to his pernicious breath."[43]

Cc. 97 and 98 have the following features in common. Both concern men with fetid breath; the *os impurum* carries the further implication that Aemilius and Victius engage in oral sex. In both, words for smell or odor precede the first mention of the names of Catullus' victims (*olfacerem Aemilio* 2; *putide Victi* 1). In both, the theme of gaping holds a place of prominence, at the center of c. 97 (7–8) and the end of c. 98 (6). Common to both is the obscene expression *culum lingere*. Finally, both use language drawn from the country (*ploxenum* 97.6; *crepidas carpatinas* 98.4) to intimate that the principals are lacking in *venustas*.[44]

The cycle contains two other political lampoons; the one is directed against Caesar (93), the other against Mamurra (94).

Interestingly, Catullus paired each squib with a Lesbia poem (85 and 86).

Poems 85~93

Cc. 85 and 93 are two "of the best known of the epigrams" of Catullus.[45] The poems, each consisting of a single couplet, are joined by the opposing themes of passion for Lesbia and indifference toward Caesar:

> Odi et amo. quare id faciam, fortasse requiris?
> nescio, sed fieri sentio et excrucior.
>
> Nil nimium studeo, Caesar, tibi velle placere,
> nec scire utrum sis albus an ater homo.

The first verses of cc. 85 and 93 exhibit similar components: a neuter monosyllabic pronoun (*id, nil*), a trisyllabic adverb (*fortasse, nimium*), and a preponderance of verbs, four in 85 (*odi, amo, faciam, requiris*) and three in 93 (*studeo, velle, placere*). The second verses open with basically the same word, *nescio* in 85 and *nec scire* in 93. A rhetorical balance is common to each poem, too, with love vs. hate in 85.1 (*odi et amo*) and white vs. black (*albus an ater*) in 93.2. Finally, just as c. 85 is about sexual passion, so the indifference in c. 93 also appears to involve sex.

V. Ingemann and S. Posch argue independently that the second half of 93.2 conceals a double entendre on *albus-ater*.[46] The Greek equivalent λευκός-μέλας offers parallels that suggest an erotic use of white and black in Catullus' poem. In an erotic sense λευκός and μέλας are epithets of male homosexuals who take the passive and active parts. Λευκός suggests paleness, and as we have already seen in cc. 80 and 81, pallor can be used derogatively in reference to a submissive male. The interpretation that "Catullus is playing with the Latin translation of an ambiguous Greek expression"[47] is appealing because otherwise c. 93 is a weak poem that lacks punch. Further, an allusion to Caesar's sexual versatility creates a link with c. 57, the last poem in which Caesar is named, where he is described as both active and passive. An erotic interpretation of the proverbial *albus an ater homo* enhances too Catullus' witty placement of Caesar's name at the masculine caesura in 93.1, for the word-play on "he who has been split" now acquires semantic significance:

Nīl ni mi | ūm stu de | ō Cāe || sār ti bi | vēl le pla | cē rē
1 2 3 4 5 6

The literal cleavage of Caesar humorously accords with the double entendre on his sexual ambiguity.

Poems 86~94

Cc. 86 and 94 also are joined by contrasting themes. Catullus contraposes his discriminating taste in the one poem to Mamurra's undiscriminating taste in the other.

C. 86 compares two women who are recognized as lovely and attractive. Admitting that Quintia possesses individual attributes of beauty, Catullus denies, however, that she is totally beautiful. Rather, it is Lesbia who is the embodiment of feminine pulchritude and sex appeal.[48] While Catullus portrays himself as a connoisseur of women in c. 86, he depicts Mamurra in c. 94 as his polar opposite. The identification of Mamurra with his male organ indicates that he is a womanizer. That his sexual partners are *invenustae illepidaeque* is suggested by the proverb drawn from agriculture, *ipsa olera olla legit.*

Cc. 86 and 94 are linked additionally through word-play on proper names. In 86.4 Catullus puns on Lesbia's *cognomen* by describing her as *pulcerrima tota est* (cf. *Lesbius est pulcer* in 79.1). In 94.1 the first *Mentula*, a proper noun, is a nickname for Mamurra; the second *mentula*, a common noun, refers to a *membrum virile*:

> Mentula moechatur. Moechatur mentula? Certe.

Catullus also appears to be playing on the words for pot and vegetables in the pentameter line, which according to Varro are etymologically related (*L.L.* V.108):

> Hoc est quod dicunt: ipsa olera olla legit.

The enclosing of *olera* by *ipsa...olla*, as well as the elaborate elision *ipsolerolla*, metaphorically suggests the sexual act. To quote J. Ferguson, "as the pot (feminine) swallows up the vegetables...the female organ swallows the male."[49]

The juxtaposition of the two Lesbia poems and the Caesar/Mamurra poems is not without significance. Catullus placed *Quintia formosa est* after *odi et amo* in an attempt to explain why he could not let go, why he could not put an end to his obsessive passion: Lesbia was irresistibly beautiful, charming, and sexy. Catullus collocated cc. 93 and 94 because they, too, are related. Both consist of a single couplet; both deal with the theme of sex; and both culminate in a proverb. Taken together they recall c. 57, the last poem in which Caesar and Mamurra appeared, which dealt also with the subject of their sexual promiscuity and versatility.[50]

Poems 83~92

The relation of the next pair, cc. 83 and 92, is obvious, for the notion that "excessive verbal abuse signifies unconscious passion" occurs nowhere else in the corpus.[51] Similar language in the opening verses further indicates a connection. Both begin with Lesbia disparaging Catullus:

Lesbia mi...mala...dicit (83.1)

Lesbia mi dicit...male (92.1)

In the first of the pair Lesbia attacks Catullus in the presence of her husband (or lover), who is delighted by the tirade. Regarding the *vir* an insensitive fool, Catullus draws a different conclusion from her hostility. He surmises that Lesbia must love him. If she were silent, she would be *sana*, free from love's passion. But because she snarls and is angry, she burns with love for him and is therefore abusive.

How does Catullus know what Lesbia feels? C. 92 supplies the answer. He knows because his symptoms are the same as hers (*quo signo? quia sunt totidem mea* 3). Although he reviles her constantly, he is passionately in love with her. The relation of the two poems, then, is responsive. Poem 92 justifies "the premise of Poem 83 that disparaging words are a sign of love."[52] What is more, it appears that the infatuation has intensified in the second of the pair, for Catullus claims here that Lesbia is always disparaging him (*Lesbia mi dicit semper male nec tacet umquam / de me* 1–2).

Word order in cc. 83 and 92 merits comment. In c. 83 Catullus reinforces the notion of a love triangle by quite literally placing himself between Lesbia and her man: *Lesbia mi praesente viro* (1) and *mule,...nostri oblita* (3). Conversely, in c. 92 Catullus embraces Lesbia: *de me Lesbia me* (2). The word order in the second of the pair reflects the exclusion of the figure of the rival; in c. 92 she is Catullus' Lesbia. The point of the suggestion of exclusivity, I think, is to look forward to the reconciliatory poems 107 and 109 of the next cycle. It is worth observing also that in c. 83 four of the five words for "talking" occupy the same position at the end of their verses (*dicit* 1; *taceret* 3; *obloquitur* 4; *loquitur* 6). Some critics regard *loquitur* as a weak close to c. 83. But surely the compound verb *obloquitur* at 83.4 is being repeated in its simple form of *loquitur* at 83.6 with the same sense of "to rail."[53] If so, the poem is structured around the theme of verbal abuse, which occurs in every couplet (*mala...dicit* 1; *gannit et obloquitur* 4; and *loquitur* = *obloquitur* 6).

The unity of the next poems under consideration has long been recognized.[54] Cc. 88–91 are the only group of successive poems that share the same recipient, the same theme, and the same moralizing tone. All four concern the depraved Gellius and his incestuous involvement with female relatives. Cc. 88–91 are meant to be conspicuous in order to call attention to their pivotal position. The poems form the centerpiece not only of this cycle (78b–99) but of the entire group of pieces written in elegiac couplets (65–116).[55]

Poem 88

The first of the four-poem sequence begins by bringing together themes from previous Gellius poems. The reference to Gellius' nocturnal activities (*abiectis pervigilat tunicis* 88.2) recalls the allusion to other nights apparently spent in pursuit of pleasure in 80.1–3:

> Quid dicam, Gelli, quare rosea ista labella
> hiberna fiant candidiora nive,
> mane domo cum exis...?

Likewise, the reference to Gellius' seduction of his uncle's wife in 88.3 (*patruum qui non sinit esse maritum*) calls to mind the theme of cc. 74 and 78. The point of the cross-references is to indicate that c. 88 will build on the earlier portrait of Gellius' depravity and sexual voracity. In this poem Catullus brings a new charge that he is committing incest with his mother and sister. The enormity of these sexual crimes is reflected in the elevated language in verses 5–6: "Not even limitless Tethys or Oceanus, the father of the Nymphs, can wash away the pollution" (*quantum non ultima Tethys / nec genitor Nympharum abluit Oceanus*). Gellius has reached the limits of sexual profligacy and, according to Catullus, can proceed no further, not even if he were to engage in self-fellation (*quo prodeat ultra, / non si demisso se ipso voret capite*). The shocking climax of the poem looks back to and unites Gellius' earlier roles as *irrumator* in c. 74 and fellator in c. 80. Engaged in autophagy, Gellius would be "concurrently an *irrumator* and a fellator," both passive participant and active violator.[56]

Poem 89

Continuing the theme of incest, c. 89 enumerates the same principals in the same order as in c. 88. Gellius, his mother, and his sister appear in the opening couplet, and his uncle, follows in verse 3, where *patruus* occupies the same metrical position as *patruum*:

> Quid facit is, GELLI, qui cum MATRE atque SORORE
> prurit et abiectis pervigilat tunicis?
> Quid facit is, PATRUUM... (88.1–3)
>
> GELLIUS est tenuis: quid ni? cui tam bona MATER
> tamque valens vivat tamque venusta SOROR
> tamque bonus PATRUUS... (89.1–3)

C. 89 expands the circle of Gellius' incestuous involvement to include other female relatives (*tamque omnia plena puellis cognatis* 3–4).

The poem elaborates on c. 88, too, by describing the consequences of all that sexual activity: *Gellius est tenuis.* Sexual gluttony suggested by *voret* in 88.8 results in emaciation in 89.1, 4, 6. C. 89 also resembles c. 88 in that it closes with the theme of "wickedness" (*sceleris* 88.7; *fas...non est* 89.5). But whereas c. 88 imputes guilt to Gellius alone, c. 89 includes in its indictment his kind and fit mother, his attractive sister, and his kind uncle (*tam bona..., tamque valens...tamque venusta,...tamque bonus*).[57]

Poem 90

Taking up the theme of *nefas* from the previous poem, c. 90 concentrates on the incestuous relation of Gellius and his mother (cf. *fas...non* in 89.5 with *nefando coniugio* in 90.1–2). This poem shares the grim humor of the last. As D. Lateiner observes, Catullus "jocosely" suggests "a religious purpose" for the incestuous alliance. "Not mere pleasure but a desire for a priest of the Persian type prompted Gellius and his mother."[58] The poem is constructed around words associated with "giving birth" that are etymologically related: *nascatur* (1), *gnato gignatur* (3), *gnatus* (5). The point is to stress the heinousness of this incestuous union that might produce offspring.

Poem 91

C. 91 forms the dramatic conclusion to the four-poem series by revealing the reason for Catullus' animosity. Gellius, a long-standing acquaintance, violated a trust by seducing Lesbia.[59] Betrayal of friendship constitutes an important theme in the Catullan collection. It occurs at the center of the polymetra (c. 30), and it functions as the culmination of the series of poems directed against Caelius Rufus, another rival for Lesbia's affections (cc. 77 and 100). Though one senses Catullus' posture of outrage in c. 91 is intended to be sincere, the theme is treated in a humorous and ironical vein. Catullus had not even considered Gellius a potential rival since Lesbia was neither his sister nor his mother. But to Gellius' mind his close relationship with Catullus was equivalent to a family tie, which in turn made seduction of Lesbia irresistible. The poem concludes by stating that

Gellius derives pleasure only from activities that involve wickedness. The climactic c. 91 thus wryly demonstrates that Gellius could in fact exceed the limits of sexual vice set earlier in the closing verses of c. 88.

The four-poem series presents different facets of the *scelus*-theme.[60] While cc. 89 and 90 stress Gellius' *nefas*, cc. 88 and 91, both of which are addressed to Gellius, focus on the enormity of his wickedness. In Catullus' eyes the seduction of Lesbia constituted a more serious crime than Gellius' committing incest with his relatives because he violated "the obligations of *amicitia*."[61] This is the principal point of the sequence.

Poems 88–91 combine themes found in the preceding poems of the cycle: incest, fellatio, the rival, and Catullus' obsessive love for Lesbia. Further, just as cc. 69–78 culminated in Rufus' betrayal of his friendship with Catullus by stealing Lesbia, so this cycle builds up to a similar betrayal, only with a twist. Catullus thought he could trust his amoral friend—but only because Lesbia was not a member of Gellius' family. Another parallel between the disloyal friends concerns the gravity of their transgression. In c. 77 Rufus stole what Catullus regarded as his very reason for living. In c. 91, simply for the fun of it, Gellius seduced (or attempted to seduce) Lesbia, whom Catullus indicates in 87 and 92, poems that enclose the sequence, he is deeply devoted to and in love with. The Gellius poems, although similar to the Rufus poems in several ways, differ in their intent: they are meant to shock and titillate.

Poems 82~91

C. 91 has another counterpart. It is tenuously linked with c. 82 through the theme of seduction and the figure of the rival:

> Quinti, si tibi vis oculos debere Catullum
>   aut aliud si quid carius est oculis,
> eripere ei noli, multo quod carius illi
>   est oculis seu quid carius est oculis.

Cc. 82 and 91 additionally hold in common that neither names the object of Catullus' affections. Both poems instead allude to the beloved through periphrasis, *quod carius illi oculis* in 82.2 and *hanc..., cuius me magnus edebat amor* in 91.6.

C. 82 is a four-line appeal to Quintius not to steal Lesbia.[62] The referent of *quod carius est oculis* is made clear by the similar terms Catullus uses to speak of his lady in 68.159 (*mihi quae me carior ipso est*) and later in 104.2 (*mihi quae carior est oculis*). That Quintius is in fact making advances toward Lesbia (*eripere ei noli* 3) is suggested by the repetition of language from 77.4–5 (*ei misero eripuisti omnia nostra bona / eripuisti*). There Rufus stole Lesbia from Catullus.

C. 82 is a slight poem constructed around a single phrase. Perhaps the most interesting feature is its position in the corpus. Catullus appears to be hinting at the meaning of the poem by enclosing it with two other pieces involving rivals, Furius in c. 81 and Lesbia's "husband" in c. 83.

Poems 87~96

C. 87 also concerns Lesbia. The poem is the last in a sequence of three that deal with Catullus' love for her. While c. 85 sets in opposition the strongly conflicting emotions of love and hate, c. 86 attempts to account for the obsessive quality of the love: Lesbia alone epitomizes the ideal woman both physically and intellectually. C. 87 in turn carries over the notion of uniqueness and applies it to the unconventional nature of Catullus' feelings. His love and extreme devotion to his lady are without parallel:

> Nulla potest mulier tantum se dicere amatam
> vere, quantum a me Lesbia amata mea est.
> nulla fides ullo fuit umquam foedere tanta,
> quanta in amore tuo ex parte reperta mea est.

C. 96, the counterpart to c. 87, too concerns a poet's deep love for his lady. The circumstances of the two poems, however, are quite different, for the mistress of the poet Licinius Calvus is dead. In c. 96 Catullus attempts to console his close friend on his loss by exploring the idea of a love that transcends death:[63]

> Si quicquam mutis gratum acceptumve sepulcris
> accidere a nostro, Calve, dolore potest,

quo desiderio veteres renovamus amores
  atque olim missas flemus amicitias,
certe non tanto mors immatura dolori est
  Quintiliae, quantum gaudet amore tuo.

J.T. Davis summarizes the message of the poem as follows: "If the feeling of the living can touch the dead, then the real meaning of grief is that it expresses a love in which even the dead can rejoice."[64] Catullus attempts to define Calvus' love for Quintilia in terms of the physical and nonphysical (*amores* and *amicitias*), just as he defined his own love for Lesbia in c. 87 in much the same way by combining *amor* and *fides*.[65] In addition, the expression *tanto... / quantum gaudet amore tuo* in the final couplet of c. 96 echoes *tanta / quanta in amore tuo* in the final couplet of c. 87. The possessive adjective *tuo*, which refers to the beloved, has an objective force in both instances, meaning "love for you." By subtly equating the two love affairs through use of similar language, Catullus' empathy with his friend seems all the more sincere and poignant.

C. 96 apparently was written in response to a poem Calvus wrote on the death of Quintilia.[66] The literary character of c. 96 thus creates a link with c. 95, which is addressed to a friend who espoused the same poetic values as Calvus and Catullus.

Poems 84~95

C. 95 celebrates the publication of Cinna's *Zmyrna*, an epyllion nine years in the making that dealt with the subject of the incestuous passion of Zmyrna for her father.[67] Catullus compliments his friend on his achievement by contrasting his poem to the long-winded work of inferior writers. He faults Hortensius Hortalus for celerity of composition in verses 3–4 and Volusius for writing historical epic in the manner of Ennius in verses 7–8. The *Annales* of Volusius was attacked earlier in c. 36, where it was condemned for its rusticity and assigned to the flames. Interestingly c. 95 also combines lack of *venustas* with a fiery end to Volusius' epic. The reference to the mouth of the Po river in Northern Italy where the *Annales* will perish suggests the rusticity of both the poetry and its author. The fate of Volusius' voluminous *volumen*[68] as loose wrappers for fish alludes to a method of Roman cookery by which a fish is wrapped in moistened paper and cooked until the paper begins to burn.[69]

C. 95 is a programmatic statement that alludes to the Callimachean ideal of artistic refinement and composition on a small scale as it contrasts good poetry with bad. The couplet that follows, 95b, also is programmatic; it alludes to the Callimachean ideal of composing on a small scale for a small audience. What is more, not only does 95b deal with the same theme as c. 95, but it does so in the same way, by setting a good poet against an offensive one. The question that now arises is this: Do the two pieces belong together, with 95b forming the conclusion of c. 95? I think that the question can best be answered by looking at the structure, shown in figure 5.4 below.

The poem appears to exhibit a ring-composition arrangement, with verses 5–8 functioning as the pivot. Three pairs of antithetical ideas join the central verses. The *Zmyrna*, representative of the comparatively short, polished poem in verse 5, is set against the *Annales*, representative of the long-winded, traditional type of epic in verse 7. The future and long-lived fame of Cinna's work in verse 6 contrasts with the ignominious end to Volusius' history in verses 6–7. Finally, the two rivers, used as metaphors for style and originality, invite comparison. "The broad familiar Po with its mud and flotsam" in verse 7 forms the antithetical complement to "the exotic Satrachus, deep-channelled, swift and clear" in verse 5.[70] I suggest that *Zmyrna mei Cinnae* in 95.1 and *parva mei...monimenta sodalis* in 95b.1–poet and poem–form another pair. Together the two verses appear to act as a frame for the reunified poem.

There are problems, however, with 95b following directly on verse 8. Separatists point out that the repetition of *at* in successive couplets is difficult stylistically,[71] and *parva mei mihi* does not follow logically on *et laxas...tunicas*.[72] I would argue that these difficulties are the result of a gap in the text. The structure appears to indicate a lacuna between 95 and 95b. It seems odd that *Zmyrna mei Cinnae* and *parva mei monimenta sodalis* form the only parallel that joins the opening and closing verses.

ZMYRNA MEI CINNAE nonam post denique messem
quam coepta est nonamque edita post hiemem,
milia cum interea quingenta Hortensius uno
. . . .
ZMYRNA cavas SATRACHI penitus MITTETUR AD UNDAS,
Zmyrnam cana DIU saecula pervolvent.
at Volusi ANNALES PADUAM MORIENTUR AD IPSAM
et laxas scombris SAEPE dabunt tunicas.

95b PARVA MEI mihi sint cordi MONIMENTA SODALIS
at populus tumido gaudeat Antimacho.

Figure 5.4 Ring-Composition Structure of Poem 95

The text of the poem clearly has suffered in the course of transmission. Verse 4 is missing, and *sodalis* at the end of 95b.1 is a supplement.[73] Structure, stylistic considerations, lack of transition, and a poorly preserved text all strongly suggest the loss of a couplet after *et laxas...tunicas*. Because Catullus alternated in successive couplets the *Zmyrna* of Cinna and the work of an objectionable poet, it seems reasonable to suppose that the missing verses concerned Cinna's poem:[74] Cinna (1–2), Hortensius (3–4), Cinna (5–6), Volusius (7–8), Cinna? (9–10), Cinna vs. Antimachus (11–12). Possibly, too, the lost verses, like 95b, may have been couched in the present tense. If so, the poem would exhibit a triadic structure of perfect proportions:[75]

verses 1–4:	poem composed in *past*
verses 5–8:	its *future* immortality
verses 9–12:	*present* appreciation by Catullus and lack of appreciation by the *vulgus*

The figures of Cinna and the objectionable poet, who appear in separate couplets in the rest of the poem, are neatly joined in the final verses of the reunified poem. Not only does 95b give a satisfactory close to Catullus' praise of Cinna's achievement—which *et laxas scombris...tunicas* fails to do—but it forms the perfect conclusion to a poem developed around antithetical ideas.[76]

C. 84, the counterpart to c. 95, concerns proper use of the letter 'h.'[77] By the first century B.C. the Latin aspirate appears to have been disappearing from popular speech. The influence of Greek loan words "and social pretension combined strongly to rehabilitate it, not only in those words where it belonged but even in others where it did not (e.g. *pulcher*)."[78] And so correct usage of the aspirate comes to distinguish the *urbani* from the *inurbani*. Catullus' poem concerns a certain Arrius of humble birth (probably Q. Arrius, a mediocre orator mentioned by Cicero in the *Brutus* 242), whose misplacement of initial aspirates marks him as a social climber.

The poem begins with two of Arrius' frequent mispronunciations. Arrius was accustomed to say *chommoda* for *commoda* and *hinsidias* for *insidias*:

> Chommoda dicebat, si quando commoda vellet
> dicere, et insidias Arrius hinsidias,

Word order in verse 2 merits comment. As J. Ferguson observes, *insidias Arrius hinsidias* "implies that he [Arrius] is caught in his own trap."[79] The second couplet elaborates on this implication by revealing the reason for the ridicule. Like other victims of Catullan censure, Arrius is guilty of self-delusion. He thinks he has spoken wonderfully, especially when he has uttered *hinsidias* as emphatically as possible:

> et tum mirifice sperabat se esse locutum,
> cum quantum poterat dixerat hinsidias.

Verses 5–6 sarcastically impute Arrius' lack of culture to servile beginnings. He comes from a family of individuals who were not free, all of whom aspirated incorrectly:

> credo, sic mater, sic liber avunculus eius,
> sic maternus avus dixerat atque avia.

Catullus' singling out of the *avunculus* as *liber* = *libertinus* is consistent with his treatment of the uncle as a comic figure elsewhere in the elegiac epigrams (cf. Catullus' treatment of the *patruus* in cc. 74, 78, 88, and 89). In the second half of the poem we learn that Arrius has gone East and, consequently, everyone's ears have had a rest. His departure, however, was the calm before the storm, so to speak. After a while a chilling message arrived. As a result of Arrius' blast of mis-aspiration, the Ionian waves have been converted to Hionian (a pun on Greek χιονέους meaning "wintry"[80]).

Cc. 84 and 95 thus attack individuals with literary or social ambitions. The one poem criticizes the prolix Hortensius and the rural Volusius as it praises Cinna; the other criticizes the affectations of the unsophisticated Arrius, a petty politician, who wishes to appear urbane. Catullus suggests the rustic character of two of the victims by references to their origins. Volusius hails from a town near the mouth of the Po (7–8); Arrius comes from a long line of social climbers (5–6). Arrius shares with Hortensius the quality of excessiveness: Hortensius is guilty of prolixity, Arrius of hyperaspiration. The poems are linked also through geographical references. C. 95 mentions the Satrachus and the Po rivers, c. 84 Syria and the Ionian sea. Interestingly, Cyprus, the home of the Satrachus River, and Syria are neighbors. Finally, if I am right that there is a couplet missing between 95 and 95b, the poems are of equal length, twelve verses apiece. Cc. 84 and 95 form one of the most interesting pairs in the third part of the corpus. Although ostensibly the poems are quite different, they clearly are constructed around similar ideas.

Before we turn to the linear order of cc. 78b–99, it is worth observing that while poems in the first half of the cycle are largely amatory, those in the second half are not. The reason is that the proportion of poems on love and on other subjects is inverted in the two parts, as figure 5.5 below illustrates. In the first half of the cycle there are eight poems about Lesbia or Juventius and four on other topics; in the second half there are three poems about Lesbia or Juventius and eight on other topics (counting 91 twice).

Linear Structure of Poems 78b–99

The cycle begins with a series of poems about rivals. Cc. 78b, 79, 82, and 83 concern Lesbia's relationships with various men, while c. 81 concerns a successful rival for Juventius. C. 80, the only

LESBIA/JUVENTIUS POEMS		OTHER	
78b	Lesbia		
79	Lesbia		
		80	Gellius
81	Juventius		
82	Lesbia		
83	Lesbia		
		84	Arrius
85	Lesbia		
86	Lesbia		
87	Lesbia		
		88	Gellius
		89	Gellius
		90	Gellius
91	Lesbia	91	Gellius
92	Lesbia		
		93	Caesar
		94	Mamurra
		95	Cinna/Hortensius/Volusius
		96	Calvus
		97	Aemilius
		98	Victius
99	Juventius		

Figure 5.5 Distribution of Lesbia and Juventius Poems in 78b–99

non-rival poem of the opening six, functions as a transition between the Lesbia and Juventius poems. The theme of oral sex here looks back to 78b and c. 79; the theme joined with that of homosexuality looks forward to c. 81. Another sequence of Lesbia poems soon follows on the first. In cc. 85 through 87 Catullus describes his intense feelings for Lesbia and his unparalleled devotion to her as he attempts to account for the obsessive nature of his love. A poem ridiculing Arrius intrudes between Lesbia poems 82/83 and 85 through 87. C. 84 appears to separate poems about rivals for Lesbia from poems about Lesbia and Catullus. Cc. 88–91 form the most conspicuous series of related poems in the cycle. All four concern Gellius' incestuous affairs with his female relatives. The culmination of the tetrad, c. 91, recalls the theme of *fides* from the conclusion of c. 87, a Lesbia poem. C. 87 describes Catullus' loyalty to Lesbia; c. 91 recounts Gellius' disloyalty regarding Lesbia. The reference to the love affair at 91.6–7 points forward to the final Lesbia poem in this cycle. C. 92 has as its theme verbal abuse as an indication of unconscious passion.[81] Strong feelings of love for Lesbia in c. 92 contrast with indifference toward Caesar in c. 93. This last poem, a monodistich, is followed by another monodistich, c. 94. The one poem ridicules Caesar by suggesting that he plays both the passive and active roles in a homosexual relation; the other attacks Mamurra for his sexual immorality and undiscriminating taste. C. 94 paves the way for the not dissimilar subject of c. 95. Here Catullus intimates that those lacking good taste will prefer the long-winded works of Volusius and Hortensius to the small, carefully crafted epyllion of Cinna. The subject of Cinna's poem accords with that of the Lesbia/Lesbius poems, 78b and 79, and the Gellius poems, 88–91, all of which deal with the theme of incest. C. 96 is directed to another poet-friend of Catullus, Licinius Calvus, and was written apparently in response to a poem Calvus wrote on the death of his mistress. Cc. 95 and 96 both treat the theme of pleasure and that of "premature" death (*morientur* 95.7, *gaudeat* 95b.2; *gratum, gaudet* 96.1, 6; *mors immatura* 96.5). The next poems conclude the series of poems in this sequence that deal with political figures.[82] Cc. 97 and 98 concern the extremely foul mouths of Aemilius and Victius. C. 99 continues the theme of the *os impurum*.[83] Here Juventius reacts childishly to a stolen kiss as though Catullus were a prostitute who indulged in fellatio. His immature behavior cures the poet of his passion for the boy (this is the point of the reference to hellebore in v. 14). Theme and position neatly coordinate in this final Juventius poem. Dismissal of Juventius here sets the stage for reconciliation with Lesbia in poems 100–111.

Poems 100–111

100. Aufillena/Aufillenus
101. Brother's death
102. Pledge of silence
103. Prostitution
104. Catullus has never written obscenities against Lesbia
105. Mentula, symbolic of obscene verse
106. Prostitution
107. Reconciliation with Lesbia
108. Cominius' tongue to go first
109. Reconciliation with Lesbia
110. Aufillena
111. Aufillena

Figure 5.6 Ring Structure of Poems 100–111

Like cc. 78b–99, cc. 100–111 are ordered in a ring composition (shown above in figure 5.6). The last complete cycle of elegiac epigrams is enclosed by three poems that refer to Aufillena. She is the central figure in cc. 110 and 111 and the object of Quintius' affections in c. 100. Another correspondence assists in defining the cycle. Cc. 101, 107, and 109 are related through the antithetical themes of loss and restoration: reunion with Lesbia in cc. 107 and 109 counterbalances the death of Catullus' brother in c. 101. The remaining six poems make up three pairs. Cc. 102 and 108 are enigmatic pieces that set Catullus' silence against Cominius' malicious tongue. Cc. 104 and 105 deal with the incompatibility of love and obscenity, while cc. 103 and 106 hold in common the figure of the pimp.

Poems 103~106

Cc. 103 and 106, slight poems of four and two verses respectively, are related through the theme of prostitution.[84] In the one Silo, whose identity is unknown to us, has accepted a large amount of money from Catullus, apparently in order to act as intermediary in an amorous intrigue. Now because he refuses to return the money, Catullus accuses him of behaving like a greedy *leno*. In the other a handsome boy is seen in the company of an auctioneer. The logical conclusion to be drawn from this scenario is that the *praeco* is serving as the boy's pander. Silo and the *praeco* thus appear to be playing similar parts in the two poems as procurers.

Poems 104~105

Cc. 103~106 frame another pair of slight poems of four and two verses respectively. C. 104 is a Lesbia poem that attacks an unnamed addressee, while c. 105 derides the literary pretensions of Mamurra, referred to by the nickname Mentula.

C. 104 inverts the theme of c. 92. There verbal abuse indicated unconscious passion. Here extreme passion makes verbal abuse impossible:

> Credis me potuisse meae maledicere vitae,
>   ambobus mihi quae carior est oculis?
> non potui, nec, si possem, tam perdite amarem:
>   sed tu cum Tappone omnia monstra facis.

In c. 104 Catullus responds to criticism of an anonymous addressee by asserting that he could not write violent lampoons against Lesbia because he is so desperately in love with her.[85] The end-words in verses 1–3 of the poet's response reinforce the intensity of feelings. In verse 1 Lesbia is identified with his life (*vita*); in verse 2 she is dearer to him than his sight (*oculis*); and in verse 3 she is the object of his great passion (*tam perdite amarem*). The final verse shifts from Lesbia to the meddlesome accuser. Here defense turns to offense, as Catullus charges him with committing every enormity with Tappo.

C. 105 mocks the literary aspirations of Mamurra (which were alluded to earlier in 57.7). Catullus wittily describes his attempts at versification as a sexual assault on the Muses:[86]

> Mentula conatur Pipleium scandere montem:
>   Musae furcillis praecipitem eiciunt.

In verse 1 the Prick undertakes to mount the slopes of poetry. The description of Mamurra's ambition in terms of an attempted rape on women who inspire poetry seems to suggest that he is trying his hand at writing erotic verse. In verse 2 the Muses respond in kind to this act of aggression by turning Mentula's own weapon against him. They expel him, driving him HEADlong, with instruments resembling a phallus (*furcillis*).[87] The agricultural associations of *scando* and *furcillis* suggest rusticity and lack of urbanity.[88] These implied notions recall Mamurra's undiscriminating taste and the horticultural proverb that Catullus applied to him in c. 94.

The incompatibility of love and obscenity thus appears to connect cc. 104 and 105. In the one Catullus protests that he cannot write obscenities against Lesbia because of his intense love for her. In the other the Muses reject Mentula's attempts at writing erotic verse because as a personified phallus he "stands...for the idea of obscene poetry."[89]

Poems 102~108

In writing on cc. 97 and 98, P.Y. Forsyth demonstrates how corresponding poems can illuminate the identity of unknown persons.[90] She argues that the similar attacks on Aemilius and Victius (= Vettius) would be meaningful to a Roman audience, who would be aware of a connection between the two individuals. In B.C. 59 Vettius charged a certain L. Aemilius Paullus, along with other leading senators, of attempting to murder Pompey. To the best of our knowledge, he is the only Aemilius with whom Vettius had any dealings. Accordingly, it seems possible that L. Aemilius Paullus has the dubious distinction of being the recipient of the coarsest epigram in the collection. The relation of cc. 102 and 108, which are tenuously linked by the antithetical themes of silence and a malicious tongue, may resolve similar problems of identification.

We know neither the occasion nor the circumstances of c. 102:

> Si quicquam tacito commissum est fido ab amico,
> cuius sit penitus nota fides animi,
> meque esse invenies illorum iure sacratum,
> Corneli, et factum me esse puta Arpocratem.

We also do not know the identity of the person to whom Catullus pledges his confidence, whether he is Cornelius Nepos of c. 1,

Cornelius of c. 67, an adulterer who in fact has something to hide, or some other Cornelius. C. 108, the counterpart to c. 102, may assist in resolving at least the problem of the identity of the poem's addressee. (Unfortunately, c. 102 is so obscure that we cannot do much more than this.)

C. 108 describes a gruesome end for an individual named Cominius. Admittedly, the name is common at Rome,[91] but we happen to know of a Cominius in public life whose unpopularity apparently stemmed from his association with a Cornelius. A certain P. Cominius prosecuted the ex-tribune C. Cornelius twice, once in B.C. 66 and again in B.C. 65. On the first occasion P. Cominius "and his brother were mobbed by the *populares*"[92] and, because of their prosecution of Cornelius, both individuals were greatly disliked. The fate of dismemberment that Catullus has in mind for P. Cominius fits with his unpopularity and makes it appear probable that he may be the target of the invective. If so, the identity of the subject of c. 102 is surely C. Cornelius, the object of his attentions.[93] In accordance with this interpretation, cc. 102 and 108 may be the earliest poems in the collection, since they refer to events that took place in the mid-60's B.C.[94]

Poems 101~107~109

C. 101, the first in the next group of related poems, looks back to cc. 65, 68a, and 68b, where Catullus reveals that he had a brother who died in the Troad of Asia Minor. Presumably on his way home from Bithynia in B.C. 56 Catullus visited the grave. C. 101 dramatizes the distant journey to pay final tribute. We are to imagine Catullus standing by the grave site, as he performs "the formal rites of a traditional ceremony"[95] that involve a ritual farewell to his brother and an offering of gifts. Plain, straightforward language movingly expresses pain and loss. Indeed, c. 101 achieves much of its effect through verbal repetition, which gives shape to the poem.

As figure 5.7 below illustrates, c. 101 is constructed around Catullus' brother. He is addressed as *frater* in verses 2, 6, and 10, and is referred to by *te* and *tete ipsum* in verses 3 and 5. The poem is framed by triple repetition of *multus* in verses 1, 9, and 10, and of

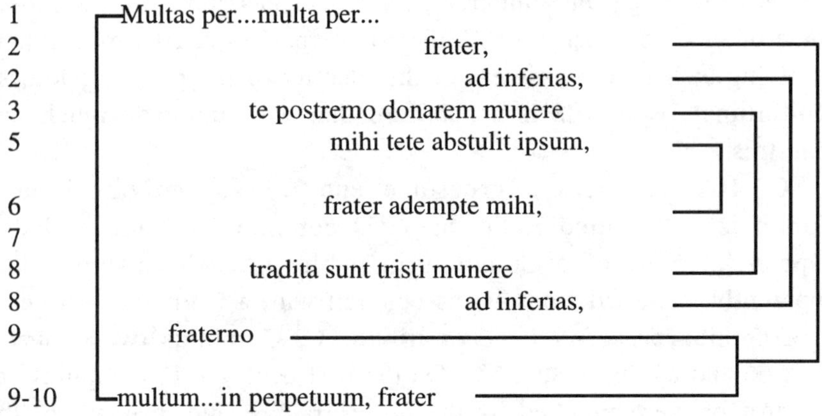

Figure 5.7 Ring-Composition Structure of Poem 101

per in verses 1 and 10 (*multas per...multa per multum...per-petuum*). Within this frame the noun *munus* links verses 3 and 8, the phrase *ad inferias* verses 2 and 8. In addition, the notion of giving, *tradita sunt* in verse 8, echoes *donarem* in verse 3. The loss of the brother occupies the center. Catullus' brother is taken away from him in an elaborate chiasmus: "Fate from me took you yourself,...brother stolen from me" (*fortuna mihi tete abstulit ipsum...frater adempte mihi*). The disposition of the repeated words coordinates with the theme of deprivation. Verse 6 separates the brothers (*frater adempte mihi*), who appeared together in verse 5 (*mihi tete*).[96]

In c. 68b we saw that Catullus came to terms with his grief by transferring "his love for his dead brother to 'rehabilitated' Lesbia."[97] The relation of cc. 101, 107, and 109 is reminiscent of 68b, for here, as there, Lesbia's love is intended to compensate Catullus for his loss.

Cc. 107 and 109 are the last love poems in the collection. Their position is interesting because both have reconciliation with Lesbia as their subject. In the first of the pair Catullus describes his feelings of ecstasy on her expected return. In the second the rapturous mood dissipates and anxiety intrudes, as Catullus worries that the reunion will not last. In c. 107 Lesbia, of her own accord, returns to Catullus. The reaction of her lover is a combination of disbelief and elation.

1 OPTANTIque
1 UMQUAM

3 NOBIS
3 CARIUS auro
4 quod TE RESTITUIS, LESBIA, MI CUPIDO.

5 RESTITUIS CUPIDO..., IPSA REFERS TE
6 NOBIS.
6 o lucem CANDIDIORE nota!
7 me uno vivit FELICIOR, aut magis
7 UMQUAM
8 OPTANDAM vitam ducere quis poterit?

Figure 5.8 Ring-Composition Structure of Poem 107

Pure happiness and gratification pervade the poem. As possibly the most rapturously joyful piece in the entire collection, c. 107 works well as the antithetical complement to the sorrowful c. 101. We saw in the poem on the brother's death how verbal repetition enhanced the mood of sadness. In c. 107 repeated language is used again but to an opposite effect, to contribute to a mood of joy and incredulity. As with c. 101, many of the verbal parallels serve to unify the poem in a ring-composition structure, which is illustrated in figure 5.8 above.[98]

C. 107 is enclosed by two sets of pairs, *optantique* and *optandam* in verses 1 and 8 and *umquam* in verses 1 and 7. The repeated *nobis* links verses 3 and 6; comparative adjectives, *carius*, *candidiore*, and *felicior,* join verses 3, 6, and 7. For our purposes, the most important parallels occur at the center, where Catullus states three times that his lady has returned to him (*te restituis, restituis, ipsa refers te*) and twice how he longed for her (*mi cupido, cupido*). It is significant that the language in the central verses of both cc. 101 and 107 is arranged in a pattern of chiasmus. Plainly we are meant to see a responsive relation between the idea of restoration in the one poem (*te restituis mi cupido restituis cupido...ipsa refers te*) and that of loss in the other (*mihi tete abstuli ipsum...frater adempte mihi*). As in c. 68b, Lesbia is to serve as a substitute for the dead brother.

C. 109 continues the theme of reconciliation:

Iucundum, mea vita, mihi proponis amorem
  hunc nostrum inter nos perpetuumque fore.
di magni, facite ut vere promittere possit,
  atque id sincere dicat et ex animo,
ut liceat nobis tota perducere vita
  aeternum hoc sanctae foedus amicitiae.

Verbally the poem resumes where c. 107 left off by repeating the noun *vita*, which in 109.1 is applied to Lesbia as a term of endearment. The noun *vita* occurs in the poem again with a general sense several verses later, where, as in c. 107, it is collocated with the verb *ducere* (*optandam vitam ducere quis poterit?* 8). Forms of *nos* (*nostrum, nos, nobis*) recall the repetition of *nobis* in verses 3 and 6 of c. 107, where the duplication of the personal pronoun served a similar structural purpose of framing the central verses. There, however, *nobis* signified Catullus, while here it signifies Catullus and Lesbia.

The organization of c. 109 is simple and obvious. In verses 1–2 Lesbia pledges a love that is to be happy and everlasting. In verses 3–6 Catullus responds to her pledge with a combination of doubt and hope. His anxiety that she might not mean what she says is reflected by the pleonasm of *vere, sincere*, and *ex animo*.[99] What is more, Catullus feels compelled to redefine slightly in the final couplet what Lesbia offered him in the first. He replaces passion (*amorem* 1) with commitment (*sanctae amicitiae* 6) and mutual love (*[amorem] hunc nostrum inter nos* 2) with mutual obligation (*foedus* 6). He reinforces also the notion of an everlasting love (*amorem perpetuum* 1–2) by repeating the idea of "lifelong" twice (*tota vita, aeternum* 5–6).

C. 109 forms the perfect close to the story of Catullus' on-again off-again relation with Lesbia. This is how we are meant to remember Catullus the lover—passionately in love (*cupido*), hopeful, yet skeptical that Lesbia can be true to him. The advantage of ending with reconciliation instead of recrimination is that the story of the love affair can fall back on itself and begin again with the *passer* poems (2, 3). C. 109 also provides a satisfying close to the amatory elegiac epigrams because here for the first time Catullus finally articulates his concept of ideal love.[100] For him it is a love that is lasting and that is firmly rooted in friendship and in mutual obligation.

As was stated above, cc. 101, 107, and 109 recall the themes and language of 68b.[101] Yet the death of the brother seems more tragic here. The reason that this is so has to do not only with the reenactment of Catullus' physical presence at the grave site to bid his brother farewell, but with his counterbalancing the loss with his ecstatic reconciliation with Lesbia. Catullus appears to be setting himself up for more pain, for at this point in the collection we know and he knows that Lesbia is incapable of keeping her promise to be true to him.

The poet, however, indicated through cross-references to other poems that we are not to perceive Catullus the lover in c. 109 as a naïve romantic. The adjective *cupidus*, which occurs in the elegiac epigrams only in cc. 70 and 107,[102] creates a link between the first and the last pair of love poems in this section, cc. 70~72 and cc. 107~109. The point of the reminiscence is to undercut Catullus' delirious happiness in 107 (*quod te restituis, Lesbia, mi cupido, / restituis cupido atque insperanti* 4–5) and to reaffirm his skepticism in 109 by having the reader recall how "Lesbia's [earlier] promise of love...proved to be illusory and false."[103] Catullus also reinforces his doubt regarding Lesbia's promise of a lasting commitment through the juxtaposition of c. 109 to c. 110, which concerns a woman who fails to keep her promise to Catullus. Lesbia's *promittere* of 109.3 is tellingly echoed by the repeated *promisiti...promisse* in 110.3, 5.[104]

Poems 100~110~111

C. 110 censures a woman by the name of Aufillena for taking Catullus' money and then refusing to have sex with him. This eight-line poem falls neatly into two parts. In the first part (vv. 1–4) Aufillena is contrasted with *bonae amicae*: "Obliging mistresses are always praised, since they receive payment and fulfill their contractual obligations." In the second part (vv. 5–8) Aufillena is unfavorably compared to a *meretrix avara* of the lowest sort: her behavior is more detestable than that of "a grasping whore who has prostituted herself with her entire body," since the whore at least does not withhold sexual favors after being paid. The point of the comparisons to *bonae amicae* and a *meretrix avara,* of course, is to suggest that, if

Aufillena is not already an *amica*, she is on the point of becoming a demimondaine.[105] Even her name, Aufil-LENA, associates her with the world's oldest profession.[106] It thus comes as a surprise to discover in the very next poem that the lady in reality is a Roman matron.

C. 111, like c. 110, begins with an address to Aufillena, followed by a reference to women who deserve praise:[107]

> Aufillena, bonae semper laudantur amicae: (110.1)

> Aufillena, viro contentam vivere solo,
> nuptarum laus ex laudibus eximiis: (111.1–2)

In c. 110, a mistress who is sexually obliging is extolled, while in c. 111 a woman who is *univira* is held in the highest esteem. Aufillena, of course, fits neither category, since in the first of the pair she fails to keep her promise and in the second she is accused not only of being promiscuous but of engaging in incest with an uncle:

> sed cuivis quamvis potius succumbere par est,
> quam matrem fratres ex patruo <parere>.

Through her uncle Aufillena begets brothers for her children and cousins for herself. As M.H. Lindgren observes, "the references to *nuptarum* and *matrem* emphasize that she is betraying her obligations to both husband and children by her actions."[108] Catullus thus caps his attack on Aufillena, who is depicted as merely "dishonest" in c. 110, by portraying her as "utterly corrupt" in 111.[109]

Cc. 110 and 111 are related to c. 100 through the figure of Aufillena, who appears in the very first verse of all three poems. Her lover Quintius may furnish an additional link between cc. 100 and 111. It seems likely that he is alluded to in c. 111 either as the cuckolded husband (1) or as the incestuous *patruus* (4), since he is not the target of c. 100 and since Catullus always repays a wrong (in c. 82 Quintius attempted to seduce Lesbia).[110] In addition, cc. 100 and 110 have in common the theme of the perfidy of an *amicus/amica*. In the previous chapter it was suggested that *unica amicitia* in 100.6 is a bitterly ironical phrase that looks back to *nostrae pestis amicitiae* in 77.6. And just as there Caelius proved to be *nequiquam credite amice*, so in c. 110 Aufillena is not an *amica* (1) but an *inimica* (3).

Caelius (Rufus) and Quintius are paired in c. 111 because they are partners in crime, so to speak. Both individuals were depicted earlier as rivals of Catullus for Lesbia's affections (cc. 77 and 82). The similar language used to describe Caelius' seduction and Quintius' attempted seduction of Lesbia (*ei misero eripuisti* 77.4; *eripere ei noli* 82.3) is intended to prepare for their appearance together in c. 100, where they are linked romantically with a brother and sister: "Caelius and Quintius, the flower of Veronese youth, are madly in love with Aufillenus and Aufillena—the former with the brother, the latter with the sister" (100.1–2). I have already shown in Chapter Four how c. 100 subtly attacks Caelius Rufus. Verbal cross-references to c. 77 recall Caelius' betrayal of friendship (cf. *nostrae pestis amicitiae* in 77.6 and *tua...unica amicitia* in 100.5–6) and the act of metaphorical cautery he performed on Catullus by stealing Lesbia from him (cf. *intestina perurens* in 77.3 and *perspecta ex igni est* 100.6).[111] The poem on the death of the brother (which looks back to 68a/b) was placed immediately after c. 100 in order to stress the heinousness of Caelius' perfidy, for after Catullus' brother died, Lesbia became his *domus*, his family, his reason for living. In c. 68b.160 he identifies her with his very life. And he repeats this idea again in cc. 104 and 109, where he refers to her in verse 1 of both poems as *mea vita*. In the discussion of c. 99 the suggestion was made that rejection of Juventius paves the way for reunion with Lesbia in cc. 107 and 109. In terms of the dramatic unity of the love poems, c. 100 may serve a similar purpose. Catullus may be eliminating his chief rival by involving him in a homosexual love affair.[112]

Linear Structure of Poems 100–111

The connection in theme between cc. 100 and 101 is reminiscent of c. 68b, where the theme of the death of the brother is combined with that of gratitude to a friend for a service rendered with regard to

Lesbia. But whereas Catullus was utterly sincere in his expression of thanks in c. 68b, he is bitterly sarcastic in thanking a former rival in c. 100. The opening poems of the cycle are linked also by the motif of brotherly love—ironical in c. 100, sincere in c. 101.[113] Cc. 101 and 102 are joined through the theme of silence. In the one poem the dead brother cannot speak (*mutam cinerem* 101.4), in the other Catullus will not speak out of a sense of loyalty (*factum me esse puta Arpocratem* 102.4). The *fides* of Catullus in c. 102 contrasts with the lack of *fides* of Silo in c. 103, who has failed to fulfill his part of a bargain. His improper behavior toward Catullus contrasts with Catullus' own proper behavior toward Lesbia in the next poem. In c. 104 he asserts to an unidentified accuser that he could never write abusive verses against a woman with whom he is so passionately in love. The relation of cc. 104 and 105 has already been discussed. Both combine the incompatibility of obscenity and love. C. 105 in turn is connected with c. 106 through the related themes of rape (*scandere* 105.1) and prostitution (*se vendere* 106.2). The notion of intense desire denoted by *discupere* in 106.2 forms a verbal link with the triple repetition of *cupidus* in 107.1, 4, 5. The word *vita*, which occurs at the end of c. 107 and the end of c. 109, acts as a frame for a poem that deals with the antithesis of life: c. 108 concerns a gruesome death imagined for the perjurer Cominius. Finally, the combined themes of keeping a promise and of being *univira*, suggested by *aeternum hoc sanctae foedus amicitiae* in c. 109, are taken up separately by cc. 110 and 111.[114] Aufillena's failure to keep a promise and her promiscuity are intended to undermine the sentimentality of the final Lesbia poem, in which Catullus' lady promises eternal love.

Poems 112–116

The elegiac epigrams conclude with a five-poem tag. Cc. 112–116 are meant to complement symmetrically the introductory five long poems (65–68b). In light of the numerous pieces in cc. 69–111 that deal with sexual material, it perhaps comes as no surprise that the phallus functions as the unifying theme of the closing sequence.

Poem 112

The final pentad begins with a slight poem that attacks a certain Naso:[115]

> Multus homo es, Naso, neque tecum multus homo <est qui>
> descendit: Naso, multus es et pathicus.

This satiric couplet obviously is constructed around the phrase *multus...es(t)*. The threefold repetition suggests wordplay; Catullus appears to be exploiting two or more meanings of the adjective *multus*.[116]

A clue to one meaning is provided by *descendere*, which sets the poem in a political context. The verb denotes "to go down to the forum" either to conduct business or to canvass votes. A sense of *multus* that complements *descendere* is "active," i.e., "politically active." M.G. Morgan, who advocates a political interpretation, analyzes the situation as follows: "Catullus is saying that Naso is active in politics, and that there is not an active man who goes down to the forum with him *as a competitor*. Naso, in other words, is an active candidate for some office, and none of his rivals is showing anything like the same amount of zeal about making friends and influencing people."[117] *Pathicus*, the final word, is intended to surprise by indicating that Naso's political aspirations conceal sexual motives. Naso is in pursuit of male lovers with whom he will play the passive and not the active part. A translation of the poem with *multus* signifying "active" then might run as follows:

> You're an active fellow, Naso, and there is not a politically
> active fellow who accompanies you to the forum: Naso,
> you're an active fellow but a passive.

A more risqué reading of the poem is prompted by a possible double entendre in *descendere* and *multus*. *Descendere* has an obscene sense equivalent to our "to go down."[118] *Multus* can mean "large," a meaning which in turn suggests "virile."[119] A sexual interpretation of c. 112, then, would set Naso's apparently extreme virility in opposition to his actual effeminacy. The following translation attempts to capture the sexual nuance:

> You're a lot of man, Naso, and there are not a lot of men
>   who go down with you: Naso, you're a lot of man and a queer.

Multus in this sense coordinates with a possible play on Naso, the *cognomen* of the addressee.[120] In art and literature the ancients noted a resemblance between the nose and the penis.[121] Catullus himself implicitly connects the two organs in the final verses of c. 13, where *nasum* occurs contrary to expectation (*nam unguentum dabo..., deos rogabis, totum ut te faciant, Fabulle, nasum* 11, 13–14). Accordingly, the name of the addressee, "Large Nose," may suggest a man who is very well-endowed. The implication that Naso is "all penis" or "a personified penis" paves the way for the paradox that he is also a *pathicus*.[122] A witty poem on a slight subject, c. 112 packs a lot of meaning into a single couplet.

Poem 113

C. 112 is closely connected verbally and thematically with the next poem:

> Consule Pompeio primum duo, Cinna, solebant
>   Maeciliam: facto consule nunc iterum
> manserunt duo, sed creverunt milia in unum
>   singula. fecundum semen adulterio.

Multus in the sense of "many" (112.1–2) anticipates the arithmetic imagery that pervades c. 113, and *descendit* in a political sense (112.2) provides an excellent transition to the reference in c. 113 to Pompey's past and recent success in being elected to the consulship (vv. 1–2).[123] C. 113 resembles the previous poem, too, in that it combines the themes of politics and sex.

The subject of c. 113 is the rapid growth of Maecilia's lovers.[124] During Pompey's first consulship (B.C. 70) Maecilia had two lovers; now, fifteen years later, on the point of his second consulship she has the same two lovers, with an addition of a thousand younger rivals for each. Although Catullus obviously is attacking Maecilia—whoever she is—for her promiscuity, the real target of the poem appears to be the unidentified pair in verses 1 and 3. This view is supported by the stress given to the repeated pronoun *duo*, which "is emphasized each time by its position in the line—before a bucolic diaeresis in line 1, before a break at the end of the second foot in line 3."[125] The shift of the poem's focus from Maecilia to the faithful pair makes the question of their identity more important. The proposal of L. Schwabe that they are Caesar and Mamurra merits serious consideration for two reasons.[126]

The first reason concerns the collocation of cc. 113 and 114. The juxtaposition of a poem about adultery and a poem about an individual, who in Catullus' eyes epitomizes adultery (Mamurra = Mentula), certainly is suggestive regarding the identity of one of the adulterous *duo*.[127] The second reason has to do with the close relation between c. 113 and the earlier c. 57, a poem that attacks Caesar and Mamurra. Both cc. 57 and 113 have as their subject adultery and sexual excess. Both occupy the fourth place from the end of a major section. Both use extensive numerical imagery to convey the ideas of singleness and duality. Lastly, both poems refer explicitly to the principal characters as a twosome. In light of these resemblances, it seems likely that the *duo* of cc. 57 and 113 are one and the same, the thoroughly dissolute Caesar and Mamurra. As for Maecilia, her name may coordinate with the poem's theme. She is a "skinny woman" as a result of all that sexual activity.

Poems 114~115

Cc. 114 and 115 have as their subject Mentula and his Italian estate. Long recognized as companion pieces, the poems differ slightly in their emphasis.[128] The first of the pair focuses on the estate, while the second focuses on the owner.[129] The complementary character of the two poems is further indicated by a parallel structure (shown in figure 5.9 on the next page).

The poems begin similarly by referring to their combined subjects. C. 114 speaks of the estate first and then the owner; c. 115 reverses the order, mentioning the owner first and then the estate:

OWNER/ESTATE	114.1	115.1–2
MENTULA'S WEALTH AND ESTATE'S ABUNDANCE	114.2	115.3–4
ENUMERATION OF RESOURCES	114.3	115.5
WEALTHY ESTATE OPPOSED TO SPENDTHRIFT OWNER	114.5–6	115.7–8

Figure 5.9 Parallel Structure of Poems 114 and 115

Firmano saltu non falso Mentula dives (114.1)

Mentula habet iuxta triginta iugera prati,
quadraginta arvi: cetera sunt maria. (115.1–2)

C. 115 elaborates on c. 114 by indicating roughly the size of the property: it is composed of 30 acres of pasture and 40 acres of arable land; the rest is marsh. The poems next make the point that Mentula is or should be (very) rich because of the estate's abundance:

Firmano saltu non falso Mentula dives
fertur, qui tot res in se habet egregias, (114.1–2)

cur non divitiis Croesum superare potis sit,
uno qui in saltu tot bona possideat, (115.3–4)

Although the language here is similar, the passages exhibit slight differences. The referent of the *qui* clause in c. 114 is the estate, while the referent of the *qui* clause in c. 115 is Mentula, and c. 115 exaggerates the idea of Mentula's wealth through comparison to the riches of Croesus. The following verse of both poems develops the theme of the estate's abundance by enumerating its resources:

aucupium omne genus, piscis, prata, arva, ferasque. (114.3)

prata arva ingentes silvas altas paludesque (115.5)

The lists coincide in content (*prata* and *arva*) as well as in style, with the single connective occurring at the very end.[130] The poems close by contrasting Mentula with his estate. C. 114 opposes the wealth of the estate to the poverty of its owner. C. 115 opposes the size of the resources, which are just "large," to the size of Mentula, who "is largest of all":[131]

> quare concedo sit dives, dum omnia desint.
> saltum laudemus, dum modo ipse egeat. (114.5–6)

> omnia magna haec sunt, tamen ipsest maximus ultro,
> non homo, sed vero mentula magna minax. (115.7–8)

Verbal echoes also signal a connection between the final verses. *Ipse* refers to Mentula as owner in 114.6 and 115.7, and *omnia magna sunt* in 115.7 recalls *omnia desint* in 114.5.

Cc. 114 and 115 have not won high marks from critics. In the view of many, the poems are "dull" and "labored."[132] For this judgment Catullus is partly to blame. The parallel structure, which he used only here in the elegiac epigrams, does not work well in short poems with a skeletal structure; the result is that the poems are too repetitive. The other part of the blame lies with those of us who have been reading cc. 114 and 115 on a literal level only, for the poems appear to operate on a symbolic level as well.

Fields in ancient literature often function as a metaphor for female genitalia. This metaphor is complemented by that of sowing, plowing, and the plow, "symbols for male sexual activity and, in particular, the phallus."[133] And so in the context of c. 114, Mentula's estate is equivalent to an expensive mistress or mistresses, who possess "many desirable qualities, but the sexual pleasure (*fructus* 4) he [Mentula] derives [from the love-making]...is surpassed by his expenditures."[134]

C. 115 focuses on the boundless expanse of the estate: it is as vast as the sea, extending to the ends of the earth. On a metaphorical level Catullus appears to be suggesting that the opportunities for sexual activity afforded by Mentula's mistresses are many, but they are nevertheless insufficient for one who is so insatiable.

It is worth noting in support of this interpretation that Catullus may have used *saltus* in cc. 114 and 115 instead of *fundus*, the usual word for "estate,"[135] because of its etymological connection with the verb *salio*, "to leap" or "to mount."[136] Surely, too, Catullus has set up the expectation of a sexual reading of cc. 114 and 115 through the previous poems that refer to Mamurra/Mentula (29, 57, 94, 105, 113?), every one of which deals with the promiscuity of Caesar's henchman.[137]

Critics observe that *mentula magna minax* in the final verse of c. 115 "parodies an epic line from Ennius" (*Machina multa minax minitatur maxima muris* (*Ann.* 621, Skutsch).[138] It is true that the borrowing coordinates with the elevated language of verses 5–6 that serves "to emphasize the immensity of Mamurra's holdings."[139] But there is another reason, I believe, for the Ennian allusion. Words for weaponry are commonly used in ancient literature as a sexual metaphor for the penis.[140] It would be characteristic of Catullus' penchant for artistic detail to substitute *mentula* for the Ennian *machina* in 115.8 in order to foreshadow one of the nuances of *tela* in c. 116, where the noun signifies phallus as well as poem.[141] From a linear perspective it seems logical, too, for an attack on Gellius to follow an attack on Mamurra, since both individuals are repeatedly characterized in the poetry as morally bankrupt and utterly dissipated.

Poem 116

C. 116 purportedly concerns Catullus' faltering relationship with Gellius. The poet states that attempts to effect a reconciliation have been undertaken in vain. As a result of Gellius' refusal to be conciliatory, Catullus warns that he will pay the penalty. The poem is difficult because its occasion is not made explicit. And the occasion is not made explicit because the poem serves multiple structural purposes, as we shall see.

C. 116 appears motivated by Gellius' designs on Lesbia. Language reminiscent of c. 15 suggests that Gellius is to be viewed as a rival (cf. *ut nostrum insidiis caput lacessas* 15.16 and *<meum> mittere in usque caput* 116.4; *infesto pene* 15.10 and *tela [= pene] infesta* 116.4). Since *tela mittere in caput* is "a recognizable double entendre for *irrumare*," the "punishment in kind" that Catullus has in mind for Gellius in verses 7–8 is oral rape, the same punishment with which he threatens Aurelius in c. 21.[142] According to this interpretation c. 116 continues the theme of Gellius as rival from c. 91. Like cc. 15 and 21, the poem appears to be a warning to stay away from Catullus' love (as of cc. 107 and 109, he and Lesbia are together again). Taking a Priapic stance, the poet threatens Gellius simultaneously with two forms of punishment, oral rape and invective poems. This double threat provides closure to the Gellius poems[143] as well as bringing the series full circle by recalling the motif of *irrumatio* from c. 74—with a twist, of course, for in c. 116 Gellius will be the victim.[144] Attacks on rivals for Lesbia thus unify the elegiac epigrams by occupying key positions at the beginning (c. 69), middle (c. 91), and end (c. 116). By seducing, or attempting to seduce, Lesbia, Caelius Rufus and Gellius alike betray a friendship or close acquaintance with Catullus.

Poems that hold places of prominence in large collections often exhibit multiple relationships. In addition to its connection with c. 69 and the series of Gellius poems, c. 116 corresponds thematically to both c. 65 and c. 1.

Cc. 65 and 116 are *recusationes* in which one type of poetry is substituted for another.[145] In c. 65 Catullus states his intention to send Hortalus a translation of Callimachus instead of the original poem he requested. Conversely, in c. 116 Catullus was seeking poems of Callimachus to translate in order to appease Gellius, but to no avail; his rival instead will apparently receive original poems of invective. A connection between the first and last poems in elegiac couplets is signaled by a striking verbal reminiscence. The expressions *mitto tibi carmina Battiadae/tibi carmina mittere Battiadae* occur nowhere else in the corpus.[146] In light of the emphasis placed verbally and thematically on translations from Callimachus in these opening and closing pieces, it is notable that neither addressee appears to espouse Alexandrian principles. C. 95 indicates that Hortensius Hortalus is a long-winded versifier; likewise, the infelicities of c. 116 (to be discussed below) appear to parody Gellius' style[147] and thereby suggest that he, too, belongs to the old school.

C. 116 is more closely related to c. 1 than it is to c. 65. Both cc. 1 and 116 have poetry as their subject; both allude to Catullus'

Callimachean pretensions (1.1–2; 116.1–2); both make mention of erudition (1.7; 116.1) and the hard work that writing involves (1.7; 116.5); both refer indirectly to poetic inspiration (1.9–10; 116.1); both relate prayers and poetry (1.9–10; 116.6, where *preces* apparently signify poems[148]); and both have littérateurs as their recipients. The roles of these men of letters, however, are diametrically opposed. Cornelius Nepos, the author of a universal history (1.3.5–7), is a friend who encouraged the literary efforts of Catullus; his writing reflects the Callimachean qualities of refinement, conciseness, innovation, and learning that characterize Catullus' own poetry. By contrast, Gellius, a writer of invective poems (116.3–4, 6–7), is an enemy who seduced (or attempted to seduce) Lesbia (c. 91); if the stylistic oddities and archaisms in c. 116 parody his style,[149] Gellius plainly was not an adherent of Callimachean poetics. The antithetical relation between the two recipients reflects the antithetical relation between the two poems. By inverting motifs typically found in dedications, c. 116 forms the mirror image of c. 1.[150] The argument that c. 116 is "an inverted dedication," first articulated by C.W. Macleod, has won many advocates.[151] What has passed unnoticed, however, is that c. 116 literally reverses the verbal and thematic organization of c. 1. As figure 5.10 below illustrates, together cc. 1 and 116, in essence, constitute a single poem, joined by a ring-composition structure.[152]

The last three words in c. 116, *tu dabis supplicium*, echo the opening words in c. 1, *cui dono...libellum*, by repeating a pronoun, a verb for giving, and the notion of poetry (*supplicium* in 116.8 = poetry). While poetry is a gift in c. 1, it is to be a form of punishment in c. 116. The poems of Gellius described as *tela ista tua* in 116.7 and as *infesta tela* in 116.4 find their analogue in the history of Cornelius in 1.6 (*tribus cartis*) and the trifles of Catullus in 1.4 (*meas nugas*). Catullus' point appears to be to contrast his and Cornelius' literary work, which reflects Callimachean ideals, with that of Gellius, which presumably does not. The recipients of the poems, Cornelius and Gellius, form the next pair: they occupy exactly the same position of the third verse from opposite ends of the unifying structure. The correspondence between a good friend and a bitter

1	poetry as gift	Cui dono...libellum
3	addressee	Corneli
4	Cat.'s poetry	meas...nugas
6	Cornelius' history	tribus...cartis
7	labor	laboriosis
8	Cat.'s poetry	habe tibi quidquid hoc libelli
9	inspiration	<o> patrona virgo
1	inspiration	studioso animo venante requirens
1–2	Cat.'s poetry	tibi...carmina...mittere Battiadae
4	Gellius' invectives	tela infesta
5	labor	laborem
6	addressee	Gelli
7	Gellius' invectives	tela ista tua
8	poetry as penalty	tu dabis supplicium

Figure 5.10 Ring-Composition Structure of Poems 1 and 116

enemy here may explain the unusual postponement of the name of the addressee in c. 116 until the sixth verse.[153] *Laborem* in 116.5 complements *laboriosis* in 1.6; as was stated earlier, both words refer to the labor of composition. The poems of Callimachus that Catullus was going to translate for, and dedicate to, Gellius in 116.2 correspond to his own poetry book characterized by Callimachean qualities that he dedicates to Cornelius in 1.8. Finally, the "three images of seeking inspiration" in 116.1 (studioso...venante *requirens*) correspond to the Muse, the traditional source of inspiration, addressed in 1.9–10 (*<o> patrona virgo*).[154]

The ring-composition structure that unifies cc. 1 and 116 has important implications; such conscious artistry must reflect the *manum extremam* of the poet himself. And so for the often maligned c. 116, whose stylistic infelicities are explained as reflecting "an early work" or "hasty composition,"[155] it indicates that the "rather clumsy, casual, almost amateurish appearance" of the poem, with "the wholly spondaic verse 3, the change back and forth from singular to plural subject, and the suppression of the metrical role of 's' at the end of 'dabis' in verse 8" is deliberately contrived.[156] Catullus' purpose, surely, is to mimic the poetry of his enemy Gellius, which presumably was traditional, composed in an Ennian manner.[157] For the highly controversial issue of formal unity in the collection, the ring structure provides irrefutable evidence that Catullus himself is responsible for the disposition of the first and the last poems. As a frame, cc. 1 and 116 function as introduction and conclusion to the entire body of poetry, which—I am now nearly convinced—was issued in one roll.[158]

As is consistent with Catullus' practice, this thematic sequence of five ends as it began. The motifs of a pathic and erect male, which are combined in one figure in c. 112, occur as separate figures in c. 116.

The five-poem tag forms the symmetrical counterpart to the opening five poems, cc. 65–68b, in the numerical sequence that organizes the poems in elegiac couplets. But the function of cc. 112–116 is more than merely artistic. These phallic pieces are intended to respond to the recurrent theme of impotence in cc. 65–68b.

The collection closes in a manner that we moderns cannot help but find appealing. Instead of assuming the all too familiar persona as passive, whining, betrayed, or victimized, in c. 116 the poet depicts himself as virile, aggressive, vigorous, and in charge. This final glimpse of Catullus accords with the recent, unexpected turn of events in his *affaire de coeur*. Not only does Lesbia return to him (c. 107), but she does so on *his* terms (c. 109).[159] By the close of the elegiac epigrams, therefore, Catullus is ultimately victorious over all of his rivals. Despite justifiable anxiety about promises of eternal devotion, he nevertheless emerges in a position of dominance at the end. It is gratifying to see him in this role.

Chapter Six: Other Evidence

This chapter will consider other evidence, both internal and external, that Catullus himself is responsible for the present order of the transmitted text. Internal evidence that remains to be considered includes: (i) the ring arrangement and narrative continuity of the love poems, (ii) the complex system of numerical correspondence that accompanies the entire body of poetry, and (iii) the overarching chiastic structure that unifies the metrically disparate three parts by linking poems at the beginning, middle, and end. External evidence involves comparing the *Monobiblos* of Propertius and the *Odes* I–III of Horace to the *corpus Catullianum.* On the basis of striking parallels in theme and structure, it appears that both Propertius and Horace, near-contemporaries of Catullus, knew our text of the poetry and were responding to it.

The Love Poems

The Lesbia and Juventius poems together form a subpattern of major importance, for these forty-one pieces constitute over a third of the entire corpus. Although the love poems appear to be scattered indiscriminately throughout the three parts, there is method to the apparent disorder. As the diagram on page 265 illustrates, the Lesbia-Juventius poems are organized thematically along metrical lines in two rings. Cc. 24 and 81 at the center join the sequences of polymetric and elegiac poems. The pivotal function of these amatory pieces is indicated by a concomitant numerical pattern exhibiting exact equality. The sum of the verses in the participating poems in each half equals 260 respectively. As we shall see, the amatory pieces from first to last are carefully disposed so as to create a dramatic continuity, in which Catullus' tempestuous relation with Lesbia serves as the unifying theme. The role played by Juventius in this tale of grand passion is small but not insignificant, for the homosexual love poems are intended to complement and supplement the heterosexual love poems.

The Lesbia Polymetra

It has long been recognized that the opening sequence of Lesbia poems displays a meticulous order.[1] Poems 2, 3, 5, 7, 8, and 11 are arranged in the form of a miniature drama that traces the progression of Catullus' "affair with Lesbia as he wished it to be understood."[2] In cc. 2 and 3 Catullus and Lesbia are involved but the love is unfulfilled. In cc. 5 and 7 passion reaches its peak of intensity; Catullus, however, is fearful that something will go wrong. In c. 8 his fear is confirmed—Lesbia has lost interest. Finally, in c. 11 the love affair appears to be finished. Qualification is necessary here, for Catullus mentions his lady in passing in c. 13, just two poems after the resounding denunciation in c. 11. As recompense for Fabullus' catering his own dinner party, Catullus will give to him perfume, Lesbia's perfume, which was given to her by the Gods of Love. The point of this passing reference is to hint to a new reader of the book that c. 11 does not truly mark the end of the love affair; the Lesbia poems are to tell a story of an on-again, off-again relationship.[3]

The preceding interpretation of c. 13 is strengthened by c. 36, which has reconciliation as its subject. In this poem Lesbia has pledged to the Gods of Love to burn the choicest writings of the worst poet if Catullus were restored to her and if he ceased to write attacks against her. By "worst poet" Lesbia meant Catullus; Catullus wittily misconstrues her words to refer to the epic poet Volusius, whose *Annales* he assigns to the flames as a substitute for his own poetry. C. 36 is the first poem to mention Lesbia since c. 13, and it is the first poem to refer to the love affair since c. 11. The theme of reconciliation here is highly significant, therefore, because it indicates that Catullus is consciously connecting the Lesbia poems that occur in the second part of the polymetra (31–60) with those that occurred in the first part (1–30).

Verbal and thematic cross-references between poems 13 and 36 support the notion of a narrative unity. C. 36 begins by reversing the genealogy of ownership found in the closing verses of c. 13. There, at a dinner party to be held some time in the future, Fabullus is to be given perfume, which Catullus received from Lesbia, and which she originally received from the Venus and Cupid contingent (Venuses-Cupids -› Lesbia -› Catullus). Here Lesbia has pledged to the very same Gods of Love select poems of Catullus, which were given or sent to her earlier by Catullus (Catullus -› Lesbia -› Venus-Cupid). In addition, verbal repetition connects the beginning of c. 36 with the end of c. 13:

> nam unguentum dabo, quod MEAE PUELLAE
> donarunt VENERES CUPIDINESQUE,... (13.11–12)

> Annales Volusi, cacata carta,
> votum solvite pro MEA PUELLA.
> nam sanctae VENERI CUPIDINIQUE... (36.1–3)

meae puellae... Veneres Cupidines and *pro mea puella... Veneri Cupidinesque* appear at identical points in their verses, and the expression *Veneres Cupidinesque* occurs only once elsewhere, at 3.1.

The geographical section of c. 36 (12–15) also may relate to that in c. 11 (1–12), the penultimate Lesbia poem in the opening sequence. G. Williams comments on the curious inclusion and special prominence of the "Italian names" of Urii, Ancona, and Dyrrachium placed among Idalium, Cnidus, Amathus, and Golgi, "traditional Greek centres of Venus-worship." He suggests that "the context in which *all the names* (italics mine) make sense is a voyage from northern Asia Minor" to Italy;[4] in other words, the toponyms are intended to evoke Catullus' return route from Bithynia. If Williams is correct, the direction of cc. 11 and 36 is neatly inverted, as suits the themes of the two poems. In the one, travel away from Italy is used as a metaphor for separation from Lesbia; in the other, return to Italy is used as a metaphor for reunion with Lesbia.

The witty *Annales Volusi* may have been successful in effecting a reconciliation, but the very next poem indicates that the renewed relation is short-lived. In c. 37 Lesbia and Catullus are already on the "outs," and the poet attacks his lady for consorting with Egnatius in particular, an upstart from the provinces. The brevity of the reunion, signified through the interaction of cc. 36 and 37, perhaps is intended to foreshadow the coming poems of disillusion that characterize the second group of Lesbia polymetra.

In addition to its interplay with c. 36, c. 37 looks back to both poems 8 and 11 in the opening sequence. It recalls c. 11 in describing Lesbia's lovers as adulterers (*moechi* 11.17; 37.16) who number in the hundreds (*trecentos* 11.18; *centum an ducenti* 37.7); it recalls c. 8 in using identical language to convey the depth of Catullus' love for Lesbia (*amata...quantum amabitur nulla* 8.5; 37.12) and her loss of interest: *quae fugit* in the past tense in 37.11 poignantly echoes *quae fugit* in the present tense in 8.10. The striking verbal parallels between cc. 8 and 37 appear to indicate a responsive relation. The one poem closes with a series of questions: "Who now will approach you? To whom will you seem pretty? Whom now will you love? Whom will you kiss?" The other supplies the answer: "Anyone and everyone."

C. 37 also looks forward verbally and thematically to c. 51.[5] C. 37 ends with Catullus singling out one of Lesbia's lovers (Egnatius); this is precisely how c. 51 begins: *ille mi par esse deo videtur.* What is more, these poems and these poems only describe Lesbia as "seated." C. 51 opens with Lesbia sitting opposite a man who apparently is her lover (*sedens adversus* 3). This posture recalls the final image we have of her in c. 37, where she is sitting, in the sense of soliciting (*consedit*). The reminiscence is significant because it suggests that a note of bitterness underlies Catullus' description of his passionate feelings in c. 51.

A similar interpretation of c. 51 is prompted by its relation to c. 11. In perhaps the bitterest love poem of the collection, Catullus portrays Lesbia as a sex-crazed monster who embraces three-hundred lovers simultaneously, and loving none truly bursts again and again the loins of all of them. By contrast, he describes his love for her as a fragile flower grazed by a passing plow and left to die. Cc. 11 and 51 form obvious companion pieces owing to clear metrical and verbal cross-references. They are the only poems written in sapphics, and they are the only ones to use "the rare adverb" *identidem*, which occupies "the same metrical position in the stanza" at 11.19 and 51.3.[6] What is more, the projected adoption of the *vita activa*, the life of the soldier-adventurer, in stanzas 1–3 of c. 11 correlates with the repudiation of the *vita iners* in the final stanza of c. 51.[7] Reading c. 51 in light of c. 11 (and not vice versa) suggests subtle undertones of irony. And so on one level c. 51 can be construed as a "passionate confession of unrequited love,"[8] while on another level it expresses a lover's disillusionment.

C. 51 also points forward to c. 58. The two poems share verbal and thematic parallels. Both begin with anaphora of *ille/illa*, followed by the relative *qui/quam,* and both express passionate feelings. But while in c. 51 love is described in terms of physical sensations, in c. 58 feelings of love transcend physical attraction. In this poem Catullus states that he loved his lady more than he loved himself, more than he loved his family. C. 58 also diverges from c. 51 in that intensity of emotion lays the groundwork for utter condemnation. Catullus portrays his lady here as the most common of prostitutes.[9]

The close relationship of cc. 58 and 59, which are variations on the theme of debasement, was considered earlier.[10] In the second of the pair, the degradation of Lesbia reaches its nadir. Referred to as Rufa, she is portrayed in c. 59 as a *fellatrix*, who haunts cemeteries of the poor, stealing food from burning pyres (a metaphor for her indiscriminate and insatiable sexual appetite). Together cc. 58 and 59 form an antithetical counterpart to the *passer* poems, cc. 2 and 3. These damning portraits of Lesbia as one who aims to please "anyone anywhere" offer a shocking contrast to the charming picture Catullus draws of her as his beloved at the beginning of the collection.

The Juventius Polymetra

The series of Lesbia polymetra is punctuated by six Juventius poems disposed in two groups of three: 15, 21, and 24, and 38, 40, and 48 (see the diagram on page 265). The triadic organization appears deliberate, as is suggested by the way in which Catullus refers to his beloved. He specifically names Juventius in the third poems of each group (24.1; 48.1), while he alludes to him by the phrase *meos amores* in the first and second poems of each group (15.1; 21.4; 38.6; 40.7). Three of the six poems function as counterparts. Employing similar language, cc. 15, 21, and 40 warn a rival (probably the same rival) to keep hands off Juventius.[11] Two of the other Juventius poems, c. 48 and c. 38, correspond to Lesbia poems. Like cc. 5 and 7, c. 48 is about kisses; like cc. 30 and 60, c. 38 is about betrayal.[12] The last, c. 24, finds its counterpart in c. 81 of the elegiac epigrams. In both Juventius is in love with Furius.

The references to the love affair with Juventius in cc. 15, 21, and 24 and subsequently in cc. 38, 40, and 48 appear to be occasioned by the failed relationship with Lesbia in c. 11 and later in c. 37. Accordingly, it is reasonable to infer from the disposition of these poems that Juventius largely functions as a substitute for Lesbia.[13] (The *nomen* of Catullus' boy friend is in itself suggestive of his role, for the name means simply "youth.") What is more, the opening homosexual love poem, in which Catullus entrusts his boy to a flagrant pederast (c. 15), sets the tone for this series, the purpose of which is to provide comic relief from the intense emotions that characterize Catullus' obsessive preoccupation with Lesbia.[14]

As was suggested in Chapter 2, the Lesbia poems at the beginning and end of the polymetra build to a similar climax.[15] Each sequence culminates in Catullus' dismissing his lady as a nymphomaniac, incapable of commitment and unworthy of his love. At the very same time, however, that Catullus is denigrating Lesbia in the final polymetra, he is setting the stage for reconciliation. By stating in c. 58 that he loved his lady more than he loved his family and by reproaching her in c. 60 for showing lack of compassion in a recent personal tragedy (*novissimus casus* = the death of his brother), Catullus foreshadows the dramatic impulse that will reunite the lovers. In c. 68b love for Lesbia and love for the dead brother are combined in such a manner that Catullus in a sense is compensated for his loss by Lesbia's becoming his family. Transfer of affection from sibling to beloved, however, involves compromise. Reconciling himself to a relationship on Lesbia's terms, Catullus states that he will endure her occasional lapses from fidelity (68b.136). It is worth quoting T.P. Wiseman's observation on this remarkable change in attitude: "Instead of the jealous rage and the venomous attack that we might expect after the earlier poems, he [Catullus] resolves to accept the situation, showing a worldly tolerance quite new in his portrait of the affair."[16] This new-found resolve accounts for an important difference between the Lesbia poems in the polymetra and those in the elegiac epigrams. In the third part of the corpus, Catullus reacts to the infidelity of his lady with feelings of injury, disillusionment, and disappointment. Abuse and anger are directed against his rivals.

In c. 68b Catullus expresses his deep affection for Lesbia by combining two types of love, physical passion and *pietas*.[17] The conception of love here in terms of marriage, mutual obligation, and commitment prefigures the way in which Catullus will attempt to define his feelings for his lady in the coming poems. The idea of love as marriage also has important implications for Catullus' relation with Juventius. Catullus indicated earlier that homosexual affairs ended when a young man took a wife (61.125ff.). Thus, c. 68b is intended to foreshadow the few references to Juventius in the elegiac epigrams.

The Love Poems in Elegiac Meter

Both in subject and in language c. 68b is closely related to many of the Lesbia elegiac epigrams. The parallels are in fact so numerous that it seems clear that the poem was written or revised with a view to functioning as a programmatic prelude.[18] The elegiac epigram with which c. 68b is most closely linked is c. 109. These two poems that act as a frame for the love poems in the second half of the corpus correspond in a complementary manner. In the one poem Catullus accepts a relationship on Lesbia's terms, while in the other Lesbia accepts a relationship on Catullus' terms.[19] To his credit, Catullus the lover is skeptical in c. 109 that Lesbia really means what she says (although he hopes desperately that she does). The skepticism expressed here is found earlier in c. 70, the first Lesbia epigram, in which Catullus takes with a grain of salt his lady's insistence that she prefers marriage with him over anyone else. Not only is his doubt regarding the truth of her declaration in c. 70 confirmed in c. 72, but I think the vulnerability of one hopelessly in love is to be recalled in c. 107, which corresponds to both of these earlier poems (consult the diagram on page 265). In this poem of reconciliation, in which the lovers reunite at Lesbia's initiative, Catullus refers to himself twice in successive verses as *cupidus* (107.4–5). The adjective, which occurs elsewhere in the elegiac epigrams only at 70.3,[20] is deliberately pointed. The verbal cross-reference between cc. 70 and 107 makes clear that the reader is intended to recall the heartbreak of broken promises at the very moment that Catullus, a *cupidus amans*, experiences ecstatic happiness resulting from Lesbia's unexpected return.

The Lesbia poems that occur between the corresponding cc. 68b~109 and cc. 70~72~107 fall into two groups of seven poems each. The first group of seven poems deals largely with the themes of infidelity and rivals (73, 75, 76, 77, 78b, 79, 82). The second group of seven concerns real or apparent love of Lesbia for Catullus and of Catullus for Lesbia (cc. 83, 85, 86, 87, 91, 92, and 104). The dominant theme of the second group is intended to set the stage for reconciliation in cc. 107 and 109.

The fourteen poems are related to each other as follows. C. 85 reduces to a single eloquent couplet the themes of obsessive love and betrayal found in cc. 73 and 76. Cc. 77, 82, and 91 are joined by the theme of the seduction or attempted seduction of Lesbia, and cc. 77 and 91 further hold in common the theme of betrayed friendship (Rufus and Gellius). Cc. 83, 92, and 104 unite the topics of verbal abuse and passion, with the second poem elaborating on the subject of the first and with the third poem humorously inverting the point of the second. In c. 83 Lesbia abuses Catullus in her husband's presence (she must love him); in c. 92 Lesbia abuses Catullus, and Catullus abuses Lesbia (surely they love each other); in c. 104, however, Catullus denies ever verbally abusing Lesbia—he loves her too much. The relation of c. 79 (Lesbia prefers Lesbius to Catullus) and c. 86 (Catullus prefers Lesbia to Quintia) also has a witty point. Both poems pun on the family's cognomen, with *Lesbia...pulcerrima totast* echoing *Lesbius est pulcer.* Finally, cc. 75 and 87 set the infidelity of Lesbia to Catullus against the fidelity of Catullus to Lesbia.

Only two poems in the elegiac epigrams concern Juventius. The one, c. 81, forms the counterpart to c. 24. In both Catullus protests Juventius' choice of Furius as his lover. The other, c. 99, is related to the fragmentary c. 78b. These poems combine the themes of kissing and oral sex. In c. 78b Catullus attacks someone with an *os impurum* for polluting the kisses of (presumably) Lesbia. In c. 99 the shoe is on the other foot; Juventius, in rejecting a stolen kiss, acts as though Catullus were a prostitute who engaged in fellatio. Just as earlier the bitter denunciation of Lesbia in c. 11 paved the way for the introduction of Juventius in c. 15, so the termination of Catullus' affair with Juventius in this kiss-off poem prefigures reunion with Lesbia in cc. 107 and 109.

The reconciliatory cc. 107 and 109 provide a romantic close to the series of love poems. Yet our heart goes out to Catullus the lover because we know he is setting himself up for disappointment. He is too demanding; the perception of their love is not hers, but is entirely "his creation."[21] Because of his conflation of physical and familial feelings for Lesbia, the eventual dissolution of the affair will be devastating.

In writing on the originality of Catullus' Lesbia, R.O.A.M. Lyne remarks, "Catullus is, as far as we can judge, the first poet in Greek or Latin who decided to write about a particular love-affair in depth in a related collection of poems."[22] Catullus' innovative achievement, however, encompasses much more than this. The Lesbia poems (together with the Juventius poems) form a narrative unity. They tell a tale of a stormy relationship that is doomed to fail because the lovers do not have similar expectations. The homosexual and heterosexual love poems give coherence to the entire work: two-thirds of the collection is constructed around these forty-one poems. In assessing Catullus' achievement, we must bear in mind the experimental nature of the arrangement of poems long and short and of different meters, which makes his innovation of using the love poems as a frame for the corpus seem all the more remarkable.

Overarching Structure

Another way that Catullus unified his tripartite work was to create an overarching structure that joins poems at the beginning, middle, and end (see figure 6.1 on p. 238). For the discussion to follow, it is important to bear in mind that individual poems that occupy positions of structural importance in large collections often have multiple counterparts, and cycles of poems that occupy positions of structural importance often display multiple, overlapping arrangements. I make this observation because the poems that will provide a point of departure, cc. 61–68b, appear to be ordered in a ring-composition pattern, in addition to the binary and parallel structures that were examined earlier.[23] In the chiastic arrangement Catullus' masterpiece, the marriage of Peleus and Thetis, is enclosed by cc. 63 and 65/66, variations on the theme of anguish resulting from separation,[24] by cc. 62 and 67, both dialogues, and by cc. 61 and 68a/b, poems to and for Manlius.[25] Discussion will begin with the opening and closing pieces.

The relation of cc. 61 to 68a/b is largely antithetical. Although the three poems have in common the same recipient, Manlius Torquatus, and the same theme, that of marriage, cc. 68a and 68b both invert and subvert the felicitous celebration of conjugal love in c. 61. Catullus undermines the idealized relationship of Manlius and Vibia Aurunculeia that is to be based on mutual love and mutual fidelity in two ways: first, by intimating just seven poems later that the groom has been abandoned by his bride (68a.5–6) and second, by setting in opposition to Manlius' union his own non-marital involvement with Lesbia, which he depicts as a pseudo-marriage, adulterous, ill-fated, with commitment on one side only (68b.131–48). The point of the antitheses is to suggest "the instability and unreliability of all human relations," particularly those between a man and a woman.[26]

The next poems, 62 and 67, are both dialogues. In the one, choruses of young men and young women compete in an amoebean contest as they await the appearance of the bride. In the other, a personified door and unidentified interlocutor engage in scandalous gossip reminiscent of the humor and coarse banter that is characteristic of the *Fescennina iocatio,* a traditional part of a Roman wedding. A verbal reminiscence signals the relation. The opening of c. 67, *o [ianua] dulci iucunda viro, iucunda parenti* (1), echoes the end of the singing competition in c. 62, *[virgo maturo tempore] cara viro magis et minus est invisa parenti* (58). The link created between the nubile maiden in the one poem and the door addressed in language befitting a bride in the other[27] calls to mind the important role played by the house door in the Roman marriage ceremony, which J.P. Hallett describes as follows: "The Roman wedding ritual culminated in the *domum deductio*, the conducting of the bride to the entrance of her new husband's house. A bride's first act upon arrival was to grease the doorposts with wolf's fat, and to deck them with woolen fillets....She was then carried across the threshold, anything but a smooth crossing auguring badly for the future of her marriage. Thus her attention toward, and her anxiety over offending, the door of her husband's *domus* betokened a Roman bride's reverence towards her new place of residence."[28] The close association that existed in reality between a bride and the door of her new house thus strengthens a connection between cc. 62 and 67.

The poems are joined also by antithetical elements. The state of virginity that the maidens in c. 62 hold so dear is contraposed to the sexual promiscuity of the lady from Brixia in c. 67. In addition, as G.W. Most observes, filial *pietas* in the one poem and parental *impietas* in the other create "bitterly ironic balancing"; the articulation of "the proper relation between parents and children" in c. 62 (60–65) is set in sharp contrast to "the depiction of a son's cuckolding by his own father" in c. 67 (23–30).[29]

Cc. 63, 65, and 66 have as a common subject the pain of separation from family and friends. Physical distance separates Catullus from his dead brother, Berenice from her husband and "brother," and Attis from his friends, family, and home in Athens. (Catullus' brother, Berenice's husband, and Attis all are located in the same part of the world, too, either in Asia or Asia Minor.) Physical distance also separates the dedicated tress from her mistress' head.

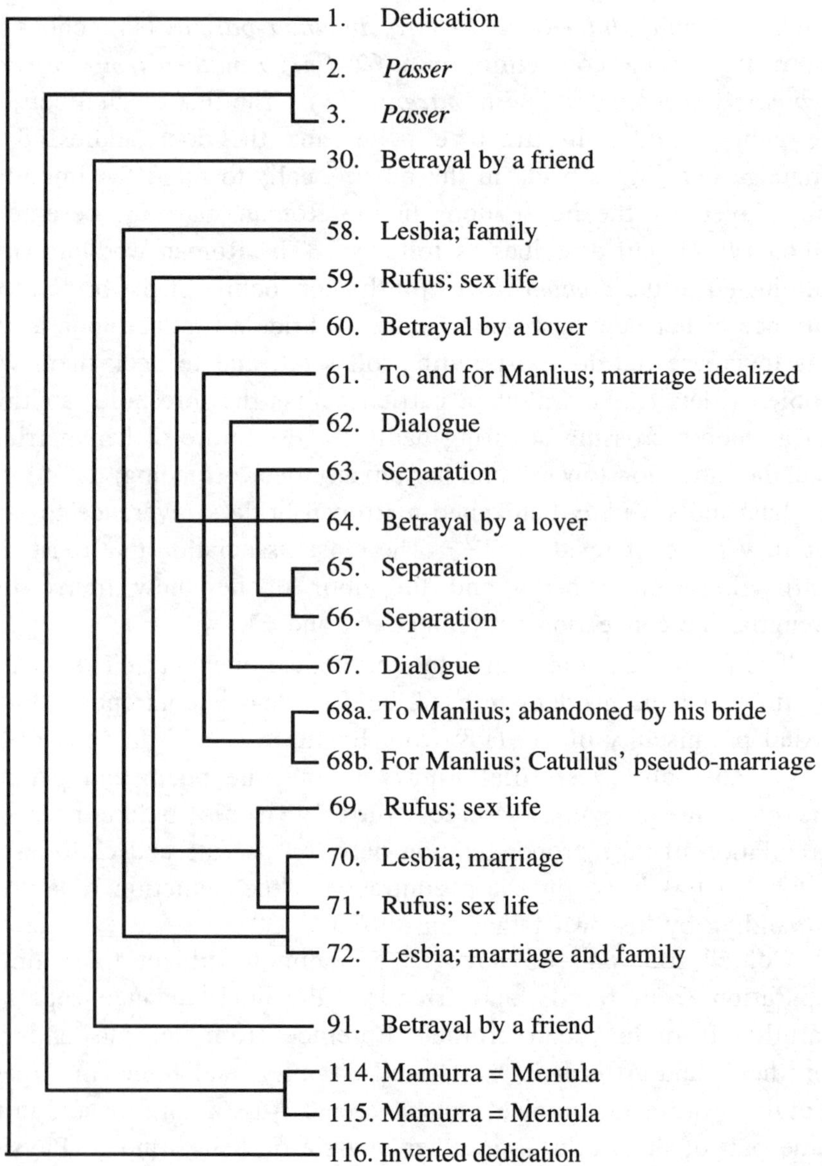

Figure 6.1 Overarching Structure of Catullan Corpus

Cc. 63 and 66 are further related through the motif of severance of a part of the body, genitalia in the one poem and a lock of hair in the other. Although the pairing of these particular body parts might seem odd to us moderns, in antiquity hair, like genitalia, was "closely associated with the seat of life itself."[30] As we shall see, the deliberateness of this connection can be shown through several parallels.

Both poems begin by referring implicitly or explicitly to the acts of severance in the opening verses. In c. 63 Attis unmans himself in verses 5–6. In c. 66 the first mention of the severed tress as *caesaries* in verse 8 evokes the idea of detachment, for popular etymology associated the CAES- element with the root for "cutting."[31] Both poems hold Venus ultimately responsible for the *disiecta membra*. In c. 63 excessive hatred of the goddess motivates Attis to emasculate himself (*corpus evirastis Veneris nimio odio* 17).[32] In c. 66 deep love for Ptolemy causes Berenice to make the vow to the gods for his safe return and to fulfill it. In both poems the severance effects radical transformations. In c. 63 not only is Attis now sexually ambiguous, but the animal imagery that pervades the poem suggests that as a result of this horrible, irreversible act he is no longer human.[33] By contrast, in c. 66 the humanized lock experiences a happier fate of apotheosis by undergoing catasterism. Finally, Attis and the lock react to their metamorphosis in similar terms. Both suffer extreme anguish over their altered state and long for a past irrevocably lost. Catullus set the comic situation of a lock of hair grieving over its separation from its sister locks and the queenly head in opposition to the tragic dehumanization and the permanent exile of the Greek Attis from home, family, and friends in order to heighten the pathos of c. 63.

C. 64 as the centerpiece combines major themes of the *carmina maiora*. It sets idealized love against love betrayed, marital commitment against non-marital involvement, and extreme happiness against utter despair. Its concerns, as those of the other eight poems, are universal and timeless, as it explores the relations "between parents and children,...between man and man, and between man and god."[34]

The *carmina maiora* are in turn ringed by a series of pieces on Rufus and Lesbia (58, 59, 69, 70, 71, and 72). Catullus' purpose is to join the beginning of the elegiac epigrams with the end of the polymetra.

The relation of cc. 59, 69, and 71 was discussed previously.[35] Linked by a common theme and a common target, all three poems attack Caelius Rufus by disclosing unsavory details of his sex life. In c. 59 he is being fellated by a *bustuaria moecha*; in c. 69 his success with the ladies is impeded by personal hygiene; and in c. 71 Rufus, now both gouty and smelly, has (somehow) managed to acquire a girl friend, but the love-making is less than satisfactory because she has to tolerate his body odor while he endures the pain of gout. The reason that Catullus inveighs against Rufus is not far to seek. C. 77, the last poem in which Rufus is named, reveals that he was one of Lesbia's lovers.

Cc. 58, 70, and 72 are bound by the complementary themes of the family and marriage.[36] C. 70 takes up the idea of a one and only relationship from c. 58:

C. 58

Caeli, Lesbia nostra, Lesbia illa,
illa Lesbia, quam Catullus unam
plus quam se atque suos amavit omnes,
nunc in quadriviis et angiportis
glubit magnanimos Remi nepotes.

C. 70

Nulli se dicit mulier mea nubere malle
  quam mihi, non si se Iuppiter ipse petat.
dicit: sed mulier cupido quod dicit amanti,
  in vento et rapida scribere oportet aqua.

In 58.2–3 Catullus states that he loved Lesbia alone more than he loved himself and more than he loved his family. In 70.1–2 Lesbia claims that she prefers to marry no one but Catullus. Two other verbal reminiscences, which occupy the same verses, strengthen the connection. *Mulier mea* in 70.1 echoes *Lesbia nostra* in 58.1, and *amanti* in 70.3 recalls *amavit* in 58.3, with Catullus in both instances serving as subject. Since c. 58 has Lesbia's sexual profligacy as its theme, the point of the relation appears to be to provide a subtle explanation for Catullus' skepticism regarding her declaration of devotion in c. 70.

Lesbia's inability to be true to Catullus is made explicit through the responsive relation of cc. 70 and 72. Catullus' doubt regarding the sincerity of Lesbia's assertion of commitment to him in the one poem is confirmed by the similar language and thought expressed in the past tense of the other:

> Nulli se dicit mulier mea nubere malle
> quam mihi, non si se Iuppiter ipse petat. (70.1–2)

> Dicebas quondam solum te nosse Catullum,
> Lesbia, nec prae me velle tenere Iovem. (72.1–2)

Presumably in c. 70 Lesbia said what she thought her lover wanted to hear.

The next verses of c. 72 call to mind c. 58, the only other poem that explicitly expresses love for Lesbia in terms of "a familial bond."[37] In c. 72 Catullus states that he loved Lesbia as though she were a member of his own family (*dilexi tum te non tantum ut vulgus amicam, / sed pater ut gnatos diligit et generos* 3–4), and in c. 58 he professes to have loved her more than he loved all of his family (*quam Catullus unam / plus quam se atque suos amavit omnes* 58.2–3). C. 72 also resembles c. 58 in that Catullus' declaration of love is followed by a jolting shift in temporal aspect. Placed at the beginning of verses 58.4 and 72.5, the adverb *nunc* forcefully returns the reader to the present and to Lesbia's promiscuous proclivities.

The interlacing of these six poems is intended to suggest the romantic involvement of Lesbia and Rufus. Their betrayal represents the epitome of *amicitia* violated since both lover and friend were simultaneously disloyal to Catullus.

The theme of betrayal is common also to c. 60. This enigmatic piece is linked tenuously to the magnificent c. 64 through similar language.[38] In creating this relationship, Catullus makes clear that he is identifying himself with Ariadne. Both he and she are victims of misplaced devotion, seduction, abandonment, and loss.

The central poems in the polymetra and elegiac epigrams deal also with the theme of betrayal.[39] Cc. 30 and 91 are directed to individuals who have been disloyal to Catullus, presumably in both instances by becoming involved with Lesbia. The poems further have in common that the perfidy of Alfenus and Gellius comes as a surprise to Catullus, although for quite different reasons. In the one Catullus trusted Alfenus because he was a good friend. In the other Catullus trusted Gellius not because of a long association but because Gellius appeared to be interested only in incestuous unions (and hence Catullus thought Lesbia was safe from his advances). The comparison makes evident that Catullus is playing with the theme of betrayed friendship by injecting a humorous twist in c. 91.

In the next poems under consideration, Catullus set forth separately themes that he combined elsewhere. The key to the connection between cc. 2~3 (*passer* poems) and cc. 114~115 (on the profligacy of Mamurra = Mentula) lies with c. 29:

> et ille nunc superbus et superfluens
> perambulabit omnium cubilia,
> ut albulus columbus aut Adoneus?
> cinaede Romule, haec videbis et feres?
> es impudicus et vorax et aleo.
> eone nomine, imperator unice,
> fuisti in ultima occidentis insula,
> ut ista vestra diffututa mentula
> ducenties comesset aut trecenties?

Here within the space of six verses Catullus equates Caesar's henchman Mamurra with a prick and a dove, a bird that not only is associated frequently with the *passer*[40] but, like the *passer*, is noted for its salaciousness.[41] The passage quoted above indicates, therefore, that to Catullus' mind amorous bird and penis are complementary images.

It should be observed that the association of *passer* and *mentula* would not have seemed odd to an ancient audience. Not only were phalluses in antiquity early and often conceived as birds, or furnished with wings,[42] but the lexicographer Festus supplies direct evidence for an obscene connection between the sparrow and the penis: *strutheum in mimis praecipue vocant obscenam partem virilem, <a> salacitate videlicet passeris, qui Graece strouthos dicitur.*[43]

Because sparrows can stand for male genitalia, the symmetry of cc. 2~3 and 114~115 has a further implication. Recent literature on the *passer* poems repeatedly has addressed the issue of whether the sparrow symbolizes the phallus of the poet.[44] Although an obscene reading is not essential to the appreciation of the sparrow poems, the relation of cc. 2~3 to 114~115 lends support to proponents of a double entendre.

The penis poems that enclose the collection are suggestive of its largely sexual content. Perhaps, too, through the phallic imagery this angry young poet is showing his contempt for the upper class of Roman society, which was so conservative and so unreceptive to new ideas and to newcomers.

The close relationship of cc. 1 and 116 was examined in the previous chapter.[45] The last of Catullus quite literally is the mirror image of the first, since c. 116 reverses the order of ideas and themes found in c. 1. The ring-composition structure that fuses dedication and inverted dedication into a single entity is significant because it offers clear proof that c. 1 functions as an introduction to the entire work.

Mathematical Symmetry

A third technique that Catullus used to integrate his poetry collection was to create a numerical pattern that encompasses all three parts. But before this piece of evidence is introduced, some preliminary discussion is necessary.

Mathematical symmetry is a characteristic feature of Latin poetry books of the first century B.C. It is found first in Catullus and last in Ovid and is used even by Lygdamus and Sulpicia of the *corpus Tibullianum*.[46] On an esoteric level mathematical symmetry reflects the *doctrina* or conscious artistry associated with this period of intense intellectual activity.[47] On a practical level it provides an invaluable tool for the literary critic interested in artistic arrangement. Taken together with verbal and structural clues, mathematical symmetry provides strong, if not definitive, evidence that the poet himself created the present order of his poetry collection.

There are two basic types of numerical patterns. The one type generally occurs in works of fifteen poems or fewer; in it the sum of, or the difference between, the number of verses in corresponding poems creates a pattern of near or exact equality. For example, in the *Eclogues* of Virgil, the sum of the verses in cc. 1 and 9 = 150, cc. 2 and 8 = 181, cc. 3 and 7 = 181, and cc. 4 and 6 = 149; in Tibullus, Book 1, the difference between the verses in cc. 1 and 10 = 10, cc. 3 and 9 = 10, cc. 2 and 8 = 20, 4 and 7 = 20, and 5 and 6 = 10. This type of numerical scheme reaffirms the pairing of thematically related poems and at the same time furnishes clear evidence that a ring arrangement functions as the primary organizing pattern (vis-à-vis a bipartite or tripartite structure, which is secondary). The other type of numerical scheme generally occurs in collections of more than fifteen poems. In it the sum of, or the difference between, the number of verses in groups of poems creates a pattern of near or exact equality. For example, Propertius' *Monobiblos* is organized in four groups or panels of five poems each. A numerical scheme of near equality reaffirms the interplay between cc. 1–5 (A^1) and 15–19 (A^2) and between cc. 6–9 (B^1) and 10–14 (B^2): A^1 = 89 distichs, B^1 = 71, B^2 = 70, A^2 = 88. This type of numerical scheme indicates that units of thematically related poems have been correctly identified. In some instances the numerical correspondence involves both addition and subtraction. For example, in the *Monobiblos* a second numerical scheme indicates that cc. 20–22, a coda of three poems, form an integral part of the book.[48] Here the difference between the totals of verses in the inner panels (B) and in the outer panels (A) equals the total of verses in the three-poem tag (C). Hence, $[A^1 + A^2] - [B^1 + B^2] = C$ or, more simply, A (177 distichs) – B (141) = C (36).

Mathematical symmetry performs another function. Because numerical patterns reaffirm interplay between individual poems or groups of poems, they generally exclude pieces without symmetrical counterparts and thereby indicate that non-corresponding poems, too, have been identified correctly.[49] For example, in the *Epodes* of

Horace the theme of the thirteenth poem, "to live for today," does not occur elsewhere in the book. The suspicion that this epode lacks a companion piece is reaffirmed by its omission from a numerical scheme in which there is near equality between the total verses in *Epodes* 1 through 8 (304) and those in *Epodes* 9 through 17 (303). Non-corresponding poems are a characteristic feature of collections consisting of more than ten poems. Their purpose is to provide a slight inconcinnity in a structure that would have been too symmetrically perfect.

A final point needs to be made before mathematical symmetry in the *corpus Catullianum* can be considered. Very large collections may have multiple overlapping numerical patterns. In Horace's *Odes* I–III, for example, the series of poems concerning Bacchus, Mercury, and Faunus, who are important gods for Horace, all display numerical correspondence. In addition, numerical schemes are characteristic of the poems that provide a frame for the three books and of those, too, that occupy key positions at the end of Books I and II and the beginning of Book III. Finally, a numerical pattern that embraces the three books as a whole reaffirms that all the poems that serve a structural function (those described in the preceding sentence) have been correctly identified.[50]

Mathematical symmetry in the poetry of Catullus is equally dazzling. As we saw earlier in this chapter, the love poems are accompanied by a numerical pattern exhibiting exact equality.[51] Its purpose is to indicate that the series of Lesbia and Juventius poems function as a pivot around which the other poems in 1–60 and 65–116 revolve. The mathematical symmetry concomitant to the long poems and poems written in elegiac couplets also was introduced previously.[52] A numerical pattern characteristic of smaller collections reaffirms the correspondences and structural integrity of cc. 61–68b, which divide along metrical lines into 61–64 and 65–68b. Catullus appears to have used this particular type of pattern here and only here because of the important function served by this magnificent group as the centerpiece of the corpus. Owing to its complex character the scheme is best illustrated by a mathematical equation: [64 (408) – 61~62 (309)] + [68a~b (160) – 65~66 (118)] = [63 (93) + 67 (48)].

Simply put: If the difference between the number of verses in each group of poems that act as a frame is added together (99 + 42), the total equals the sum of the verses in the central two poems (93 + 48). All other numerical schemes in the corpus involve the number of verses in *groups* of thematically related poems, and as in the long poems, all involve addition and subtraction. In the elegiac epigrams the difference between the totals of verses in the first (A) and second (B) cycles equals the total in the third (C): B, 148, – A, 82, = C, 66. The numerical pattern reaffirms the thematic delineation of the elegiac epigrams into 69–78, 78b–99, and 100–111. Another numerical pattern embraces all the poems in elegiac couplets. In this scheme the difference between the totals of verses in the introductory five long poems and in the three complete cycles of elegiac epigrams nearly equals the sum of the verses in the five-poem tag: 65–68b, 326 verses, – cc. 69–111, 296, is nearly equal to cc. 112–116, 28.[53] This numerical pattern is particularly significant for the long poems in elegiac couplets. It provides clear evidence that cc. 65–68b are to be taken with the other poems in elegiacs as well as with cc. 61–64.

Mathematical symmetry in the polymetra is problematical, however, because of the loss of poems and parts of poems that belonged to the second cycle. We possess only a few verses of 14b; we presumably lack the counterpart to 14b; and we presumably lack a counterpart for cc. 23 and 24.[54] The figure on the following page shows how the second cycle of polymetric poems was possibly arranged, with a gap of two poems between *O Colonia* and *Aureli, pater esuritionum*. The subject of the counterpart to 14b probably was poetry, that of the counterpart to cc. 23~24 homosexuality.[55]

Because these major losses are confined to a single cycle, we can reconstruct the numerical scheme that Catullus created for the polymetra if the following assumptions are made. First, since the organization of cc. 1–60 in many ways resembles that of cc. 69–116, chances are that the numerical patterns operate similarly. In other words, presumably the numerical scheme in the polymetra, as the one that accompanies the elegiac epigrams, involves cycles of poems and is based on addition and subtraction. Second, since later Latin poets

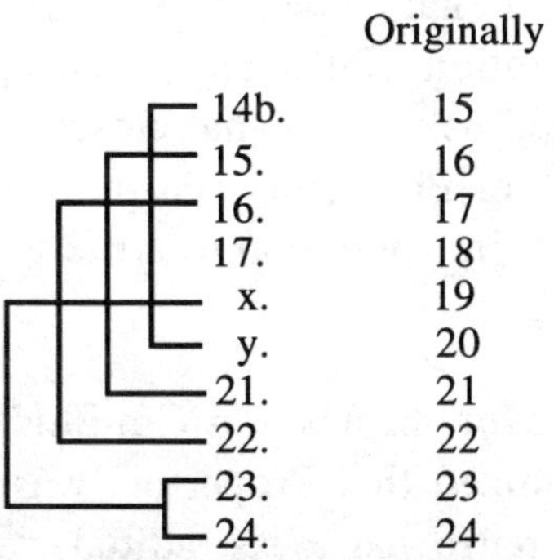

exclude non-corresponding poems from numerical patterns (as was discussed above), it seems reasonable to suppose that Catullus followed the same procedure with cc. 17, 30, and 48. Working under these premises, we can now restore mathematical symmetry to this part of the corpus. If thirty-six verses are added to the second cycle for the verses missing from 14b and from the lost poems indicated on the chart above by x and y, a pattern exhibiting exact equality emerges: If the total verses in the second and fourth polymetric cycles are subtracted from the total verses in the first and last polymetric cycles, the difference equals the total verses in the central cycle: [1–14 (252) + 45–60 (168)] – [15–24 (143) + 34–44 (180)] = 25–33 (97), or, more simply, 420 – 323 = 97.[56] Further evidence that the second cycle of polymetric poems originally contained approximately 143 verses can be offered by a final numerical scheme that embraces all the corresponding poems in the collection.[57] It works as follows. If the total verses in the polymetra (according to my calculations), X, are subtracted from the total verses in the long poems, Y, the difference equals the total verses in the three complete cycles of elegiac epigrams, Z: Thus, Y (1136) – X (840) = Z (296).[58]

Mathematical symmetry is one of several clues that reinforce structural design. But for a collection whose arrangement has often been denied to the poet, the complex network of mathematical schemes that overlap and interrelate one to another bears enormous significance. It is too contrived to be the result of chance. It is too elaborate to reflect the hand of anyone but the poet himself.

We now turn to the external evidence. Propertius and Horace, who belong to the next generation of Roman poets, appear to have read and studied a text of Catullus' poems that closely resembles our own, for both the *Monobiblos* of Propertius and the *Odes* I–III of Horace show striking parallels in theme and structure to the *corpus Catullianum.*

Propertius' Monobiblos and Catullus 69–116

It is generally recognized that Propertius was greatly influenced by Catullus. Propertius borrowed ideas, attitude, and language about love from Catullus. In the *Monobiblos* he took the Catullan technique of "dramatic reenactment" found in the Lesbia polymetra and used it in "virtually every Cynthia poem"; in addition, he adapted, and used extensively in this work, Catullus' use of mythical narrative to illuminate personal experience.[59] Propertius himself acknowledges his debt to his poetic predecessor at the outset of the *Monobiblos.* Here by alluding to an epigram of Meleager in the opening verses of the first poem, just as Catullus had in the dedicatory poem to Cornelius Nepos, he indicates that he is situating the *Monobiblos* "in the wake of Catullus' poetry."[60] So pervasive is Catullus' influence that even the structure of the *Monobiblos* appears to be modeled on that of the elegiac epigrams.

The elegiac epigrams of Catullus and the *Monobiblos* of Propertius are the only extant bodies of Latin poetry in which poems that lack symmetrical counterparts, which usually appear singly and sporadically, are combined as a group in order to form a concluding segment (112–116 and 1.20–22). Although the postponement of these poems until the end is notable, two other parallels make the possibility of imitation seem certain. The first concerns the themes of the poems that make up the tag. Both series contain all political poems but one (the political themes in Propertius 1.21 and 1.22 are especially conspicuous because of the exclusive amatory content of elegies 1.1–1.19), and the single non-political poems coalesce in having a literary subject. Propertius 1.20 and c. 116 are similarly addressed to men of literature, Cornelius Gallus and Gellius, and they similarly exhibit archaic features of language which are so striking that they appear to imitate consciously the style of the addressees.[61] The second parallel concerns the double numerical pattern. In both works poems in the coda are included in the second numerical pattern, but are excluded from the first, which reaffirms the identification of units of thematically related poems. In the first numerical pattern in Catullus, the difference between the total verses in the first and second cycles (148 and 82) equals the total in the third (66). In the second numerical pattern in Catullus, which involves cc. 65–68b, the difference between the total verses in the long poems in elegiac meter and those in the three complete cycles of elegiac epigrams (326 and 296) is nearly equal to the total verses in the five-poem tag (28). Likewise, in Propertius, one numerical pattern exhibits near equality, the other exact equality. In the first numerical pattern in the *Monobiblos*, the sum of the distichs in panel A^1 = 89, B^1 = 71, B^2 = 70, and A^2 = 88. In the second numerical pattern, the difference between the total distichs in panels A and B equals the total in panel C, the three-poem tag (177 – 141 = 36). To sum up, the postponing of poems that lack symmetrical counterparts until the end, the resemblance in themes displayed by these poems (political and literary), and the similarly complex double numerical pattern that both includes and excludes the tag poems clearly indicate imitation on the part of Propertius. His text of the third part of the *corpus Catullianum*, therefore, must have resembled our own.

It is thus possible to see the *Monobiblos* as a distillation of the entire Catullan *oeuvre*. Propertius borrowed the technique of dramatic reenactment from the Lesbia polymetra, the use of myth to illuminate personal experience from the central poems, and the structure of the poetry book from the elegiac epigrams.

Horace's Odes I–III and the Corpus Catullianum

The relation of Horace's *Odes* I–III to the Catullan collection bears even greater significance because of the similarity in size and general organization. The two bodies of poetry are of approximately equal length (around 2300 and 2450 verses), each consisting of three distinct parts. What is more, the structural integrity of these tripartite works is indicated in both instances through linkage of first and last poems. Horace's *Odes* 1.1 and 3.30 are related through meter and theme. The only pieces in the collection written in the first asclepiad, they treat the subject of the poet's immortality. In the one Horace aspires to immortality; in the other he has achieved it. Catullus 1 and 116 are related through theme and structure. C. 1 is a dedication, c. 116 an inverted dedication. While Horace employed a distinctive meter to indicate that his opening and closing pieces function as a frame, Catullus used structure to a similar end. Cc. 1 and 116 in essence form a single artistic whole through the chiastic organization that joins these contrasting poems.[62] It seems likely that Horace made obvious in his *Odes* a relationship that is subtle in the poetry of Catullus.

Both collections culminate in a series of poems whose structural integrity is readily observable. Catullus 61–68b all are comparatively long, and all are concerned directly or indirectly with the subject of marriage. *Odes* 3.1 through 3.6 all are in the alcaic (a sequence of poems in the same meter does not occur elsewhere in the three books), and all six poems treat civic issues. Fifty-eight poems precede the Roman Odes; approximately fifty-eight poems precede the *carmina maiora*. In addition, the thematic and structural importance of both cycles is indicated through the type of numerical scheme that occurs here. These cycles, and these cycles only in the two collections, are accompanied by the sort of pattern that generally is found in small bodies of poetry (like Virgil's *Eclogues*), where the sum of, or the difference between, the verses in corresponding poems creates a pattern. As we have already shown, numerical correspondence in the long poems of Catullus is quite intricate. In order to rival the complexity, Horace created four numerical patterns to accompany each of the four thematic schemes in which he ordered *Odes* 3.1–3.6.[63]

The collections begin with a similar thematic sequence. The opening poem is a dedicatory/programmatic piece (c. 1; *Odes* 1.1); it is followed by a poem displaying hymnic characteristics. In c. 2 of Catullus, the *passer* is deified; in *Odes* 1.2 Octavian is Mercury incarnate. A piece that personifies a ship occupies the fourth place in Catullus and the third in Horace. Catullus' ship has just returned from the East, while Virgil's ship is setting sail for the East. Catullus' poem ends with the *phaselus'* dedicating itself to Castor and Pollux. Horace's ode begins with his asking Castor and Pollux, along with Venus and Aeolus, to guide Virgil's ship to safety. The theme of *carpe diem*, combined with love, occurs in the next poems. Catullus 5 and *Odes* 1.4 in turn are followed by amatory pieces, in which a beloved is not identified. In c. 6 Catullus suspects that his friend Flavius is involved with some "hot little tart" (*febriculosum scortum*); in *Odes* 1.5 Horace wants to know who is the latest victim of the charms of Pyrrha, who radiates sexual passion, too, with a name deriving from the Greek for "fire." The opening sequences of themes bear sufficient resemblance to suggest imitation. Horace created a clear connection with the *corpus Catullianum* at the outset in order to place himself in a tradition in which he is both successor to and rival with his illustrious Latin predecessor.

The collections are organized similarly. Catullus arranged his poems in successive cycles. In order to unify the three parts, he created an overarching chiastic structure that joins poems holding prominent places at the beginning, middle, and end. Horace also arranged his poems in successive cycles. But instead of imposing a chiastic structure on a cyclic arrangement, Horace combined the two techniques (see the figure on page 253). Poems in the first half of the corpus (1.1–2.6) that find their counterparts in the second half (2.7–3.30) form an overarching structure. These poems, which are organized in groups of five or six, in turn form cycles (e.g., *Odes* 1.1–1.6 find their counterparts in 3.25–3.30, 1.15–1.19 in 3.12–3.16, 1.20–1.24 in 3.7–11, and 2.1–2.6 in 2.7–2.12). The other poems have a readily discernible cyclic organization since their thematic complements are in close proximity within each of the three books (e.g., *Odes* 1.7–1.10 find their counterparts in 1.11–1.14; *Odes* 3.17–3.19 in 3.20–3.23, etc.).

In both collections meter is employed as a structural tool. Catullus used meter to organize and define three major sections of his poetry. Poems 1–60 largely are composed in hendecasyllables; poems 65–116 all are in elegiac couplets; and cc. 61–64 are metrically mid-way between the other two groups, with 62 and 64 in dactylic hexameters and 61 in a combination of pherecratics and glyconics, the latter of which are truncated equivalents to the hendecasyllable. Horace used meter to organize and define smaller units of poems. For example, the Roman Odes all are in alcaics; *Odes* 2.2 through 2.11, the center, alternate sapphic and alcaic; *Odes* 1.30 and 1.38, which open and close the final cycle in Book I, are eight-line poems in sapphics; and so forth. Catullus introduced the principal meters of the polymetra in the first eleven poems. Improving on his predecessor, Horace introduced the principal meters of the entire collection in the first nine poems.[64]

The collections display other parallels. In both works certain poems function as a frame for the corpus—in Catullus, the love poems and in Horace, poems on poetry, politics, and friendship—and in both works these pivotal poems are accompanied by a numerical pattern. In both works numerical sequences function as an organizing tool. Catullus used the pattern 5 - 10 - 12 - 10 - 12 - 5 to order the third part of his *oeuvre*. Taking Catullus' innovative use of mathematical symmetry a step further to embrace the whole, Horace used the pattern 6 - 1 - 5 - 5 - 1 - 6 to order the odes in each half (1.1–2.6, 2.7–3.30) that form an overarching structure for the three books.[65] Horace also attempted to surpass his predecessor by doubling the six numerical patterns found in the poetry of Catullus. To the best of my knowledge, no other extant collection of poetry from antiquity contains as many numerical patterns as the *Odes* I–III of Horace.[66]

The poetry collections coincide in other details. In both, the poems that open each major section feature the Muse(s) or a Muse-equivalent, and in both, the dedicatory first poem associates the Muse with the immortality of the poetry. Also in both works, striking parallels join the poems that head each half of the collection (counting c. 2 and *Odes* 1.2 as the real beginning of the first half). In Catullus, cc. 2 and 65 conclude with allusions to famous myths that involve a lover's winning the heart of his beloved by means of an apple. In Horace, *Odes* 1.2 and 2.7 portray Mercury in an unusual role as savior, of the commonwealth in the one and of the poet in the other. Finally, for both works the poets contrived extremely complex

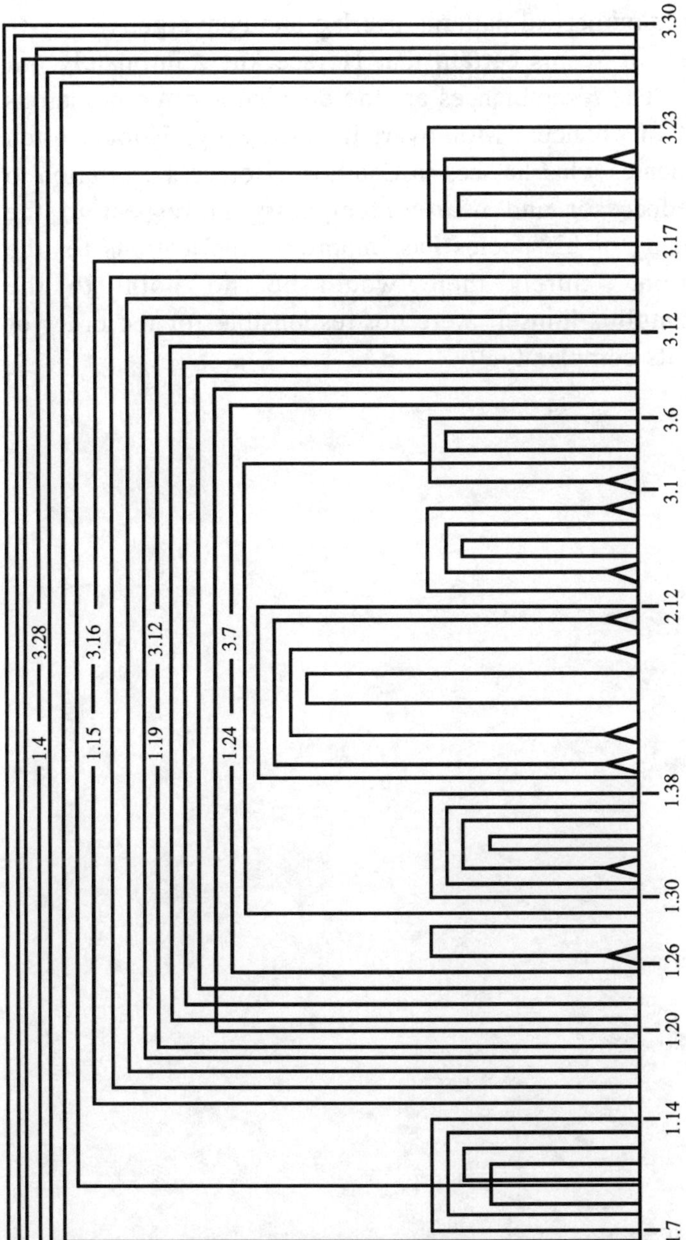

Figure 6.2 STRUCTURAL PATTERN OF THE ODES

organizations. Multiple thematic patterns underlie the primary structure; multiple numerical patterns overlap and converge.

In conclusion, it seems certain that Horace knew intimately our text of Catullus. The resemblances are too detailed and too numerous to be the result of chance. Moreover, in borrowing, Horace often refines or complicates what he sees in Catullus. Horace's aspiration to surpass his predecessor and near-contemporary in respect to the physical structuring of his poems has important implications for the Catullan Question. Surely there would be no point to the competition if Catullus himself were not responsible for the order of his poetry in all its complexity.[67]

Chapter Seven: The Epilogue

Catullus organized his poetry in nine consecutive ring structures on the basis of balanced similarities and contrasts, with a five-poem coda rounding off the whole. The formal design of the work is clearly his, for it is dazzling in its complexity. Verbal clues regularly reinforce correspondences. Mathematical symmetry accompanies and reaffirms the organization of the 118 poems (by my reckoning[1]) into units of cycles, and the pattern of exact equality that emerges from the total of verses in each of the major sections further attests to the unity of the whole.[2] The arrangement is complex and subtle; multiple thematic patterns underlie the primary structure and consequently provide additional texture to the collected work. The hand of the poet is reflected in the smallest details. The complementary character of the first and last poems further demonstrates the cohesiveness of the preserved text. Closure is achieved in c. 116 through the poem's reversing the order of ideas in c. 1.[3] The *corpus Catullianum* represents a remarkable achievement. The poets who followed Catullus learned much from his pioneering efforts.

Because cc. 1 and 116, taken together, in essence constitute a single poem, it seems clear that the dedicatory poem functions as a general introduction to the entire body of poetry. The noun *libellus* occurs in two instances only in the corpus, in c. 1 and its counterpart, c. 14.[4] Possibly Catullus is suggesting the heterogeneous content of his own *libellus* through the meaning he assigns to the word in c. 14, where it indicates an anthology of pieces.[5] The proposal that the diminutive in c. 1 is a neoteric affectation that actually refers to all the subsequent poetry receives support from the structurally versatile cc. 65–68b. These poems belong simultaneously to both cc. 61–64, of which they form an integral part, and to cc. 69–116, which they introduce.[6]

Since Catullus often signals relationships among corresponding poems through verbal clues, it is reasonable to suppose that he expected the reader to perceive the subtle artistry that he created. But like the quality of some of the poems, the arrangement is sometimes uneven. For example, in the case of cc. 78b–99 with its twenty-two poems, the cycle is almost unwieldy. In the case of cc. 45–60, the relationships among some of the poems are difficult to ascertain owing to their tenuous character. What is more, the distinct themes of love and political invective, which are combined at the end of the cycle into invective against a lover, somehow provides unsatisfactory closure to this lengthy group of 16 poems as well as to the polymetra as a whole. These infelicities are nevertheless important because they offer evidence of originality. Catullus was experimenting, and struggling, with arranging a large collection of poems in a meaningful manner. The earliest datable poems appear to belong to B.C. 65 (cc. 102 and 108).[7] The 118 poems, therefore, could have been written over a span of eleven years. This would allow time for success and failure and for the development of ideas and techniques. It is certain that Catullus wrote many poems that he discarded because he felt that they were not good enough to be included. It seems equally certain that like other first-rate poets he wrote many versions of the poems that now appear in the transmitted text. In addition, Catullus must have made perhaps many revisions in order to create the complicated system of mathematical symmetry that accompanies and forms an intrinsic part of the artistic design.

The experimental nature of the arrangement suggests to me that Catullus did not plan an edition consisting of three parts from the outset. Rather, it seems more likely that the notion of composing a large collection of poetry of various meters, themes, and lengths, and of organizing such a work into an integrated whole evolved over time. Chances are that Catullus had written a sufficient number of mostly short poems, both elegiac epigrams and polymetra, and was considering how he was going to publish these pieces when the idea occurred to him. His source of inspiration appears to have been Meleager, who published his *Garland* shortly after B.C. 100.[8]

This Hellenistic poet, who appears to have flourished a generation before Catullus, assembled and organized artistically his own poems and those of other poets from different periods into an anthology that probably was published in several books owing to its considerable size. His organizational principle seems to have been to group together poems on the same or similar themes and to intersperse his own poems with those of older poets, his pieces often being variations on theirs.[9] The sequences identified as Meleagrian in the *Greek Anthology* show a unity of theme, with verbal repetition in many instances joining one poem with the next.[10] Although it may have made sense to Meleager to place together blocks of poems that deal with the same subject, such an arrangement results in a certain unfortunate repetitiveness. Catullus saw interesting ideas and techniques in the *Garland* that he could borrow and improve on. The notion of putting together poems on similar themes was appealing. The fact that Catullus composed as well as arranged all of the poems in his *oeuvre* enabled him to create greater thematic variation in related sequences (a comparison of blocks of thematically related pieces in Catullus with those in Meleager illustrates the subtlety and sophistication of Catullus' artistry over that of his Greek antecedent).[11] It also enabled him to organize his poetry in a more complicated manner by exploiting both linear and circular structures. I suspect, too, that while the corpus of Catullus functions as a coherent unity, the anthology of Meleager did not because of its unwieldy size of around 1000 epigrams.

Meleager was interested in romantic love. He appears to have been the first ancient poet to compose a series of poems that concern the same lover (the chief objects of his affections are Zenophila, Heliodora, and Myiscus).[12] Catullus, too, was interested in romantic love and, inspired by Meleager, took his innovation several steps further. Not only does "Catullus...write about a particular love-affair in depth in a related collection of poems,"[13] but in so doing he explores sexual love in all its complexity. What is more, because the love poems, both heterosexual and homosexual (for they are complementary) coalesce as a group, they serve to unify the entire work. Making up more than a third of the corpus, they provide a frame around which the rest of the poems pivot.[14] The creation of a numerical pattern to accompany the love poems and to indicate their pivotal character appears a Catullan innovation, too.[15] The predominance of the love poems throughout the corpus suggests that even before Catullus decided to publish his best poems in their present form, as a poet he was interested primarily in love.

Pairs form the building blocks for the nine cycles and five-poem coda of thematically related pieces. According to my calculations, Catullus composed 64 of the 118 poems to function as counterparts in the primary structure (this figure is modest; he probably composed more than that). The chart on page 260 lists corresponding poems with close relationships. Catullus wrote some of these poems contemporaneously to function as pairs (possibly, for example, cc. 12 and 13; 50 and 51; 70 and 72; 83 and 92), while he wrote other poems at a later time to function as complements to earlier ones (for instance, c. 1 is later than c. 14; c. 68a is probably later than c. 65). Chances are that corresponding poems that do not display a close relationship were not conceived as pairs (e.g., cc. 26 and 31, 86 and 93, 82 and 91, etc.). It seems reasonable to speculate that when Catullus began to organize his poetry, he had preconceived ideas about what themes would dominate in each cycle so that he could leave space for poems that he would write at some point in the future. For example, a majority of the poems that belong to the first cycle, cc. 1–14, probably were in place by the end of B.C. 56, with the exception of cc. 1 and 11, which appear to have been written shortly before the collection was published. The nearly completed cycle would have enabled Catullus to compose and fill out the final group of polymetra with poems that echo many of the themes found in the first (many of the poems in cc. 45–60 appear to be relatively "late").

Within the polymetra O. Skutsch identified two groups of hendecasyllables that appear to belong roughly to the same period of composition. In cc. 2 through 26, 13 of 16 poems in hendecasyllables consistently open in the first foot with a spondee base; in cc. 27 through 58 and c. 1, 15 of 23 poems in hendecasyllables open in the first foot with either an iambic or trochaic variation.[16] The significance of this observation is that the hendecasyllables in cc. 2 through 26 appear to be earlier than c. 1 and the majority of the hendecasyllables in cc. 27 through 58, in which Catullus has relaxed his technique.

It is difficult to talk about relative chronology in the elegiac epigrams because so few of the poems can be dated. Cc. 102 and 108 appear to be the earliest poems in the entire work; the references to Cornelius and Cominius suggest the year B.C. 65. The connection between Aemilius and Vettius in cc. 97 and 98 may indicate a date of B.C. 59,[17] and if the *vir* in c. 83 refers to Lesbia's husband, Q. Metellus Celer, this poem may refer to the same year or an earlier one. The Caelius Rufus poems (cc. 69, 71, 77, and 100) appear to belong to B.C. 56 because as a group they allude to his prosecution in the spring of this year. The final poem, c. 116, is probably late, owing to its close relationship with c. 1, which as the dedication was probably one of the last pieces written for the collection. Accordingly, even if a majority of the elegiac epigrams predate the polymetra, Catullus appears to have been writing both kinds of poems during the same period. It seems clear, too, that the two groups of short poems are intended to bear a certain thematic resemblace to each other. For this reason similar themes occur in similar positions—the polymetra and elegiac epigrams both begin with a closely connected sequence of Lesbia poems and end with a series of political invectives.

Cc. 61–68b surely represent some of the latest pieces, as is suggested by their lofty themes, by their technical brilliance, and by their involved organization. As the central panel, they epitomize the major concern of Catullus' poetry, which has to do with different kinds of relationships—those between male friends, those between lover and beloved, between parents and children, husbands and wives, and men and gods—and the moral obligations that these relationships impose.

It is important to bear in mind that even if the guesswork about Catullus' organizational procedure and about the relative chronology is roughly accurate, much rewriting and reworking must have taken

cc. 1~14	Gift of a *libellus* (parallel structure)
cc. 2~3	*Passer* poems
cc. 5~7	Kiss poems (parallel structure)
cc. 6~10	*Scorta* poems (parallel structure)
cc. 12~13	Symposia (parallel structure)
cc. 15~21	Warnings to Aurelius
cc. 23~24	Furius' poverty
cc. 25~33	Thieving *cinaedi*
cc. 27~32	Hard drinking/hard loving (parallel structure)
cc. 28~29	Provinces (parallel structure)
cc. 37~39	Egnatius
cc. 38~40	Juventius
cc. 41~43	Amiana
cc. 50~51	Love and poetry (ring-composition structure)
cc. 53~56	Anecdotes (parallel structure)
cc. 58~59	Lesbia (parallel structure)
cc. 61~62	Marriage hymns
cc. 65~66	Covering letter and concomitant poem
cc. 65~68a	Covering letters (parallel structure)
cc. 68a~68b	Covering letter and concomitant poem
cc. 69~71	Rufus the stinker
cc. 70~72	Lesbia; verbal commitment
cc. 73~76	Betrayal by Lesbia
cc. 74~78	Gellius and his uncles
cc. 78a~99	Fellatio and kisses
cc. 83~92	Unconscious passion
cc. 88~91	Gellius and the enormity of his *scelera*
cc. 89~90	Gellius and incest
cc. 97~98	Foul mouths of Aemilius and Victius
cc. 101~107~109	Reconciliation with Lesbia compensates for loss of brother
cc. 100~110~111	Aufillena
cc. 114~115	Mentula (parallel structure)

Figure 7.1 Poems Written to Form Pairs in the Primary Structure

place before the collection was issued in its final form. This observation is prompted by the qualities of *labor* and *doctrina,* meticulous workmanship combined with erudition and sophistication, which the New Poets so esteemed, by the complicated character of the arrangement itself, and by the equally complicated system of numerical patterns. And it is the complexity of the *corpus Catullianum* that is one of its most remarkable features. Linear and circular structures coalesce in harmony. Thematic subpatterns complement the primary structure. The theme of love unifies and gives coherence to the whole. Sophisticated and complicated numerical patterns accompany and reinforce the design of the poetry in a way that I suspect was not witnessed before Catullus' time. In the hands of this very accomplished poet, form and meaning are intimately bound. Structure often illuminates problems of text and interpretation. At the very least it deepens an appreciation of the individual poems.

It has long been recognized that Catullus was an innovator and a pioneer. Because the extent of his originality has been underestimated, his achievement and importance in the history of Latin literature needs to be reassessed. This collection—which is unlike any other that has survived from antiquity, and I suspect was *sui generis* even in Catullus' day—is, among other things, a bold and brilliant experiment in structural organization. This experiment, which largely succeeds, intimidated some of Catullus' successors while it challenged others. Clearly Catullus deserves the acclaim that often has been accorded to him as one of Rome's greatest poets.

1.2	read *arido* for *arida*
2.9	read *posse* for *possem*
3.16	read *quod, miselle passer*, for *o miselle passer*
14.16	read *salse* for *false*
22.6	read *novae bibli* for *novi libri*
25.5	read *conviva cum ebriosior se tendit oscitanter* for *cum diva mulier aries ostendit oscitantes*
26.1	read *nostra* for *vestra*
29.23	read *urbis o piissimi* for *urbis opulentissime*
32.1	read *Ipsithilla* for *Ipsitilla*
41.1	read *Amiana* for *Ameana*
54.2	read *Hirri* for *et eri*
	read *rustica et* for *rustice*
55.3	read *in Campo* for *Campo*
55.4	read *sacellis* for *libellis*
55.8	read *serenas* for *sereno*
55.9	read *avelli sinite* for *avelte, sic*
55.13	read *Herculi* for *Herculei*
55.11	read *nudum sinum reducens* for *nudum reduc...*
55.22	read *sim ego particeps* for *sim particeps*
58.5	read *magnanimos* for *magnanimi*
58b.2-3	invert verses *non Ladas* and *non si*
58b.5	read *plumipedes* for *plumipedas*
58b.7	read *vinctos* for *iunctos*
58.5	read *magnanimos* for *magnanimi*
61.16	read *Vibia* for *Iunia*
64.395	read *Ramnusia* for *Amarunsia*
68.157	read *auctor* for *aufert*
71.4	read *apte* for *a te*
73.6	read *quae* for *qui*
90.5	read *gnatus for gratus*
95b.1	supply *sodalis*
100.6	read *perspecta est igni tum* for *perspecta ex igni est*
107.7	read *umquam* for *hac est*
107.8	read *optandam vitam ducere* for *optandus vita dicere*
111.4	supply *parere*
112.1	read *<est qui>* for *<est quin>*
112.2	read *descendit* for *te scindat*
115.5	read *altasque paludes* for *saltusque paludesque*
116.5	read *acta* for *amitha*

Arrangement of the Love Poems

	No. of Verses
2. *Passer;* unfulfilled love	13
3. *Passer;* unfulfilled love	18
5. Kissing (Lesbia)	13
7. Kissing (Lesbia)	12
8. Affair is disintegrating; who will love Lesbia?	19
11. Destructive character of Lesbia's love	24
13. Reference to Lesbia intimates that affair is not over; gift-giving	14
15. Aurelius warned to keep hands off Juventius	19
21. Aurelius warned again: hands off Juventius	13
24. Catullus protests Juventius' love for Furius	10
30. Betrayal by Alfenus	12
36. Reconciliation; giving of poetry	20
37. Response to Poem 8: everyone will love Lesbia	20
38. Betrayal by Cornificius (Juventius)	8
40. Ravidus warned to desist (Juventius)	8
48. Kissing poem (Juventius)	6
51. Destructive character of love for Lesbia	16
58. Lesbia = whore of lowest sort	5
59. Lesbia (= Rufa) = *bustuaria moecha*	5
60. Betrayal by Lesbia	5
68b. Catullus accepts love on Lesbia's terms	120
70. Catullus, a man in love, should be skeptical of Lesbia's words	4
72. Skepticism confirmed	8
73. Pain resulting from Catullus' unrequited devotion	6
75. Lesbia's infidelity	4
76. Pain resulting from Catullus' unrequited devotion	26
77. Rufus seduced Lesbia	6
78b. Kisses taken at a price	6
79. Lesbia prefers Lesbius	4
81. Catullus protests Juventius' love for Furius	6
82. Quintius has attempted to seduce Lesbia	4
83. Lesbia verbally abuses Catullus (she must love him)	6
85. Theme of 73 and 76 reduced to a couplet	2
86. Catullus prefers Lesbia	6
87. Catullus' profession of love and fidelity	4
91. Gellius seduced Lesbia	10
92. Lesbia maligns Catullus, and Catullus Lesbia	4
99. Kisses taken at a price; Catullus cured of love for Juventius	16
104. Catullus could never malign Lesbia	4
107. Catullus, a man in love, is reconciled with Lesbia	8
109. Lesbia accepts love on Catullus' terms	6

Sum of verses = 260

Ring Arrangement of the Catullan Corpus

1. Gift of a *novus libellus*
2 + 2b. *Passer*: solace
3. *Passer* : grief
4. Homecoming of Catullus
5. Kiss Poem
6. Flavius' *scortum*
7. Kiss poem
8. Kisses no more
9. Homecoming of Veranius
10. Varus' *scortum*
11. Journey away from home
12. Symposium: boorishness
13. Symposium: urbanity
14. Gift of a *novus libellus*

15. Warning to Aurelius
16. Biographical fallacy
    17. Colonia and her bridge
21. Second warning to Aurelius
22. Biographical fallacy
23. Furius' poverty
24. Furius' poverty

RIVALS

25. To thieving *cinaedus*, Thallus
26. Catullus' villa
27. Hard drinking
28. Misuse of gubernatorial power
29. Misuse of gubernatorial power
    30. Betrayal by a friend
31. Catullus' villa
32. Hard loving
33. To thieving *cinaedi*, Vibennius, Sr. and Jr.

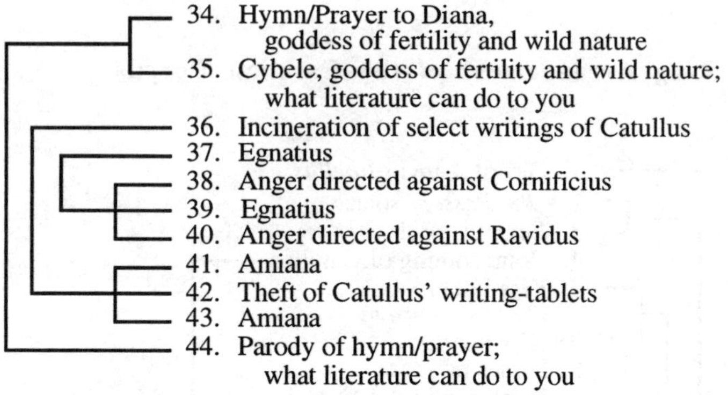
34. Hymn/Prayer to Diana,
goddess of fertility and wild nature
35. Cybele, goddess of fertility and wild nature;
what literature can do to you
36. Incineration of select writings of Catullus
37. Egnatius
38. Anger directed against Cornificius
39. Egnatius
40. Anger directed against Ravidus
41. Amiana
42. Theft of Catullus' writing-tablets
43. Amiana
44. Parody of hymn/prayer;
what literature can do to you

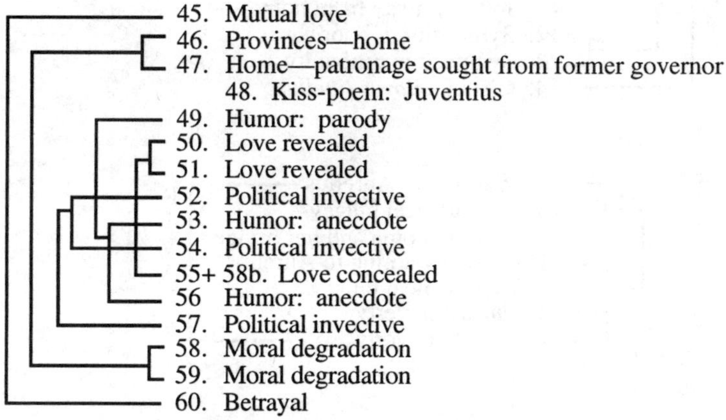
45. Mutual love
46. Provinces—home
47. Home—patronage sought from former governor
48. Kiss-poem: Juventius
49. Humor: parody
50. Love revealed
51. Love revealed
52. Political invective
53. Humor: anecdote
54. Political invective
55+ 58b. Love concealed
56 Humor: anecdote
57. Political invective
58. Moral degradation
59. Moral degradation
60. Betrayal

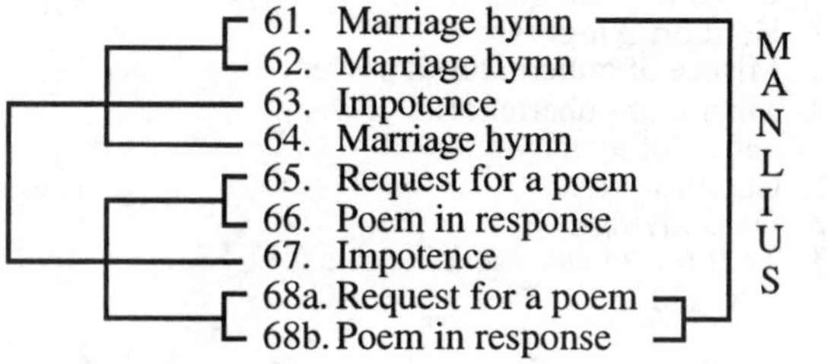
61. Marriage hymn
62. Marriage hymn
63. Impotence
64. Marriage hymn
65. Request for a poem
66. Poem in response
67. Impotence
68a. Request for a poem
68b. Poem in response
MANLIUS

69. Rufus the stinker
70. Lesbia's preference for Catullus
71. Rufus the stinker
72. Lesbia's former preference for Catullus
73. Disillusionment
74. Gellius and Uncle
75. Betrayal by Lesbia
76. Disillusionment
77. Rufus' affair with Lesbia
78. Uncle and Gellius

RIVALS

78b. Oral sex; kissing
79. Oral sex; kissing
80. Paleness
81. Paleness
82. Seduction of Lesbia
83. Lesbia abuses Catullus
84. Hyperaspiration and rusticity
85. Intensity of Catullus' love
86. Discriminating taste
87. Catullus' love and fidelity toward Lesbia
88. Gellius: *scelus*
89. Gellius: *nefas*
90. Gellius: *nefas*
91. Gellius: *scelus*; seduction of Lesbia
92. Lesbia abuses Catullus and Catullus Lesbia
93. Indifference toward Caesar
94. Undiscriminating taste
95 + 95b. Prolixity and rusticity
96. Calvus' love and devotion to Quintilia
97. Stinking Aemilius
98. Stinking Victius
99. Oral sex; kissing

100. Aufillena
101. Brother's death
102. Pledge of silence
103. Prostitution
104. Catullus has never written obscenities against Lesbia
105. Mentula, symbolic of obscene verse
106. Prostitution
107. Reconciliation with Lesbia
108. Cominius' tongue to go first
109. Reconciliation with Lesbia
110. Aufillena
111. Aufillena

112–116 form a five-poem tag.

Notes

Chapter One: Introduction

1 J.D. Minyard, "The Source of the Catulli Veronensis Liber," *CW* 81 (1988) 347–50.

2 Most Catullan specialists today appear willing to concede that the ordering of at least part of the collection (1–50 or 1–51) reflects the poet's hand. For an extensive bibliography on the Catullan question, see T.K. Hubbard, "The Catullan Libellus," *Philologus* 127 (1983), especially pages 218–23, notes 1–21.

Additional bibliography now includes: M. Pulbrook, "The Lesbia Libellus of Catullus," *Maynooth Review* 10 (1984) 72–84; J. Ferguson, "The Arrangement of Catullus' Poems," *LCM* 11.1–2 (1986) 2–6, 18–20; Minyard (above, note 1) 343–53; H. Dettmer, "Design in the Catullan Corpus: A Preliminary Study," *CW* 81 (1988) 371–81; J.K. King, "Catullus' Callimachean Carmina, cc. 65–116," *CW* 81 (1988) 383–92; and P.Y. Forsyth, "Catullus 14B," *CW* 83 (1989) 81–85;

3 Terms used in *A.P.* 4.1 (= G-P 3926) appear to indicate that the *Garland* included poems in lyric meters (A.L. Wheeler, *Catullus and the Traditions of Ancient Poetry* [Berkeley 1934] 38).

4 *Ibid.* 40.

5 On the date, see A. Cameron, *The Greek Anthology*: *From Meleager to Planudes* (Oxford 1993) 56.

6 Catullus 1.1, "To whom shall I give my charming new book?" (*Cui dono lepidum novum libellum*) echoes Meleager *A.P.* 4.1 (=G-P 3926), "To whom, dear Muse, shall you bring this song rich in every kind?" (Μοῦσα φίλα, τίνι τάνδε φέρεις πάγκαρπον ἀοιδάν;). On *A.P.* 7.195 and 196 serving as a model for Catullus 2, see J.D. Bishop, "Catullus 2 and its Hellenistic Antecedents," *CP* 61 (1966) 158–67. On the relation of Catullus 3 to *A.P.* 7.207, see R.F. Thomas, "Sparrows, Hares, and Doves: A Catullan Metaphor and its Tradition," *Helios* 20 (1993) 131–42. For Meleager's *Garland*, see J. Geffcken, *RE* XV 481–88; and now Cameron, *The Greek Anthology* (above, note 5) 1–56.

7 Catullus' experiment enabled Horace, his successor, to use meter as an organizing tool in the *Odes* I–III in a more sophisticated fashion.

8 *Catullus*: *The Complete Poetry* (Ann Arbor 1964) xi.

9 Catullus' innovations are difficult to assess because he is the only one of the New Poets whose work survives.

10 *Clio's Cosmetics*: *Three Studies in Greco-Roman Literature* (Leicester 1979) 177.

11 C.W. Macleod, "The Artistry of Catullus 67," *Collected Essays of C.W. Macleod* (Oxford 1983) 192, note 1.

12 The programmatic character of c. 116 is discussed by C.W. Macleod in "Catullus 116," *CQ* 23 (1973) 304–09. On the close relation of cc. 1 and 116, see pages 223–26.

13 The four Gellius poems, which together form the centerpiece of the poems in elegiac meter, culminate in c. 91.

14 There is often, however, little agreement where these sequences begin and end. For the present discussion it is important only that critics have recognized that poems tend to form unified blocks that coalesce through one or more predominant themes.

15 For the best discussion of the relationships among these poems, see C.P. Segal, "The Order of Catullus, Poems 2–11," *Latomus* 27 (1968) 305–21.

16 For cc. 12–14 as transitional poems, see P.Y. Forsyth, "Gifts and Giving: Catullus 12–14," *CW* 78 (1985) 571–74.

17 E.A. Schmidt suggests that cc. 35, 36, 37, 42, and 44 make up a "Zyklus der Ding-Apostrophen" ("Catulls Anordnung seiner Gedichte," *Philologus* 117 [1973] 221–24).

18 M.B. Skinner, *Catullus' Passer: The Arrangement of the Book of Polymetric Poems* (New York 1981) 74–75. She, however, sees these final poems as "a jumble of…unfinished verses."

19 R. Ellis, *A Commentary on Catullus*, 2nd ed. (Oxford 1889) 208.

20 T.P. Wiseman, *Catullus and his World: A Reappraisal* (Cambridge 1985) 169. For discussion of 69–92, see pages 164–73, and also pages 25–28 of his earlier work, *Catullan Questions* (Leicester 1969). For 93–116, see *A Reappraisal* 173–75 and *Catullan Questions* 28–29.

21 As a matter of convenience, this study will use the symbol ~ to signify "corresponding."

22 For principles of book arrangement, see H. Dettmer, *Horace: A Study in Structure* (Hildesheim 1983) 1–75.

23 The name of the addressee of c. 68 is problematical. On identifying Manius or Mallius of c. 68a as Manlius of c. 61, see T.P. Wiseman, *Cinna the Poet and Other Roman Essays* (Leicester 1974), 88–89, 102–03.

24 "Catullan Libellus" 226–31.

25 V.P. McCarren, *A Critical Concordance to Catullus* (Leiden 1977) 136, 20, and 97.

26 For a discussion of the verbal parallels that join cc. 6~10 and 12~13, see pages 29–33 and 33–38. The technique of creating a parallel structure to indicate the complementary character of corresponding poems appears to be Hellenistic. See R.B. Egan, "Two Complementary Epigrams of Meleager (*A.P.* 7.195 and 196)," *JHS* 108 (1988) 24–32, who notes a parallel arrangement of two of Meleager's poems.

27 The expression *Veneri Cupidinique* occurs only once elsewhere, at 36.3, where it indicates a connection between cc. 13 and 36.

28 J.R. Heath, "Catullus 11: Along for the Ride," Coll. Latomus 206 (1989) 109. Heath further observes that "the allusion [to cc. 5 and 7] is even stronger if, as some have argued, the *basia* words were introduced to Roman poetry by Catullus."

29 Segal, "The Order" 316.

30 B. Heck (*Die Anordnung der Gedichte des Gaius Valerius Catullus* [Diss. Tübingen 1950] 38–41) and K. Barwick ("Zyklen bei Martial und in den kleinen Gedichten des Catull," *Philologus* 102 [1958] 314), for example, pair cc. 8 and 11 on the grounds that both are "dismissal poems."

31 On the principle of imbalance, see F.O. Copley, "The Structure of Catullus c. 51 and the Problem of the *Otium*-Strophe," *GB* 2 (1974) 28. I disagree, however, with his view that the *otium*-strophe should be detached from c. 51.

32 See Dettmer, *Horace* (above, note 22) 25–30.

Chapter Two: The Polymetra

1 Page 3.

2 Cc. 5~7, 6~10, 12~13, and 1~14.

3 E. von Leutsch ("Catull. c. 14b," *Philologus* 35 [1876] 695) and K.P. Schulze ("Catullforschungen," *Festschrift zu der 2. Säcularfeier des Friedrichs-Werderschen Gymnasiums zu Berlin* [Berlin 1881] 194–214) appear to be the first to recognize the unity of cc. 1–14.

4 The symmetrical relation of cc. 2/3 and 12/13 is signaled by a verbal clue. *Veneres Cupidinesque* (3.1; 13.12) occurs elsewhere only at 36.3

(McCarren, *A Critical Concordance* 198), where the expression serves to link additionally cc. 13 and 36. For a discussion, see pages 228–29.

5 "Catullus 5 and 7: A Study in Complementaries," *AJP* 89 (1968) 301.

6 For bibliography prior to 1982, see B. Arkins, "Further Thoughts on Catullus 1," *LCM* 8.2 (1983) 18. Additional secondary literature now includes: E. Link, *Poetologisches bei Catull, Erlanger Studien* vol. 39 (1982) 97–161; H. Dettmer, "A Fresh Look at Catullus 1.9," *LCM* 9.5 (1984) 74–75; and E.B. Holtsmark, "A Note on Logotactic Iconicity (Catullus 1 and 47)," *LCM* 12.9 (1987) 130–31.

7 For previous literature that rejects a dual significance, see P. Levine, "Catullus c. 1: A Prayerful Dedication," *CSCA* 2 (1969) 209, note 2.

8 Cf. *novum* (v. 1) and *iam tum, ausus es unus Italorum* (v. 5); *libellum* (vv. 1, 8) and *omne aevum tribus...cartis* (v. 6); and *arido...pumice expolitum* (v. 2) and *doctis...laboriosis* (v. 7). Levine (*ibid.* 211–13) appears to be the first to notice these parallels.

9 See pages 226 and 255–56.

10 The relation of cc. 1 and 14 has been noted previously by T.P. Wiseman, *Cinna the Poet and other Roman Essays* (Leicester 1974) 60; G.N. Sandy, "Indebtedness, *Scurrilitas*, and Composition in Catullus (Cat. 44, 1, 68)," *Phoenix* 32 (1978) 74–76; and Hubbard, "Catullan Libellus" 226–27.

11 G.N. Sandy, "Catullus 16," *Phoenix* 25 (1971) 56.

12 T. Bergk, "Philologischen Thesen," *Philologus* 12 (1857) 581; H.A.J. Munro, *Criticisms and Elucidations of Catullus*, 2nd ed. (London 1905) 1–5; and G.P. Goold, "*O Patrona Virgo*," *Polis and Imperium: Studies in Honor of Edward Togo Salmon*, ed. by J.A.S. Evans (Toronto 1974) 253–64, and "Two Notes on Catullus 1," *LCM* 6.9 (1981) 233–38.

13 The secondary literature on figure 2.3 includes FOR reading *o patrona virgo*: F.O. Copley, "Catullus, c. 1," *TAPA* 82 (1951) 200–06; F. Cairns, "Catullus 1," *Mnemosyne* 22 (1969) 153–58; Levine, "A Prayerful" (above, note 7) 209–16; W. Clausen, "Catulli Veronensis Liber," *CP* 71 (1976) 37–43; M. Monbrun, "Quelques remarques sur le c. 1 de Catulle," *Pallas* 23 (1976) 31–38; Arkins, "Further Thoughts," (above, note 6) who refers to P. White's study, "*Amicitia* and the Profession of Poetry in Early Imperial Rome," *JRS* 68 (1978) 74–92; and Dettmer, "A Fresh Look" (above, note 6); and AGAINST reading *o patrona virgo*: C.J. Fordyce, *Catullus: A Commentary* (Oxford 1961) *ad* 1.9; D. Singleton, "A Note on Catullus' First Poem," *CP* 67 (1972) 192–96; and Goold, "*O Patrona Virgo*" (above, note 12).

14 For a discussion, see J.D. Bishop, "Catullus 2 and its Hellenistic Antecedents," *CP* 61 (1966) 158–67; and D. Korzeniewski, "Elemente hymnischer Parodie in der Lyrik Catulls," *Helikon* 18–19 (1978–79) 230–36.

15 On the deliberateness, see also E.H. Guggenheimer's very interesting study, "Acoustic Symmetry in Catullus," *Dialectica* 24 (1970) 194.

16 The ring patterning also is significant because it indicates that *et*, and not *ut*, is to be read at 2.7.

17 In poems 2 and 3, I have adopted Vossius' *posse* in 2.9, which I think is preferable to the manuscript's reading of *possem*, and G.P. Goold's *quod, miselle passer*, in 3.16 for the generally accepted reading of *o miselle passer* ("Catullus 3.16," *Phoenix* 23 [1969] 186–203).

On the correspondence of cc. 2 and 3, see B. Németh, "Further Notes on Catullan Poetry (c.2, c.2a, c.3; c.11, c.51)," *ACD* 9 (1973) 41–48; B. Arkins, *Sexuality in Catullus* (Hildesheim 1982) 81–84; and A.S. Fotiou, "Catullus' Passer Poems: Meaning and Form," *GB* 9 (1980) 111–21.

18 For a discussion of the sexual language, see Fotiou, "Catullus' Passer Poems" (above, note 17) 112–14.

19 Arkins, *Sexuality in Catullus* 81–82.

20 McCarren, *A Critical Concordance* 136.

21 The other instances are at 10.32 and 66.75 (McCarren, *ibid.* 183–84).

22 "Catullus 2B from a Structural Perspective," *CW* 78 (1984) 107–10; and "Closure in the Lesbia Polymetra 1–13," *CW* 82 (1989) 375–77.

For recent literature on this issue, see note 2 of "Catullus 2B," to which should be added T. Wirth, "Catull c. 2: *Passer* und *Malum* als Zeichen der Liebe," *RhM* 129 (1986) 36–53.

23 On two-to-two correspondences, see H. Dettmer, *Horace: A Study in Structure* (Hildesheim 1983) 19–21, 64–65.

24 Recent critics who embrace this view include Hubbard, "Catullan Libellus" 228–29; S.G.P. Small, *Catullus: A Reader's Guide to the Poems* (Lanham and London 1983) 167, note 14; Wiseman, *Catullan Questions* 25, note 3; and P.Y. Forsyth, *The Poems of Catullus: A Teaching Text* (Lanham and London 1986) introd. to 2b.

25 It is difficult to determine how much reworking of the text occurred prior to publication. But in collections exhibiting a complicated system of numerical patterns, as we shall see is characteristic of this one, it is reasonable to assume that many revisions may have taken place.

26 For discussion of the relationship between cc. 2 and 65, see my "Catullus 2B" (above, note 22).

27 Cf. also the language common to 2.11–13, 61.52–53, and 65.19–24 (Wiseman, *A Reappraisal* 121, notes 96 and 97).

28 Pages 242–43.

29 The expression and its variation, *carior/-us est oculis*, occur five times elsewhere: 14.1; 82.2, 3–4, 4; and 104.2 (McCarren, *A Critical Concordance* 130–31); in three of the five instances, the "eyes" are Catullus'. It is worth noting, too, that *passer...quem plus illa oculis suis amabat* at 3.4–5 is echoed by *Lesbia quam Catullus unam / plus quam se atque suos amavit* at 58.2–3. The verbal cross-reference heightens the poignancy of Catullus' *cri de coeur* in the latter poem.

30 On this point, cf. E.A. Fredericksmeyer's remark, "Above all else in life she [Clodia = Lesbia] craved pleasure, and pleasure for her, meant sexual pleasure" ("The Beginning and the End of Catullus' *Longus Amor*," *SO* 58 [1983] 65).

31 B. Mills, *The Unheroic Muse* (Berkeley 1978) 37.

32 The best study of the relation of cc. 5 and 7 is Segal's "Catullus 5 and 7" (above, note 5). The following discussion owes much to his excellent article.

33 By placing *mala lingua* in the nominative, instead of the ablative case, Catullus stresses syntactically the closing phrase of the poem (K. Quinn, "*Docte Catulle*" in *Critical Essays on Roman Literature*: *Elegy and Lyric*, ed. by J.P. Sullivan [London and Cambridge, Mass. 1962] 46).

34 "The hard rhythm, produced by the incision at the end of every single line, is in keeping with the hard tone of the whole poem" (E. Fraenkel, "Two Poems of Catullus," *JRS* 51 [1961] 52). Fraenkel apparently is the first to observe the lack of enjambment.

35 On the thematic relation of c. 8 to 5 and 7, see especially Segal, "The Order" 311, 315–16. On Catullus' debt to Menander, see R.F. Thomas, "Menander and Catullus 8," *RhM* 127 (1984) 308–16.

36 "*Miser* in erotic context describes the lover whose will and reason are altogether subject to his passion" (A.W. Allen, "Elegy and the Classical Attitude toward Love: Propertius 1.1," *YCS* 11 [1950] 259).

37 For a discussion of the language of computation, see especially N.T. Pratt, "The Numerical Catullus 5," *CP* 51 (1956) 99–100; R.E. Grimm, "Catullus 5 Again," *CJ* 59 (1963) 15–22; and F. Cairns, "Catullus' *Basia* Poems (5, 7, 48)," *Mnemosyne* 26 (1973) 15–22.

38 *Metaformations*: *Soundplay and Wordplay in Ovid and Other Classical Poets* (Ithaca and London 1985) 120.

39 Segal, "The Order" 316.

40 See S. Bertman ("Oral Imagery in Catullus 7," *CQ* 28 [1978] 477–78) for oral imagery as a unifying element in c. 7.

41 On the structure, see R.L. Rowland, "*Miser Catulle*: An Interpretation of the Eighth Poem of Catullus," *G&R* 13 (1966) 20.

42 *Ibid.* 19.

43 On their correspondence, see Segal, "The Order" 316, 318; and H.D. Rankin, "The Progress of Pessimism in Catullus, Poems 2–11," *Latomus* 31 (1972) 750.

44 I follow those critics who believe that c. 4 describes Catullus' return from Bithynia. For a defense of this view, see L. Richardson, Jr., "Catullus 4 and Catalepton 10 Again," *AJP* 93 (1972) 215–17. Some of the curious details in this poem can be explained through the poem's correspondence to c. 66 in the ring ordering of personified inanimate objects (for which, see pages 82–85).

45 H.J. Mette, "Catull Carm. 4," *RhM* 105 (1962) 153–57.

46 S. Levin, "A Dying Man's Farewell, Parodied by Catullus," *CW* 69 (1976) 374–75; and J.C. Yardley, "Catullus 11: the End of a Friendship," *SO* 56 (1981) 67.

47 "Style and Content in Catullus 45," *CP* 60 (1965) 259, note 15.

48 For further discussion of this point, see page 97.

49 M. Pulbrook, "The Lesbia Libellus of Catullus," *Maynooth Review* 10 (1984) 76.

50 For literature, see D.R. Sweet, "Catullus 11: a Study in Perspective," *Latomus* 46 (1987) 510–11, note 1; Sweet discusses this issue in detail on pages 523–26.

51 Furius' poverty is the subject of cc. 23, 24, and 26, and in cc. 15 and 40 Catullus equates Aurelius' infatuation with Juventius as madness (*furorque vecors* 15.14; *vecordem...rixam* 40.4). On the identity of Ravidus of c. 40 as Aurelius, see page 288, note 192.

52 On the correspondence of cc. 6 and 10, see Segal, "The Order" 318; Rankin, "The Progress of Pessimism" 751 (above, note 43); and H. Offermann, "Zu Catulls Gedichtcorpus," *RhM* 120 (1977) 272. The following discussion is based on my study of 6 and 10 that appeared in *LCM* 10.2 (1985) 29–30.

53 On the meaning and connotations of *lepor*, see R. Seager, "*Venustus, Lepidus, Bellus, Salsus*: Notes on the Language of Catullus," *Latomus* 33 (1974) 893–94.

54 Following Baehrens, Morgan observes that "the epithet [*febriculosi*] serves to typify the girl as a prostitute of the lowest social level" ("*Nescio Quid Febriculosi Scorti*: A Note on Catullus 6," *CQ* 27 [1977] 338).

55 Ellis, *A Commentary ad loc.*; and Fordyce, *Catullus ad loc.*

56 McCarren, *A Critical Concordance* 169.

57 *Ibid.* 81.

58 *Ibid.* 74.

59 Segal, too, notes the parallelism of the beds ("The Order" 318).

60 M.B. Skinner, "Semiotics and Poetics in Catullus 6," *LCM* 8.9 [1983] 141–42. R.M. Nielsen also interprets c. 6 as a statement about poetry ("Catullus, c. 6: on the Significance of too Much Love," *Latomus* 43 [1984] 104–10).

61 Morgan, *"Nescio Quid"* (above, note 54) 340. Catullus' debt to Hellenistic antecedents in c. 6 is discussed also by M. Carilli, "Le *Nugae* di Catullo e l'epigramma greco," *ASNP* 5 (1975) 937–39.

62 Segal, "The Order" 316–18.

63 That c. 12 is in fact picking up from where c. 10 left off is suggested by a verbal cross-reference: *neglegentiorum* in 12.3 echoes *neglegentem*, the final word of c. 10. For a discussion of the relation of cc. 10 and 12, see Hubbard, "Catullan Libellus" 230.

64 On the correspondence of cc. 12 and 13, see K. Barwick, "Zyklen bei Martial und in den kleinen Gedichten des Catull," *Philologus* 102 (1958) 316; Wiseman, *Catullan Questions* 9, note 4; Seager, "*Venustus, Lepidus, Bellus, Salsus*" 891; Forsyth, *A Teaching Text* introd. to c. 13; H. Dettmer, "*Meros Amores.* A Note on Catullus 13.9," *QUCC* N.S. 23 (1986) 87–91; and A. Richlin, "Systems of Food Imagery in Catullus," *CW* 81 (1988) 358.

65 A. Ernout and A. Meillet, *Dictionnaire étymologique de la langue latine: Histoire des mots*, vol. 1, third ed., rev. (Paris 1951) 90–91. In this connection, W. Clausen suggests that "the *cognomen* [*Marrucinus*] is probably a fiction, invented by Catullus for this poem and put first to emphasize the contrast between Asinius 'Marrucinus', the provincial boor, and Asinius Pollio, his urbane and witty brother" ("Catulliana," in *Vir Bonus Discendi Peritus*: *Studies in Celebration of O. Skutsch's Eightieth Birthday*, ed. by N. Horsfall [London 1988] 13).

66 J. Pokorny, *Indogermanisches etymologisches Wörterbuch*, vol. I.1 (Berlin and Munich 1959) 106. Fabullus is a diminutive of Fabius.

67 For *puer*, see Pokorny, *ibid.* vol. I.2, 843.

68 For a defense of *differtus*, see G.P. Goold, "A New Text of Catullus," *Phoenix* 12 (1958) 93–94.

69 For a discussion, see M. Marcovich, "Catullus 13 and Philodemus 23," *QUCC* N.S. 11 (1982) 133–36.

70 Marcovich, *ibid.*; and W.H. Bernstein, "A Sense of Taste: Catullus 13," *CJ* 80 (1985) 129.

71 Hubbard, "Catullan Libellus" 226.

72 On this point, see also R.O.A.M. Lyne, *Selections from Catullus: Handbook* (Cambridge 1975) 30–33.

73 Cf. also the language at 12.16–17, *haec amem necesse est / ut Veraniolum meum et Fabullum*, and 14.1, *ni te* [= *Calvum*] *plus oculis meis amarem.*

74 Segal, "The Order" 316.

75 "The picture [in 11.17–18]...is of a gross Scylla-like figure engulfing her lovers in one gargantuan embrace" (G.S. Duclos, "Catullus 11: Atque in perpetuum, Lesbia, ave atque vale," *Arethusa* 9 [1976] 80–81).

76 On the *cena adventicia,* see R.G.M. Nisbet and M. Hubbard, *A Commentary on Horace*: *Odes, Book I* (Oxford 1970) introd. *ad Odes* 1.36.

77 On the relation of cc. 12 through 14, see also H. Offermann, "Einige Gedanken zum Aufbau des Catull-Corpus," *Eranos* 76 (1978) 54; P.Y. Forsyth, "Gifts and Giving: Catullus 12–14," *CW* 78 (1985) 571–74; and Hubbard, "Catullan Libellus" 230–31.

The interaction of these three poems suggests that *salse* (and not *false*) is the correct reading at 14.16. It is worth noting that the element of wit figures also in c. 50, another verse epistle to Licinius Calvus, which has many features in common with c. 14, as B. Németh demonstrates ("Catullan Twin Poems [c. 50–c. 14]," *ACD* 10–11 [1974–75] 45–53, especially 51–52).

78 Segal, "The Order" 308; and Forsyth, *A Teaching Text* introd. to c. 11.

79 For secondary literature on 14b and a detailed discussion of the fragment's history, see Hubbard, "Catullan Libellus" 231–33.

80 In only one other Catullan poem (22.11) is a derivative of *horreo* associated with the writing of poetry (McCarren, *A Critical Concordance* 76).

81 K. Quinn, *Catullus: The Poems*, 2nd ed. (London 1973) introd. to 14b.

82 On 14b as a transitional poem, see Wiseman, *Catullan Questions* 7; Skinner, *Catullus' Passer* 44; and Forsyth, *A Teaching Text* introd. to c. 14b.

83 On the connection between the Lesbia and Juventius poems, see also H.D. Rankin, "Poem 16 of Catullus," *SO* 51 (1976) 93.

84 E.T. Merrill, *Catullus* (Cambridge, Mass. 1893, 1951) xxix.

85 Literature on the Aurelius-Furius poems includes Barwick, "Zyklen bei Martial und Catull" (above, note 64) 315; L. Richardson, Jr., "*Furi et Aureli, Comites Catulli*," *CP* 58 (1963) 93–106; E. Schäfer, *Das Verhältnis von Erlebnis und Kunstgestalt bei Catull* Hermes Einzelschriften 18 (1966) 25–28; Schmidt, "Catulls Anordnung" 219–21; Offermann, "Einige Gedanken" 41–43; Skinner, *Catullus' Passer* 43–48; L. Tromaras, "Die Aurelius- und Furius-Gedichte Catulls als Zyklen (cc. 11, 15, 16, 21, 23, 24, 26)," *Eranos* 85 (1987) 41–47; Arkins, *Sexuality in Catullus* 104–13; and P.Y. Forsyth, "Catullus 14B," *CW* 83 (1989) 81–85.

86 J. Ferguson, *Catullus* (Lawrence 1985) 65.

87 For principles of arrangement common to Latin poetry books of the first century B.C., see Dettmer, *Horace* (above, note 23 of this chapter) 1–75.

88 See pages 246–47.

89 On the relationship of cc. 15 and 21, see also Schäfer, *Das Verhältnis* (above, note 85) 26–27; Schmidt, "Catullus Anordnung" 220–21; Offermann, "Einige Gedanken" 42; Arkins, *Sexuality in Catullus* 108–11; S. Lilja, *Homosexuality in Republican and Augustan Rome*, Commentationes Humanarum Litterarum 74 (1983) 53–54; and Tromaras, "Die Aurelius- und Furius-Gedichte" (above, note 85) 43–44.

90 In fact, only in cc. 15 and 21 does Catullus refer to Juventius as a *puer*.

91 M.H. Lindgren, *Non Bona Dicta*: *Obscenity in the Poetry of Catullus* (Diss. University of Iowa 1983) 56.

92 E. Adler, *Catullan Self-Revelation* (New York 1981) 56–57.

93 Cairns, "Catullus' *Basia* Poems" (above, note 37) 19. For cc. 16 and 22 as statements about poetry, see Sandy ("Catullus 16" [above, note 11] 54–57), the first to note a connection between the poems.

94 C. 16 is a difficult poem. For a succinct discussion of its problems, see A. Richlin, *The Garden of Priapus*: *Sexuality and Aggression in Roman Humor* (New Haven and London 1983; rev. Oxford 1992) 248, note 9.

95 C. 16 undoubtedly is intended to look back to c. 5 (and c. 7). These are the only kiss poems that an ancient reader unrolling his book would have met thus far. Through the cross-reference "Catullus is absolving himself from the conventional *mollitia* of an erotic poet" (Skinner, *Catullus' Passer* 54).

96 Ferguson, *Catullus* 70.

97 Richlin (*The Garden of Priapus* 146) and Rankin ("Poem 16" [above, note 83] 93) also note a connection between cc. 11 and 16.

98 Sandy, "Catullus 16" (above, note 11) 56.

99 I follow R.G.M. Nisbet ("Notes on the Text of Catullus," *PCPHS* 204 [1978] 96–97) in reading *novae bibli* instead of *novi libri* in 22.6, and in taking the phrase as a genitive with *cartae regiae.*

100 It is unlikely that Varus of cc. 10 and 22 is to be identified with Alfenus of c. 30. In Catullus, poems that feature the same individual(s) usually exhibit similar themes. Cc. 10 and 22 concern the quality of *venustas*, whereas c. 30 is about betrayal.

101 Tromaras also notes verbal parallels that interconnect cc. 14, 14b, 16, and 22 ("Die Aurelius- und Furius-Gedichte" [above, note 85] 45, note 17).

102 "*Furi et Aureli*" 98.

103 On the connection of cc. 13 and 23, see also Richlin, "Systems of Food Imagery in Catullus" (above, note 64) 358–59.

104 C.W. Macleod, "Parody and Personalities in Catullus," *CQ* 23 (1973) 297.

105 H.D. Rankin, "A Note on Some Implications of Catullus 16.11–13," *Latomus* 29 (1970) 120.

106 On this point, see also O. Harnecker, "Des Catullus Juventiuslieder," *Jahrb. f. class. Philol.* 133 (1886) 273–79, especially 278.

107 K. Quinn, *Catullus*: *An Interpretation* (London 1973) 242. On this point, see also Macleod, who repeatedly stresses the comic intent of the homosexual poems ("Parody and Personalities" 294–303).

108 The other two non-corresponding poems are cc. 30 and 48. C. 17 is non-corresponding in the primary ring structure; in a subpattern it functions as counterpart to c. 67 (see pages 83–84).

109 Whether adulterers were actually "radished" or not (J. Roy, "Traditional Jokes about the Punishment of Adulterers in Ancient Greek Literature," *LCM* 16.5 [1991] 73–76), the association of the punishment with poor men may be part of the traditional joke.

110 Cf. *pudicum/-i* in 16.4, 8 and *pudentem*, *pudice*, and *pudenter* in 15.2, 5, 13; *castum* in 16.5 and *castum* in 15.4; *non dico...sed* in 16.10 and *non dico...verum* in 15.6, 9; and *nequeunt movere lumbos* in 16.11 and *quem* (= *penem*)...*moveto* in 15.11.

111 Both G.P. Goold (*Catullus* [London 1983] 241) and Richlin (*Garden of Priapus* 155–56) suggest that the phrase *tibi flagella conscribillent* in verse 11 refers to the "lash" inflicted by the poem itself.

112 Secondary literature on the textually corrupt verse 5 is immense. For a brief review of principal readings, see T.D. Papanghelis, "Crux Catulliana (A Note on 25.5)," *Latomus* 39 (1980) 409–10. Papanghelis' emendation, *conviva cum ebriosior se tendit oscitanter,* which I adopted, is attractive from a structural perspective because it accords well with the coming theme of inebriation in c. 27.

113 I am convinced that Veranius and Fabullus made two trips abroad, one to Spain and the other to Macedonia. The reference to Spain in 25.7 appears to be serving a purely structural purpose: it recalls the appearance of the two friends in cc. 9 and 12 and anticipates their appearance in c. 28.

114 McCarren, *A Critical Concordance* 134.

115 I am indebted to C. Hogarth, formerly of Fountain Valley School, for this point.

116 "Obscenity in Catullus," *Ramus* 6 (1977) 23.

117 Skinner, *Catullus' Passer* 30.

118 The manuscripts are divided between *vestra* (O) and *nostra* (GR). After much vacillating, I finally decided that the point of the poem is more witty if the villa belongs to Catullus.

A poem by Furius Bibaculus (fr. 2, Morel) on a similar subject has many parallels in common with Catullus 26. For a discussion, see W.A. Heidel, "Catullus and Furius Bibaculus," *CR* 15 (1901) 216; E.H. Green, "Furius Bibaculus," *CJ* 35 (1940) 353–55; and J.W. Loomis, "M. Furius Bibaculus and Catullus," *CW* 63 (1969) 114.

119 *Catullus* introd. to c. 26.

120 D.O. Ross, Jr., *Style and Tradition in Catullus* (Cambridge, Mass. 1969) 99–100, note 231.

121 Ellis, *A Commentary ad* 26.4.

122 On the genre, see J. Moore-Blunt, "Catullus 31 and Ancient Generic Composition," *Eranos* 72 (1974) 106–18; and F. Cairns, "*Venusta Sirmio*: Catullus 31," *Quality and Pleasure in Latin Poetry*, ed. by T. Woodman and D. West (Cambridge 1974) 1–17.

123 C. Witke, "Verbal Art in Catullus 31," *AJP* 93 (1972) 241–44.

124 R.J. Baker, "Catullus and Friend in Carm. 31," *Mnemosyne* 23 (1970) 33–41; and "Catullus and Sirmio," *Mnemosyne* 36 (1983) 316–23.

125 For other humorous features, see Cairns, "*Venusta Sirmio*" (above, note 122) 17. Moore-Blunt observes that Catullus uses the choliambic meter for poems that are either obscene or jocular ("Catullus 31" [above, note

122] 115). It is worth comparing c. 31 to c. 44, a humorous poem also written in limping iambics, in which Catullus personifies his Sabine villa.

126 C. 31 holds this place in the corpus, too, because it participates in two thematic subpatterns. It functions as counterpart to c. 9 in the poems concerned with the provincial experiences of Catullus and his friends, Fabullus and Veranius (see pages 64–65), and it functions as counterpart to c. 44 in the poems to or about personified objects (see pages 83–84).

127 Small, *Catullus* 14. In fact, "drunkenness was traditionally second only to adultery…in the catalogue of sins unforgiveable in a married woman" (Wiseman, *A Reappraisal* 134).

128 For a discussion of the theme of the excluded lover in c. 32, see J.R. Heath, "The Supine Hero in Catullus 32," *CJ* 82 (1986) 28–31.

129 Along similar lines cc. 25 and 32 both seem to look back to c. 5. *Severos* (27.6) recalls the *senum severiorum* of 5.2 (*severi* occurs in these two places only in Catullus); and the counting of *fututiones* (32.7–8) brings to mind the counting of kisses in 5.7–10 (on the connection between the two enumerations, see Cairns, "Catullus' *Basia* Poems" [above, note 37] 21–22).

130 The name is transmitted in the manuscripts in various forms. For a review of emendations, see C.L. Neudling, *A Prosopography to Catullus* (Oxford 1955) 87; and T.P. Wiseman, "Catullus' *Belle De Jour*," *Filologia e forme letterarie* 2 (Urbino 1987) 375–76. Because Catullus puns so frequently on proper names, the proposal of R.O. Fink that we read *Iphathylla*, a joking metathesis for *ithyphalla*, is not unattractive ("Catullus, Carmen 32," *CW* 76 [1983] 292–94). Such a paronomasia would accord neatly with the final image of the poem (*pertundo tunicamque palliumque*).

131 I owe this idea to A. Gratwick ("Ipsithilla: A Vulgar Name. Catullus, 32.1," *Glotta* 44 [1966–67] 174–76), who at one time was of the opinion that Ipsithilla's name meant "Little Grape" (although he repudiates this view now, in *CQ* 41 [1991] 548, note 2). Seeing the element *psith-* in Ipsithilla's name creates another link with Postumia, who is compared to a drunken grape (*ebrioso acino* 4).

132 Wiseman, *Catullan Questions* 8.

133 E.g., F. Cairns, "Catullus 27," *Mnemosyne* 28 (1975) 27.

134 Critics who see a relation between cc. 28~29 include E. Badian, "Mamurra's Fourth Fortune," *CP* 72 (1977) 322; Offermann, "Einige Gedanken" 39–40; Skinner, *Catullus' Passer* 29; Forsyth, *A Teaching Text* introd. to c. 29; and J. Ferguson, "The Arrangement of Catullus' Poems" *LCM* 11.1 (1986) 5.

135 I follow Merrill in taking the dramatic setting of the poem to be Rome, where Catullus greets Veranius and Fabullus immediately on their arrival (*Catullus* [above, note 84] introd. to c. 28).

136 M.B. Skinner, "Parasites and Strange Bedfellows: A Study in Catullus' Political Imagery," *Ramus* 8 (1979) 146.

137 On the adjectives *superbus* and *superfluens*, Merrill observes that "both adjectives refer to his [Mamurra's] wealth" (*Catullus* [above, note 84] *ad loc.*).

138 Neudling appears the first to propose that 29.1–10 are directed to Pompey (*A Prosopography* 89, 143). His proposal is supported by A. Cameron, "Catullus 29," *Hermes* 104 (1976) 155–63; and K. Quinn, "Pompey, Caesar and Catullus 29," *AFLNice* 50 (1985) 261–68.

139 J.N. Adams, *The Latin Sexual Vocabulary* (London 1982) 13.

140 For critics who espouse this view, see above, note 138.

141 For arguments that *malum* is not an interjection at 29.21, see J.D. Minyard, "Critical Notes on Catullus 29," *CP* 66 (1971) 180–81.

142 Minyard, however, defends the reading of the text (*ibid.* 174–81). Most commentators accept *urbis* as genuine. Mynors, however, is a notable exception.

143 The spondee *nunc Galliae* at the beginning of verse 20 also is problematical. As for the spondaic *Mamurra* in the first foot of verse 3, most critics allow Catullus the liberty, practiced by other Latin poets, of shortening or lengthening the quantity of a syllable in a proper name to fit the meter.

144 Skinner, "Parasites and Strange Bedfellows" (above, note 136) 151–52, note 31.

145 The principal emendations of 29.23 are enumerated in C. Deroux, "Un nouveau personnage Catullien: de la philologie à l'histoire," *RBPh* 55 (1977) 56–57, note 3.

146 I discussed the relation of cc. 28~29 and its significance for the textual problem at 29.23 in *Syllecta Classica* 2 (1990) 23–27.

147 Adler, *Catullan Self-Revelation* 88.

148 C. Witke, *Enarratio Catulliana: Carmina 50, 30, 65, 68* (Leiden 1968) 10; D.W.T.C. Vessey, "Thoughts on Two Poems of Catullus: 13 and 30," *Latomus* 30 (1971) 52; and M.L. Daniels, "Personal Revelation in Catullus 64," *CJ* 62 (1967) 352–53.

149 "Thoughts on Two Poems" (above, note 148) 50.

150 Skinner, *Catullus' Passer* 29.

151 Vessey, "Thoughts on Two Poems" (above, note 148) 50.

152 To the best of my knowledge, no one has noticed that all of the provincial poems are meant to be read together. For a discussion of the relation of some of these poems, see M.C.J. Putnam, "Catullus' Journey (Carm. 4)," *CP* 57 (1962) 10–19 (on cc. 4, 31, and 46); R.M. Nielsen, "Catullus 9 and 31: The Simple Pleasure," *Ramus* 8 (1979) 165–73; and my "Catullus 13: A Nose is a Nose is a Nose," *Syllecta Classica* 1 (1989) 82–83. In the last piece I argue that c. 13 imitates *A.P.* 11.44 of Philodemus, an intimate of Piso, and thus provides a witty transition from the Spain poems, 9 and 12, to the Piso poems, 28 and 47.

153 Cf. *venistine domum ad tuos penates* (9.3) and *venimus larem ad nostrum* (31.9); *visam te incolumem* (9.6) and *te...inviso,...videre te in tuto* (31.4, 6); *quid me laetius est* (9.11) and *o quid...est beatius* (31.7); and the elaborate address of affection to Veranius in 9.1–2 (*Verani, omnibus e meis amicis / antistans mihi milibus trecentis*) and Sirmio in 31.1–3 (*Paene insularum, Sirmio, insularumque / ocelle, quascumque in liquentibus stagnis / marique vasto fert uterque Neptunus*).

154 Others who have noticed that poems within cc. 34–44 are carefully ordered include: Wiseman, *A Reappraisal* 148–51; Schmidt, "Catulls Anordnung" 221–24; Clausen, "Veronensis Liber" (above, note 13) 39; Offermann, "Zu Catulls Gedichtcorpus" 274–77; Ferguson, "The Arrangement" (above, note 134) 6; and P.Y. Forsyth, "The Lady and the Poem: Catullus 35–42," *CJ* 80 (1984) 24–26.

155 Skinner, *Catullus' Passer* 31.

156 *A Teaching Text* introd. to c. 34.

157 G. Williams, "Phases in Political Patronage of Literature in Rome," in *Literary and Artistic Patronage in Ancient Rome*, ed. by B.K. Gold (Austin 1982) 11–12; and Wiseman, *A Reappraisal* 96–101.

158 Cf. *magna progenies* at 34.6 and *Magna...Mater* at 35.18; and *montium domina* at 34.9 and *Dindymi dominam* at 35.14. Dindymus is a mountain in Phyrgia sacred to Cybele.

159 Wiseman, *A Reappraisal* 97.

160 *Catullus ad* 44.2ff.

161 For c. 44 as a parody of a prayer, see Williams, *Tradition and Originality* 137–40; and C.P. Jones, "Parody in Catullus 44," *Hermes* 96 (1968) 379–83. For secondary literature on c. 44, see D.B. George, "Catullus 44: The Vulnerability of Wanting to Be Included," *AJP* 112 (1991) 247, notes 1 and 2.

162 For the literary pun on *frigus*, see now M.F. Williams, "Amor's Head-Cold (*Frigus* in Catullus 45)," *CJ* 83 (1988) 130–31.

It is worth noting that humor is a common element of all the polymetra that deal with the issue of literature (cf. 1, 6, 14, 16, 22, 35, 36, 38, 44, 49, and 50).

163 Skinner, *Catullus' Passer* 30.

164 "A Literary Chill: Catullus 44," *CW* 62 (1969) 354–56.

165 Although the subject of c. 14 is similar to that of cc. 35 and 44, Catullus is more concerned there with describing his immediate reaction to Calvus' gift and his desire for revenge than he is in describing symptoms that resulted from his reading the anthology.

166 For previous literature on c. 35, see F.O. Copley, "Catullus, 35," *AJP* 74 (1953) 149–60; J.M. Fisher, "Catullus 35," *CP* 66 (1971) 1–5; H.A. Khan, "Catullus 35 and the Things Poetry Can Do to You," *Hermes* 102 (1974) 475–90; S. Onetti and G. Maurach, "Catullus 35," *Gymnasium* 81 (1974) 481–85; R. Heine, "Zu Catull c. 35," in *Catull,* ed. by R. Heine, "Wege der Forschung," vol. 308 (Darmstadt 1975) 62–84; V. Buchheit, "Dichtertum und Lebensform in Catull c. 35/36," in *Lebendige Romania*: *Festschrift für Hans-Wilhelm Klein,* ed. by A. Barrera-Vidal *et al.* (Göppingen 1976) 47–64; J. Basto, "Caecilius, Attis and Catullus 35," *LCM* 7.3 (1982) 30–34; and E.A. Fredricksmeyer, "Catullus to Caecilius on Good Poetry (C. 35)," *AJP* 106 (1985) 213–21 (who reviews earlier studies on pages 213–15).

167 That the repeated *incohata* contains a *tacita censura* of Caecilius' poem was first suggested by E. Baehrens (*Catulli Veronensis Liber,* vol. 1, rev. by K.P. Schulze [Leipzig 1893] 205) and later argued forcefully by Copley ("Catullus, 35" [above, note 166] 154–60). For other instances of Catullus creating similar situations in which to contrast good writer with bad, cf. 1~14 and 16~22.

168 On the relation of cc. 35 and 36, see also Buchheit ("Dichtertum und Lebensform" [above, note 166] 60–64), Skinner (*The Passer* 31), Forsyth ("The Lady" [above, note 154] 25), and J.B. Solodow, "Forms of Literary Criticism in Catullus: Polymetric vs. Epigram," *CP* 84 (1989) 316–19.

169 Catullus appears to be glossing the Latin *ANnALes VOLVsi* with the Greek *cacata carta.* The temptation to see verbal play at 36.1 and 20 is enhanced by the possibility that *Annales* is Catullus' nickname for Volusius' historical work, which he uses both here and later in c. 95 (M.G. Morgan suggests this interesting idea only to reject it in "Catullus and the *Annales Volusi,*" *QUCC* N.S. 4 [1980] 65–66).

170 Ferguson, *Catullus* 108.

171 On c. 42, see Fraenkel, "Two Poems of Catullus" (above, note 34) 46–51; and Williams, *Tradition and Originality* 196–99.

172 Quinn, for example, seeing c. 42 as a "follow-up" to c. 37, identifies Lesbia as the "rotten whore" (*An Interpretation* 100–01).

173 *Tradition and Originality* 223. Because c. 36 is a complicated piece that skillfully blends several themes, it is pointless to argue that one theme predominates over another (cf. V. Buchheit, "Catulls Dichterkritik in c. 36," *Hermes* 87 [1959] 309, who contends that the principal concern of the poem is literary criticism).

174 Cf. Arkins' closing remark on c. 36: "The humorous, bantering tone and the reconciliation suggest that all is well with the lovers" (*Sexuality in Catullus* 79).

175 On the etymology of *ignis* < *egnis*, see Pokorny, *etymologisches Wörterbuch*, vol. I.1 (above, note 66) 293.

176 On the correlation of the two types of retaliation, see Lindgren, *Non Bona Dicta* 57; and Small, *Catullus* 54.

177 *Celtiber(-ia)*, *defricare*, and the words for "urine" that close cc. 37 and 39 (*urina*, *lotium*) do not occur elsewhere in the Catullan collection (McCarren, *A Critical Concordance* 26, 40, 99, and 208).

178 On the correspondence of cc. 41 and 43, which have long been recognized as companion pieces, see P.Y. Forsyth, "The Ameana Cycle of Catullus," *CW* 70 (1977) 445–50; M.B. Skinner, "*Ameana, Puella Defututa*," *CJ* 74 (1978–79) 110–14; and Lindgren, *Non Bona Dicta* 38–41.

179 The phrase, which occurs only here in the poetry (McCarren, *A Critical Concordance* 39), signals the poems' correspondence.

180 Fordyce, *Catullus* 191.

181 I. Opelt, *Die lateinischen Schimpfwörter und verwandte sprachliche Erscheinungen, Eine Typologie* (Heidelberg 1965) 26–27 (cited by Skinner, "*Ameana*" [above, note 178] 110–11 in notes 3 and 5).

182 Skinner, "*Ameana*" (above, note 178) 113.

183 *Ibid.* 112.

184 *Non Bona Dicta* 39.

185 Ellis, *A Commentary ad* 41.1; and Neudling, *Prosopography* 3–4.

186 If Amiana is the unidentified woman of c. 42, there are two additional parallels. Both she and Egnatius are described as *moechi* (37.16; 42.3, 11–12, 19–20), and are derided for their smile or grin (39.2, 7, 14–16; 42.8–9).

187 "Catullus, c. 38," *TAPA* 87 (1956) 125–29. S. Baker uses Copley's study as a point of departure to discuss the pun on *me hercule et laboriose* in verse 2 ("Catullus 38," *CP* 55 [1960] 37–38).

188 "c. 38" (above, note 187) 128.

189 Quinn, *The Poems ad* 38.3.

190 Cf. *meos amores* (15.1, 40.7); *populo* (15.6), *vulgi* (40.5); *qua lubet...vis* (15.11–12), *vis qualubet* (40.6); *paratum* (15.12), *parat* (40.4); *te mala mens,...in tantam impulerit, sceleste, culpam* (15.14–15), *te mala mens...agit praecipitem in meos iambos* (40.1–2); *vecors* (15.14), *vecordem* (40.4); *miserum* (15.17), *miselle* (40.1); *attractis pedibus patente porta / percurrent raphanique mugilesque* (15.18–19), *cum longa...poena* = *pene* (40.8).

191 Neudling's succinct analysis of the usage of *meos amores* is worth quoting: "The phrase is twice used of Juventius (15.1; 21.4), never of Lesbia, and the parallels [*suos amores*, 10.1; 45.1; 64.27; and *tuos amores*, 6.16] do not refer to Lesbia" (*A Prosopography* 155).

For an opposing view that the expression alludes to the affair with Lesbia, see Quinn, *The Poems ad* 38.6; Wiseman, *Catullan Questions* 15; and Forsyth, "The Lady and the Poem" (above, note 154) 25.

192 The name Ravidus is unattested (Neudling, *A Prosopography* 155). The close relation between cc. 15 and 40, however, suggests that Ravidus is Aurelius. The vocative *Ravide*, in fact, is virtually an anagram of *Aureli*: Rau-/Aur-, -ide/-eli. Unfortunately, because the antepenultimate syllable must be short, meter prevents emending the text to *Aureli*. Perhaps the best solution to this difficulty has been offered by Richardson, who proposes that Ravidus is Aurelius' *cognomen* ("*Furi et Aureli*" 102).

193 The phrase is borrowed from Wiseman, *A Reappraisal* 156. "Tavern," *taberna*, at 37.1 and 36.15 links the beginning of c. 37 with the end of c. 36. The word occurs only once elsewhere, later at 37.10 (McCarren, *A Critical Concordance* 183).

The point is worth making that cc. 36 and 37 initiate a series of poems that begin and/or end with obscene or scatological references: *cacata carta* (36.1, 20); *mentulas, cun-i-cul-osae, urina* (37.3, 18, 20); *loti* (39.21); *poena* = *pene* (40.8); and *defututa* (41.1).

194 Lindgren, *Non Bona Dicta* 57.

195 *morbum* (39.7); *mala mens* (40.1); *non est sana* (41.7); *salve* (43.11); and *orationem...plenam veneni et pestilentiae...hic me gravedo frigida et frequens tussis / quassavit usque* (44.11–14).

196 Richardson, "*Furi et Aureli*" 102.

197 Schmidt suggests that the personified objects, beginning with c. 31 and ending with c. 44, form a cycle ("Catulls Anordnung" 221–23).

198 On the relation of cc. 17 and 67, which similarly owe their inspiration to primitive folk ideas, see also H.D. Rankin, "Catullus and Incest," *Eranos* 74 (1976) 116–17; and Goold, *Catullus* 240.

199 On the relation of cc. 31 and 44, see also Skinner, *Catullus' Passer* 30; and Schmidt, "Catulls Anordnung" 222.

200 Critics are divided whether the scraps of verse begin at c. 51 or at c. 52. *C. 51:* Clausen, "Catulli Veronensis Liber" (above, note 39) 40; J. van Sickle, "The Book-Roll and Some Conventions of the Poetic Book," *Arethusa* 13 (1980) 15–16; Hubbard, "Catullan Libellus" 218–37; Pulbrook, "The Lesbia Libellus" (above, note 49) 77; and Goold, *Catullus* 245–46. *C. 52:* Segal, "The Order" 307, note 1; Skinner, *Catullus' Passer* 74–92; and Forsyth, *A Teaching Text* 9.

201 Seven of the last nine poems (I take 58b with 55) are less than 8 lines in length (52, 53, 54, 56, 58, 59, 60).

202 Skinner, *Catullus' Passer* 74–75.

203 *Ibid.*

204 Wiseman, *A Reappraisal* 155.

205 For a survey of theories, see E.A. Fredricksmeyer, "Catullus 49, Cicero, and Caesar," *CP* 68 (1973) 268–73. For additional bibliography on the poem, see C. Deroux, "Le plus mauvais de tous les poètes et le meilleur de tous les avocats," Coll. Latomus 187 (1985) 124–25, note 1.

206 The current trend is to view the poem as ironical. For references to interpretations of the poem as sincere, see C. Deroux, "Catulle et Cicéron ou les raisons d'un silence," *LEC* 53 (1985) 221, note 2.

207 McCarren, *A Critical Concordance* 71. In addition to the verbal echo, parody of Cicero's and Sestius' oratorical style may be an additional feature common to the poems. A connection between cc. 44 and 49 is seen also by V. Buchheit ("Literarische Kritik an T. Annius Cimber [Verg. *Catal.* 2], Cicero [Cat. C. 49] und Sestius [Cat. C. 44]," *Forschungen zur Römischen Literatur* vol. 1, ed. by W. Wimmel [Wiesbaden 1970] 42, note 31, and 43).

208 E.S. Gruen, "Cicero and Licinius Calvus," *HSCP* 71 (1966) 218.

209 McCarren, *A Critical Concordance* 44. *Differtus* is the correct reading at 12.9, as was demonstrated in our discussion of cc. 12 and 13 on page 35.

210 K.M.W. Shipton, "Catullus 51: Just Another Love Poem?" *LCM* 5.4 (1980) 73.

211 *Ibid.* 73–76.

212 Wiseman, *A Reappraisal* 155.

213 Catullan self-address in successive poems is striking because the instances in which Catullus addresses himself are very few (8.1, 19; 46.4; 51.13; 52.1, 4; 76.5; and 79.2).

214 J.N. Adams, "Words for 'Prostitute' in Latin," *RhM* 126 (1983) 329.

215 To the best of my knowledge, Lindgren is the first to suggest that *sella in curuli...sedet* at 52.2 may have pejorative sexual connotations (*Non Bona Dicta* 33, note 16).

216 Lesbia is mentioned only in passing at 43.7.

That *sedens adversus...te [sedentem]* in 51.3 is meant to recall *puella...consedit* in 37.11, 14 is suggested not only by the relative proximity of the two Lesbia poems, but by the fact that Lesbia is described as sitting nowhere else in the poetry.

217 E. Bickel, "Salaputium: Mentula Salax," *RhM* 96 (1953) 94–95. Since Calvus is known to have been of small stature, "the joke is in the paradoxical obscenity" between the small man who is a large phallus (Lateiner, "Obscenity" 24).

218 On this identification, see Ellis, *Catullus* 185.

219 For a succinct discussion of the problem of what sexual activity the *pupulus* is engaged in, see Richlin, *Garden of Priapus* 249–50, note 23.

220 For discussion of the epic character of 56.6–7, see W.C. Scott, "Catullus and Cato (c. 56)," *CP* 64 (1969) 27–28.

221 For the restoration of 58b to 55, see pages 109–11. I follow F. Peachy in placing 58b after verse 14 ("Catullus 55," *Phoenix* 26 [1972] 258–67). The latest advocate of integrating 55 and 58b is G.P. Goold (*Interpreting Catullus* [London 1974] 15–21), who places the fragment after verse 13.

222 In commenting on *si placet Dionae*, Ross writes: "It is tempting to speculate on a possible connection with Caesar here" (*Style and Tradition* [above, note 121] 100, note 231).

223 D.H. Garrison, *The Student's Catullus*, 2nd. ed (Norman and London 1995) *ad* 57.9.

224 On the insulting character of Caesar's "perfect friendship with Mamurra," see Skinner, "Parasites and Strange Bedfellows" (above, note 136) 142–44.

225 According to Quinn, "*Catullus* is possibly a diminutive formed from *Cato*" (*The Poems ad* 56.3).

226 On the relation of poems 58–60, see O. Weinreich, "Catull c. 60," *Hermes* 87 (1959) 88–90; and Wiseman, *A Reappraisal* 156–57.

227 Weinreich, *ibid.* 75–84.

228 G. Lieberg, *Puella Divina* (Amsterdam 1962) 280.

The reference to the offspring of the Scylla in c. 60 almost seems a natural consequence of all the seamy sex that takes place in cc. 56 through 59. In c. 56 Catullus pedicates a *pupulus* caught in the act of making c. 57 the theme of pedication is picked up by *pathico* in verse 2; in 57.7 the sexually versatile Caesar and Mamurra "are doing it" on a study couch (*in lecticulo*); in c. 58 Lesbia "is doing it" in crossroads and alleys (*in quadriviis et angiportis*); and in c. 59 Rufa "is doing it" in graveyards of the poor (*in sepulchretis*).

229 Segal, for example, observes: "The end of the group of first sixty poems presents obvious difficulties, not only because of the unfinished state of poems like 58b, but also because it is hard to imagine Catullus placing so inconsequential a poem as c. 59 in so emphatic a position" ("The Order" 306).

230 D.F. Bright, *"Non Bona Dicta*: Catullus' Poetry of Separation," *QUCC* 21 (1976) 115; and Sweet, "Catullus 11" (above, note 50) 517.

231 On their similar features, see especially Bright, *ibid.* 105–06, 108–10, 116–17.

232 Richlin, *The Garden of Priapus* 152.

233 Levin, "A Dying Man's Farewell" (above, note 46) 374–75; and Yardley, "Catullus 11" (above, note 46) 67.

234 Duclos, "Catullus 11: Atque In Perpetuum" (above, note 75) 80–81; Fredricksmeyer, "Catullus' *Longus Amor*" (above, note 30) 79; and especially R.T. Scott, "On Catullus 11," *CP* 78 (1983) 40–41. The Scylla occurs only once elsewhere in the poetry, at 64.156 (McCarren, *A Critical Concordance* 169).

235 On this point, see also Quinn, *An Interpretation* 101.

236 I am grateful to C. Hogarth for discussion and helpful suggestions regarding the thematic relation of these poems.

237 McCarren, *A Critical Concordance* 70. *Gemellus* makes his first attested appearance in Latin literature in these Catullus poems (*ThLL* 6 s.v. 1735).

The *gemelli* Castor and Pollux coordinate with the *gemelli* Caesar and Mamurra in that one twin of each pair is mortal, the other "divine." The subtle identification of Caesar and Castor may have some basis in reality. According to Suetonius (*Divus Julius* 10), the aedile Bibulus made the following comment about his colleague Caesar: "The Temple of the Heavenly Twins in the Forum is always simply called 'Castor's'; and I always play Pollux to Caesar's Castor when we give a public entertainment together" (*Suetonius: The Twelve Caesars*, trans. by R. Graves, Penguin Classics).

238 On this point, see H.A. Khan, "Catullus 45: What Sort of Irony?" *Latomus* 27 (1968) 4, 11–12; and Skinner, *Catullus' Passer* 77, 80.

239 Skinner, *Catullus' Passer* 77.

240 "Catullus 45" (above, note 238) 3–12.

241 S. Baker, "The Irony of Catullus' 'Septimius and Acme'," *CP* 53 (1958) 110–12; and Ross, "Catullus 45" (above, note 47) 256–59. Other proponents of an ironical reading of the poem include: D. Singleton, "Form and Irony in Catullus 45," *G&R* 18 (1971) 180–87; Quinn, *An Interpretation* 228; Skinner, *Catullus' Passer* 77, 80; Small, *Catullus* 66–67; Ferguson, *Catullus* 130–32; and R. Newton, "Acme and Septimius Recounted: Catullus 45," *Syllecta Classica* 7 (1996) 99–105.

242 Ross ("Catullus 45" [above, note 47] 259, note 14) apparently is the first to notice geographical similarities between the two poems: Catullus refers to India nowhere else in the polymetra, and to Britain "only in these poems and in [c.] 29."

243 This verbal connection is tentatively suggested by Ross (*ibid.*).

244 Ferguson, *Catullus* 131.

245 McCarren, *A Critical Concordance* 97.

246 "c. 60" (above, note 226) 75–83.

247 *Profectus* occurs only here in Catullus' poetry (McCarren, *A Critical Concordance* 147). On the military implications of the phrase *a bono auspicio*, see H. Dietz, "Zu Catulls Gedicht von Acme und Septimius," *SO* 44 (1969) 42–47.

248 Skinner, *Catullus' Passer* 77.

249 Richlin, *The Garden of Priapus* 149.

250 "Parasites and Strange Bedfellows" (above, note 136) 141.

251 *The Poems* introd. to c. 47. All of the Veranius and Fabullus poems (9, 12, 13, 28, 47) appear to be set in Rome.

252 Catullus, who is guilty of the same behavior as his friends, at least turns to other *nobiles amicos* in attempting to cadge a dinner invitation, as c. 44 illustrates, although, admittedly, as a *novus homo* Sestius is not in the same league as Piso.

253 The term is borrowed from P. Pucci, "Il carme 50 di Catullo," *Maia* 13 (1961) 249.

254 Weinreich, "c. 60" (above, note 226) 89; and Wiseman, *A Reappraisal* 156.

255 Catullus also connects Veranius and Fabullus with Lesbia of c. 58 through the similar phrases *in trivio* (47.7) and *in quadriviis* (58.4).

256 Other critics have tried to identify a single motive for the composition of the poem. For secondary literature, see above, note 205.

257 The relation of c. 49 to cc. 44 and 53 is discussed on pages 86–87.

258 This tripartite classification of political, personal, and literary "reasons why Catullus might be at loggerheads with Cicero" is borrowed from Ferguson (*Catullus* 139–40).

259 As J. Ferguson observes, even though the references to the *neoteri* (*Tusc.* 3.19.45; *Att.* 7.2.1) "postdate Catullus' death by some years....Cicero's critical opinions were not evolved suddenly in the last years of his life, and there is no evidence that they suffered radical change" ("Catullus and Cicero," *Latomus* 25 [1966] 871).

260 Through the recollection in 49.2–3 of Juventius poems 21.2–3 (and 24.2-3), Catullus appears to be creating another link between the poem to Cicero and the preceding poem to Juventius (c. 48).

261 On this point, see C. Pascal, *Poeti e personaggi Catulliani* (Catania 1916) 136–39; Skinner, *Catullus' Passer* 78–79; and Small, *Catullus* 58.

262 Owing to the political character of this final sequence of polymetra and to the great stress placed on the hilarity of the incident—the first four verses of this seven-line poem are devoted to the subject of its humor—the humorless politician Marcus Cato seems a more likely candidate as the poem's recipient than the scholar-poet Valerius Cato.

263 The Latin *deus* and the Greek *Dione*, a feminine form of Ζεύς, Διος, derive from the same Indo-European root (Pokorny, *etymologisches Wörterbuch* [above, note 66] vol. I.1, 184–86).

264 The sexual activity in which the *pupulus* is engaged is a subject of controversy. Following M.B. Skinner, I understand *cunnum* as the object of *trusantem* and *puellae* as a dative "equivalent to a posssessive genitive" ("Supplementary Note on the Latin Sexual Language: Catullus 56.5–6," *LCM* 7.9 [1982] 140).

265 Ferguson, *Catullus* 163.

266 "Catullus and Cato" (above, note 220) 26–29. Scott cites as evidence *Pro Cael.* 36, where Cicero refers to Clodius as *pusio*, "little boy" and *Att.*

2.1.4 and 2.22.1, where Cicero refers to Clodius as *Pulchellus,* "the Little Beauty."

Some take the *pupulus* to be Camerius of the previous poem (e.g., A.D. Booth, "Camerius the Catamite [Catullus 55 & 58b]," *LCM* 6.5 [1981] 135–36; and Goold, *Catullus* 247).

267 On this point, cf. Seneca, *Controv.* 7.4.6: Calvus, qui diu cum Cicerone iniquissimam litem de principatu eloquentiae habuit, usque eo violentus actor et concitatus fuit, ut in media eius actione surgeret Vatinius reus et exclamaret: "rogo vos, iudices, num si iste disertus est, ideo me damnari oportet?"

268 O. Hezel, *Catull und das griechische Epigramm* (Stuttgart 1932) 51, note 3.

269 On the symmetry of c. 52, see also A. Traina, "Strutture catulliane: Il c. 52," *AFLNice* 50 (1985) 269–72.

270 Vatinius suffered from boils (Cicero, *In Vatinium* 39), an affliction Catullus transfers to Nonius.

271 Skinner, "Parasites and Strange Bedfellows" (above, note 136) 143.

272 The subject of the improvised poetry is hinted at through the erotic language in verses 2–5 (*lusimus, delicatos, versiculos, ludebat*).

273 Macleod, "Parody and Personalities" 294; and Skinner, *Catullus' Passer* 82–85.

274 M. Lavency, "L'Ode à Lesbie et son billet d'envoi," *AC* 34 (1965) 175–82; G.C. Giardina, "La composizione del liber e l'itinerario poetico di Catullo," *Philologus* 118 (1974) 225, 231; and J. Clack, "*Otium tibi Molestum Est*—Catullus 50 and 51," *CB* 52 (1976) 50–53.

Other critics who see a close relation between cc. 50 and 51 include: L. Ferrero, *Un' introduzione a Catullo* (Turin 1955) 63–69; D.F.S. Thompson, "Catullus and Cicero: Poetry and the Criticism of Poetry," *CW* 60 (1967) 230; C.P. Segal, "Catullan *Otiosi*: The Lover and the Poet," *G&R* 17 (1970) 25–31; Skinner, *Catullus' Passer* 81; T.E. Kinsey, "Catullus 51," *Latomus* 33 (1974) 376; and J.F. Finamore, "Catullus 50 and 51: Friendship, Love, and *Otium*," *CW* 78 (1984) 11–19.

275 Cc. 14 and 50 have numerous features in common (Németh, "Catullan Twin Poems" [above, note 77] 44–53). The point of their close relation may be to indicate that the humorous c. 50 with the accompanying c. 51 represents a sort of one-upmanship on Catullus' part for his friend's earlier prank of sending him an anthology of bad poetry as a Saturnalia gift (cf. especially the theme of retribution that occurs at the end of both poems). C. 50, of course, also has a serious purpose, as is suggested by the combination of the important themes of friendship and poetry.

276 For secondary literature on the *otium*-strophe, see Finamore, "Catullus 50 and 51" (above, note 274) 11, notes 1, 2, and 3.

277 The idea that c. 51 was the first poem that "Catullus sent, or showed, his mistress" appears to have been popularized by Quinn (*An Interpretation* 57) and to have been proposed first by L.P. Wilkinson, in *L'influence grecque sur la poésie latin de Catulle à Ovide*, ed. by J. Bayet, Fond. Hardt (Geneva 1953) 47–48.

278 It is important to note, too, that c. 51 is meant to be read in light of c. 11, the only other poem in the Sapphic meter (cf. also the pointed repetition of *identidem* at 51.3 from 11.19). If the reverse were true, c. 51 would have preceded c. 11.

279 On this point, see page 87.

280 *scribens versiculos uterque nostrum / ludebat numero modo hoc modo illoc* (50.4–5). The same observation, of course, applies to c. 51.

281 "Catullus 55," (above, note 221) 259.

There is one additional deviation from the OCT, besides those taken from Peachy's reconstruction of the text. Following Goold, I read *sacellis* for *libellis* at verse 5 (*Interpreting Catullus* [above, note 221] 18).

The topographical references appear to alternate degrees of size: Campus Minor, Circus Maximus; shrines (*sac-ellis)*, temple of Jupiter Maximus; Jupiter Maximus in turn forms a link with Pompeius Magnus and his portico. I owe this observation to Barbara McCauley, a former student.

282 "Catullus 55" (above, note 221) 260. There is a simple explanation for how 58b came to be detached from c. 55. The resemblance between 55.14 and 58b.10 (*te...amice*) may have caused the scribe to believe that he had already copied 58b.1–10. When he came to realize his mistake, he included the verses several poems later. Others who combine cc. 55 and 58b include: O. Bianco, "Catullo, C. 55 e 58a," *RCCM* 6 (1964) 33–44; P. Oksala, *Adnotationes Criticae ad Catulli Carmina* (Helsinki 1965) 59–61; H.A. Khan, "An Interpretational Crux: Catullus 55 and 58a," *AC* 36 (1967) 116–31; and Goold, *Interpreting Catullus* (above, note 221) 15–21. Critics disagree, however, at what verse in c. 55 the fragment 58b is to be incorporated. From the perspective of the poem's structure, Peachy's insertion after verse 14 seems superior to all other proposals.

283 Ferguson, *Catullus* 169.

284 Khan, "Catullus 55 and 58a" (above, note 282) 120.

285 On this point, see W. Ferrari, "Il carme 51 di Catullo," *ASNP* 7 (1938) 70; and D.A. Kidd, "The Unity of Catullus 51," *AUMLA* 20 (1963) 307.

286 Khan, "Catullus 55 and 58a" (above, note 282) 125.

287 J.F. Killeen, "Catullus C. 55," *Siculorum Gymnasium* 29 (1976) 261.

288 F.O. Copley, "Catullus 55, 9–14," *AJP* 73 (1952) 295–97.

289 H. Comfort, "Parody in Catullus 58a," *AJP* 56 (1935) 45–49.

290 Khan, "Catullus 55 and 58a" (above, note 282) 127–28. Keeping the tongue in the mouth would deprive Camerius of using it in love-play.

291 Macleod, "Parody and Personalities" 296.

292 Németh, "Catullan Twin Poems" (above, note 77) 45–53.

293 McCarren, *A Critical Concordance* 42.

294 Their connection is discussed in great detail by Fredricksmeyer, "Catullus' *Longus Amor*" (above, note 30) 63–88, especially 80–81.

295 In conjunction with this proposal, it is worth noting that the adverb *pulcre*, which occurs in the first and final lines of c. 57, appears to point backward to Clodius Pulcher of c. 56 and forward to Clodia (Pulchra) of c. 58.

Chapter Three: The Central Poems

1 On the unity, see especially G. Lieberg, "L'ordinamento ed i reciproci rapporti dei carmi maggiori di Catullo," *RFIC* 36 (1958) 23–47; E. Schäfer, *Das Verhältnis von Erlebnis und Kunstgestalt bei Catull* Hermes Einzelschriften 18 (1966) 73–77; Wiseman, *Catullan Questions* 20–25; Schmidt, "Catulls Anordnung" 236–37; G.W. Most, "On the Arrangement of Catullus' *Carmina Maiora*," *Philologus* 125 (1981) 109–25 (the pattern of arrangement proposed by Most is discussed below, pages 236–39); and Newman, *Roman Catullus* 204–47.

2 A.L. Wheeler, *Catullus and the Traditions of Ancient Poetry* (Berkeley 1934) 211.

3 T.P. Wiseman, *Clio's Cosmetics: Three Studies in Greco-Roman Literature* (Leicester 1979) 177 and note 10; and *A Reappraisal* 183–84.

4 C. 61 is in glyconics; c. 62 is in lyric hexameters; c. 64 is in epic hexameters; and c. 63 is in galliambics. The glyconics of c. 61 create a metrical link with 1–60, for the meter of the poem is virtually the same as the hendecasyllabic found in many of the polymetra (W. Clausen, "Catulli Veronensis Liber," *CP* 71 [1976] 40).

5 Owing to the often sorry state of the text, numerical correspondence in the Catullan collection can be only relatively accurate. In the long poems c. 62 has suffered the loss of 7 or 8 verses following verse 33, depending upon whether 58b (an insertion by Muretus) is counted; and line references

to c. 61 acknowledge the lacunae indicated in Mynors' text. I do not, however, assume a lacuna between verses 141 and 142 of c. 68b. Instead, I believe that verse 142 is corrupt.

6 For a discussion of mathematical symmetry in Latin poetry books, see H. Dettmer, *Horace: A Study in Structure* (Hildesheim 1983) 1–75.

7 Pages 243–47.

8 Wheeler, *Traditions of Ancient Poetry* (above, note 2) 270, note 1; O. Weinreich, *Catull: Sämtliche Gedichte* (Zurich 1969) 49; Wiseman, *Catullan Questions* 20–21; V. Tufte, *The Poetry of Marriage* (Los Angeles 1970) 21–36; and Small, *Catullus* 93, 96.

9 *The Poetry of Marriage* (above, note 8) 30, 36.

10 On c. 61, see Wheeler, *Traditions of Ancient Poetry* (above, note 2) 191–213; L. Ferrero, *Interpretazione di Catullo* (Turin 1955) 283–313; Williams, *Tradition and Originality* 199–202; P. Fedeli, *Catullus' Carmen 61* (Amsterdam 1983, rev. in English; Fribourg 1972, repr. 1981 Italian); Ferguson, *Catullus* 175–79; Small, *Catullus* 88–92; Adler, *Catullan Self-Revelation* 121–25; and O. Thomsen, *Ritual and Desire: Catullus 61 and 62 and Other Ancient Documents on Wedding and Marriage* (Denmark 1992) 17–150. The name of Torquatus' bride is problematical. To circumvent the difficulty of the girl's having a double *gentilicium* (the manuscripts read *vinia*, *iunia*, and *iullia*), I follow Neudling in adopting R. Syme's solution of reading Vibia, a feminine Oscan *praenomen* (*A Prosopography* 185).

11 Fordyce, *Catullus* 237.

12 On c. 62, see Wheeler, *Traditions of Ancient Poetry* (above, note 2) 213–17; Ferrero, *Interpretazione* (above, note 10) 314–39; E. Fraenkel, "*Vesper adest*," *JRS* 45 (1955) 1–8; Williams, *Tradition and Originality* 201–02; D.A. Kidd, "Hesperus and Catullus 62," *Latomus* 33 (1974) 22–33; E.S. Stigers, "Retreat from the Male: Catullus 62 and Sappho's Erotic Flowers," *Ramus* 6 (1977) 83–102; W.R. Nethercut, "The Art of Catullus 62," Coll. Latomus 164 (1979) 229–38; S. Commager, "The Structure of Catullus 62," *Eranos* 81 (1983) 21–33; Ferguson, *Catullus* 181–84; Small, *Catullus* 84–88; Adler, *Catullan Self-Revelation* 125–28; and Thomsen, *Ritual and Desire* 151–230.

13 *A Commentary* 209.

14 On their close connection, see especially Thomsen, *Ritual and Desire* 155–77; and Lieberg, "carmi maggiori di Catullo" (above, note 1) 23–28.

15 Wheeler, *Traditions of Ancient Poetry* (above, note 2) 215.

16 Adler, *Self-Revelation* 126; and Thomsen, *Ritual and Desire* 157.

17 Thomsen, *Ritual and Desire* 156.

18 Adler, *Self-Revelation* 124.

19 *Ibid.* 127.

20 "The Structure" (above, note 12) 29.

21 Fedeli, *Carmen 61* (above, note 10) 53.

22 Thomsen interprets *parentes* to refer to both "the father and mother (of the bride)" (*Ritual and Desire* 209–16).

23 Commager, "The Structure" (above, note 12) 26.

24 Newman, *Roman Catullus* 214.

25 Wiseman assigns verses 46–75 of c. 61 to a female choir and 124–83 to a male choir (*A Reappraisal* 119, note 88).

26 In c. 62, however, there is the addition of the Latin *ades*. "The effect…is to revitalize the refrain as invocation" (Thomsen, *Ritual and Desire* 196).

27 Adler, *Catullan Self-Revelation* 125. In conjunction with this point, it is worth quoting an observation made by J. Redfield: "We can understand why the bride is the star of the wedding. It is her initiation; virginity is not properly a quality of males" ("Notes on the Greek Wedding," *Arethusa* 15 [1982] 191).

28 Thomsen, *Ritual and Desire* 158.

29 J. Granarolo, *L'Oeuvre de Catulle: aspects religieux, éthiques et stylistiques* (Paris 1967) 132–33; and D. Konstan, *Catullus' Indictment of Rome: The Meaning of Catullus 64* (Amsterdam 1977) 6–7.

Catullus moved the celebration of the wedding from the traditional location on Mount Pelion to Peleus' palace at Pharsalus, I suspect, because the *domus* functions as a unifying motif of the central poems.

30 Fordyce, *Catullus ad loc.*

31 L.C. Curran, "Catullus 64 and the Heroic Age," *YCS* 21 (1969) 189.

32 McCarren, *A Critical Concordance* 169.

33 Thomsen, *Ritual and Desire* 239, note 20.

34 F. Klingner, "Catulls Peleus-Epos," *SBAW* vol. 6 (Munich 1956) 82–83.

35 Curran, "Catullus 64" (above, note 31) 175.

36 Quinn, *The Poems ad* 64.163; and J. Glenn, "Ariadne's Daydream (Cat. 64.158–63)," *CJ* 76 (1980–81) 112–13.

37 Lieberg, "carmi maggiori di Catullo" (above, note 1) 33–36; M.C.J. Putnam, "The Art of Catullus 64," *HSCP* 65 (1961) 169–70, 174, 177–78; Schäfer, *Das Verhältnis* (above, note 1) 102–03; Granarolo, *L'Oeuvre* (above, note 29) 143–44; P.Y. Forsyth, "The Marriage Theme in Catullus 63," *CJ* 66 (1970) 66–69; G.N. Sandy, "Catullus 63 and the Theme of Marriage," *AJP* 92 (1971) 188–89; and Wiseman, *A Reappraisal* 180–81.

38 "The Art of Catullus 64" (above, note 37) 169–70.

39 Sandy, "The Theme of Marriage" (above, note 37) 188.

40 Putnam, "The Art of Catullus 64" (above, note 37) 188.

41 Sandy, "The Theme of Marriage" (above, note 37) 193.

42 Critics who see the poem as mirroring the poet's experience with Lesbia include: G. Highet, *Poets in a Landscape* (New York 1957) 26–27; P.W. Harkins, "Autoallegory in Catullus 63 and 64," *TAPA* 90 (1959) 102–16; R. Bagg, "Some Versions of Lyric Impasse in Shakespeare and Catullus," *Arion* 4 (1965) 84–87; P.Y. Forsyth, "Catullus: the Mythic Persona," *Latomus* 35 (1976) 555–66; T.J. Sienkewicz, "Catullus—Another Attis?" *CB* 57 (1981) 37–43; Ferguson, *Catullus* 191; Arkins, *Sexuality in Catullus* 152–56; Wiseman, *A Reappraisal* 180–82; B-M. Näsström, *The Abhorrence of Love. Studies in Rituals and Mystic Aspects in Catullus' Poem of Attis* (Stockholm 1989) 22, 25–26, 92; J.A. Lobell, "An Unconventional Reading of Catullus 63," *Brown Classical Journal* 8 (1992) 18–22; and M.B. Skinner, "*Ego Mulier*: The Construction of the Male Sexuality in Catullus," *Helios* 20 (1993) 118–21. Professor Skinner kindly sent me a copy of her paper before it appeared in print.

C. 64 has been subject to similar biographical exegesis. In this instance the close relation of 60.1–3 to 64.154–57 clearly indicates that Catullus is identifying his own situation with that of Ariadne. For a discussion of the similarities between the two passages, see Putnam, "The Art of Catullus 64" (above, note 37) 176–77.

43 *A Reappraisal* 181.

44 *Ibid.*

45 Brother = light/life (*lumen*) and brother = *domus* (93–96); by the poem's end, Lesbia = light/life (*lux*), hence Lesbia = *domus*.

46 M.R. Salzman, "Cicero, The *Megalenses* and the Defense of Caelius," *AJP* 103 (1982) 301.

47 *Poets in a Landscape* (above, note 42) 27.

48 Ferguson, *Catullus* 191.

49 Bagg favors a quasi-autobiographical interpretation for other reasons that are worth mentioning: "1) The poem contains the castration and reversal of

sex visible in 11 and 68 and 64. 2) Catullus was in the habit of projecting himself into his mythic poems, explicitly in 68, and in 64 seemingly identifying his loss with Ariadne's....[And] 3) Catullus has altered the myth so that it presents a worshipper violently disillusioned and homesick, after his self-mutilation rite, and this change accords with 11 and his revulsion with Lesbia" ("Shakespeare and Catullus" [above, note 42] 84).

50 Schmidt ("Catulls Anordnung" 237) and Forsyth (*A Teaching Text* 12) also note a connection between these pieces.

51 McCarren, *A Critical Concordance* 179.

52 F.O. Copley, *Exclusus Amator: A Study in Latin Love Poetry* (Baltimore 1956) 157–58, note 27.

53 E.g., the door speaks instead of being spoken to; it abuses others instead of being abused; it receives praise instead of reproach for being shut; etc. ("Some Neglected Aspects of Catullus 67," *Hermes* 117 [1989] 472–73).

54 G.N. Sandy, "The Imagery of Catullus 63," *TAPA* 99 (1968) 389–99.

55 W. Kroll suggests, quite plausibly, that the phrase *in novissimo casu* in 60.4 alludes to the death of the brother (*C. Valerius Catullus* [Leipzig and Berlin 1923] *ad loc.*).

56 C. Witke, *Enarratio Catulliana: Carmina 50, 30, 65, 68* (Leiden 1968) 19–20; and Adler, *Catullan Self-Revelation* 79–81.

57 This appears to be the point of Catullus' statements, *scriptorum non magna est copia apud me,...huc una ex multis capsula me sequitur*, in verses 33 and 36.

58 I take 68a.27–29 as referring to Verona and to Catullus' sleeping alone there. On the similar situations of Catullus and Manlius, see C.J. Tuplin, "Catullus 68," *CQ* 31 (1981) 114–16.

59 J. Wohlberg ("The Structure of the Laodamia Simile in Catullus 68b," *CP* 50–51 [1955–56] 45), F. Della Corte (*Due studi catulliani* [Genoa 1951] 137–38), and F.O. Copley ("The Unity of Catullus 68: A Further View," *CP* 52 [1957] 29–32) suggest that 68b is a revision of an earlier poem that was contained in the single box of books Catullus brought from Rome. I cannot agree with this view for reasons that will become clear in Chapter Six. Since Catullus comes to terms with his brother's death through this very original composition, I think the reader is to assume a change of mind resulted from the same obligations of friendship that motivated a translation of the *Lock of Berenice*.

60 Copley, "The Unity of Catullus 68" (above, note 59) 29–32.

61 On the relation of 65 and 68a, see Lieberg, "carmi maggiori di Catullo" (above, note 1) 44–45; Witke, *Enarratio Catulliana* (above, note 56) 20,

29, 33–34; and K.M.W. Shipton, "Catullus 68," *LCM* 3.3 (1978) 58–61. I disagree, however, with Shipton's conclusion that cc. 65 and 68a are addressed to the same individual.

62 The image of shipwreck here also recalls that of being storm-tossed in 65.4 (*mens animi, tantis fluctuat ipsa malis*).

63 "Catullus' Callimachean Carmina" 384. For c. 65 as an introduction to the following poems in the elegiac meter, see also Wiseman, *Catullan Questions* 17–18 and *Clio's Cosmetics* 176; and E. Block, "Carmen 65 and the Arrangement of Catullus' Poetry," *Ramus* 13 (1984) 48–59.

64 Adler, *Catullan Self-Revelation* 79.

65 For 68a as a separate poem, see also M.B. Skinner, "The Unity of Catullus 68: The Structure of 68a," *TAPA* 103 (1972) 495–512; K. Vretska, "Das Problem der Einheit von Catull c. 68," *WS* 79 (1966) 315–20; and T.P. Wiseman, *Cinna the Poet and Other Roman Essays* (Leicester 1974) 90–91.

66 "Catullus c. 68: A New Perspective," *CSCA* 9 (1976) 71. My interpretation of the relation of 68a and 68b is much indebted to Levine's excellent analysis.

67 On the relation between the *domus* of Protesilaus and Laodamia and the *domus* of Lesbia and Catullus, compare the similar language in 73–74 and 143–44:

coniugis ut quondam flagrans ADVENIT amore
  Protesilaeam Laudamia DOMUM
nec tamen illa mihi dextra deducta paterna
  fragrantem Assyrio VENIT odore DOMUM.

68 For *munus* referring to the pleasures of love, cf. 61.234–35: *munere assiduo valentem / exercete iuventam.*

69 Cf. *iucundum lumen* = the brother (93) with *lux mea* = Lesbia (132, 160), and *omnia tecum una perierunt gaudia nostra* (95) with *qua viva vivere dulce mihi est* (160).

70 J.P. Elder, "Notes on Some Conscious and Subconscious Elements in Catullus' Poetry," *HSCP* 60 (1951) 127, 129, quotation taken from the latter page.

71 Wiseman, *A Reappraisal* 163.

72 On these points, see also T.E. Kinsey, "Some Problems in Catullus 68," *Latomus* 26 (1967) 52.

73 Wiseman, *A Reappraisal* 166.

74 On the relation between the language and thought in these verses, see also E. Courtney, "Three Poems of Catullus," *BICS* 32 (1985) 95. The change of addressee at the conclusion of the poem can be paralleled on a smaller scale by c. 1.

75 For my interpretation of the benediction in verses 155–60, I again am indebted to Levine, "A New Perspective" (above, note 66) 73.

The text at verse 157 is corrupt, *et qui principio nobis †terram dedit aufert†*, but I think not irreparably so. The problem appears to involve *aufert* only, for, as Levine observes, "the image in *terram dedit* is an appropriate complement to the nautical simile characterizing the service rendered by Allius to Catullus" in verses 63–66 ("A New Perspective" [above, note 66] 76). Since verses 156–58 look back to verses 63–69 in repetition of language, thought, and metaphor as well as reference to Allius' *officium*, Rossbach's emendation of *aufert* to *auctor* is attractive for two reasons. First, the noun is cognate with *auxilium*, which Catullus used of Allius in verse 66 (*tale fuit nobis Allius auxilium*). Second, *auctor* can refer to a consenting witness to a marriage (*OLD*, s.v. 3.b), which well accords with Allius' role in the "nuptials" of Catullus and Lesbia (which are suggested symbolically by the language in vv. 70–72, 133–34, and 143–46). *Auctus* is associated with marriage twice in the poetry of Catullus, at 64.25 and 66.11.

76 Similar features that connect cc. 65 and 66 are noted by King ("Catullus' Callimachean Carmina" 385, 387–88), quotation taken from page 387.

77 Cf. *semper...semper* in 65.11–12 with *invita...invita* in 66.39–40, *me afore...afore me* in 66.75–76, and *semper...semper* in 66.87–88 (W. Clausen, "Catullus and Callimachus," *HSCP* 74 [1970] 91–93).

78 King, "Catullus' Callimachean Carmina" 385.

79 D.A. Kidd, "Some Problems in Catullus 66," *Antichthon* 4 (1970) 40.

On the relation of cc. 66 and 68b, see also M.C.J. Putnam, "Catullus 66.75–88," *CP* 55 (1960) 226–27; M. Puelma, "Die Aitien des Kallimachos als Vorbild der römischen Amores-Elegie," *MH* 39 (1982) 232–35; and C.W. Macleod, "The Artistry of Catullus 67," in *Collected Essays of C.W. Macleod* (Oxford 1983) 194, note 1. My own discussion owes much to Macleod's observations.

80 Kidd, "Some Problems" (above, note 79) 40.

81 Lewis-Short, s.v. I.1. Goold, in fact, translates *lux* as "star" at 68b.160 (*Catullus* 189).

82 T.D. Papanghelis, "A Note on Catullus 68.156–157," *QUCC* N.S. 11 (1982) 144–45. F. Della Corte (*Personaggi catulliani,* 2nd ed. [Florence 1976] 133) apparently was the first to draw attention to the similar passages, as A.W. Allen observes ("Catullus 68.157," *Maia* 53 [1991]

193–94). The resemblance between 66.49–50 and 68b.157 offers additional support of Rossbach's emendation of *aufert* to *auctor*, which is paralleled in meaning by *institit*.

83 "The Artistry" (above, note 79) 194, note 1.

84 On the relation of cc. 66 and 67, see L. Richardson, Jr., "Catullus 67: Interpretation and Form," *AJP* 88 (1967) 423–24; Macleod, "The Artistry" (above, note 79) 192–93; Puelma, "Die Aitien" (above note 79) 231–32; P. Levine, "Catullus c. 67: The Dark Side of Love and Marriage," *ClAnt* 4 (1985) 70–71; and King, "Catullus' Callimachean Carmina" 388.

85 Levine, "Dark Side of Love" (above, note 84) 69.

86 Macleod, "The Artistry" (above, note 79) 192.

87 "Dark Side of Love" (above, note 84) 71.

88 On their relation, see also Macleod, "The Artistry" (above, note 79) 193–94.

89 J.P. Hallett, "*Ianua iucunda*: The Characterization of the Door in Catullus 67," Coll. Latomus 168 (1980) 110.

90 Murgatroyd, "Some Neglected Aspects" (above, note 53) 471–78; and K.M.W. Shipton, "A Successful Komos in Catullus," *Latomus* 44 (1985) 503–20.

91 Puelma, "Die Aitien" (above, note 79) 234–35.

92 Tufte, *The Poetry of Marriage* (above, note 8) 30.

93 Wiseman, *A Reappraisal* 119.

94 Quinn, *An Interpretation* 250. His interpretation of the Attis poem is supported by Skinner ("*Ego Mulier*" [above, note 42] 112–13).

95 Quinn (*An Interpretation* 250–53) notes the connection.

96 Hymenaeus and Catullus' Attis hold in common, too, that both are *pueri delicati*. In traditional myth Hymenaeus is depicted as "a beautiful youth, *eromenos* of various gods" (Thomsen, *Ritual and Desire* 94).

97 "Catullus 63 and the Theme of Marriage" (above, note 37) 192.

98 Richardson, "Catullus 67" (above, note 84) 432–33; and Levine, "The Dark Side" (above, note 84) 65.

99 Wiseman, *Catullan Questions* 22.

100 "Catullus 67" (above, note 84) 433. In support of his interpretation, Richardson notes that the scandalous content of the poem and the spirited exchange between the interlocutor and the door accord with what Horace has to say about the early form of the Fescennines: *Fescennina per hunc*

inventa licentia morem / versibus alternis opprobria rustica fudit (*Epistle* 2.1.145–46).

101 K. Gutzwiller, "Callimachus' Lock of Berenice: Fantasy, Romance, and Propaganda," *AJP* 113 (1992) 370.

102 *Ibid.* 372

103 Newman, *Roman Catullus* 226.

104 Thomsen, *Ritual and Desire* 89. On the close association of Hymenaeus and Hesperus, see J. Diggle, "*Elegiae in Maecenatem* 129–32," *Latomus* 27 (1968) 175–80.

105 "The Art of Catullus 64" (above, note 37) 190.

106 In conjunction with this point, it is worth observing that according to one version of the story, the marriage of Peleus and Thetis turns out not to be altogether happy (64.379–80, in fact, allude to estrangement).

107 G.B. Townend, "The Unstated Climax of Catullus 64," *G&R* 30 (1983) 26.

108 "Comparison is the cardinal trope of hymenaeal, with mythic, or divine, models proposed for bride and groom, and with analogies from the work of nature" (D.C. Feeney,"'Shall I Compare Thee…?' Catullus 68b and the Limits of Analogy," *Author and Audience in Latin Literature*, ed. by T. Woodman and J. Powell [Cambridge 1992] 33-34).

109 The view that 68a and 68b sever Manlius' dual role in c. 61 as recipient and sometimes addressee is shared by G. Pennisi, "Il carme 68 di Catullo," *Emerita* 27 (1959) 235–36; Wiseman, *Cinna the Poet* (above, note 65) 102–03; Most, "Catullus' *Carmina Maiora*" 116–17; Ferguson, *Catullus* 175; and Newman, *Roman Catullus* 228–29.

110 It is essential to the theme of 68b and its programmatic content that Lesbia have a husband, whether her marital status is based on fact (the poem, then, is early and has been reworked) or is invented as fiction.

111 61.17–19, 21–25, 34–35, 87–89, 106–09, 193–95, 228–30 and 68.53–56, 57–62, 63–66, 73–130, 109–18, 119–24, and 125–28. I count 68.57–66 and 119–28 as double similes.

112 "'Shall I Compare Thee…?'" (above, note 108) 33.

113 *Ibid.* 33–44.

114 Wiseman, *A Reappraisal* 119.

115 *Roman Catullus* 245.

Chapter Four: Caelius Rufus

1 C. 73 is not included among the Caelius Rufus poems because I read *quae* (= Lesbia) instead of *qui* in verse 6 (O. Skutsch, "Metrical Variations and Some Textual Problems in Catullus," *BICS* 16 [1969] 42). This emendation was first proposed by T. Birt ("Zu Catull's Carmina minora," *Philologus* 63 [1904] 469).

2 The evidence that Lesbia was a Clodia is based on the authority of Apuleius (*Apol.* 10). That she was one of Publius Clodius' three sisters is suggested by 79.1, where Catullus puns on the *cognomen* Pulcher (*Lesbius est pulcer*). On the traditional identification, see, for example, H.D. Rankin, "'Clodia II,'" *AC* 38 (1969) 501–06; Quinn, *An Interpretation* 131–53; C. Deroux, "L'identité de Lesbie," *ANRW* 1.3 (1973) 390–416; and Arkins, *Sexuality in Catullus* 50–53.

3 For a discussion of this textual problem, see R.G. Austin, *M. Tulli Ciceronis Pro M. Caelio Oratio*, 3rd ed. (Oxford 1960) 146–47; and D.M. Madsen, *The Life and Political Career of Marcus Caelius Rufus* (Diss. University of Washington 1981) 17–21.

4 For the most recent study of this prosopographical issue, see B. Arkins, "Caelius and Rufus in Catullus," *Philologus* 127 (1983) 306–11.

5 *Cinna the Poet and other Roman Essays* (Leicester 1974) 106–07.

6 *Catullus* (Cambridge, Mass. 1893, 1951) xxxix.

7 *An Interpretation* 74–75; and "The Irony of Catullus 100," *CW* 70 (1977) 313–17. On this issue, see also Forsyth's comments on the individual Caelius and Rufus poems in her *A Teaching Text*.

8 Briscoe, review of "T.P. Wiseman's *Catullan Questions*," *JRS* 61 (1971) 304; and Austin, *Pro M. Caelio Oratio* (above, note 3) 149.

9 For Catullus' referring to the same individual by his *nomen* in one poem and *cognomen* in another, cf. the Licinius Calvus poems (14, 50, 53, 96).

10 For reading *magnanimos* in preference to the manuscript's *magnanimi*, see now B. Arkins ("Catullus 58.5," *LCM* 2.10 [1977] 237–38) and O. Skutsch ("Catullus 58.4–5," *LCM* 5.1 [1980] 21).

11 McCarren, *A Critical Concordance* 120.

12 On the life of Caelius Rufus, see F. Münzer, *RE* 3.1 1266–72; Austin, *Pro M. Caelio Oratio* (above, note 3) v–xvi; M. Volponi, "Celio Rufo ingeniose nequam," Mem. 1st Lombardo, *Classe di Lettere* 31.3 (1970) 197–280 (unavailable); S.B. Jackson, "Marcus Caelius Rufus," *Hermathena* 126 (1979) 55–67; and Madsen, *Life and Political Career* (above, note 3).

13 On this point cf. D.F. Bright, who suggests that "49 and 58 may relate to similar circumstances" ("*Non Bona Dicta*: Catullus' Poetry of Separation," *QUCC* 21 [1976] 108).

14 H.A.J. Munro, *Criticisms and Elucidations of Catullus* (London 1905) 134; and Ellis, *A Commentary* 205.

15 For a similar interpretation of *Bononiensis*, cf. Ellis' translation: "Rufa has found a Rufus to be kind to" (*A Commentary* 205). On the sexual meaning of *bonus*, see s.v. *OLD*, 4a; and P. Pierrugues, *Glossarium Eroticum Linguae Latinae* (Paris 1826; 2nd ed., Berlin 1908) 97, 99.

16 For a discussion of the politico-social implications of the word *bonus*, see U. Paananen, *Sallust's Politico-Social Terminology* (Helsinki 1972) 59–64.

17 On the political connotations of *Remus* and *Romulus* in Catullus, cf. the occurrences of the words at 28.15; 29.5, 9; and 49.1; for *boni* signifying "persons of rank" elsewhere in Catullus, cf. 37.14, 19.

18 On the thematic relation of cc. 58 and 59, see also O. Weinreich, "Catull c. 60," *Hermes* 87 (1959) 89–90; and Wiseman, *A Reappraisal* 156.

19 On a metaphorical meaning of *tundo*, see Arkins, *Sexuality in Catullus* 6; J.N. Adams, "Words for 'Prostitute' in Latin," *RhM* 126 (1983) 336; and Lindgren, *Non Bona Dicta* 26.

Glubo, a *hapax legomenon*, metaphorically refers to retracting the foreskin. Whether the *retractio praeputi* occurs prior to masturbation or to fellatio, however, is a subject of controversy. For literature, see F.W. Lenz, "Catulliana," *RCCM* 5 (1963) 62–67, especially 63–64; R.J. Penella, "A Note on *(de)glubere*," *Hermes* 104 (1976) 118–20; J.G. Randall, "Mistresses' Pseudonyms in Latin Elegy," *LCM* 4.4 (1979) 29–30; B. Arkins, "*Glubit* in Catullus 58.5," *LCM* 4.5 (1979) 85–86; H.D. Jocelyn, "Catullus 58 and Ausonius, *Ep.* 71," *LCM* 4.5 (1979) 87–91; Skutsch, "Catullus 58.4–5" (above, note 10) 21; and J.G. Randall, "*Glubit* in Catullus 58: retractio," *LCM* 5.1 (1980) 21–22.

20 On a possible connection between the epithets *semiraso* and *magnanimos*, see D.O. Ross, Jr., *Style and Tradition in Catullus* (Cambridge, Mass. 1969) 21–22.

21 Weinreich, "Catull c. 60" (above, note 18) 89. Lesbia's name appears in five polymetric poems: cc. 5, 7, 43, 51, and 58 (McCarren, *A Critical Concordance* 96).

22 On Rufus' determining Rufa, cf. Lesbia's determining Lesbius in c. 79.

23 McCarren, *A Critical Concordance* 63.

24 Randall ("Mistresses' Pseudonyms" [above, note 19] 28) and E. Wirshbo ("'Lesbia': A Mock Hypocorism?" *CP* 75 [1980] 70) independently suggest that "both sublime and lewd connotations" (Wirshbo) prompted Catullus' choice of the pseudonym Lesbia. In my opinion it seems more likely that a disillusioned, bitter Catullus later took advantage of the less than flattering connotation of the name.

25 It is tempting to see Catullus playing on the setting of c. 59, *in sePULCHRetis* (a *hapax legomenon*), as part of his subtly revealing the identity of Rufa-Lesbia as the widow Clodia Metelli. For wordplay on the PULCHR- element of *sepulchretis*, cf. the tomb inscription of Claudia (Pulchra?), which dates to the late 2nd century B.C.: *Heic est sePULCHRum hau PULCHRum PULCRai feminae* (A. Ernout, *Recueil de textes latins archaïques* [Paris 1947] no. 133 77–78). For a discussion of the inscription, see F. Ahl, *Metaformations: Soundplay and Wordplay in Ovid and other Classical Poets* (Ithaca and London 1985) 43. It is worth noting that Catullus puns on the *cognomen* of Lesbia's family in another poem, 86.5, where he describes her as *PULCHERrima tota*.

26 The correspondence of cc. 58 and 59 suggests that the emendation of *Rufus* to *Rufulus* in 59.1 is correct. The disparaging masculine diminutive looks back to the feminine diminutive *Lesbilla*, the result of the elided *Lesbia illa* in 58.1–2.

27 Wiseman, *A Reappraisal* 20. If c. 59 were not a scathingly obscene *diffamatio*, it would be tempting to suggest that the description of Lesbia as "Bolognese" in c. 59 is intended to anticipate Catullus' identifying her with his home and family in Verona in c. 68b.

28 On Caelius' good looks, *Pro Caelio* 6, 36, 77.

29 "The question of degradation was most acute where the oral mode was involved; thus *fellator*—or *fellatrix*, of a woman—was the most contemptuous of insults" (Wiseman, *A Reappraisal* 11).

30 Lindgren (*Non Bona Dicta* 27) offers the interesting suggestion that c. 59 is a parody of a sepulchral epigram. Verses 1–2 contain "the three basic elements of functional epitaphs": place of origin (*Bononiensis*), the name of the decedent (*Rufa*), and patronymic (here *uxor Meneni* is the equivalent). "The final three lines describe not the admirable qualities of the deceased woman,...but rather her deplorable habit of stealing food from corpses."

31 On the derivation of *femina*, see A. Walde, *Lateinisches Etymologisches Wörterbuch* (Heidelberg 1910) 281. Popular etymology also connects *femur* (69.2) with the Latin root FE- (Isid., *Orig.* 11.1.106).

32 On the relation between oral sex and eating, Adams, *LSV* 139, 141.

33 On identifying Rufus of c. 69 with the *iste aemulus* of c. 71, see W. Kroll, *C. Valerius Catullus* (Leipzig and Berlin 1923) 143–44; Wiseman, *Cinna the Poet* (above, note 5) 107, note 15; and Arkins, *Sexuality in Catullus* 40–41. I construe Catullus as the addressee of the poem, and I follow R.A. Kaster ("A Note on Catullus, c. 71.4," *Philologus* 121 [1977] 308–12) in reading *apte* for the corrupt *ate* at verse 4.

34 McCarren, *A Critical Concordance* 8.

35 It is tempting to see a sexual nuance in *pereo* ("to experience orgasm").

36 The phrase *exercere amores/em* occurs only at 68.69 and 71.3 (McCarren, *A Critical Concordance* 59). S.J. Heyworth suggests that Catullus used the plural *vestrum* at 71.3, instead of the singular *tuum*, in order to signify Rufus' "appropriation" of his love ("Notes on Propertius Books I and II," *CQ* 34 [1984] 395).

37 "*Bellus* [is] an old word (a diminutive made from *bonus*)" (Fordyce, *Catullus ad* 3.14).

38 On Catullus' use of "contorted and harsh" language and numerous elisions to convey his bitterness toward Rufus, see Ferguson, *Catullus* 259.

39 "*Mala Bestia* in Catullus 69.7–8," *CW* 73 (1979) 155–64.

40 Our source is Pliny, *N.H.* 27.4 (cited by Noonan, *ibid.* 160): constat omnium venenorum occissimum esse aconitum et tactis quoque genitalibus feminini sexus animalium eodem die inferre mortem. Hoc fuit venenum quo interemptas dormientis a Calpurnio Bestia uxores M. Caelius accusator obiecit; hinc illa atrox peroratio eius in digitum.

41 Noonan, "*Mala Bestia*" (above, note 39) 160.

42 *Ibid.* 163–64.

43 On the foul smell, cf. Pliny *N.H.* 27.9, who makes the following comment on the etymology of *myoctonon*, another name for aconite: nec defuere qui [aconitum] myoctonon appellare mallent, quoniam procul et e longinquo odore mures necat.

44 McCarren, *A Crictical Concordance* 34.

45 Fordyce, *Catullus ad* 77.6.

46 Noonan, "*Mala Bestia*" (above, note 39) 163, note 25.

47 Quinn (*The Poems* 412) apparently is the first to suggest that *vita* in 77.5 alludes to Lesbia.

48 On this point, see Skutsch ("Metrical Variations" [above, note 1] 42) and Quinn (*The Poems ad* 77.6), the latter of whom observes, "One is tempted to accord *amicitiae* the meaning it has in 109.6."

49 "Catullus 76: The Summing Up," *Athenaeum* 46 (1968) 65–71. On the similar language, cf. *miser/miserum* in 76.12, 19 and *misero* in 77.4; *eripite* in 76.20 and *eripuisti* in 77.4–5; *pestem* in 76.20 and *pestis* in 77.6; and *subrepens* in 76.21 and *subrepsti* in 77.3.

50 *Ibid.* 67.

51 Khan follows Palmer in reading *perspecta est igni tum* in the textually troubled 100.6 (*ibid.* 70), a reading that I adopt in the quoted text.

52 The expression *eripere ei/ei eripuisti* occurs only here (McCarren, *A Critical Concordance* 51).

53 The identification of Caelius and Quintius as rivals of Catullus in turn makes sense of the curious question, *cui faveam potius*, in 100.5; we would not expect Catullus to declare his support for either individual.

54 Khan, "The Summing Up" 69.

55 For such an interpretation, see Forsyth, "The Irony" (above, note 7) 313–17; Ferguson, *Catullus* 309; and P. Levine, "Catullus c. 100: A Potent Wish for a 'Friend' in Need," *Maia* 39 (1987) especially 34–39.

56 *Felix* is related to the Latin verb *fello*, "to suck" (Walde, *Wörterbuch* [above, note 31] 280). I am indebted to my colleague E.B. Holtsmark for this point. For references to *possum* used in a sexual sense, see Levine, "A Potent Wish" (above, note 55) 38, note 28.

57 Catullus' expression of "gratitude" to Caelius in c. 100 can be construed as recalling also his expression of "gratitude" to Cicero in c. 49, which together with c. 58 initiates the cycle of Caelius Rufus poems.

58 This detail is striking because the plural possessive modifies Lesbia in only one other poem, 43.7.

59 Catullus associates Lesbia with the BON- instead of the MAL- element even in c. 11, where Furius and Aurelius are to deliver a few *non bona dicta*.

60 *A Prosopography* 39.

61 *Catullus* 262.

62 *CIL* 5.3441, 3570, and 3689.

63 On this point, see Bright, "*Non Bona Dicta*" (above, note 13 of this chapter) 108. When the trial took place, Catullus may have been on his way home from Bithynia. Even so, he could easily have acquired a copy of the published version of Cicero's speech when he returned to Rome (Quinn, *An Interpretation* 197).

64 The individual poems have been the subject of little critical exegesis. See section C of Roman numeral VI in J.P. Holoka's *Gaius Valerius Catullus: A Systematic Bibliography* (New York and London 1985). Secondary literature on c. 58 has been concerned chiefly with text and interpretation of verse 5: are we to read *magnanimi* or *magnanimos*? and what sexual activity does *glubit* denote?

Chapter Five: The Elegaic Epigrams

1 McCarren, *A Critical Concordance* 20.

2 King, "Catullus' Callimachean Carmina" 390–91. The thesis of King's article is that cc. 65–68b function as an introduction to cc. 69–116.

3 Four verses have been added to "B," two for the opening distich of 78b and another two for the verses I will propose to have been lost between 95 and 95b, which I construe as a single poem. For a discussion of mathematical symmetry in the *corpus Catullianum*, see pages 245–47. Propertius appears to be imitating the ordering of 69–116 in his *Monobiblos*, where poems 20 through 22 do not participate in the ring arrangement of 1–19 but function as a tag instead.

4 This scheme represents a slight revision of a symmetrical arrangement I proposed in "Design in the Catullan Corpus: A Preliminary Study," *CW* 81 (1988) 376–77.

5 The Propertian *Monobiblos* offers an analogue for tag poems participating in a numerical pattern. There the difference between the total of verses in B [poems 6–14] and that in A [poems 1–5, 15–19] equals the total of verses in C [20–22], a three-poem tag.

6 McCarren, *A Critical Concordance* 20.

7 For a less apparent reason, see pages 161–64.

8 C. 71 also resembles in certain respects Meleager, *A.P.* 5.8 (= G-P 4348): Νὺξ ἱερὴ καὶ λύχνε. For discussion of the double allusion, see Newman, *Roman Catullus* 248–50.

9 For a discussion of the sexual overtones of *nubere*, see Williams, *Tradition and Originality* 404; and of *nosse*, see H.A. Khan, "A Note on the Expression *solum...nosse* in Catullus," *CP* 62 (1967) 35–36.

10 Arkins, *Sexuality in Catullus* 70.

11 "*Qui potis est, inquis?* Audience Roles in Catullus," *Arethusa* 19 (1986) 203.

12 On reading *quae* in verse 6, see page 305, note 1.

13 O. Weinreich, *Catull: Sämtliche Gedichte* (Zurich 1969) 51.

14 Several critics have noticed the relation of cc. 73 and 76: O. Skutsch, "Metrical Variations and Some Textual Problems in Catullus," *BICS* 16 (1969) 42; D.O. Ross, Jr., *Style and Tradition in Catullus* (Cambridge, Mass. 1969) 88; Goold, *Catullus* 259; H.A. Khan, "Catullus 76: The Summing Up," *Athenaeum* 46 (1968) 68–69; and Ferguson, *Catullus* 252–53. Ferguson observes many of the parallels noted in the following discussion.

15 Their relation is observed by Khan, "The Summing Up" 65–69; and Adler, *Catullan Self-Revelation* 94–95.

16 Khan, "The Summing Up" 67.

17 I take *nostrae vitae* and *nostrae amicitiae* in verses 5–6 to refer also to Lesbia and the love affair, in addition to taking the expressions to refer to Catullus' own life and his friendship with Rufus.

18 Adams, *LSV* 127. The only article devoted solely to c. 74 is the excellent study of K.F. Kitchell, "*Et patruum reddidit Arpocratem*: a Reinterpretation of Catullus, c. 74," Coll. Latomus 180 (1983) 100–10. My discussion of cc. 74 and 78 is indebted also to F.V. Hickson's study, "*Patruus*: Paragon or Pervert? The Case of a Literary Split Personality," *Syllecta Classica* 4 (1992) 22–24.

19 Seager, "*Venustus, Lepidus, Bellus, Salsus*" 892.

20 For example, the collocation of *bene velle* occurs only in 72.8, 73.1, and 75.3 (McCarren, *A Critical Concordance* 21); *alarum* occurs only in 69.6 and 71.1 (McCarren 8) and the expression *bella puella cubet* only in 69.8 and 78.4 (McCarren 20); the Jupiter image occurs in the elegiac epigrams only in 70.2 and 72.2 (McCarren 89, 92–93); *pestis* only in 69.9, 76.20, and 77.6 in the elegiac epigrams (McCarren 140); *crudelis* only in 69.9 and 77.5 in the elegiac epigrams (McCarren 34); etc.

21 Lesbia poems: 78b, 79, 82, 83, 85, 86, 87, 91, 92; oral sex: 78b, 79, 80, 81, 88, 93, 97, 98, 99; and incest: 78b?, 79, 88, 89, 90, 91, 95.

22 For the history of the separation of c. 78 and 78b, see G. Milanese ("Su Catullo, carme 78. Unità, ideologia, linguaggio," *Maia* 40 [1988] 251–61), who reconsiders the question of whether the fragment 78b constitutes part of a separate poem.

23 McCarren, *A Critical Concordance* 180. For discussion of Catullus' use of *basium, suavium, and osculum*, see Ross, *Style and Tradition in Catullus* (above, note 14) 105.

24 Both verbal expressions occur only here in the poetry (McCarren, *A Critical Concordance* 83, 167). *Comminxit* in 78b.2 is an emendation of

manuscript O's *connuxit* and manuscript X's *coniunxit* made by Scaliger on the basis of the similar language in 99.10. Even so, the phrase *saliva spurca* occurs nowhere else (McCarren 167).

25 "Catullus 79," *Latomus* 44 (1985) 377–82. For c. 79, see also M.B. Skinner, "Pretty Lesbius," *TAPA* 112 (1982) 197–208.

26 W. Kroll (*C. Valerius Catullus* [Leipzig and Berlin 1923] *ad* 78b.2) suggests that the reference in both poems is to cunnilingus.

27 The description *purae pura puellae suavia*, is, of course, ironical. On the *os impurum*, see Richlin, *The Garden of Priapus* especially 26–31; and Adams, *LSV* 213.

28 For c. 99, see O. Harnecker, "Des Catullus Juventiuslieder," *Jahrb. f. kl. Philol.* 133 (1886) 274–76; Richardson, "*Furi et Aureli*" 95–96; Adler, *Catullan Self-Revelation* 54–56; H.A. Khan, "Catullus 99 and the Other Kiss-Poems," *Latomus* 26 (1967) 609–18, especially 614–18; J.C.D. Marshall, "Catullus 99," *CW* 65 (1971) 57–58; and Ferguson, *Catullus* 307–08.

29 Apparently first noted by R. Ellis, who discusses the medical terminology on pages 339–40 of his 1878 commentary on Catullus (cited by Marshall [above, note 28] on page 57, note 1).

30 On this point, compare c. 11, where the combination of dismissal of Lesbia and the introduction of Furius and Aurelius is preparatory to the series of homosexual love poems in cc. 15–24.

31 On the poem's structure, see F. Stoessl, "Catulls Gelliusepigramme," *Antidosis: Festschrift f. W. Kraus zum 70. Geburtstag* (Vienna 1972) 417.

32 Lindgren, *Non Bona Dicta* 67.

33 For the combination of rumors and allusions to *fellatio/irrumatio*, see Adams, *LSV* 212, note 3 (who cites F.C. Forberg, *Antonii Panormitae Hermaphroditus, primus in Germania edidit et apophoreta adiecit F.C.F.* [Coburg 1824] 287).

34 "Gellius and the Lover's Pallor: A Note on Catullus 80," *Arion* 5 (1966) 26.

35 Seager, "*Venustus, Lepidus, Bellus, Salsus*" 894.

36 The exceptions are: E. Baehrens, *Catulli Veronensis Liber,* vol. 2, rev. by K.P. Schulze (Leipzig 1893) *ad* c. 81; Kroll, *Catullus* (above, note 26) *ad* c. 81; and Richardson, *"Furi et Aureli"* 104.

37 It is tempting to see a pun on the entire word (PIS = to crush, AUR = gold). Furius' complexion thus resembles the name of the Umbrian city.

38 On this point, scc Richlin, *Garden of Priapus* 26–31, 150–51.

39 For c. 97, see J. Whatmough, "Pudicus Poeta: Words and Things," in *Poetic, Scientific, and Other Forms of Discourse*, Sather Classical Lectures 29 (Berkeley and Los Angeles 1956) 45–49; Seager, "*Venustus, Lepidus, Bellus, Salsus*" 893; Lateiner, "Obscenity in Catullus" 21–22; Richlin, *Garden of Priapus* 150–51; and Arkins, *Sexuality in Catullus* 41–42. On Aemilius' identity, see Neudling, *A Prosopography* 1; and P.Y. Forsyth, "Order and Meaning in Catullus 97–99," *CW* 72 (1979) 407–08.

40 Arkins, *Sexuality in Catullus* 41–42.

41 McCarren, *A Critical Concordance* 35. On the correspondence of cc. 97 and 98, see Forsyth, "Order and Meaning" (above, note 39) 403–08; and Lindgren, *Non Bona Dicta* 59–60.

42 Most recently, Forsyth ("Order and Meaning" [above, note 39] 406–08) has argued for this identification.

43 *Non Bona Dicta* 60.

44 For another possible parallel between the two poems, see Forsyth ("Order and Meaning" [above, note 39] 408), who argues that the juxtaposition of cc. 97 and 98 is intended to recall an actual connection between Aemilius and Victius (= Vettius).

45 Ferguson, *Catullus* 279 and 295.

46 V. Ingemann, "*Albus an ater*—A Double Entendre in Catullus 93?" *C&M* 33 (1981–82) 145–50; and S. Posch, "*Albus an ater homo*: zu Catull c. 93," *Serta Philologica Aenipontana* 3 (1979) 319–36.

47 Ingemann, *ibid.* 148.

48 On poem 86, see K. Quinn, *Latin Explorations*: *Critical Studies in Roman Literature* (London 1963) 66–73; and T.D. Papanghelis, "Catullus and Callimachus on Large Women," *Mnemosyne* 44 (1991) 372–86, the latter of whom interprets the poem as programmatic, as contraposing "a Neoteric Lesbia" to "an un-Neoteric Quintia."

49 *Catullus* 297. For an obscene interpretation of the proverb, see V. Buchheit, "Ludicra Latina," *Hermes* 90 (1962) 254–55; and Lindgren, *Non Bona Dicta* 77–78.

50 On the close connection of cc. 93 and 94, see Posch, "*Albus an ater homo*" (above, note 46) 336, note 68.

51 The correspondence is noted by most commentators. In addition, there is the discussion of Arkins (*Sexuality in Catullus* 74–75) and of J.P. Holoka ("Self-Delusion in Catullus 83 and 92," *CW* 69 [1975] 119–20).

52 Quinn, *The Poems* introd. to c. 92.

53 W. Clausen made this same point many years ago in "Silva Coniecturarum," *AJP* 76 (1955) 49–51, where he cites other examples of this stylistic feature.

54 Literature on the Gellius poems includes: G. Rettig, *Catulliana III: De Epigrammatis in Gellium Scriptis* (Bern 1871) 1–15 (unavailable); K. Barwick, "Zyklen bei Martial und in den kleinen Gedichten des Catull," *Philologus* 102 (1958) 317; E. Schäfer, *Das Verhältnis von Erlebnis und Kunstgestalt bei Catull* Hermes Einzelschriften 18 (1966) 28–33; Stoessl, "Catulls Gelliusepigramme" (above, note 31) 408–24; P.Y. Forsyth, "The Gellius Cycle of Catullus," *CJ* 68 (1972–73) 175–77; Schmidt, "Catulls Anordnung" 228–33; H.D. Rankin, "Catullus and Incest," *Eranos* 74 (1976) 117–19; Offermann, "Einige Gedanken" 43–45; Arkins, *Sexuality in Catullus* 34–39; and Lindgren, *Non Bona Dicta* 64–70.

55 For repetition and slight variation of the same theme in a group of poems that form the center, cf. Horace, *Odes* 2.2–2.11.

56 Lindgren, *Non Bona Dicta* 68.

57 *Ibid.* For c. 89, see also Macleod, "Parody and Personalities" 303.

58 "Obscenity in Catullus" 19–20.

59 Or perhaps he only attempted to seduce her—Catullus is not explicit here. Either way, Gellius betrayed Catullus.

60 On the interrelationships among these poems, see also Schäfer, *Das Verhältnis* (above, note 54) 31.

61 Forsyth, "The Gellius Cycle" (above, note 54) 177.

62 The single study devoted to c. 82 is that by P.Y. Forsyth ("Catullus 82," *CJ* 70 [1975] 33–35), who argues that the traditional interpretation of c. 82 as a rival poem is correct.

63 For literature on c. 96, see E. Fraenkel, "Catulls Trostgedicht für Calvus," *WS* 69 (1956) 278–88; H. Tränkle, "Neoterische Kleinigkeiten," *MH* 24 (1967) 93–99; Williams, *Tradition and Originality* 187–90; and J.T. Davis, "*Quo desiderio*: The Structure of Catullus 96," *Hermes* 99 (1971) 297–302.

64 "*Quo desiderio*" (above, note 63) 300.

65 Cf. also the combination of *amor* and *amicitia* in c. 109.

66 A single verse from the poem survives: *forsitan hoc etiam gaudeat ipsa cinis* (frag. 16, Morel).

67 For literature on c. 95, see W. Clausen, "Callimachus and Latin Poetry," *GRBS* 5 (1964) 188–91; D.F.S. Thomson, "Interpretations of Catullus—II," *Phoenix* 18 (1964) 30–36; J.B. Solodow, "On Catullus 95," *CP* 82

(1987) 141–45 and "Forms of Literary Criticism in Catullus: Polymetric vs. Epigram," *CP* 84 (1989) 312–19; and J.D. Noonan, "Myth, Humor and the Sequence of Thought in Catullus 95," *CJ* 81 (1985) 299–304.

68 Just as earlier Catullus punned on Volusius' name by glossing *AN(n)ALes VOLV-si* with *cacata carta*, so here he plays on the root VOLV- by placing the verb *pervolvent* and the *nomen Volusius* in close proximity. In contrast to the *Zymrna* of Cinna, the *Annales* of VOLVsi will not be unrolled to long be read (*perVOLVent*) by white-haired generations (*Zmyrnam cana diu saecula pervolvent / at Volusi annales Paduam morientur ad ipsam* 6–7).

69 Thomson, "Interpretations of Catullus" (above, note 67) 34–36. U.E. Paoli, whose interpretation of c. 95 Thomson develops, also observes that the theme of incineration may be a common element of cc. 36 and 95 alike ("Note di filologia reale su Catullo, Orazio, Marziale," *SIFC* N.S. 10 [1932] 37).

70 Clausen, "Callimachus and Latin Poetry" (above, note 67) 189.

71 Ferguson, *Catullus* 300.

72 E. Fraenkel, "Review of Fordyce, *Catullus*," *Gnomon* 34 (1962) 263.

73 Critics supply *sodalis* to fill the lacuna on the basis of *meus sodalis—Cinna est Gaius* in 10.29–30. I am convinced this restoration is correct, for it is characteristic of Catullus to create verbal or thematic cross-references between poems that refer to the same individuals.

74 This structure was first noted by J.P. Elder, "Catullus 1, His Poetic Creed, and Nepos," *HSCP* 71 (1966) 148, note 7.

75 This is F. Bellandi's analysis of the poem's structure with my addition of a couplet in the present tense ("Sulla struttura del C. 95 di Catullo," *Sileno* 4 [1978] 185–98).

76 Solodow, "On Catullus 95" (above, note 67) 144–45.

77 For literature on c. 84, see N.I. Herescu, "Autour de l'ironie de Catulle," *Revista Classica* 13–14 (1941–42) 133–37; Neudling, *A Prosopography* 7–11; E.S. Ramage, "Note on Catullus' Arrius," *CP* 54 (1959) 44–45; Fordyce, *Catullus* 373–77; H.B. Rosén, "Arrius' Speech Again (Catullus 84)," *Mnemosyne* 14 (1961) 224–32; B. Einarson, "On Catullus 84," *CP* 61 (1966) 187–88; D.N. Levin, "Arrius and his Uncle," *Latomus* 32 (1973) 587–94; B.A. Marshall and R.J. Baker, "The Aspirations of Q. Arrius," *Historia* 24 (1975) 220–31; and Ferguson, *Catullus* 275–77.

78 Goold, *Catullus* 260.

79 *Catullus* 276.

80 Einarson, "On Catullus 84," (above, note 77) 187–88. E. Harrison ("Catullus 84," *CR* 29 [1915] 198–99) apparently was the first to observe the wordplay.

81 Disparagement of Lesbia here creates a link with c. 104, the next Lesbia poem, where the poet denies ever maligning his darling.

82 These figures include Caesar, Mamurra, Hortensius, Calvus, Aemilius, and Victius = Vettius. Hortensius and Calvus, both orators and poets, obviously knew each other; along with Cicero they delivered speeches in defense of Sestius in B.C. 56.

83 On the relation among these three poems, see Forsyth, "Order and Meaning" (above, note 39) 407–08.

84 Literature on c. 103 includes: Neudling, *A Prosopography* 163–64; W. de Grummond, "A Note on Catullus 103," *CP* 66 (1971) 188–89; C. Gnilka, "Catulls Spottgedicht auf Silo," *RhM* 118 (1975) 130–35; M.B. Skinner, "Gentleman's Agreement: Catullus 103," *CP* 76 (1981) 39–40; and I. Schmid, "Catull c. 103—ein politisches Epigramm?" *RhM* 127 (1984) 317–25. On c. 106: E.W. Bushala, "A Note on Catullus 106," *HSCP* 85 (1981) 131–32; and Arkins, *Sexuality in Catullus* 44–45.

85 On this point, compare Quinn, who writes: "It is clear that Catullus is not talking about the kind of cutting remark that reveals the attempt to conceal passion (as in Poems 83 and 92): he means the kind of attack that relieves passion, violently abusive lampoon" (*The Poems ad* 104.3).

86 For this interpretation of c. 105, see Lindgren, *Non Bona Dicta* 78–80; Ferguson, *Catullus* 321; Lateiner, "Obscenity in Catullus" 22; and R. Boughner, "Mentula in Catullus, c. 105," *CB* 59 (1983) 29–32.

87 For the play on *praecipitem*, with *prae* suggesting *praeputium* and *caput* the male organ, see Boughner ("c. 105" [above, note 86] 30), who proposes that "the Muses...are attempting a castration"; for *furcilla* as a metaphor for the penis, see Adams' discussion of farm implements, *LSV* 24–25.

88 *Scandere* ("to mount") is used of animal copulation (Adams, *LSV* 205–06).

89 Lateiner, "Obscenity in Catullus" 22.

90 "Order and Meaning" (above, note 39) 408.

91 Neudling, *A Prosopography* 48.

92 Fordyce, *Catullus* introd. *ad* c. 108.

93 L. Schwabe appears the first to propose a connection between Cominius of c. 108 and Cornelius of c. 102 (*Quaestionum Catullianarum Liber I* [Giessen 1862] 317–23).

94 An early date for c. 102 might explain some of the poem's "infelicities" (on this point, see Fordyce, *Catullus* introd. *ad* c. 102).

95 Quinn, *The Poems* introd. *ad* c. 101. Studies of c. 101 include: Quinn, *Latin Explorations* 80–83; P.M. Stark, "Two Poems to a Dead Brother: Catullus and Thomas Merton," *CB* 38 (1962) 81–83; and N. Howe, "The 'Terce Muse' of Catullus 101," *CP* 69 (1974) 274–76.

96 Ferguson, *Catullus* 312.

97 J.P. Elder, "Note on Some Conscious and Subconscious Elements in Catullus' Poetry," *HSCP* 60 (1951) 129.

98 Unfortunately, the text of this splendid poem is in sorry shape. Except for *carior* in verse 3, I have adopted the readings and punctuation suggested by R.O.A.M. Lyne ("The Text of Catullus 107," *Hermes* 113 [1985] 498–500). I discussed the structure of the poem earlier in "Catullus 107.7–8," *CW* 80 (1987) 371–73.

99 Arkins, *Sexuality in Catullus* 72.

100 L. Cahoon, "Love's Illusions Lost: A Comparison of Catullus and Marcabru," *Classical and Modern Literature* 4 (1984) 227.

101 *frater adempte mihi* (68a.20, 68b.92, 101.6); *se...intulit* (68b.70–71), *se...contulit* (68b.132), and *refers te* (107.5); *qua viva vivere* (68b.160), *quis vivit...vitam* (107.7–8), and *mea vita....tota...vita* (109.1, 5); and *me carior ipso* (68b.160) and *carius auro* (107.3).

102 McCarren, *A Critical Concordance* 36–37.

103 Offermann, "Zu Catulls Gedichtcorpus" 300.

104 On the relation of cc. 109 and 110, see Offermann, *ibid.*; and Ferguson, "The Arrangement" 20.

105 Quinn, *An Interpretation* 240.

106 P.Y. Forsyth, "Quintius and Aufillena in Catullus," *CW* 74 (1980–81) 221. If Catullus is punning on the -LENA ("seductress") element of the woman's name, is he punning also on FIL-, which is related to FELL-, the root for "to suck" and AU- = an assimilated form of the preposition *ab*, "off"? If so, the elements of her name, which signify a prostitute who performs fellatio, would coordinate well with Catullus' comparing her to a whore *quae sese toto corpore prostituit* in 110.8. My colleague E.B. Holtsmark points out to me that the element FIL- may additionally suggest Greek PHIL-, which accords with the themes of *amor* and *amicus/a* in cc. 100 and 110.

107 For literature on cc. 110 and 111, see Forsyth, *ibid.*; F. Stoessl, "Aus Catulls Frühzeit," *Hermes* 101 (1973) 453–56; Quinn, *An Interpretation*

240–41; Adler, *Catullan Self-Revelation* 104–05; Arkins, *Sexuality in Catullus* 9–12; and Lindgren, *Non Bona Dicta* 43–45.

108 *Non Bona Dicta* 44.

109 Arkins, *Sexuality in Catullus* 11–12.

110 Forsyth tentatively suggests that Quintius is Aufillena's husband ("Quintius and Aufillena" [above, note 106] 222), Stoessl that he is her uncle ("Aus Catulls Frühzeit" [above, note 107] 451).

111 Khan, "The Summing Up" (above, note 14) 69–71.

112 On this point, see also P.Y. Forsyth, "The Irony of Catullus 100," *CW* 70 (1977) 316.

113 Forsyth, *ibid.* 316; and Ferguson, *Catullus* 309.

114 "The concept of the eternity of the marriage-bond is...a corollary of *univira*" (G. Williams, "Some Aspects of Roman Marriage Ceremonies and Ideals," *JRS* 48 [1958] 25).

115 Textual problems plague c. 112. I accept Scaliger's supplement of *est qui* in verse 1 and read *descendit* with manuscript V in verse 2.

116 Important discussions of c. 112 include: H.A. Khan, "Three Epigrams of Catullus (Carm., 114, 115, 112)," Coll. Latomus 101 (1969) 9–11; M.G. Morgan, "Catullus 112: A *Pathicus* in Politics," *AJP* 100 (1979) 377–80; P.Y. Forsyth, "Catullus 112," *CW* 77 (1983) 65–68; and Lindgren, *Non Bona Dicta* 85–86. Critics, however, do not agree either on the significance of *multus* ("talkative" or "tedious" or "active" or "large") or on whether the adjective sustains the same meaning in all three instances or only in the first and third.

117 "A Pathicus" (above, note 116) 380 .

118 Lateiner, "Obscenity in Catullus" 25.

119 For *multus* meaning "large," cf. Ovid, *Amores* 2.4.33–34. Catullus may be indicating that Naso = Mentula through a verbal cross-reference to c. 115; cf. *multus homo es, Naso* with *ipsest maximus..., non homo, sed vero mentula magna* (7–8).

Proponents of the interpretation of *multus* = "virile" in c. 112 include: Lateiner, "Obscenity in Catullus" 25; Lindgren, *Non Bona Dicta* 85–86; and Ferguson, *Catullus* 337. Khan ("Three Epigrams," [above, note 116] 9–11) appears the first to propose the idea of physical size suggesting virility, but talks himself out of it by the end of his discussion. *Multus* with a sexual nuance would apply to Naso in the first and third instance; in the second instance the adjective would signify "many."

120 Lindgren, *Non Bona Dicta* 86; and Newman, *Roman Catullus* 169 and 266.

121 See, for example, Adams, *LSV* 35; and M.I. Davies, "The Tickle and Sneeze of Love," *AJA* 86 (1982) 117.

122 Forsyth ("Catullus 112" [above, note 116] 67–68) offers a different interpretation. She maintains that *multus* with the sense of "talkative," having "a mouth that's always open," sets the reader up for a *fellatio* joke at the end: "Naso has a mouth that's always open, and, of course, an open mouth is useful for more than just talking!" Although her interpretation is possible, I think the poem is more witty if *multus* contrasts with *pathicus*.

123 Neudling raises the interesting possibility that the anonymous political figure in 112.1–2, to whom "Naso attached himself," may in fact allude to Pompey: "*neque tecum multus homo qui descendit* could satirize Pompey's well-known aloofness and silence..., and the charge of homosexuality is one which Catullus and his friend Calvus levelled at Pompey with notorious effect" (*A Prosopography* 131–32).

124 The best treatment of c. 113 is that by Lindgren (*Non Bona Dicta* 45–47). My discussion is indebted to some of her ideas.

125 Quinn, *The Poems ad* 113.3.

126 *Quaestionum Catullianarum* (above, note 93) 210–21. Others, who like Schwabe emend *Maeciliam* to *Mucillam* (or *Moecillam*), identify Caesar and Pompey as the *duo*, since Pompey was once married to Mucia and Caesar was her lover (e.g., Quinn, *The Poems* introd. to c. 113; and Herescu, "Autour de l'ironie" [above, note 77] 132–33).

127 If the proposal regarding the identity of the *duo* is correct, all three elegiac epigrams that close with a proverb (94, 95, 113) refer to Mamurra and/or Caesar.

128 For discussion of cc. 114 and 115, see P. Harvey, "Catullus 114–115: Mentula, bonus agricola," *Historia* 28 (1979) 329–55; and Lindgren, *Non Bona Dicta* 80–84. By comparing the known sizes of ancient estates of this period, Harvey demonstrates that "Mentula's *saltus Firmanus* was neither poor nor unusual" (page 329). Lindgren suggests that the poems can be read on a metaphorical as well as a literal level.

129 Ferguson, *Catullus* 341.

130 For arguments that the manuscript reading of *saltusque* in 115.5 needs to be emended, see Fordyce, *Catullus ad loc.*; and Ross, *Style and Tradition in Catullus* (above, note 14) 103, note 243.

131 Ellis, *A Commentary ad* 115.7.

132 E.g., Kroll, *Catullus* (above, note 26) introd. to c. 115; and Fordyce, *Catullus* introd. to c. 114.

133 E.A. Fredricksmeyer, "The Beginning and the End of Catullus' *Longus Amor*," *SO* 58 (1983) 73. For discussion of the metaphors, see Adams, *LSV* 82–85, 154–55.

134 Lindgren, *Non Bona Dicta* 81.

135 Harvey, "Catullus 114–115" (above, note 128) 330–31.

136 Adams, *LSV* 206. On the etymological connection, see Ernout-Meillet, *Dictionnaire étymologique de la langue latine: Histoire des mots*, vol. 2, 3rd ed., rev. (Paris 1951) s.v. *salio*, p. 1139 (cited by Harvey, "Catullus 114–115" [above, note 128] 330, note 3).

137 Lindgren, *Non Bona Dicta* 82.

138 Ferguson, *Catullus* 343.

139 Ross, *Style and Tradition* (above note 14) 103

140 Adams, *LSV* 19–22.

141 K.F. Kitchell, "Catullus 116.7: *Amitha/Micta*," *CW* 80 (1986) 6–7; and Richlin, *Garden of Priapus* 149–50.

142 Richlin, *ibid.* 150.

143 Cf. the final Aurelius poem, c. 40, which combines the themes of a stiff penalty and invective poems. Catullus here refers to Aurelius as Ravidus (above, page 288, note 192).

144 On the function of c. 116 in the series of Gellius poems, see Forsyth, "The Gellius Cycle" (above, note 54) 177.

145 On the relation of cc. 65 and 116, see especially P.Y. Forsyth, "Comments on Catullus 116," *CQ* 27 (1977) 352–53; and King, "Catullus' Callimachean Carmina" 385–87.

146 McCarren, *A Critical Concordance* 20.

147 Baehrens (*Veronensis Liber* [above, note 36] *ad* 116.3, 8) appears to be the first to make this suggestion.

148 King, "Catullus' Callimachean Carmina" 386, note 15.

149 These include: the wholly spondaic verse 3, the suppressed 's' of *dabis* in verse 8, *uti* in verse 2, and the instrumental *qui* in verse 3 (C.W. Macleod, "Catullus 116," *CQ* 23 [1973] 307 and note 1 on the same page).

150 In c. 116 "Catullus, like other dedicators, speaks of the thought and effort he has expended for his addressee's benefit; but here it has all been wasted. Dedicators often profess that their work has been written to honour or to acquire a friendship; but Catullus' was meant first to pacify an enemy and now delivers a threat" (Macleod, *ibid.* 308).

151 For example, J. van Sickle, "Poetics of Opening and Closure in Meleager, Catullus, and Gallus," *CW* 75 (1981) 68; Forsyth, "Catullus 116" (above, note 145) 352–53 (Van Sickle and Forsyth interpret the poem as functioning as the conclusion to the poems in elegiac couplets only); Wiseman, *A Reappraisal* 185; Newman, *Roman Catullus* 45; and B. Arkins, "Crucial Constants in Catullus: Callimachus, the Muses, Friends and Enemies," *LCM* 17.8 (1992) 117.

152 I discussed the chiastic arrangement of cc. 1 and 116 in *Syllecta Classica* 5 (1994) 29–33. The only other Catullan pair joined by a ring-composition structure are cc. 50 and 51 (page 108).

153 "The name of the addressee is not normally delayed beyond the second line, and is often the opening word of the poem" (Quinn, *The Poems ad* 116.6). In conjunction with this point, it is worth noting that Gellius is named in the first line of six of the eight poems that make up this series (74, 80, 88, 89, 90, and 91), and he is alluded to in the second line of c. 78. I am indebted to J.D. Minyard for this observation.

154 Arkins, "Crucial Constants" (above, note 151) 117.

155 Quinn, *The Poems* introd. to c. 116; and Kroll, *Catullus* (above, note 26) introd. to c. 116.

156 The quote is taken from page 9 of J.D. Minyard's unpublished monograph, *The Last of Catullus*. In this study that deals with the Catullan Question, Minyard explores the issue of whether c. 116 "can give closure to the entire collection" in its present order. The author with characteristic modesty did not feel the study was "good enough" to be published at the time he kindly sent me a copy of it.

157 Hence, the point of the allusion to Ennius' *Annales* in the closing words of the poem (*hoc nec tu: nam mi calido dabi' sanguine poenas* 95, Skutsch) and of the only wholly spondaic hexameter to occur outside Ennius (116.3).

158 After years of wavering on this issue, I now believe that the noun *libellus* in c. 1 refers to the entire work for two reasons. First, c. 1 is the only formal dedicatory poem in the collection. Second, cc. 65–68b cannot be detached from either cc. 61–64 or cc. 69–116; owing to their pivotal function, these five poems belong simultaneously to both groups.

159 On cc. 107 and 109, Wiseman writes, "They are the last love poems in the entire three-volume collection, and they are unlike anything we have met so far" (*A Reappraisal* 173). These poems provide an element of resolution in the sense that we can imagine the tempestuous fluctuations in the love affair continuing *in perpetuum*.

Chapter Six: Other Evidence

1 R. Westphal (*Catull's Gedichte in ihrem geschichtlichem Zusammenhange,* 2nd ed. [Breslau 1870] 4–5) was the first to recognize the unity of the Lesbia poems in 2–11. For a discussion of this sequence of related poems, see Segal, "The Order" 305–21; Williams, *Tradition and Originality* 469–70; H.D. Rankin, "The Progress of Pessimism in Catullus, Poems 2–11," *Latomus* 31 (1972) 744–51; and Skinner, *Catullus' Passer* 39–43.

2 Williams, *Tradition and Originality* 469.

3 It is the view also of H. Tränkle ("Neoterische Kleinigkeiten," *MH* 24 [1967] 101–03) and H. Offermann ("Zu Catulls Gedichtcorpus," *RhM* 120 [1977] 269–302) that all the Lesbia poems display a deliberate order.

4 *Tradition and Originality* 223.

5 Since Catullus did not provide c. 43 with a symmetrical counterpart, as he did for every other Lesbia/Juventius poem, chances are that he did not view *Salve, nec minimo* as a "Lesbia poem." It is worth noting in this regard that even in the single verse in which his lady is mentioned (7), Amiana holds the place of prominence, at the begining of the verse: *tecum Lesbia nostra comparatur?*

6 Wiseman, *A Reappraisal* 154.

7 E.A. Fredricksmeyer, "The Beginning and the End of Catullus' *Longus Amor*," *SO* 58 (1983) 81.

8 Quinn, *An Interpretation* 58.

9 C. 58 also looks back to c. 37. The expression *unam / plus quam se atque suos amavit omnes* at 58.2–3 parallels *amata tantum quantum amabitur nulla* at 37.12, and the milieu of 37.14–15 and 58.4–5 and the inhabitants are clearly similar. In both, Lesbia is consorting with the privileged class of Rome in seedy places, a brothel in the one, and highways and byways in the other.

10 See pages 154–58.

11 See page 288, note 192.

12 Although c. 30 does not refer explicitly to Lesbia, the verbal parallels it holds in common with the Ariadne section of c. 64 suggest that the *amorem* of verse 8 alludes to the love affair with Lesbia.

13 O. Harnecker ("Des Catullus Juventiuslieder," *Jahrb. f. class. Philol.* 133 [1886] 273–79) is the first to propose that the Juventius poems are intended to complement the Lesbia series.

14 Quinn, *An Interpretation* 242; and Macleod, "Parody and Personalities" 302–03.

15 See page 92.

16 *A Reappraisal* 162. It is important to reiterate that Lesbia is married in 68b because Catullus wishes her to be so. Her marital status need not be based on reality.

17 G. Williams, *Figures of Thought in Roman Poetry* (New Haven and London 1980) 59–60.

18 "The themes of most of the subsequent epigrams that concern Lesbia appear variously in poem 68, which functions almost as programmatic to them" (Williams, *ibid.* 61).

Cc. 70, 72, and 73 ("one and only") take up the theme of marriage; 73, 76, and 85 deal with unrequited love (cf. 68b.51–66); 75, 77, and 91 concern infidelity (cf. *rara...furta* 68b.136); and 83 mentions a husband (cf. 68b.146). Lesbia is identified with Catullus' life in 77, 104, and 109 (cf. 68b.160). She is described as precious in 82 and 104 and his dearest possession in 77 (cf. 68b.158–59). 107 refers to reconciliation with Lesbia as a "red-letter day" (cf. 68b.147–48); 78b describes immortal fame in terms similar to that found in 68b.46 (*haec carta loquatur anus*); and 68b and 77 use the same language to describe the loss of the brother to death and the loss of Lesbia to another (cf. *ei misero frater adempte mihi* 68b.92; *ei misero eripuisti omnia nostra bona* 77.4).

19 Wiseman, *A Reappraisal* 162 and 174.

20 McCarren, *A Critical Concordance* 37. The referent of *cupido* in 107.1 is indefinite.

21 R.O.A.M. Lyne, *The Latin Love Poets: From Catullus to Horace* (Oxford 1980) 29.

22 *Ibid.* 21.

23 Pages 115–16 and 128–29. We know that the binary structure is primary because of the concomitant numerical pattern.

24 D.A. Kidd, "Some Problems in Catullus 66," *Antichthon* 4 (1970) 40.

25 This ring pattern was discovered by Most, "Catullus' *Carmina Maiora*" 109–25.

26 *Ibid.* 119.

27 Wiseman, *Catullan Questions* 22.

28 "*Ianua iucunda*: The Characterization of the Door in Catullus 67," Coll. Latomus 168 (1980) 109.

29 "Catullus' *Carmina Maiora*" 119.

30 A.S. Pease, *Publi Vergili Maronis Aeneidos liber quartus* (Cambridge, Mass. 1935) *ad* 4.608.

31 *a caedendo dicta est 'caesaries'; ergo tantum virorum est* (Servius *Aeneid* 1.590). On this etymology, cf. also Servius Auctus *Aeneid* 8.659 and Isid., *Orig.* 11.1.29.

It is noteworthy, too, that *caesaries* occurs only here (McCarren, *A Concordance* 23); elsewhere Catullus uses *capillus, coma,* or *crinis* (McCarren 24, 29, 34).

32 The idea of associating hatred for Venus with rite of passage is echoed in c. 66 (*estne novis nuptis odio Venus*? 15).

33 E.g., *stimulatus* (4), *vaga pecora* (13), *reboant* (21), *remugit* (29), *iuvenca* (33), etc. (G.N. Sandy, "The Imagery of Catullus 63," *TAPA* 99 [1968] 389–99).

34 Most, "Catullus' *Carmina Maiora*" 119, 120.

35 Pages 158–60.

36 On the relation of cc. 58, 70, and 72, see also Quinn, *An Interpretation* 78.

37 T.P. Wiseman, *Cinna the Poet and Other Roman Essays* (Leicester 1974) 116. On the relation of cc. 58 and 72, see also P. McGushin, "Catullus' *Sanctae Foedus Amicitiae*," *CP* 62 (1967) 90; and Arkins, *Sexuality in Catullus* 65–66.

38 Striking verbal parallels in 60.1–3 and 64.154–56 suggest a deliberate connection despite the great disparity in length of the two poems: *te genuit...leaena* in 64.154 echoes *te leaena...procreavit* in 60.1, 3 (*leaena* apparently first appears in Latin literature here—see Ellis, *A Commentary ad loc.*); the desolate setting of *sola sub rupe* in 64.154 evokes that of *montibus Libystinis* in 60.1; and the monster Scylla occurs in 60.2 and 64.156 and nowhere else in Catullus (McCarren, *A Concordance* 169).

39 Newman, *Roman Catullus* 183.

40 E.g., Plautus, *Cas.* 138; Pliny the Elder, *N.H.* 10.52.107; Pliny the Younger, *Ep.* 9.25.3; Martial 1.7.5; and Apuleius, *Met.* 6.6.

41 *columbae et turtures octonis annis vivunt. contra passeri minimum vitae, cui salacitas par* (Pliny, *N.H.* 10.52.107).

42 J. Henderson, *The Maculate Muse: Obscene Language in Attic Comedy* (New Haven 1975) 128–29; G. Giangrande in P. Howell's *A Commentary on Book One of the Epigrams of Martial* (London 1980) 122–23; and H. Herter, "Phallos" *RE* 19.2 (1938) 1723–26. For pictorial representations of winged phalluses, see, for example, J. Ward-Perkins and A. Claridge, *Pompeii AD 79*, vol. 2 (Boston 1987) 188.

43 W.M. Lindsay, *Sexti Pompei Festi De Verborum Significatu quae supersunt cum Pauli Epitome* (Leipzig 1913) 410.

44 For the latest discussion in favor of a metaphorical reading of cc. 2 and 3, see R.F. Thomas, "Sparrows, Hares, and Doves: A Catullan Metaphor and its Tradition," *Helios* 20 (1993) 131–42.

45 Pages 223–26.

46 For a detailed discussion of mathematical symmetry from Virgil's *Eclogues* to Ovid's *Amores,* with bibliography, see H. Dettmer, *Horace: A Study in Structure* (Hildesheim 1983) 1–75.

47 Numerical correspondence appears to have originated with the Alexandrians. Darcy Thomas, a former student, discovered two numerical schemes in Theocritus, *Idylls* 1–10, which resemble those found in Virgil's *Eclogues* by O. Skutsch ("Symmetry and Sense in the *Eclogues,*" *HSCP* 73 [1969] 153–69). In the pattern that accompanies the corresponding idylls, the sum of the verses in 1 and 10 = 210, in 3 and 7 = 211, in 2 and 6 = 212, and in 4 and 5 = 213. In the other pattern, the sum of the verses in the outer and inner pairs (1~10 and 4~5) equals the sum of the verses in the central two pairs (3~7 and 4~6), 423 apiece. The double numerical scheme is highly significant because it reaffirms the prevailing view that *Idylls* 8 and 9 are spurious and additionally suggests that *Idylls* 1–10 apparently formed a book, with *Idyll* 10 functioning as an envoi poem.

48 On the thematic relationship of poems 20–22 to the rest of the book, see G.O. Hutchinson, "Propertius and the Unity of the Book," *JRS* 74 (1984) 103–06.

49 The exceptions are the tag poems at the end of Propertius' *Monobiblos* and of Catullus' elegiac epigrams. These poems, which are excluded from the first numerical pattern, are included in the second.

50 For an overview of the twelve numerical patterns in Horace's *Odes* I–III, see Dettmer, *Horace* (above, note 46) Appendix A, 525–29, 534–37.

51 Pages 227 and 265.

52 Pages 116–17 and 173–74.

53 Since all the other numerical patterns in the corpus appear to exhibit exact equality, we are faced with two possibilities here: either a couplet was lost from one of the final pieces, or the pattern of inequality was deliberately contrived to create a slight asymmetry of the sort characteristic of the ring patterns in which not all poems have symmetrical counterparts.

54 Experience with ring structures in other Latin poetry books indicates that c. 14b and cc. 23~24 must have a symmetrical counterpart. It is indeed remarkable that poems have been lost precisely where Muretus inserted

additional poems. I can offer no explanation for this extraordinary coincidence.

55 I am convinced that c. 17 was meant to be non-corresponding in the primary structure, not so much because of the unusual character of this poem directed to a provincial town with a rickety bridge, but because if it had a companion piece, it should have occurred in the second half of the cycle (cc. 21–24).

56 Catullus' pairing of these cycles makes sense because thematic parallels link the final cycle of polymetra with the first, and the fourth cycle with the second. The central cycle stands apart from the other four in that it contains no explicit reference to either of Catullus' principal love affairs.

57 In other words, this numerical pattern excludes the single non-corresponding poems in the polymetra, 17, 30, and 48, and the five-poem tag in the elegiac epigrams.

58 I should stress that all of these figures are only *relatively* accurate owing to the often sorry state of the manuscript. Nevertheless, the overlapping and complex character of the numerical schemes indicates that the total must very closely reflect Catullus' own total.

59 Lyne, *The Latin Love Poets* (above, note 21 of this chapter) 102–03.

60 P. Fedeli, "Allusive Technique in Roman Poetry," *MPhL* 7 (1986) 21–22. While Catullus alludes to the opening of Meleager's *Garland* (*A.P.* 4.1), Propertius alludes to an epigram on Meleager's passion for Myiscus (*A.P.* 12.101.1–4).

61 In Catullus 116, for example, there is the wholly spondaic verse 3 and the suppression of the final 's' of *dabis* in verse 8; in Propertius, poem 20 we find *nullae*, instead of *nulli,* in verse 35 and the infinitive expressing purpose with a verb of motion in verses 23 and 24 (D.O. Ross, Jr., *Backgrounds to Augustan Poetry: Gallus, Elegy and Rome* [Cambridge 1975] 78–79).

62 See page 225.

63 See Dettmer, *Horace* (above, note 46 of this chapter) 534–35.

64 J. Ferguson, "The Arrangement of Catullus' Poems," *LCM* 11.1 (1986) 3.

65 See Dettmer, *Horace* (above, note 46) 130–31.

66 *Ibid.*, Appendix A, 525, 534–47.

67 It is worth observing that in Latin poetry it is not uncommon to find that a literary debt to a predecessor is indicated structurally as well as

thematically. In addition to the examples provided above, the arrangement of Horace's *Epodes* closely resembles that of Callimachus' *Iambi* (for Callimachus, see D.L. Clayman, *Callimachus' Iambi* [Leiden 1980] 48–49; for the *Epodes*, see Dettmer, *Horace* [above, note 46] Chapter 2); and Tibullus clearly modeled the organization of his first book of elegies on that of Virgil's *Eclogues* (both books are composed of ten poems).

Chapter Seven: The Epilogue

1 1–60 = 60 poems, counting 14b as a remnant of a separate poem, and counting the missing counterpart to 14b, and the missing counterpart to cc. 23~24; 69–116 = 49 poems, counting 78b as a separate poem and counting 95 and 95b as one poem; and 61–68 = 9 poems, counting 68a and 68b as separate poems.

2 For mathematical symmetry in the *corpus Catullianum*, see pages 245–47.

3 Pages 223–25.

4 I read *sacellis* in 55.4 (see page 295, note 281).

5 Wiseman also believes that Catullus' use of the word *libellus* in c. 14 has significance for its meaning in c. 1 (*Catullan Questions* 31). As for the problem of *nugae*, "frivolous stuff," referring to all the poetry, I think F.O. Copley is correct in suggesting that Catullus is using the very term that his detractors were calling his poems ("Catullus, c. 1," *TAPA* 82 [1951] 203).

6 For arguments that the collection in three parts could have formed a single roll, see J.D. Minyard, "The Source of the Catulli Veronensis Liber," *CW* 81 (1988) 343–53.

7 Pages 208–09.

8 The general consensus is that the first verse of the introductory c. 1 of Catullus alludes to the first verse of the introduction to Meleager's *Garland* (*A.P.* 4.1). By nodding to Meleager in this very important programmatic piece, Catullus is both placing himself within a tradition and indicating that he intends to respond to his Greek predecessor's work. Lest we miss the point, Catullus follows with another two poems (cc. 2 and 3) in which he again appears to be directly influenced by Meleager (*A.P.* 7.195 and 196, and *A.P.* 7.207). For secondary literature on Catullus' indebtness to these poems of Meleager, see page 271, note 5.

9 A.S.F. Gow and D.L. Page, *The Greek Anthology: Hellenistic Epigrams*, vol. 1 (Cambridge 1965) xxvi.

10 Gow-Page provide a table of Meleagrian sequences that have been identified by Stadtmüller and Weisshäupl (*ibid.*, page xxv).

11 Although Catullus undoubtedly was influenced by the architectonic schemes that unify the poetry of the Alexandrians, his arrangement exhibits greater complexity because poems are not paired strictly on a one-to-one basis (for the arrangement of the *Iambi* of Callimachus, for example, see D.L. Clayman, *Callimachus' Iambi* [Leiden 1980] 48–49).

12 D.H. Garrison, *Mild Frenzy: A Reading of the Hellenistic Love Epigram,* Hermes Einzelschriften 41 (1978) 91. On Catullus' debt to the series of erotic poems of Meleager, see also Williams, *Tradition and Originality* 553–54.

13 R.O.A.M. Lyne, *The Latin Love Poets: From Catullus to Horace* (Oxford 1980) 21.

14 Quinn comes close to making a similar observation by claiming "primacy of importance to the Lesbia poems" and by consigning the rest (of the short poems) "to the status of background" (*An Interpretation* 49–50, 204–05).

15 Page 227.

16 "Metrical Variations and Some Textual Problems in Catullus," *BICS* 16 (1969) 38. The exceptions in cc. 2 through 26 are: 2.4, 3.12, 3.17, and 7.2; the poems that do not admit any variations in cc. 27 through 58 include: 28, 33, 43, 46, 47, 48, 56, and 57. I have benefited from Hubbard's discussion of Skutsch's findings ("Catullan Libellus" 234).

17 P.Y. Forsyth, "Order and Meaning in Catullus 97–99," *CW* 72 (1979) 408.

BIBLIOGRAPHY

Adams, J.N. *The Latin Sexual Vocabulary* (London 1982).

_____. "Words for 'Prostitute' in Latin," *RhM* 126 (1983) 321–58.

Adler, E. *Catullan Self-Revelation* (New York 1981).

Ahl, F. *Metaformations: Soundplay and Wordplay in Ovid and Other Classical Poets* (Ithaca and London 1985).

Allen, A.W. "Catullus 68.157," *Maia* 53 (1991) 193–94.

_____. "Elegy and the Classical Attitude toward Love: Propertius 1.1," *YCS* 11 (1950) 255–77.

Arkins, B. "Caelius and Rufus in Catullus," *Philologus* 127 (1983) 306–11.

_____. "Catullus 58.5," *LCM* 2.10 (1977) 237–38.

_____. "Crucial Constants in Catullus: Callimachus, the Muses, Friends and Enemies," *LCM* 17.8 (1992) 115–18.

_____. "Further Thoughts on Catullus 1," *LCM* 8.2 (1983) 18–20.

_____. "*Glubit* in Catullus 58.5," *LCM* 4.5 (1979) 85–86.

_____. *Sexuality in Catullus* (Hildesheim 1982).

Austin, R.G. *M. Tulli Ciceronis Pro M. Caelio Oratio*, 3rd ed. (Oxford 1960).

Badian, E. "Mamurra's Fourth Fortune," *CP* 72 (1977) 320–22.

Baehrens, E. *Catulli Veronensis Liber,* 2 vols., rev. by K.P. Schulze (Leipzig 1893).

Bagg, R. "Some Versions of Lyric Impasse in Shakespeare and Catullus," *Arion* 4 (1965) 64–95.

Baker, R.J. "Catullus and Friend in Carm. 31," *Mnemosyne* 23 (1970) 33–41.

_____. "Catullus and Sirmio," *Mnemosyne* 36 (1983) 316–23.

Baker, S. "Catullus 38," *CP* 55 (1960) 37–38.

_____. "The Irony of Catullus' 'Septimius and Acme'," *CP* 53 (1958) 110–12.

Barwick, K. "Zyklen bei Martial und in den kleinen Gedichten des Catull," *Philologus* 102 (1958) 284–318.

Basto, J. "Caecilius, Attis and Catullus 35," *LCM* 7.3 (1982) 30–34.

Bellandi, F. "Sulla struttura del C. 95 di Catullo," *Sileno* 4 (1978) 185–98.

Bergk, T. "Philologischen Thesen," *Philologus* 12 (1857) 578–81.

Bernstein, W.H. "A Sense of Taste: Catullus 13," *CJ* 80 (1985) 127–30.

Bertman, S. "Oral Imagery in Catullus 7," *CQ* 28 (1978) 477–78.

Bianco, O. "Catullo, C. 55 e 58a," *RCCM* 6 (1964) 33–44.

Bickel, E. "Salaputium: Mentula Salax," *RhM* 96 (1953) 94–95.

Birt, T. "Zu Catull's Carmina minora," *Philologus* 63 (1904) 425–71.

Bishop, J.D. "Catullus 2 and its Hellenistic Antecedents," *CP* 61 (1966) 158–67.

Block, E. "Carmen 65 and the Arrangement of Catullus' Poetry," *Ramus* 13 (1984) 48–59.

Bömer, F. "Claudia Quinta," *MDAI(R)* 71 (1964) 146–51.

Booth, A.D. "Camerius the Catamite (Catullus 55 & 58b)," *LCM* 6.5 (1981) 135–36.

Boughner, R. "Mentula in Catullus, c. 105," *CB* 59 (1983) 29–32.

Bright, D.F. "*Non Bona Dicta*: Catullus' Poetry of Separation," *QUCC* 21 (1976) 105–19.

Briscoe, J. "T.P. Wiseman's *Catullan Questions*," *JRS* 61 (1971) 303–04.

Buchheit, V. "Catull an Cato von Utica (c. 56)," *Hermes* 89 (1961) 345–56.

_____. "Catulls Dichterkritik in c. 36," *Hermes* 87 (1959) 309–27.

_____. "Dichtertum und Lebensform in Catull c. 35/36," *Lebendige Romania: Festschrift für Hans-Wilhelm Klein,* ed. by A. Barrera-Vidal *et al.* (Göppingen 1976) 47–64.

_____. "Literarische Kritik an T. Annius Cimber (Verg. *Catal.* 2), Cicero (Cat. C. 49) und Sestius (Cat. C. 44)," *Forschungen zur Römischen Literatur*, vol. 1, ed. by W. Wimmel (Wiesbaden 1970) 37–45.

_____. "Ludicra Latina," *Hermes* 90 (1962) 252–56.

Bushala, E.W. "A Note on Catullus 106," *HSCP* 85 (1981) 131–32.

Cahoon, L. "Love's Illusions Lost: A Comparison of Catullus and Marcabru," *Classical and Modern Literature* 4 (1984) 215–30.

Cairns, F. "Catullus 1," *Mnemosyne* 22 (1969) 153–58.

_____. "Catullus 27," *Mnemosyne* 28 (1975) 24–29.

_____. "Catullus' *Basia* Poems (5, 7, 48)," *Mnemosyne* 26 (1973) 15–22.

_____. "*Venusta Sirmio*: Catullus 31," *Quality and Pleasure in Latin Poetry,* ed. by T. Woodman and D. West (Cambridge 1974) 1–17.

Cameron, A. "Catullus 29," *Hermes* 104 (1976) 155–63.

_____. *The Greek Anthology: from Meleager to Planudes* (Oxford 1993).

Carilli, M. "Le *Nugae* di Catullo e l'epigramma greco," *ASNP* 5 (1975) 925–53.

Clack, J. "*Otium tibi Molestum Est* — Catullus 50 and 51," *CB* 52 (1976) 50–53.

Clausen, W. "Callimachus and Latin Poetry," *GRBS* 5 (1964) 181–96.

_____. "Catulliana," *Vir Bonus Discendi Peritus: Studies in Celebration of O. Skutsch's Eightieth Birthday*, ed. by N. Horsfall (London 1988) 13–17.

_____. "Catulli Veronensis Liber," *CP* 71 (1976) 37–43.

_____. "Catullus and Callimachus," *HSCP* 74 (1970) 85–94.

_____. "Silva Coniecturarum," *AJP* 76 (1955) 47–62.

Clayman, D.L. *Callimachus' Iambi* (Leiden 1980).

Comfort, H. "Parody in Catullus 58a," *AJP* 56 (1935) 45–49.

Commager, S. "The Structure of Catullus 62," *Eranos* 81 (1983) 21–33.

Copley, F.O. "Catullus, c. 1," *TAPA* 82 (1951) 200–06.

_____. "Catullus, c. 38," *TAPA* 87 (1956) 125–29.

_____. "Catullus 35," *AJP* 74 (1953) 149–60.

_____. "Catullus 55, 9–14," *AJP* 73 (1952) 295–97.

_____. *Catullus: The Complete Poetry* (Ann Arbor 1964).

_____. *Exclusus Amator: A Study in Latin Love Poetry* (Baltimore 1956).

_____. "The Structure of Catullus c. 51 and the Problem of the *Otium*-Strophe," *GB* 2 (1974) 25–37.

_____. "The Unity of Catullus 68: A Further View," *CP* 52 (1957) 29–32.

Corte, F. Della. *Catullo: Le poesie* (Milan 1977).

_____. *Due studi catulliani* (Genoa 1951).

_____. *Personaggi catulliani*, 2nd ed. (Florence 1976).

Courtney, E. "Three Poems of Catullus," *BICS* 32 (1985) 85–100.

Curran, L.C. "Catullus 64 and the Heroic Age," *YCS* 21 (1969) 169–92.

_____. "Gellius and the Lover's Pallor: A Note on Catullus 80," *Arion* 5 (1966) 24–27.

Daniels, M.L. "Personal Revelation in Catullus 64," *CJ* 62 (1967) 351–56.

Davies, M.I. "The Tickle and Sneeze of Love," *AJA* 86 (1982) 115–18.

Davis, J.T. "*Quo desiderio*: The Structure of Catullus 96," *Hermes* 99 (1971) 297–302.

DeAngeli, E.S. "A Literary Chill: Catullus 44," *CW* 62 (1969) 354–56.

Deroux, C. "Catulle et Cicéron ou les raisons d'un silence," *LEC* 53 (1985) 221–46.

_____. "Le plus mauvais de tous les poètes et le meilleur de tous les avocats," Coll. Latomus 187 (1985) 124–38.

_____. "L'identité de Lesbie," *ANRW* 1.3 (1973) 390–416.

_____. "Un nouveau personnage Catullien: de la philologie à l'histoire," *RBPh* 55 (1977) 56–78.

Dettmer, H. "Catullus 2B from a Structural Perspective," *CW* 78 (1984) 107–10.

_____. "Catullus 6 and 10," *LCM* 10.2 (1985) 29–30.

_____. "Catullus 13: A Nose is a Nose is a Nose," *Syllecta Classica* 1 (1989) 75–85.

_____. "Catullus 107.7–8," *CW* 80 (1987) 371–73.

_____. "Closure in the Lesbia Polymetra 1–13," *CW* 82 (1989) 375–77.

_____. "Design in the Catullan Corpus: A Preliminary Study," *CW* 81 (1988) 371–81.

_____. "The First and Last of Catullus," *Syllecta Classica* 5 (1994) 29–33.

_____. "A Fresh Approach to Catullus 29.23," *Syllecta Classica* 2 (1990) 23–27.

_____. "A Fresh Look at Catullus 1.9," *LCM* 9.5 (1984) 74–75.

_____. *Horace: A Study in Structure* (Hildesheim 1983).

_____. "*Meros Amores*. A Note on Catullus 13.9," *QUCC* N.S. 23 (1986) 87–91.

Dietz, H. "Zu Catulls Gedicht von Acme und Septimius," *SO* 44 (1969) 42–47.

Diggle, J. "*Elegiae in Maecenatem* 129–32," *Latomus* 27 (1968) 175–80.

Duclos, G.S. "Catullus 11: Atque in perpetuum, Lesbia, ave atque vale," *Arethusa* 9 (1976) 77–90.

Egan, R.B. "Two Complementary Epigrams of Meleager (*A.P.* 7.195 and 196)," *JHS* 108 (1988) 24–32.

Einarson, B. "On Catullus 84," *CP* 61 (1966) 187–88.

Elder, J.P. "Catullus 1, His Poetic Creed, and Nepos," *HSCP* 71 (1966) 143–49.

_____. "Notes on Some Conscious and Subconscious Elements in Catullus' Poetry," *HSCP* 60 (1951) 101–36.

Ellis, R. *A Commentary on Catullus*, 2nd ed. (Oxford 1889).

Ernout, A. and Meillet, A. *Dictionnaire étymologique de la langue latine: Histoire des mots,* 2 vols., 3rd ed., rev. (Paris 1951).

Fedeli, P. "Allusive Technique in Roman Poetry," *MPhL* 7 (1986) 17–30.

_____. *Catullus' Carmen 61* (Amsterdam 1983, rev. in English; Fribourg 1972, repr. 1981 Italian).

Feeney, D.C. "'Shall I Compare Thee...?' Catullus 68b and the Limits of Analogy," *Author and Audience in Latin Literature*, ed. by T. Woodman and J. Powell (Cambridge 1992) 33–44.

Ferguson, J. "The Arrangement of Catullus' Poems," *LCM* 11.1–2 (1986) 2–6, 18–20.

_____. *Catullus* (Lawrence 1985).

_____. "Catullus and Cicero," *Latomus* 25 (1966) 871–72.

Ferrari, W. "Il carme 51 di Catullo," *ASNP* 7 (1938) 59–72.

Ferrero, L. *Interpretazione di Catullo* (Turin 1955).

_____. *Un' introduzione a Catullo* (Turin 1955).

Finamore, J.F. "Catullus 50 and 51: Friendship, Love, and *Otium*" *CW* 78 (1984) 11–19.

Fink, R.O. "Catullus, Carmen 32," *CW* 76 (1983) 292–94.

Fisher, J.M. "Catullus 35," *CP* 66 (1971) 1–5.

Fordyce, C.J. *Catullus: A Commentary* (Oxford 1961).

Forsyth, P.Y. "The Ameana Cycle of Catullus," *CW* 70 (1977) 445–50.

_____. "Catullus 14B," *CW* 83 (1989) 81–85.

_____. "Catullus 79," *Latomus* 44 (1985) 377–82.

_____. "Catullus 82," *CJ* 70 (1975) 33–35.

_____. "Catullus 112," *CW* 77 (1983) 65–68.

_____. "Catullus: the Mythic Persona," *Latomus* 35 (1976) 555–66.

_____. "Comments on Catullus 116," *CQ* 27 (1977) 352–53.

_____. "The Gellius Cycle of Catullus," *CJ* 68 (1972–73) 175–77.

_____. "Gifts and Giving: Catullus 12–14," *CW* 78 (1985) 571–74.

_____. "The Irony of Catullus 100," *CW* 70 (1977) 313–17.

_____. "The Lady and the Poem: Catullus 35–42," *CJ* 80 (1984) 24–26.

_____. "The Marriage Theme in Catullus 63," *CJ* 66 (1970) 66–69.

_____. "Order and Meaning in Catullus 97–99," *CW* 72 (1979) 403–08.

_____. *The Poems of Catullus: A Teaching Text* (Lanham and London 1986).

_____. "Quintius and Aufillena in Catullus," *CW* 74 (1980–81) 220–23.

Fotiou, A.S. "Catullus' Passer Poems: Meaning and Form," *GB* 9 (1980) 111–21.

Fraenkel, E. "Catulls Trostgedicht für Calvus," *WS* 69 (1956) 278–88.

_____. "Review of Fordyce, *Catullus*," *Gnomon* 34 (1962) 253–63.

_____. "Two Poems of Catullus," *JRS* 51 (1961) 46–53.

_____. "*Vesper adest*," *JRS* 45 (1955) 1–8.

Fredricksmeyer, E.A. "The Beginning and the End of Catullus' *Longus Amor*," *SO* 58 (1983) 63–88.

_____. "Catullus 49, Cicero, and Caesar," *CP* 68 (1973) 268–78.

_____. "Catullus to Caecilius on Good Poetry (C. 35)," *AJP* 106 (1985) 213–21.

Garrison, D.H. *Mild Frenzy: A Reading of the Hellenistic Love Epigram*, Hermes Einzelschriften 41 (1978).

_____. *The Student's Catullus,* 2nd ed. (Norman and London 1995).

George, D.B. "Catullus 44: The Vulnerability of Wanting to Be Included," *AJP* 112 (1991) 247–50.

Giardina, G.C. "La composizione del liber e l'itinerario poetico di Catullo," *Philologus* 118 (1974) 224–35.

Glenn, J. "Ariadne's Daydream (Cat. 64. 158–63)," *CJ* 76 (1980–81) 110–16.

Gnilka, C. "Catulls Spottgedicht auf Silo," *RhM* 118 (1975) 130–35.

Goold, G.P. *Catullus* (London 1983).

_____. *Interpreting Catullus* (London 1974).

_____. "A New Text of Catullus," *Phoenix* 12 (1958) 93–116.

_____. "*O Patrona Virgo,*" *Polis and Imperium: Studies in Honor of Edward Togo Salmon*, ed. by J.A.S. Evans (Toronto 1974) 253–64.

_____. "Two Notes on Catullus 1," *LCM* 6.9 (1981) 233–38.

Gow, A.S.F. and Page, D.L. *The Greek Anthology: Hellenistic Epigrams,* vol. 1 (Cambridge 1965).

Granarolo, J. *L'Oeuvre de Catulle*: *aspects religieux, éthiques et stylistiques* (Paris 1967).

Gratwick, A. "Catullus 32," *CQ* 41 (1991) 547–51.

_____. "Ipsithilla: A Vulgar Name. Catullus, 32.1," *Glotta* 44 (1966–67) 174–76.

Green, E.H. "Furius Bibaculus," *CJ* 35 (1940) 348–56.

Grimm, R.E. "Catullus 5 Again," *CJ* 59 (1963) 15–22.

Gruen, E.S. "Cicero and Licinius Calvus," *HSCP* 71 (1966) 215–33.

de Grummond, W. "A Note on Catullus 103," *CP* 66 (1971) 188–89.

Guggenheimer, E.H. "Acoustic Symmetry in Catullus," *Dialectica* 24 (1970) 185–95.

Gutzwiller, K. "Callimachus' Lock of Berenice: Fantasy, Romance, and Propaganda,"*AJP* 113 (1992) 359–85.

Hallett, J.P. "*Ianua iucunda*: The Characterization of the Door in Catullus 67," Coll. Latomus 168 (1980) 106–22.

Harkins, P.W. "Autoallegory in Catullus 63 and 64," *TAPA* 90 (1959) 102–16.

Harnecker, O. "Des Catullus Juventiuslieder," *Jahrb. f. class. Philol.* 133 (1886) 273–79.

Harrison, E. "Catullus 84," *CR* 29 (1915) 198–99.

Harvey, P. "Catullus 114–115: Mentula, Bonus Agricola," *Historia* 28 (1979) 329–55.

Heath, J.R. "Catullus 11: Along for the Ride," Coll. Latomus 206 (1989) 98–116.

_____. "The Supine Hero in Catullus 32," *CJ* 82 (1986) 28–36.

Heck, B. *Die Anordnung der Gedichte des Gaius Valerius Catullus* (Diss. Tübingen 1950).

Heidel, W.A. "Catullus and Furius Bibaculus," *CR* 15 (1901) 215–17.

Heine, R. "Zu Catull c. 35," in *Catull*, ed. by R. Heine, "Wege der Forschung," vol. 308 (Darmstadt 1975) 62–84.

Henderson, J. *The Maculate Muse: Obscene Language in Attic Comedy* (New Haven 1975).

Herescu, N.I. "Autour de l'ironie de Catulle," *Revista Classica* 13–14 (1941–42) 128–37.

Herter, H. "Phallos," *RE* 19.2 (1938) 1723–26.

Heyworth, S.J. "Notes on Propertius Books I and II," *CQ* 34 (1984) 394–405.

Hezel, O. *Catull und das griechische Epigramm* (Stuttgart 1932).

Hickson, F.V. "*Patruus*: Paragon or Pervert? The Case of a Literary Split Personality," *Syllecta Classica* 4 (1992) 21–26.

Highet, G. *Poets in a Landscape* (New York 1957).

Holoka, J.P. *Gaius Valerius Catullus: A Systematic Bibliography* (New York and London 1985).

_____. "Self-Delusion in Catullus 83 and 92," *CW* 69 (1975) 119–20.

Holtsmark, E.B. "A Note on Logotactic Iconicity (Catullus 1 and 47)," *LCM* 12.9 (1987) 130–32.

Howe, N. "The 'Terce Muse' of Catullus 101," *CP* 69 (1974) 274–76.

Howell P. *A Commentary on Book One of the Epigrams of Martial* (London 1980).

Hubbard, T.K. "The Catullan Libellus," *Philologus* 127 (1983) 218–37.

Hutchinson, G.O. "Propertius and the Unity of the Book," *JRS* 74 (1984) 99–106.

Ingemann, V. "*Albus an ater*—A Double Entendre in Catullus 93?" *C&M* 33 (1981–82) 145–50.

Jackson, S.B. "Marcus Caelius Rufus," *Hermathena* 126 (1979) 55–67.

Jocelyn, H.D. "Catullus 58 and Ausonius, *Ep.* 71," *LCM* 4.5 (1979) 87–91.

Jones, C.P. "Parody in Catullus 44," *Hermes* 96 (1968) 379–83.

Kaster, R.A. "A Note on Catullus, c. 71.4," *Philologus* 121 (1977) 308–12.

Khan, H.A. "Catullus 35 and the Things Poetry Can Do to You," *Hermes* 102 (1974) 475–90.

_____. "Catullus 45: What Sort of Irony?" *Latomus* 27 (1968) 3–12.

_____. "Catullus 76: The Summing Up," *Athenaeum* 46 (1968) 54–71.

_____. "Catullus 99 and the Other Kiss-Poems," *Latomus* 26 (1967) 609–18.

_____. "An Interpretational Crux: Catullus 55 and 58a," *AC* 36 (1967) 116–31.

_____. "A Note on the Expression *solum...nosse* in Catullus," *CP* 62 (1967) 34–37.

_____. "Three Epigrams of Catullus (Carm., 114, 115, 112)," Coll. Latomus 101 (1969) 1–11.

Kidd, D.A. "Hesperus and Catullus 62," *Latomus* 33 (1974) 22–23.

_____. "Some Problems in Catullus 66," *Antichthon* 4 (1970) 38–49.

_____. "The Unity of Catullus 51" *AUMLA* 20 (1963) 298–308.

Killeen, J.F. "Catullus C. 55," *Siculorum Gymnasium* 29 (1976) 253–64.

King, J.K. "Catullus' Callimachean Carmina, cc. 65–116," *CW* 81 (1988) 383–92.

Kinsey, T.E. "Catullus 51," *Latomus* 33 (1974) 372–78.

_____. "Some Problems in Catullus 68," *Latomus* 26 (1967) 35–53.

Kitchell, K.F. "Catullus 116.7: *Amitha/Micta*" *CW* 80 (1986) 1–11.

_____. "*Et patruum reddidit Arpocratem*: a Reinterpretation of Catullus, c. 74," Coll. Latomus 180 (1983) 100–10.

Klingner, F. "Catulls Peleus-Epos," *SBAW* vol. 6 (Munich 1956) 1–92.

Konstan, D. *Catullus' Indictment of Rome: The Meaning of Catullus 64* (Amsterdam 1977).

Korzeniewski, D. "Elemente hymnischer Parodie in der Lyrik Catulls," *Helikon* 18–19 (1978–79) 228–57.

Kroll, W. *C. Valerius Catullus* (Leipzig and Berlin 1923).

Lateiner, D. "Obscenity in Catullus," *Ramus* 6 (1977) 15–32.

Lavency, M. "L'Ode à Lesbie et son billet d'envoi," *AC* 34 (1965) 175–82.

Lenz, F.W. "Catulliana," *RCCM* 5 (1963) 62–70.

Leutsch, E. von. "Catull. c. 14b," *Philologus* 35 (1876) 695.

Levin, D.N. "Arrius and his Uncle," *Latomus* 32 (1973) 587–94.

Levin, S. "A Dying Man's Farewell, Parodied by Catullus," *CW* 69 (1976) 374–75.

Levine, P. "Catullus c. 1: A Prayerful Dedication," *CSCA* 2 (1969) 209–16.

_____. "Catullus 67: The Dark Side of Love and Marriage," *ClAnt* 4 (1985) 62–71.

_____. "Catullus c. 68: A New Perspective," *CSCA* 9 (1976) 61–88.

_____. "Catullus c. 100: A Potent Wish for a 'Friend' in Need," *Maia* 39 (1987) 33–39.

Lieberg, G. "L'ordinamento ed i reciproci rapporti dei carmi maggiori di Catullo," *RFIC* 36 (1958) 23–47.

_____. *Puella Divina* (Amsterdam 1962).

Lilja, S. *Homosexuality in Republican and Augustan Rome*, Commentationes Humanarum Litterarum 74 (1983).

Lindgren, M.H. *Non Bona Dicta: Obscenity in the Poetry of Catullus* (Diss. University of Iowa 1983).

Lindsay, W.M. *Sexti Pompei Festi De Verborum Significatu quae supersunt cum Pauli Epitome* (Leipzig 1913).

Link, E. *Poetologisches bei Catull*, Erlanger Studien vol. 39 (1982).

Lobell, J.A. "An Unconventional Reading of Catullus 63," *Brown Classical Journal* 8 (1992) 18–22.

Loomis, J.W. "M. Furius Bibaculus and Catullus," *CW* 63 (1969) 112–14.

Lyne, R.O.A.M. *The Latin Love Poets: From Catullus to Horace* (Oxford 1980).

_____. *Selections from Catullus: Handbook* (Cambridge 1975).

_____. "The Text of Catullus 107," *Hermes* 113 (1985) 498–500.

McCarren, V.P. *A Critical Concordance to Catullus* (Leiden 1977).

McGushin, P. "Catullus' *Sanctae Foedus Amicitiae*," *CP* 62 (1967) 85–93.

Macleod, C.W. "The Artistry of Catullus 67," *Collected Essays of C.W. Macleod* (Oxford 1983).

_____. "Catullus 116," *CQ* 23 (1973) 304–09.

_____. "Parody and Personalities in Catullus," *CQ* 23 (1973) 294–303.

Madsen, D.M. *The Life and Political Career of Marcus Caelius Rufus* (Diss. University of Washington 1981).

Marcovich, M. "Catullus 13 and Philodemus 23," *QUCC* N.S. 11 (1982) 131–38.

Marshall, B.A. and Baker, R.J. "The Aspirations of Q. Arrius," *Historia* 24 (1975) 220–31.

Marshall, J.C.D. "Catullus 99," *CW* 65 (1971) 57–58.

Merrill, E.T. *Catullus* (Cambridge, Mass. 1893, 1951).

Mette, H.J. "Catull Carm. 4," *RhM* 105 (1962) 153–57.

Milanese, G. "Su Catullo, carme 78. Unità, ideologia, linguaggio," *Maia* 40 (1988) 251–61.

Mills, B. *The Unheroic Muse* (Berkeley 1978).

Minarini, A. "Note di onomastica catulliana," *Mnemosynum: studi in onore di Alfredo Ghiselli* (Bologna 1989) 425–39.

Minyard, J.D. "Critical Notes on Catullus 29," *CP* 66 (1971) 174–81.

_____. "The Source of the Catulli Veronensis Liber," *CW* 81 (1988) 343–53.

Monbrun, M. "Quelques remarques sur le c. 1 de Catulle," *Pallas* 23 (1976) 31–38.

Moore-Blunt, J. "Catullus 31 and Ancient Generic Composition," *Eranos* 72 (1974) 106–18.

Morgan, M.G. "Catullus and the *Annales Volusi*," *QUCC* N.S. 4 (1980) 59–67.

_____. "Catullus 112: A *Pathicus* in Politics," *AJP* 100 (1979) 377–80.

_____. "*Nescio Quid Febriculosi Scorti*: A Note on Catullus 6," *CQ* 27 (1977) 338–41.

Most, G.W. "On the Arrangement of Catullus' *Carmina Maiora*," *Philologus* 125 (1981) 109–25.

Münzer, F. "Caelius Rufus," *RE* 3 1266–72.

Munro, H.A.J. *Criticisms and Elucidations of Catullus*, 2nd ed. (London 1905).

Murgatroyd, P. "Some Neglected Aspects of Catullus 67," *Hermes* 117 (1989) 471–78.

Näsström, B-M. *The Abhorrence of Love. Studies in Rituals and Mystic Aspects in Catullus' Poem of Attis* (Stockholm 1989).

Németh, B. "Catullan Twin Poems (c. 50–c. 14)," *ACD* 10–11 (1974–75) 45–53.

_____. "Further Notes on Catullan Poetry (c.2, c.2a, c.3; c.11, c.51)," *ACD* 9 (1973) 41–56.

Nethercut, W.R. "The Art of Catullus 62," Coll. Latomus 164 (1979) 229–38.

Neudling, C.L. *A Prosopography to Catullus* (Oxford 1955).

Newman, J.K. *Roman Catullus and the Modification of the Alexandrian Sensibility* (Hildesheim 1990).

Newton, R. "Acme and Septimius Recounted: Catullus 45," *Syllecta Classica* 7 (1996) 99–105.

Nielsen, R.M. "Catullus 9 and 31: The Simple Pleasure," *Ramus* 8 (1979) 165–73.

_____. "Catullus, c. 6: on the Significance of too Much Love," *Latomus* 43 (1984) 104–10.

Nisbet, R.G.M. and Hubbard, M. *A Commentary on Horace*: *Odes, Book I* (Oxford 1970).

Nisbet, R.G.M. "Notes on the Text of Catullus," *PCPHS* 204 (1978) 92–115.

Noonan, J.D. "*Mala Bestia* in Catullus 69.7–8," *CW* 73 (1979) 155–64.

_____. "Myth, Humor and the Sequence of Thought in Catullus 95," *CJ* 81 (1985–86) 299–304.

Offermann, H. "Einige Gedanken zum Aufbau des Catull-Corpus," *Eranos* 76 (1978) 35–64.

_____. "Zu Catulls Gedichtcorpus," *RhM* 120 (1977) 269–302.

Oksala, P. *Adnotationes Criticae ad Catulli Carmina* (Helsinki 1965).

Onetti, S. and Maurach, G. "Catullus 35," *Gymnasium* 81 (1974) 481–85.

Opelt, I. *Die lateinischen Schimpfwörter und verwandte sprachliche Erscheinungen. Eine Typologie.* (Heidelberg 1965).

Paananen, U. *Sallust's Politico-Social Terminology* (Helsinki 1972).

Paoli, U.E. "Note di filologia reale su Catullo, Orazio, Marziale," *SIFC* N.S. 10 (1932) 23–37.

Papanghelis, T.D. "Catullus and Callimachus on Large Women," *Mnemosyne* 44 (1991) 372–86.

_____. "Crux Catulliana (A Note on 25.5)," *Latomus* 39 (1980) 409–11.

_____. "A Note on Catullus 68.156–57," *QUCC* N.S. 11 (1982) 139–49.

Pascal, C. *Poeti e personaggi Catulliani* (Catania 1916).

Peachy, F. "Catullus 55," *Phoenix* 26 (1972) 258–67.

Pease, A.S. *Publi Vergili Maronis Aeneidos liber quartus* (Cambridge, Mass. 1935).

Pedrick, V. "*Qui potis est, inquis?* Audience Roles in Catullus," *Arethusa* 19 (1986) 187–207.

Penella, R.J. "A Note on *(de)glubere*," *Hermes* 104 (1976) 118–20.

Pennisi, G. "Il carme 68 di Catullo," *Emerita* 27 (1959) 89–109, 213–38.

Pierrugues, P. *Glossarium Eroticum Linguae Latinae* (Paris 1826; 2nd ed., Berlin 1908).

Pokorny, J. *Indogermanisches etymologisches Wörterbuch*, 2 vols. (Berlin and Munich 1959).

Posch, S. "*Albus an ater homo*: zu Catull c. 93," *Serta Philologica Aenipontana* 3 (1979) 319–36.

Pratt, N.T. "The Numerical Catullus 5," *CP* 51 (1956) 99–100.

Pucci, P. "Il carme 50 di Catullo," *Maia* 13 (1961) 249–56.

Puelma, M. "Die Aitien des Kallimachos als Vorbild der römischen *Amores*-Elegie," *MH* 39 (1982) 221–46.

Pulbrook, M. "The Lesbia Libellus of Catullus," *Maynooth Review* 10 (1984) 72–84.

Putnam, M.C.J. "The Art of Catullus 64," *HSCP* 65 (1961) 165–205.

_____. "Catullus 22.13," *Hermes* 96 (1968) 552–58.

_____. "Catullus 66.75–88," *CP* 55 (1960) 223–28.

_____. "Catullus' Journey (Carm. 4)," *CP* 57 (1962) 10–19.

Quinn, K. *Catullus: An Interpretation* (London 1973).

_____. *Catullus: The Poems*, 2nd ed. (London 1973).

_____. "*Docte Catulle*" in *Critical Essays on Roman Literature Vol. 1: Elegy and Lyric*, ed. by J.P. Sullivan (London and Cambridge, Mass. 1962) 31–63.

_____. *Latin Explorations* : *Critical Studies in Roman Literature* (London 1963).

_____. "Pompey, Caesar and Catullus 29," *AFLNice* 50 (1985) 261– 68.

Ramage, E.S. "Note on Catullus' Arrius," *CP* 54 (1959) 44–45.

Randall, J.G. "*Glubit* in Catullus 58: Retractio," *LCM* 5.1 (1980) 21–22.

_____. "Mistresses' Pseudonyms in Latin Elegy," *LCM* 4.4 (1979) 27–35.

Rankin, H.D. "Catullus and Incest," *Eranos* 74 (1976) 113–21.

_____. "'Clodia II'," *AC* 38 (1969) 501–06.

_____. "A Note on Some Implications of Catullus, 16.11–13," *Latomus* 29 (1970) 119–21.

_____. "Poem 16 of Catullus," *SO* 51 (1976) 87–94.

_____. "The Progress of Pessimism in Catullus, Poems 2–11," *Latomus* 31 (1972) 744–51.

Redfield, J. "Notes on the Greek Wedding," *Arethusa* 15 (1982) 181–201.

Richardson, L., Jr. "Catullus 4 and Catalepton 10 Again," *AJP* 93 (1972) 215–22.

_____. "Catullus 67: Interpretation and Form," *AJP* 88 (1967) 423–33.

_____. "*Furi et Aureli, Comites Catulli,*" *CP* 58 (1963) 93–106.

Richlin, A. *The Garden of Priapus: Sexuality and Aggression in Roman Humor* (New Haven 1983; rev. New York 1992).

_____. "Systems of Food Imagery in Catullus," *CW* 81 (1988) 355–63.

Rosén, H.B. "Arrius' Speech Again (Catullus 84)," *Mnemosyne* 14 (1961) 224–32.

Ross, D.O., Jr. *Backgrounds to Augustan Poetry: Gallus, Elegy and Rome* (Cambridge 1975).

_____. "Style and Content in Catullus 45," *CP* 60 (1965) 256–59.

_____. *Style and Tradition in Catullus* (Cambridge, Mass. 1969).

Rowland, R.L. "*Miser Catulle*: An Interpretation of the Eighth Poem of Catullus," *G&R* 13 (1966) 15–21.

Roy, J. "Traditional Jokes about the Punishment of Adulterers in Ancient Greek Literature," *LCM* 16.5 (1991) 73–76.

Salzman, M.R. "Cicero, The *Megalenses* and the Defense of Caelius," *AJP* 103 (1982) 299–304.

Sandy, G.N. "Catullus 16," *Phoenix* 25 (1971) 51–57.

_____. "Catullus 63 and the Theme of Marriage," *AJP* 92 (1971) 185–95.

_____. "The Imagery of Catullus 63," *TAPA* 99 (1968) 389–99.

_____. "Indebtedness, *Scurrilitas*, and Composition in Catullus (Cat. 44, 1, 68)," *Phoenix* 32 (1978) 68–80.

Schäfer, E. *Das Verhältnis von Erlebnis und Kunstgestalt bei Catull* Hermes Einzelschriften 18 (1966).

Schmid, I. "Catull c. 103—ein politisches Epigramm?" *RhM* 127 (1984) 317–25.

Schmidt, E.A. "Catulls Anordnung seiner Gedichte," *Philologus* 117 (1973) 215–42.

Schulze K.P. "Catullforschungen," Festschrift zu der 2. Säcularfeier des Friedrichs-Werderschen Gymnasiums zu Berlin (Berlin 1881) 194–214.

Schwabe, L. *Quaestionum Catullianarum Liber I* (Giessen 1862).

Scott, R.T. "On Catullus 11," *CP* 78 (1983) 39–42.

Scott, W.C. "Catullus and Cato (c. 56)," *CP* 64 (1969) 24–29.

Seager, R. "*Venustus, Lepidus, Bellus, Salsus*: Notes on the Language of Catullus," *Latomus* 33 (1974) 891–94.

Segal, C.P. "Catullan *Otiosi*: The Lover and the Poet," *G&R* 17 (1970) 25–31.

_____. "Catullus 5 and 7: A Study in Complementaries," *AJP* 89 (1968) 284–301.

_____. "The Order of Catullus, Poems 2–11," *Latomus* 27 (1968) 305–21.

Shipton, K.M.W. "Catullus 51: Just Another Love Poem?" *LCM* 5.4 (1980) 73–76.

_____. "Catullus 68," *LCM* 3 (1978) 57–64.

_____. "A Successful Komos in Catullus," *Latomus* 44 (1985) 503–20.

Sickle, J. van. "The Book-Roll and Some Conventions of the Poetic Book," *Arethusa* 13 (1980) 5–42.

_____. "Poetics of Opening and Closure in Meleager, Catullus, and Gallus," *CW* 75 (1981) 65–75.

Sienkewicz, T.J. "Catullus—Another Attis?" *CB* 57 (1981) 37–43.

Singleton, D. "Form and Irony in Catullus 45," *G&R* 18 (1971) 180–87.

_____. "A Note on Catullus' First Poem," *CP* 67 (1972) 192–96.

Skinner, M.B. "*Ameana, Puella Defututa*," *CJ* 74 (1978–79) 110–14.

_____. *Catullus' Passer: The Arrangement of the Book of Polymetric Poems* (New York 1981).

_____. "*Ego Mulier*: The Construction of the Male Sexuality in Catullus," *Helios* 20 (1993) 107–30.

_____. "Gentleman's Agreement: Catullus 103," *CP* 76 (1981) 39–40.

_____. "Parasites and Strange Bedfellows: A Study in Catullus' Political Imagery," *Ramus* 8 (1979) 137–52.

_____. "Pretty Lesbius," *TAPA* 112 (1982) 197–208.

_____. "Semiotics and Poetics in Catullus 6," *LCM* 8.9 (1983) 141–42.

_____. "Supplementary Note on the Latin Sexual Language: Catullus 56.5–6," *LCM* 7.9 (1982) 140.

_____. "The Unity of Catullus 68: The Structure of 68a," *TAPA* 103 (1972) 495–512.

Skutsch, O. "Catullus 58.4–5," *LCM* 5.1 (1980) 21.

_____. "Metrical Variations and Some Textual Problems in Catullus," *BICS* 16 (1969) 38–43.

_____. "Symmetry and Sense in the *Eclogues*," *HSCP* 73 (1969) 153–69.

Small, S.G.P. *Catullus: A Reader's Guide to the Poems* (Lanham and London 1983).

Solodow, J.B. "Forms of Literary Criticism in Catullus: Polymetric vs. Epigram," *CP* 84 (1989) 312–19.

_____. "On Catullus 95," *CP* 82 (1987) 141–45.

Stark, P.M. "Two Poems to a Dead Brother: Catullus and Thomas Merton," *CB* 38 (1962) 81–83.

Stigers, E.S. "Retreat from the Male: Catullus 62 and Sappho's Erotic Flowers," *Ramus* 6 (1977) 83–102.

Stoessl, F. "Aus Catulls Frühzeit," *Hermes* 101 (1973) 442–63.

_____. "Catulls Gelliusepigramme," *Antidosis: Festschrift f. W. Kraus zum 70. Geburtstag* (Vienna 1972) 408–24.

Sweet, D.R. "Catullus 11: a Study in Perspective," *Latomus* 46 (1987) 510–26.

Syndikus, H.P. *Catull: Eine Interpretation*, 3 vols. (Darmstadt 1984, 1987, 1990).

Thomas, R.F. "Menander and Catullus 8," RhM 127 (1984) 308–16.

_____. "Sparrows, Hares, and Doves: A Catullan Metaphor and its Tradition," *Helios* 20 (1993) 131–42.

Thomsen, O. *Ritual and Desire: Catullus 61 and 62 and Other Ancient Documents on Wedding and Marriage* (Denmark 1992).

Thomson, D.F.S. "Catullus and Cicero: Poetry and the Criticism of Poetry," *CW* 60 (1967) 225–30.

_____. "Interpretations of Catullus—II," *Phoenix* 18 (1964) 30–36.

Townend, G.B. "The Unstated Climax of Catullus 64," *G&R* 30 (1983) 21–30.

Tränkle, H. "Neoterische Kleinigkeiten," *MH* 24 (1967) 87–103.

Traina, A. "Strutture catulliane: Il c. 52," *AFLNice* 50 (1985) 269–72.

Tromaras, L. "Die Aurelius- und Furius-Gedichte Catulls als Zyklen (cc. 11, 15, 16, 21, 23, 24, 26)," *Eranos* 85 (1987) 41–47.

Tufte, V. *The Poetry of Marriage* (Los Angeles 1970).

Tuplin, C.J. "Catullus 68," *CQ* 31 (1981) 113–39.

Vessey, D.W.T.C. "Thoughts on Two Poems of Catullus: 13 and 30," *Latomus* 30 (1971) 45–55.

Volponi, M. "Celio Rufo ingeniose nequam," Mem. 1st Lombardo, *Classe di Lettere* 31.3 (1970) 197–280 (unavailable).

Vretska, K. "Das Problem der Einheit von Catull c. 68," *WS* 79 (1966) 313–30.

Walde, A. *Lateinisches Etymologisches Wörterbuch* (Heidelberg 1910).

Ward-Perkins, J. and Claridge, A. *Pompeii AD 79*, vol. 2 (Boston 1987).

Weinreich, O. "Catull c. 60," *Hermes* 87 (1959) 75–90.

_____. *Catull: Liebesgedichte und sonstige Dichtungen* (Hamburg 1960).

_____. *Catull: Sämtliche Gedichte* (Zurich 1969).

Westphal, R. *Catull's Gedichte in ihrem geschichtlichem Zusammenhange,* 2nd ed. (Breslau 1870).

Whatmough, J. "Pudicus Poeta: Words and Things," in *Poetic, Scientific, and Other Forms of Discourse*, Sather Classical Lectures 29 (Berkeley and Los Angeles 1956) 29–55 .

Wheeler, A.L. *Catullus and the Traditions of Ancient Poetry* (Berkeley 1934).

White, P. "*Amicitia* and the Profession of Poetry in Early Imperial Rome," *JRS* 68 (1978) 74–92.

Williams, G. *Figures of Thought in Roman Poetry* (New Haven and London 1980).

_____. "Phases in Political Patronage of Literature in Rome," in *Literary and Artistic Patronage in Ancient Rome*, ed. by B.K. Gold (Austin 1982) 3–27.

_____. "Some Aspects of Roman Marriage Ceremonies and Ideals," *JRS* 48 (1958) 16–29.

_____. *Tradition and Originality in Roman Poetry* (Oxford 1968).

Williams, M.F. "Amor's Head-Cold (*Frigus* in Catullus 45)," *CJ* 83 (1988) 128–32.

Wirshbo, E. "'Lesbia': A Mock Hypocorism?" *CP* 75 (1980) 70.

Wirth, T. "Catull c. 2: *Passer* und *Malum* als Zeichen der Liebe," *RhM* 129 (1986) 36–53.

Wiseman, T.P. *Catullan Questions* (Leicester 1969).

_____. *Catullus and his World: A Reappraisal* (Cambridge 1985).

_____. "Catullus' *Belle De Jour*," *Filologia e forme letterarie* 2 (Urbino 1987) 375–76.

_____. *Cinna the Poet and other Roman Essays* (Leicester 1974).

_____. *Clio's Cosmetics: Three Studies in Greco-Roman Literature* (Leicester 1979).

Witke, C. *Enarratio Catulliana: Carmina 50, 30, 65, 68* (Leiden 1968).

_____. "Verbal Art in Catullus 31," *AJP* 93 (1972) 239–51.

Wohlberg, J. "The Structure of the Laodamia Simile in Catullus 68b," *CP* 50–51 (1955–56) 42–46.

Yardley, J.C. "Catullus 11: The End of a Friendship," *SO* 56 (1981) 63–69.

Index of Passages

General Index